MARTYRS OF HOPE

MARTYRS OF HOPE

Seven U.S. Missioners in Central America

Donna Whitson Brett and Edward T. Brett

ORBIS BOOKS
Maryknoll, New York 10545

ORBIS BOOKS
Maryknoll, New York 10545

Founded in 1970, Orbis Books endeavors to publish works that enlighten the mind, nourish the spirit, and challenge the conscience. The publishing arm of the Maryknoll Fathers and Brothers, Orbis seeks to explore the global dimensions of the Christian faith and mission, to invite dialogue with diverse cultures and religious traditions, and to serve the cause of reconciliation and peace. The books published reflect the views of their authors and do not represent the official position of the Maryknoll Society. To learn more about Maryknoll and Orbis Books, please visit our website at www.maryknollsociety.org.

Library of Congress Cataloging-in-Publication Data

Names: Brett, Donna Whitson, author.
Title: Martyrs of hope : seven U.S. missioners in Central America / Donna Whitson Brett and Edward T. Brett.
Description: Maryknoll : Orbis Books, 2018. | Includes bibliographical references and index.
Identifiers: LCCN 2018011850 (print) | LCCN 2018027934 (ebook) | ISBN 9781608337590 (e-book) | ISBN 9781626982932 (pbk.)
Subjects: LCSH: Missionaries—Central America—Biography. | Missionaries—United States—Biography. | Christian martyrs—Central America—Biography. | Catholic Church—Missions—Central America. | Central America—Church history—20th century.
Classification: LCC BV2842 (ebook) | LCC BV2842 .B729 2018 (print) | DDC 266/.023730728 [B]—dc23
LC record available at https://lccn.loc.gov/2018011850
ISBN 9781608337590 (ebook)

I believe that Good will win over evil,
that Creativity will win over destruction
and that Peace will win over war. . .
My belief in Jesus who makes all things new is growing.
God has never abandoned me—
I've felt alone and lonely
but I'm learning to wait and He is present even in this mess.

—Carol "Carla" Piette, MM
El Salvador, 1980

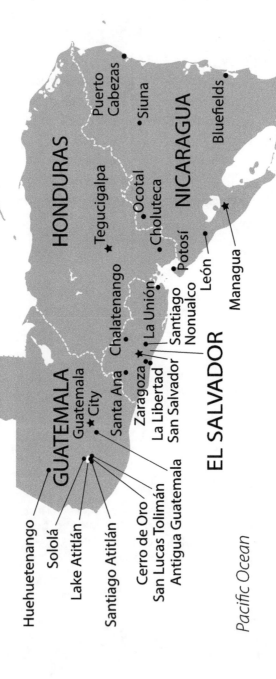

Caribbean Sea

HONDURAS

Puerto
Cabezas

Siuna

NICARAGUA

Tegucigalpa

Ocotal

Choluteca

Bluefields

Potosí

León

Managua

La Unión

Santiago
Nonualco

Chalatenango

GUATEMALA

Guatemala
City

Santa Ana

Zaragoza

La Libertad

San Salvador

EL SALVADOR

Huehuetenango

Sololá

Lake Atitlán

Santiago Atitlán

Cerro de Oro

San Lucas Tolimán

Antigua Guatemala

Pacific Ocean

Contents

Preface

We can trace our interest in Central America to a morning in February 1982 when we heard over the radio that James Miller, a Christian Brother from Wisconsin, had been gunned down at a mission school in Huehuetenango, Guatemala. Ed was then teaching at the College of Santa Fe, an institution run by the Christian Brothers in Santa Fe, New Mexico, and several members of the faculty and administration there had known Jim well. At a memorial Mass, Greg Robertson read a long letter he and his wife, Maura, had recently received from Jim. It described his work with the Mayan Indians, "the forgotten ones of Guatemala," as he called them, and his strong desire to remain in Huehuetenango in spite of increasing risk to his safety. Later, no one we asked could explain why Miller had been killed, apparently by a right-wing death squad, when his views could hardly have been considered radical or even leftist.

Moved by Jim's testimony, we researched Guatemala's recent history to write an article about him. What we found was disturbing. The thousands of civilians murdered in that troubled nation from the mid-1960s until Brother Jim's death in 1982 included not only Miller but also hundreds of other churchpeople—a few North American, European, and Guatemalan religious, but largely poor Indian catechists. Many had endured torture. They were targeted not because they advocated revolution or violence, but because, in one sense, they *were* subversive, for they were laboring against the status quo—a long-entrenched system of injustice that kept a majority of Guatemalans poor and powerless to change their fate.

Our research did not end with Jim Miller, but led to an investigation of ten other U.S. missioners who had been murdered in Central America in the mid to late 1970s and early 1980s. Our study resulted in a book, *Murdered in Central America: The Stories of Eleven U.S. Missionaries*, which was published in 1988 by Orbis Books.

Writing that book changed our lives. We were moved by these churchpeople who, guided by the gospels and by the teachings of the

ix

Second Vatican Council, were willing to risk their lives in a nonviolent struggle for justice for the marginalized people of the isthmus. Other research projects dealing with the oppression of the poor in Central America and the murders of religious personnel who spoke out on their behalf grew out of that early interest. As a history professor, Ed made several visits to the isthmian countries; he also developed courses on Central America and its relationship with the U.S., which he taught regularly at La Roche College in Pittsburgh. Donna returned to college to earn a master's degree at the University of Pittsburgh, where she studied Latin American history. During the 1980s and '90s, we belonged to organizations attempting to change the United States' shortsighted policy toward Central America. We and our two daughters took part in more than a few activities aimed at ending American military aid to right-wing dictatorships in that region. In short, following our attendance at James Miller's memorial Mass in Santa Fe, our concern for the people of Central America has grown, as has our heartfelt hope that justice for its people will be achieved.

While we were researching *Murdered in Central America* in the 1980s, Ronald Reagan was reelected president by one of the greatest landslides in modern U.S. history and was at the height of his popularity. In the name of a misguided form of anticommunism, Reagan and Congress were enabling brutal military dictatorships in Guatemala and El Salvador. And they were financing a violent counterrevolution (spearheaded by the "contras") that sought to topple the new Sandinista administration in Nicaragua, where the people had recently overthrown the decades-long Somoza regime. We wished to present our readers with the stories of courageous U.S. missioners who had come to identify with the poor of Central America and for that reason had been murdered at the hands of the very right-wing armies and dictators our own government was supporting. By placing these eleven missioners within the historical and cultural context of the lands where they served, we hoped to open our readers' hearts to Central Americans who were dying violent deaths as they struggled for a more just society. We reasoned that by seeing this struggle through the eyes of fellow citizens working closely with the people, Americans would conclude that our policy in the isthmus was morally bankrupt, counterproductive, and in need of change.

In the three decades since our book was published much has changed. The wars in Central America have ended. The Soviet Union has disintegrated, along with its totalitarian-communist ideology. The Sandinistas have come to power through democratic elections in Nicaragua, as has the Farabundo Martí National Liberation Front

(FMLN) in El Salvador. The Catholic Church has its first Latin American pope, a man who deeply admires the missionary martyrs of his native region and embraces the church's obligation to "hear the cry of the poor" as an essential part of being Christian. Yet Americans—especially those not yet born in the 1980s—still know very little about the struggles for justice in Central America in the last quarter of the twentieth century and the adverse role played by our government then.

The pool of resources available on the martyrs has expanded and become more readily accessible for journalists and scholars since 1988 when *Murdered in Central America* was published. Important primary sources—original correspondence from the missioners to family and friends, audiocassette tapes, retreat notes, reports, and other documents—have been carefully collected by Maryknoll and other religious congregations and can be found in their archives. Judith M. Noone, MM, deserves special note here. Immediately following the deaths in 1980 of Maryknoll Sisters Carla Piette, Ita Ford, and Maura Clarke, she painstakingly began to collect their letters and tapes, as well as recollections by family members, lifelong friends, and other Maryknoll sisters. These have been organized and catalogued in the Maryknoll Archives and are a treasure trove for scholars and other researchers.

In addition, investigative findings—the most notable of which are the Moakley Report, commissioned by the U.S. Congress, and the United Nations Truth Commission Report—were published in the 1990s, shedding valuable new light on the violence that took place in El Salvador during its civil war. Too, some missioners who had worked with the U.S. martyrs could not be interviewed then for their own safety because they were still working in the isthmus. Now their recollections and insights are available.

Partly as a result of the accessibility of these new sources, several fine biographies of particular U.S. martyrs have appeared since the publication of *Murdered in Central America*. All are excellent studies focusing on a single individual. Yet in most of these works, the question of why thousands of churchpeople (only a handful of whom were U.S. citizens) were murdered throughout Central America in the late 1970s and early 1980s is secondary to the life of the missionary martyr being treated. In other words, the authors do not completely unravel the complex origins of the violent realities of Central America nor do they devote detailed analysis to explain why the poor were so often under attack, along with those who stood with them—whether foreign or native religious personnel and catechists; labor, peasant, or community leaders; professors, medical professionals, or politicians. Moreover, most of these studies—there are a few exceptions—explore the culpability of the United States' involvement in only a passing way.

For all these reasons—and because *Murdered in Central America* is now somewhat dated—we decided to revise and update our 1988 book. The stories of all eleven of the martyrs in our first book remain quite worthy of attention, but with so much new information available we were not able to include them all. *Martyrs of Hope* tells the stories of seven missioners. Since the Vatican has recently beatified Father Stanley Rother and declared him the first official U.S. martyr in history, he was an obvious choice. Similarly, we chose Brother James Miller, a Christian Brother whose cause for beatification is under consideration (as we write, an announcement appears to be imminent). Both were martyred in Guatemala. The brutal murders in El Salvador of four church-women—Sisters Dorothy Kazel, Ita Ford, and Maura Clarke, and lay missioner Jean Donovan—have moved the hearts and raised the consciousness of U.S. citizens, Catholics and non-Catholics alike, more than any other martyrs of the region. Therefore, their stories must be retold here as well.

In this book we have added a companion of the four churchwomen, Sister Carla Piette, who was not included in our 1988 book because she was not a martyr in the traditional sense (one who is killed out of "hatred for the faith"). However, in his apostolic letter of July 11, 2017, Pope Francis created a new pathway to sainthood that is not martyrdom but is similar to it. Persons who were not murdered for their witness but who put their lives in danger out of compassion for others and died as a result are now eligible for beatification and canonization under this new category. In Francis's own words: "It is certain that their heroic offering of life, suggested and sustained by charity, expresses a true, full and exemplary imitation of Christ and, therefore, is worthy of that admiration which the community of the faithful usually reserved for those who have voluntarily accepted the martyrdom of blood or have exercised the Christian virtues to a heroic degree."[1] Although we are not theologians or canon lawyers, it seems to us that Carla—who selflessly jeopardized her life to aid the refugees of war in El Salvador and as a result died in a flash flood—meets these new criteria for sainthood.

We have also added new chapters that trace the accomplishments and the setbacks in the struggle for a just and equitable society in Guatemala and El Salvador after the deaths of the seven American missioners up to the present. We include here the shameless complicity of the United States government, especially during the presidency of Ronald Reagan, in covering up massacres and assassinations, including those of the martyrs mentioned above. We do so based on concrete evidence that is largely indisputable and is not biased speculation.

We began this study intending to "revise and update" *Murdered in Central America*. Yet as we neared the end of our project, we realized that what we had written was much more than a revision. *Martyrs of Hope* is essentially a different book that contains extensive information not found in our 1988 book.

This is a time in history when the Catholic Church has suffered from a variety of scandals and when some of its leaders seem more concerned with preserving the prestige and power of the church as an institution than with serving the poor and marginalized. We are living in an age when it should be obvious that the church, in order to remain relevant, must reevaluate its priorities so that it places emphasis more on "serving" than on "judging." Our Central American martyrs stand tall as models for this church of the future. They were ordinary human beings, flawed in some ways as we all are, who opened themselves to "the cry of the poor" and, as a result, were transformed. They became the embodiment of what the scriptures and the Second Vatican Council have called us all to be. They are the prophetic daughters and sons of Vatican II who give us hope and ideals to live by and to pass on to the next generations. They were capable of inspiring thousands nearly four decades ago and are no less so today.

Acknowledgments

Without the help of the missioners' coworkers, friends, and relatives, this book—and its 1988 counterpart—could not have been written, and we extend our deepest gratitude to those who contributed in any way. They include those we interviewed or who helped in other ways in the 1980s. Frankie Williams, Franz and Gertrude Rother, Marita Rother, ASC, and Fathers Marvin Leven and David Monahan helped us immeasurably in our research on Father Stanley Rother. The chapter on Christian Brother James Miller was enhanced by the observations of Don Geng, Gregory and Maura Robertson, and Christian Brothers Nicholas Geimer, Stephen Markham, Gerard Pihaly, and H. Lewis Twohig. For assistance on the four churchwomen, we are indebted to William P. Ford, Joseph and Malvina Kazel, Raymond and Patricia Donovan, and former U.S. Ambassador Robert E. White; Fathers Paul Schindler, Lawrence McMahon, Edward Cleary, OP, and James Brockman, SJ; Kay Kelly, MM, Ursuline Sisters Martha Owen, Sheila Tobbe, and Barbara Sever, and Christine Rody, VSC; Josie and Frank Cuda, Mary Frances Ehlinger, and Rita Mikolajczyk, as well as Wendy Griffin, who kindly provided accommodations during our research travels in Central America in 1986 and helped us negotiate our way.

Several more have contributed their insights to this current book. Father Tom McSherry, Brother Paul Joslin, and Sister Martha Owen patiently answered our many questions by email or telephone. Indeed, we can say with certainty that this book is more accurate because of their help. Sister Marita Rother kindly sent us her reflections on her 2016 visit to Santiago Atitlán. We thank our friends Neil and Marge Himber who located and shared their notes from a 2008 trip with Ed to El Salvador and Guatemala. We are indebted to Fathers Bernard Survil and Joseph Callahan and to Susan Fitzpatrick Behrens and Frank Kendrick, all of whom helped clarify details.

Our friends Rose Marie Hogan and James Ruck listened attentively to our stories of the missioners, always contributing insightful comments, and we thank Jim and his wife, Gail Britanik, for introducing us to Brother Paul and to Joyce Hylazewski, MM, who also provided her insights. Many friends have blessed us with their enthusiasm and support for this project and we thank them as well.

Jennifer Halloran and the staff at the Maryknoll Archives could not have been more thorough and prompt with our requests, and the Maryknoll Fathers and Brothers provided us with hospitality while working in the archives. Robert Ellsberg, publisher of Orbis Books, and his staff, especially Maria Angelini, Celine Allen, and Roberta Savage, have been unfailingly patient and supportive. George Rigazzi, archdiocesan archivist of Oklahoma City, checked several details on Rother and deserves our sincere thanks. LaVerne Collins and the library staff at La Roche College—especially Caroline Horgan, the interlibrary loan director—merit our deepest appreciation.

We also owe a debt of sincere gratitude to the biographers of the seven missioners: María Ruiz Scaperlanda and Father David Monahan (Stanley Rother); Theodore Drahmann, FSC (James Miller); Cynthia Glavac, OSU (Dorothy Kazel); Ana Carrigan (Jean Donovan); Jacqueline Hansen Maggiore (Carla Piette); Jeanne Evans and Phyllis Zagano (Ita Ford); Eileen Markey (Maura Clarke); and Judith M. Noone, MM (Ita Ford, Maura Clarke, and Carla Piette).

Finally, for their enthusiastic interest, we thank our daughters, Tracy and Erin, and grandsons, Scott and Samuel, along with the Whitson and Brett families—especially Ed's sister, Peggy Hymel, who shared her memories of Brooklyn in the 1940s and '50s, where she and her brothers grew up four blocks down the street from Ita Ford.

Introduction

In Latin America, during the Cold War years of the twentieth century, Catholic priests, nuns and brothers, bishops, and lay workers were tortured and murdered by the thousands. Some have claimed that their untimely deaths occurred because a segment of the Church, infected by "communist ideology," had deviated from the traditional spiritual mission of Christianity, involving itself, instead, in radical politics. Unfortunately, such accusations have been made not only by Latin American oligarchs and military officers, but also by some political officials in the United States. Even some churchpeople—in Latin America, the United States, and the Vatican—have echoed these charges.

However, many religious people of the Cold War era who died in Latin America are no more than the latest links in a long chain of prophetic Christians dating back to the Roman Empire who suffered persecution and sometimes death because they chose to champion the cause of the poor and marginalized. This book is the story of a mere handful of such people—seven U.S. missioners who died in Guatemala and El Salvador. They represent an extremely small sample of a much larger number of modern Latin Americans who chose to follow the gospel-based example of Jesus by demanding justice for all human beings regardless of their wealth and social status.

The story of the Latin American church in the last half century—with its champions of the oppressed on the one hand, and its oligarchy, military, and collaborative churchpeople on the other—in many ways parallels the church that first came to the New World with the Spanish conquistadors in the sixteenth century. A few examples illustrate this point.

When Christopher Columbus first landed in America he knelt on the ground, gave a prayer of thanks to God, and named the island he had "discovered" San Salvador (Holy Savior). Upon encountering the indigenous population, he again gave thanks to God, because, according to historian Samuel Eliot Morison, Columbus saw: "'How easy it would be to convert these people—and to make them work for us.' In other words, enslave them but save their souls. Indeed, it seems to have been from the sailors who returned from this voyage that every Spaniard got the idea that no white man need do a hand's turn of work in the New World."[1] Columbus's vision was shared not only by conquistadors and Spanish colonists, but also by a substantial number of the Spanish clergy. Some bishops and priests became rich and powerful by giving their religious sanction to the violence perpetrated by their countrymen. Others were able to live comfortably by remaining silent when faced with atrocities.

As soon as the Spanish established their first settlement in America on the island of Hispaniola, they created the *encomienda*, a labor system that virtually enslaved the Indians. They encountered unexpected opposition, however, from a tiny group of Dominicans, especially Antonio de Montesinos. In a Sunday sermon preached on December 21, 1511, he railed at his congregation:

> Tell me by what right or justice do you hold these Indians in such a cruel and horrible servitude? On what authority have you waged such detestable wars against these peoples who dwelt quietly and peacefully on their own land—wars in which you have destroyed such infinite numbers of them by homicides and slaughters never before heard of? Why do you keep them so oppressed and exhausted, without giving them enough to eat or curing them of the sickness they incur from the excessive labor you give them? And they die, or rather, you kill them, in order to extract and acquire gold every day...Are these not men? Do they not have rational souls? Are you not bound to love them as you love yourselves? Don't you understand this?[2]

The settlers—led by Diego Columbus, governor of Hispaniola—demanded that Montesinos retract his words. He refused and his fellow Dominicans supported him. The colonists then wrote to King Ferdinand demanding that Montesinos be expelled from Hispaniola. When the king reprimanded him and informed him that he would be recalled to Spain and punished if he continued to speak "such dangerous opinions," he refused to be intimidated. He sailed to Spain where he successfully argued his case before both royal and church authorities and then returned to Hispaniola to continue his quest for justice.

Bartolomé de Las Casas went to Hispaniola in 1502, where he became an *encomendero*, with a large estate and Indians who were forced to work for him. His conversion, influenced by the sermons of Montesinos, took place around 1514, when he gave up his comforts and devoted himself to the pursuit of justice for the Indian. In 1515, now a priest, he sailed to Spain in an attempt to convince King Charles to outlaw the *encomienda*. Although he was not totally successful, he was able to have some of the system's worst abuses terminated or mitigated. In 1519 he was chosen to defend the Indians before the king in Barcelona. Arguing against him was the Bishop of Panama, Juan de Quevedo, who claimed that the Indians were slaves by nature. Much later, in 1550, in one of the most famous and important ethical debates in European history, he took on Juan Ginés de Sepúlveda, perhaps the most prestigious Spanish scholar of his day, who asserted that imperial forces had a moral right to wage war against the Indians, due to the latter's immoral character. In both debates Las Casas contended that the Indians were far more moral than the Spanish who exploited them; he was able to fortify his position by constantly referring to what he had personally witnessed in the Spanish-American colonies. Las Casas' most important contributions to the cause of justice for the Amerindian, however, were the many books and pamphlets he wrote throughout his life. They have been debated by historians, law professors, and theologians down to the present time and have served as an important source for twentieth-century liberation theologians.

In 1545 Las Casas was appointed bishop of the newly created diocese of Chiapas (today in Mexico). But after only a few months there he was driven from the region by Spanish colonists whom he had condemned for their mistreatment of the Indians. More than once, he barely avoided being seized, and possibly murdered, by his enemies. Eventually he left the Americas and returned to Spain, where his commitment to the cause of the Amerindian ended only with his death in 1566.[3]

Although Montesinos and Las Casas risked their lives for the oppressed, they avoided martyrdom. The same cannot be said for their fellow Dominican, Antonio de Valdivieso. Appointed bishop of Nicaragua in 1544, Valdivieso immediately began to clash with the governor there. The bishop sent a continuous stream of letters to the king and officials of the Spanish royal court informing them of the governor's abusive conduct toward the local Indian population. In these letters he expressed the fear that he would be murdered because of his condemnation of injustice. These fears were not unfounded. On February 26, 1550, the governor's son bribed and incited an angry mob. A former soldier then formed a "death squad" that bludgeoned Valdivieso to death.[4]

Montesinos, Las Casas, and Valdivieso are the three best known Spanish priests who risked their lives on behalf of the indigenous downtrodden. But there were many others. Cristóbal de Pedraza was appointed bishop of Comayagua (Honduras) in 1541. Arriving at his new post, he was appalled at what he witnessed. He wrote to the king, informing him that the provincial governor was selling Indians into slavery:

> [He] seized so many Indians from the land that he totally de-
> stroyed it... It was not only the misfortune of those he seized,
> but upon seeing their parents, spouses, children, brothers, sisters
> and relatives carried off, bound with rope and in chains, and put
> into ships to be sold, the few who remained fled for the hills and
> abandoned their pueblos... They died of hunger in such num-
> bers that in a pueblo of one or two thousand households not one
> person was left.[5]

Pedraza used his authority as bishop to issue decrees forbidding the employment of free Indians in the mines. Even though officials in the royal treasury denounced these decrees, the Crown decided this case in favor of the bishop.[6]

Still another defender of the Amerindians was Bishop Pablo de Torres of Panama (1547–1554), who excommunicated the Spanish *encomenderos* for their brutality toward the Indians only to be condemned himself by Archbishop Jerónimo de Loaysa and forced to return to Spain, where he was accused of treason and forbidden ever again to enter Panama.[7]

Unfortunately, the prophetic efforts of these and other early colonial churchmen did not survive as a widespread movement. Whereas the Spanish monarch Charles V was, on the whole, sympathetic to the cause of the clerical protectors of the indigenous population, his son Philip II was more concerned with the religious wars in Europe. When financial pressures increased on the Spanish monarchy because of these costly wars, concern for Indian welfare dwindled. If oppression of the Amerindians produced more gold and silver to be used to destroy "Protestant heretics," the king reasoned, so be it.

Nevertheless, throughout the following centuries, the rare prophetic voices of a few churchmen refused to be silent. In the seventeenth century the Carmelite priest Vázquez de Espinosa criticized the Spanish for plying Indians with alcohol to trick them into entering workhouses. Once inside they were enslaved and never permitted to leave. For years and sometimes for their whole lives, their wives and children would know nothing of what had happened to them.[8] He further revealed that Incas in Peru were forced to stay deep within the mines all week without seeing the light of day except on Sundays, when they were allowed to attend

Mass, and that they were given no food but that which their wives brought to the mines for them.[9]

In the eighteenth century the Mexican Jesuit theologian Francisco Javier Alegre denounced the African slave trade, while Pedro José Márquez, also a Mexican Jesuit, argued that the concepts of racial superiority and inferiority were philosophically absurd.[10]

The little-known Padre Manuel de Jesús Subirana was another champion of Indian rights. In the 1850s he was sent from Cuba to the province of Yoro in Honduras to proselytize among the Hicaque Indians. Upon his arrival he found the Hicaques exploited by *ladinos* (sometimes called *mestizos*, a mixture of Indian and Caucasian) through forced labor and debt peonage. He was appalled and determined to ameliorate their condition. He complained to national Honduran authorities, accusing local *ladinos* of exploiting the Indians economically and also of beating the men, robbing the women and boys, and raping the girls. When the governor of Yoro forced Hicaques to transport sarsaparilla to the coast for his personal gain, fourteen of them died from exhaustion and disease. Subirana vigorously protested this abuse and was able to convince the central government to limit the governor's power.

Subirana succeeded in his efforts to have Hicaque debts cancelled; he also taught them that they had a legal right to freedom and therefore could refuse to work for unfair wages. He declared null and void any contracts between Hicaques and *ladinos* that were not signed in his presence or that of another authorized by him. Subirana's most significant effort was his work in obtaining land and titles of ownership for the Hicaques in 1864. Unfortunately, after his death in November of that year, his projects were taken over by priests who collaborated with the governor. Consequently, by the late nineteenth century, the Hicaques had lost their best land to *ladinos*. Thus the fifteen years or so of Subirana's work proved to be little more than an interlude. Hicaque culture and economic well-being was again being undermined and, as a result, many Indians fled to the more inaccessible mountain regions, where they could at least live with a modicum of freedom.[11]

As stated above, priests like Vázquez de Espinosa, Alegre, Márquez, and Subirana were rare in post-sixteenth-century Latin America. Many clergymen in the seventeenth and eighteenth centuries served as apologists for the power structure, and those who did not tended to remain silent in the face of unjust political institutions. In the anticlerical Liberal period of the nineteenth and twentieth centuries—at least prior to 1960—the Church, faced with serious problems of its own, concerned itself little with ameliorating the horrible conditions of the marginalized majority. At best, some churchmen displayed what might be termed a "benevolent" approach to missionary work. Perhaps the best known churchman to take this approach was the Jesuit, Pedro Claver, who came to the port of Cartagena, Colombia, from Spain in 1610. Cartagena was the major slave market in Spanish America; about a thousand black slaves were shipped there each month. Claver would board every ship once it docked. The ships arrived with large numbers of slaves who were near death. Claver would first baptize the dying and next hand out food, brandy, and tobacco to those who had survived the voyage. He trained blacks who spoke the various African dialects as catechists, and it is said, perhaps with some exaggeration, that in his forty-four-year ministry he baptized more than three hundred thousand slaves. Yet, in all those years, Padre Pedro never once spoke against the institution of slavery:

> Claver accepted slavery as an inevitable though regrettable element in the social system. It was with the slaves as victims of the social system rather than with the system itself that he was concerned. His life was dedicated to reforming the individual rather than to reforming the system. His heroic predecessor at Cartagena, Father [Alonso de] Sandoval, combined Claver's love for the individual slave with [the nineteenth-century English Protestant abolitionist, William] Wilberforce's hatred of slavery. He collected all the relevant facts about the slave trade and wrote a book which is one of the most effective attacks on this infamous traffic and is still an invaluable source book for historians of slavery.[12]

While Claver remained mute when confronted with the immoral institution of slavery, Sandoval, although not as outspoken as the earlier sixteenth-century defenders of the Indians, wrote occasionally with a flash of insight reminiscent of Montesinos and Las Casas:

> [The slaves] arrive looking like skeletons; they are led ashore, completely naked, and are shut up in a large court of enclosure ... and it is a great pity to see so many sick and needy people denied all care or assistance, for as a rule they are left to lie on the ground, naked and without shelter...I recall that I once saw two of them, already dead, lying on the ground on their backs like animals, their mouths open and full of flies, their arms crossed as

if making the sign of the cross...and I was astounded to see them dead as a result of such great inhumanity.[13]

It is interesting to note that whereas Pedro Claver was canonized in 1888, Sandoval not only has not been canonized but is all but forgotten except by a few historians.

In summary, throughout its history the Latin American church has always had prophetic clergy who fought for the rights of the downtrodden. Their numbers were somewhat substantial in the sixteenth century. But from the seventeenth through the mid-twentieth century they were relatively rare. The post-sixteenth-century Latin American church primarily labored for the salvation of the soul of the individual. It did this through a parish structure that placed primary emphasis on dispensing the sacraments. Its clergy preached homilies against personal sins such as drunkenness and fornication; little was ever said against political, social, and economic institutional structures that robbed the masses of their human dignity. At its best, the Church ignored the injustices emanating from these structures; at its worst, it indirectly supported them by encouraging the oppressed to accept their lot with humility and passivity. Resignation to the miseries of this life, the masses were told, would merit them a place in heaven. In short, it was God's will that they suffer in this life, but they could take heart, for their sufferings would end once they entered the gates of heaven.

Such ecclesiastical attitudes began to break down in the post–World War II era. But change became more rapid as a result of Pope John XXIII's *aggiornamento*, his call for the renewal and modernization of the Catholic Church culminating in Vatican II (1962–1965). The Council taught that championing human development and social justice went hand in hand with saving souls. The scriptures stressed not only the hereafter, but justice and dignity in this world as well. Strong emphasis was placed on the social encyclicals of Popes Leo XIII and Pius XI as well as on the social teachings of Pius XII. John XXIII issued two encyclicals himself, *Mater et Magistra* and *Pacem in Terris*, which further extended the views of his predecessors. As Edward Cleary noted:

John spoke about just wages and strikes as did previous popes. But he also discussed economic aid, the use of farm surpluses at the international level, and in a forceful statement asked the well fed to look after the undernourished "without imperialistic aggrandizement." He called for the state to take a more active role, and even talked about state ownership...

The encyclical goes beyond the Catholic world; it addressed all Christians and all persons of good will...John also opened a new topic: he warned against colonialism and new forms of imperialism.[14]

At a time when poverty and repression were escalating throughout the developing world, the conciliar fathers issued *Gaudium et Spes* (The Church in the Modern World). Perhaps the most important document of Vatican II, it condemned the hoarding of wealth and power for the benefit of a small segment of society. It further noted that the right to private property is not an unlimited ownership. But, more important, it stipulated that all persons are entitled to the basic earthly necessities of life, and that therefore when individuals or their families are in extreme need they are morally justified in taking from the excessive wealth of others.

Perhaps as important as its contents, *Gaudium et Spes* introduced a radically new methodology to Catholic theological study. Instead of the traditional top-down way of discussing theological or biblical principles and then applying them to the problems of the day, it reversed the process. It now began with an analysis of the current situation, and then turned to theology and sacred scripture for reflection on that situation. *Gaudium et Spes* also went beyond the traditional theological and philosophical approach, employing the social and behavioral sciences in its analysis.[15]

Following their return from the Council, the Latin American bishops agreed to hold a general bishops' conference at Medellín, Colombia, in order to apply the principles of Vatican II to the Latin American situation. After two years of preparation, the conference was held in 1968. Its importance cannot be overstated. Using the methodology of *Gaudium et Spes*, it changed the direction of the Latin American church from one aligned, at least indirectly, with the power structure to one that sided with the poor and marginalized. As Cleary stated:

> The final document would say, in brief, that the church is a sinful church in a sinful (unjust) society, one marked by structural inequalities. Latin America, it went on, is a region suffering from two massive evils: external dominance and internal colonialism. Change was obviously called for and the church wished to take part in the change. The church chose the side of the poor. It must reach out to them, and to the whole continent. This would be accomplished through evangelization and lay participation (*pastoral de conjunto*) from which grassroots communities (*comunidades de base*) would emerge.[16]

Comunidades de base were the key element in the Church's siding with the masses. Using the consciousness-raising techniques created by Paulo Freire for educating the poor, the Church began training catechists. They, in turn, formed small, grassroots groups of twenty to thirty *campesinos* (peasants) and urban poor for Bible study and prayer. Biblical passages were read and the group then reflected on them, rooting them in the actualities of their everyday lives. The catechist served as coordinator rather than leader. Eventually the group members learned about themselves from a gospel-based orientation. They realized that it was not God's will that they suffer. As God's people they were not created to serve the rich, but to have human dignity. They realized that they had a right to basic physical necessities for themselves and their families and that they were not inferior to the wealthy. In studying the gospel of Luke, for instance, they learned that Jesus called the rich landowner who hoarded his grain a fool (12:16–21) and that he said, "It is easier for a camel to pass through the eye of a needle than for a rich man to enter the kingdom of God" (18:25). Other books of the scriptures revealed more about God's commitment to the poor and exploited:

> They interpret the exodus as applying to them. They read Amos about helping the widow and the orphaned. And they reflect on Jesus as the one who came to liberate them. They are quick to catch on that liberation is more than spiritual. Often their discussion centers on not having to live in the unfavorable conditions that they once thought unchangeable. Health, education and landownership become topics of reflection, replacing resignation and suffering, as in the past.[17]

Since basic Christian community members often helped organize or joined labor unions, agrarian organizations, and cooperatives and took part in nonviolent protests demanding human rights, many of the Latin American elites soon concluded that the Medellín-based church was responsible for this new activism of the poor. Consequently, in several countries, the military and security forces were turned against the clergy. Priests began to be kidnapped, tortured, and killed, causing the more conservative bishops and clergy to call for the Church to return to its former state of "political noninvolvement." Thus, the Church became divided. It seemed that the conservatives might prove successful when they gained control of the agenda for the upcoming Latin American bishops' conference to be held at Puebla, Mexico in 1979. The Medellín-oriented progressives, however, aided by the writings of the theologians of liberation, not only reaffirmed the commitments of Medellín but actually expanded them. They more clearly and vigorously pledged the Church to the service of the downtrodden by calling on it to make "a preferential option for the poor."

One more outgrowth of Pope John's *aggiornamento* must be mentioned, since it directly bears on the lives of those included in this book. In 1961, as the Church was preparing for Vatican II, Pope John issued a call for the Catholic churches of the United States, Canada, and Europe to commit 10 percent of their priests and religious to mission work in Latin America.[18] As a result of this plea, hundreds of North Americans—priests, religious nuns and brothers, and laypeople—pledged themselves to this apostolate. Many Europeans did the same. Entering a world of widespread and extreme poverty for the first time, they reacted in different ways. A small minority, fearing communist undertones in the demands of the marginalized for change, sided with the conservative faction of the Latin American bishops. The majority, however, committed themselves to the poor, some in a more radical way that questioned the legitimacy of the economic and socio-political realities of the day and others in more low-keyed, non-"politicized" ways. Many missionaries took great pains to avoid any activity that could be construed as "political," only to find that they still were looked on with suspicion by the powerful. As Father Stanley Rother remarked to a journalist not long before he was shot to death in Guatemala: "To shake the hand of an Indian is [considered] a political act."[19] Although the post-Vatican II missioners cannot be cast in the same mold, it was not uncommon for them to go through a transformation process. They often began their mission work with the traditional goal of catechizing those they served and providing them with the sacraments. But as they immersed themselves in the lives of the people and experienced their misery, they were changed. They became part of that long chain of prophetic missionaries who heard the cry of the poor and demanded justice for them, just as Montesinos, Las Casas, Valdivieso, and others had done before them in the sixteenth century. What follows are the stories of seven of these missioners.

CHAPTER 1

Stanley Rother

Diocesan Priest

Stanley Rother

It was July, fiesta time in Santiago Atitlán, a picturesque indigenous town on the southern shore of Lake Atitlán in Guatemala. In the past, tourists would be arriving, crossing the deep, dark blue lake by launch, enchanted by three volcanic mountains and refreshed by the "eternal spring" temperature. But there were few visitors in 1981; their numbers had dwindled as word had spread that the army was abducting and murdering Indians in the vicinity.

The Maya living in Santiago Atitlán—the Tz'utujil—had made the usual preparations for the festivities of July 25 for the feast of Santiago Apóstol (St. James the Apostle), the town's patron saint and namesake. But the army's nine-month-long encampment in a nearby field had taken a toll in human lives and seared the soul of the village with fear.

"Padre A'plas," an Oklahoma priest in his mid-forties, had suffered through months of sorrow with the people. Together, they had grown fearful witnessing the surge of repression. Like them, A'plas had helplessly watched a beloved friend being kidnapped. The muffled screams of a catechist, Diego Quic, *"Ayúdame! Ayúdame!"* ("Help me! Help me!"), had rung in the priest's ears for months. But unlike the Tz'utujils, Padre A'plas could have departed for the safe haven of Oklahoma, where Americans, unaware of the barbarity that stalked Guatemala, were farming their land, tending their cattle, and drilling for oil. There he could have become Father Stanley Rother again, pastor of a middle-class congregation—concerned about the parish building program and escalating air-conditioning bills.

But Stan remained in Guatemala among the indigenous people. Not one to court martyrdom, he once echoed the sentiments of a fellow priest: "I like martyrs, but just to read about them."[1] He told friends that he hoped to stay alive by doing nothing foolish to antagonize authorities. Yet he also wrote that "at first signs of danger, the shepherd can't run and leave the sheep fend for themselves."[2]

So in July 1981, Stan was with the people for their annual fiesta. As part of the celebration, he blessed 101 couples in marriage, an all-time record, and over 200 parishioners received first communion. But festivities had been dampened by army "recruiters" who went door-to-door forcibly rounding up teenage boys for military service.[3] Rother knew that to protest was not only futile but also dangerous. However, in spite of his careful avoidance of political entanglements, Father Stan was murdered in his rectory shortly after midnight on July 28.

The three masked murderers first attempted to abduct him, but Rother knew that torture lurked ahead for kidnapped victims. He feared not only the ordeal but what he might "confess," which might be used as evidence, however distorted, to torture and kill others. True to his resolution, revealed earlier that year to his father, that he would never let them take him from the rectory, Rother fought bare-fisted against the armed men, crying, "Kill me here!"[4] The kidnappers, unable to subdue the desperate priest with kicks and beatings, finally complied; two shots reverberated through the sleeping town and the last struggle of Padre A'plas was over.

How had Rother, a politically cautious, reticent man, apparently become a threat to the power structure in Guatemala?

Stanley Francis was born during a dust storm to Franz and Gertrude Smith Rother in a farmhouse near the town of Okarche, a small Catholic enclave in central Oklahoma, on March 27, 1935. When his father brought him to their parish church, the intractable pastor insisted that "Stanley" was not a fitting Christian name and baptized the baby "Francis Stanley." Afterwards, the Rothers quietly, but just as stubbornly, switched the names around.[5] But perhaps the pastor was unwittingly prescient: the Tz'utujil people years later found it easier to translate the Spanish word *Francisco* into their native tongue than *Estanislao* (Spanish for "Stanley") and called him "Padre A'plas"—"Father Francis" in their Mayan language.

Stan's great-grandparents on both sides had migrated to the Oklahoma Territory around 1893 after the historic land runs that opened up millions of acres of Indian Territory to settlers. The Rothers and Smiths had staked out their claims to part of the prairie. They were staunchly religious "sod-busters" of German ancestry. Oral tradition told of one-room houses and screenless windows where rattlers and bull snakes often slept on the sills. The Rothers and Smiths struggled through the bad times and prospered through the good times, and eventually their tenacity paid off. By 1926 the Rother branch owned about two thousand acres of farmland.[6]

After Stan's birth, Elizabeth, James, Carolyn (who died soon after birth), and Thomas arrived in rapid succession. The Rothers were a devout family that prayed the rosary and never missed Sunday Mass. Stan's sister Elizabeth, now Sister Marita, ASC, remembered that when there was squabbling among the siblings, her older brother was seldom involved and rarely was reprimanded by their parents, especially not by their mother.[7] Perhaps Stan, a quiet, somewhat shy boy, chose very carefully when to risk disobedience. His sister recalled: "He was good at making fudge. Anytime mom and dad were both gone, he pulled out the equipment to make the fudge. We had to eat it before they got back, which wasn't always easy."[8]

The Rothers belonged to Holy Trinity Parish in Okarche, and Stan attended Holy Trinity Elementary and High School. According to his sister, from first grade through high school, Stan was an average to good student who sometimes made the honor roll. He had many chores on the family farm, but he found time to be an altar boy, president of the Future Farmers of America, boys' athletic manager, and a member of Young Christian Students. His high school yearbook of 1953 noted beneath his senior photo: "Noise is not his specialty. Cooperation marks his personality."[9] Although an active teenager with a wide range of interests, he was quiet-spoken, not an aggressive leader—a lifelong character trait. Two weeks before his death, he jokingly remarked in a letter to friends that he could use a course in "assertiveness training."[10]

After graduating from high school, Stan told his family he wanted to study for the priesthood. His sister, one year younger, had also been thinking of religious life. The teenagers kept these thoughts to themselves and surprised each other—and their parents—by announcing their intentions around the same time.[11] Their parents were happy with their decisions, but Franz, the down-to-earth wheat farmer, betrayed some exasperation at his son's lack of foresight: "Why didn't you take Latin instead of working so hard as a Future Farmer of America?" he asked.[12] This question would prove to be more perceptive than he knew at the time.

In the fall of 1953, Stan entered St. John's Seminary in San Antonio, Texas. After two years there, he advanced to Assumption Seminary in San

Antonio, to begin the two-year curriculum in philosophy required to move on to theology. He managed to make it through—just barely. He had to repeat first-year philosophy and came close to flunking the second. He was not so fortunate, however, in first-year theology. After failing both moral and dogmatic theology, he was asked to leave the seminary. It was 1959 and he had been a seminarian for five and a half years. Sister Marita believed that Stan's academic problems were not the result of below-average ability:

> When he got to the seminary he found a lot of diverse activities that gradually took precedence over his studies. He grew up on a farm and he had his responsibilities and chores to do from little on. Like all farmers, he learned to do many things, from building, to repairing machinery, to raising crops, and he took a lot of pride in his work. When something around the seminary needed repairing, Stan would volunteer. When the trees needed trimming and the hedges needed attention, Stan volunteered. The farm boy was coming out; after all, that was the life he had known, lived and loved for 18 years. (As soon as he got home in the summer, he would be on the combine harvesting wheat or on the tractor plowing up the soil.) Consequently, his studies did suffer.[13]

In those pre–Vatican II years, extensive training in Latin was crucial for the seminarian; in fact, theology and philosophy texts used then were written in Latin. As his father foresaw, Latin would prove difficult for Stan. Father Marvin Leven, a classmate at Assumption, remembered clearly—and with annoyance—Stan's last year in San Antonio: although he struggled quite a bit academically, he was often asked by faculty and staff to do odd jobs. The young man could do almost anything: fix tractors, resolve electrical problems, repair buildings, and bind books. Stan's handiwork was requested not only during recreation time but also during study time. It is possible that for Stan, who was often humbled when it came to academic performance, these accomplishments were needed for a dose of self-confidence. So he acquiesced—and got further behind. When he was told he could not continue his studies for the priesthood, but should consider serving as a brother, Stan was greatly disappointed.

Marvin called Bishop Reed in Oklahoma City and explained the situation to his secretary. Monsignor S. F. Luecke, diocesan director of vocations, and Stan's pastor in Okarche, Edmund Von Elm, interceded on behalf of the crushed ex-seminarian. They went with Stan and his father to see the bishop, who asked Stan if he still wanted to be a priest. Stan answered, "Yes, but it's all over for me, isn't it?" Reed answered, "No, it isn't; it's not my smart priests that are my best priests." After Stan got tutoring in Latin, Reed and Luecke arranged a second chance for him at Mount St. Mary's Seminary in Emmitsburg, Maryland.[14]

At the Mount, Stan could not completely resist the temptation to use his wide array of skills. Before his first year was over, he had become one of three leaders of a group of seminarians working on the renovation of the grotto. Their work, according to Harry Flynn—then a deacon and later rector at the Mount—gave the grotto "a beauty which was really unknown before."[15] Stan also set up a book bindery, using the expertise he had gained at Assumption Seminary. But no matter what work he volunteered to do, this time Stan persevered by not allowing himself to be diverted by too many non-academic tasks. Just before Stan's graduation, the rector wrote Reed: "Mr. Rother has made excellent progress at this seminary and should be a very valuable parish priest."[16] Fortunately for Stan, he had benefited from the practice at the Mount of seminarians who were highly proficient in Latin translating textbooks into English for those who were not. He still struggled with his classwork, but as a fellow seminarian later noted, while he may have been a mediocre student, he was "a real plugger."[17] Within twenty years, the man who had entered Mount St. Mary's with a dubious academic record would receive—posthumously—the Mount's cherished Bruté Award (1982) for meritorious service.[18]

On May 25, 1963, Stanley Rother was ordained at the Cathedral of Our Lady of Perpetual Help in Oklahoma City. Ordination cards, which he had designed himself, quoted St. Augustine: "For my own sake I am a Christian; for the sake of others I am a priest."

Father Stan spent his first four years of priesthood at four different parishes. The Oklahoma City/Tulsa Diocese had just been granted at very little cost a ninety-five-acre expanse of land on Lake Texoma, provided it develop the area. So Reed assigned the new priest to St. William parish in nearby Durant. The bishop informed the pastor that Stan would have no parish obligations except to say Mass on weekends. He was to devote the rest of his time to clearing land and building cabins for a youth camp and retreat center. After two years, Stan was assigned to St. Francis Xavier parish and Holy Family Cathedral in Tulsa and then to Corpus Christi in Oklahoma City. During most of this time his primary work was devoted to construction at Lake Texoma, where he now stayed overnight on weekdays because of the long distance between his parish and the lake. He once expressed a bit of frustration that his ministry was not always sacramental, confiding to Father Dave Imming: "Here I am doing carpentry when others are doing priestly work."[19]

Stan was aware that some priests questioned his intellectual ability for "priestly work," and this hurt him deeply. His friend Marvin said that Stan's four years as a priest in Oklahoma were not the happiest for him. Rother had a "poor image of himself intellectually," and some priests criticized him for being too matter-of-fact and unassuming. Consequently, Rother did not feel secure in his ability to serve his parishioners, although, Leven added, Stan's parishioners did in fact respect him.[20]

While striving to meet his obligations to the bishop for clearing land and building cabins, he was using whatever spare time he had—and it could not have been sizable—to take courses at Southeastern State College in Durant, Oklahoma. He would receive a second college degree, a bachelor's in history, on May 26, 1966.[21] And the diocesan retreat center he built with such attention to detail was still in use fifty years later.

While he was at Corpus Christi in Oklahoma City, Rother received an offer that would radically change his life. He was invited to lunch by Ramon Carlin who, during the course of the meal, asked him to join the Oklahoma City/Tulsa mission team in Santiago Atitlán, Guatemala. Carlin, the founding pastor of the mission, had heard of Rother's abilities in farming, building, and renovation, and knew these skills were sorely needed at the mission. Stan enthusiastically accepted Carlin's invitation. Perhaps he sensed that the mission would offer him an opportunity to combine agriculture and Eucharist, construction and liturgy, carpentry and preaching the gospel. Whatever doubts the thirty-three-year-old priest may have entertained about his abilities as a pastor in Oklahoma would evaporate over time as he served the indigenous people of Santiago Atitlán. It can be said with certainty that it was not until Stan left his native land and became immersed in a remote culture that his ministry began to fit his character and diverse talents. Stan the seminarian struggled to master Latin, but Stan the priest would learn to speak not only Spanish but also the native tongue of his Tz'utujil parishioners, a language that few non-Indians were ever able to comprehend fully.

About the size of Tennessee, Guatemala—from a geographical and cultural standpoint—should be a tourist's haven. Among its lures are lush rain forests, beautiful lakes, and magnificent mountains interspersed with volcanoes. Pilfered ancient ruins dot the countryside and provide a visible link in time with the colorful fiestas and market days of today's Mayan descendants. Its many political and socioeconomic problems, however, had transformed this paradise into a land of bloodshed.

During the 1980s 45 to 50 percent of Guatemala's 8.8 million people were indigenous. Living mostly in the southern and western highlands, the Maya constituted a rural society of isolated villages in which life changed little with the passing of time. The various communities displayed a wide range of cultural and linguistic differences, including distinctive clothing. The Mayan economic mainstay was subsistence farming, with some regional specialization in handicrafts; annual per capita income was about eighty dollars, thereby ranking the Maya among the poorest and most isolated people in the Western Hemisphere.[22]

The vast majority of the remaining population were *ladinos* (sometimes called *mestizos*). The small percentage of mostly European descendants were politically conservative and controlled the country, although over the years some *ladinos* had entered their ranks. The elite considered the Maya lazy, dishonest, and biologically substandard. The more "Indian" someone was, the less civilized he or she was thought to be. To persecute the Indian population was socially acceptable to many of the privileged class, and for outsiders to come to Guatemala to labor for their spiritual and material welfare was incomprehensible and viewed with suspicion.

With the coming of independence from Spain in the 1800s, the Guatemalan elite, as in the rest of Central America, split into two factions that competed for control of the country. The Liberals envisioned themselves as progressives who favored emphasis on coffee production; they were anti-clerical and passed laws to confiscate the property of religious orders and the Indians' communal lands, so that they could be incorporated into the agro-export economy. The Conservatives favored the old aristocratic ways, when the church worked in harmony with the privileged. Although neither faction concerned itself with ameliorating the condition of the Indians and poor *mestizos*, the Conservatives at least provided a modicum of paternalistic protection. A foreign dimension was added to the country's power structure, when, in the last years of the nineteenth century, a new agricultural product, bananas, began to play a major role in the economy. Whereas coffee plantations were owned by local elites, the banana business was controlled by large U.S. companies bent on enriching their American stockholders.

Following independence, Guatemala had always been ruled by dictators who paid little attention to meaningful reform. In 1944, however, Juan José Arévalo was elected president with 85 percent of the vote. Modeling himself after U.S. President Franklin Roosevelt, he was serious about turning his nation into a twentieth-century democracy. His inauguration on March 15, 1945, ushered in a decade of social progress. The right to vote was granted to women and the illiterate; political parties (though not the Communist Party) were allowed to organize; unions were permitted; freedom of speech and assembly was allowed; social security programs were created; and government health and education programs were expanded.

In 1951, Colonel Jacobo Arbenz Guzmán was elected president with 63 percent of the vote, promising not only to continue the policies of Arévalo but to expand them by addressing the crucial problem of land inequality that Arévalo had cautiously avoided. True to his word, in 1952 Arbenz had a major land reform law passed. Over a thousand plantations were expropriated and turned over to more than a hundred thousand *campesino* (peasant) families. Former owners were to be compensated according to the land's declared tax value. Approximately 400,000 of the 550,000 acres owned by the United Fruit Company were expropriated; 85 percent of the land was uncultivated. Since this U.S. company had had its property drastically undervalued for tax purposes, it stood to lose significantly. Working with the Central Intelligence Agency and with the blessing of President Dwight Eisenhower, United Fruit branded Arbenz a communist and succeeded in toppling his democratic government in 1954. The U.S. placed the corrupt Carlos Castillo Armas in the presidency and, following his assassination in 1957, Guatemala was ruled by a long line of military dictators or civilians collaborating with the army. The nation's brief era of political progress, often referred to as the "Ten Years of Spring," had been destroyed for the sake of United Fruit Company profits.

During the short presidency of Castillo Armas, land reform ended and repression began. Expropriated land was returned to its prior owners and *campesinos* and labor union leaders who objected were murdered. Literacy programs were terminated. Agricultural exports expanded dramatically, however, along with the landholdings of the elite. From 1960 to 1974 the total annual value of the five major agro-export products increased from $105.3 million to $367.5 million. But this dramatic growth took place at the expense of subsistence farming. As the population of Guatemala rose, there was less land available for *campesinos* to grow the corn and beans necessary for their families' survival.

Within the army there was dissatisfaction among a small faction of reformers, which led to an incipient guerrilla movement. In 1966, the government commissioned Colonel Carlos Arana to destroy the rebels. Assisted by U.S. training, advisers, and equipment, his troops killed between six and eight thousand people over the next two years, nearly all of them innocent peasants, since the guerrillas never numbered over three hundred. U.S. pilots in American planes even dropped napalm on *campesinos*, and a thousand Green Berets participated in counterinsurgency operations. At this time, too, right-wing death squads were formed to assist the army, and a U.S. colonel, John Webber, played a role in their formation. When in 1970 Colonel Arana was "elected" president, kidnappings, torture, and murder intensified. From 1970 to 1975, fifteen thousand people disappeared.[23]

This, then, was Guatemala. Here Stanley Rother would serve from 1968 until his assassination in 1981.

In June 1968 Stan and Father Tom Stafford, a fellow missioner, drove the two thousand miles from Oklahoma to Guatemala in Stan's Bronco, towing a 1,000-pound rock picker.[24] The Santiago Atitlán mission had been established in March 1964, one of many founded in Latin America then in response to the call of John XXIII. The pope had made an emphatic appeal to American Catholics to send missioners to Latin America through a speech delivered by Monsignor (later Cardinal) Agostino Casaroli at the University of Notre Dame in August 1961. Of momentous importance, as Gerald M. Costello described it, "the speech . . . served as a blueprint for the United States' full-scale mission involvement in Latin America; its words set in motion a series of events that were to alter thousands of lives and change the face of the church on two continents."[25] Oklahomans had responded to this call by founding "Micatokla"—the Catholic Mission of Oklahoma—in Santiago Atitlán.

Early U.S. missioners were sometimes unrealistic in their expectations. With the best of intentions, they believed that their American know-how, efficiency, and resources would make inroads against disease, ignorance, and desperate poverty. In a few decades, they thought, the long centuries during which poor Latin Americans had come to identify the church with the wealth and power of an oppressive elite would end. Many of these missioners returned to the United States disillusioned.

If Carlin had ever entertained such notions, by the time Father David Monahan visited Micatokla in 1966 the pastor had already confronted reality:

> [Carlin] was the short fat man with the brush haircut . . . [who saw] the double reality there. He relished the complex native culture, and he had even more appreciation of the goodness and comeliness of the Indians. He admired [their] spunk and tenacity . . .
>
> He talked about the conscience problem of living in the rectory, modest by U.S. standards but far and away the best house in town, while close by women were giving birth in the dirt, and families were parceling out meager portions of corn and beans,

and malnourished babies were dying of a flu they had not the wherewithal to resist. Yet he realized that North Americans could not survive there over a long haul under other terms.[26]

Visitors came by the boatload across ten-by-fourteen-mile Lake Atitlán. The townspeople—mostly Tz'utujil Indians wearing colorful, beautifully woven clothes—captured tourists' attention, as did the market selling native handicrafts and the historic church dedicated to Santiago Apóstol. Built in 1547 by Spanish friars, it was now a national monument. But some tourists surely must have sensed the hardship of life beneath the charming façade when they saw the malnourished children, lack of sanitation, inadequate school, and absence of medical care.

Santiago Atitlán, the largest of the eleven towns around the lake, lies in the Department of Sololá. Its population, called "*Atitecos*," then numbered about 27,000 Tz'utujils and several hundred *ladinos* of mixed Spanish and Indian descent.[27] Clustered around open-air yards were myriads of small cornstalk huts with reed-thatched roofs housing three generations. Paths of volcanic sand divided the town into neighborhoods called *cantones*. Most of the population was crowded into an area of one square mile, for the Indians conserved their land for farming.

At daybreak, the men would leave to work in small fields of two or three acres that they tilled and planted using a hoe and stick. The boys later joined their fathers. Because of the land shortage, there were also plots on the steep slopes of nearby mountains. Some men supplemented their meager incomes by doing seasonal work at planting and harvesting time on large *fincas* (plantations) along the Pacific coast or in nearby mountains, earning twenty-five to seventy-five cents a day (during the 1960s) for backbreaking labor.[28]

Before the women and girls left their homes, they used a small amount of wood for a fire to cook the day's ration of black beans. Wood was carefully conserved, since it was being consumed faster than nature was replenishing it. With no ventilation within, smoke had blackened the walls of the huts, and the racking coughs of many women were probably the result of cooking tortillas and beans in these smoky dwellings. Later, the women, wearing their distinctive shawls and mostly barefoot, would walk toward the lake, some with huge baskets of dirty laundry and others with clay jugs or plastic bottles on their heads to fill with drinking water. This practice, along with heavy runoff from the village during the rainy season washing human and animal filth into the lake, accounted for most of the dysentery and intestinal worms afflicting the people. Before the

Oklahoma missioners arrived, diarrhea, flu, measles, and malnutrition killed half the children under five.

Back in the village yards, grandmothers taught the art of weaving on the backstrap loom to their granddaughters. Some of the girls practiced using palm leaves; others, using brightly colored threads, were tentatively beginning their first garments. Weaving consumed much of a woman's day—a traditional garment would take about two months from start to finish.

Some youngsters would head for the little school. There they spent two years learning Spanish from a teacher who usually lacked adequate professional training. Indian children spoke only Tz'utujil at home; with Spanish as the official language of Guatemala, it had to be mastered if progress were to be made in education. Reading and writing in Spanish would come later. Unfortunately, few completed more than two or three years of school; the fourth-grade graduate was an educated man or woman in Santiago Atitlán.

This was the reality that Carlin faced in 1964. The Oklahoma team began to tackle some issues by developing a credit union, farmers' and weavers' cooperatives, and a health clinic. The team reached out to four remote *fincas*, and villagers were trained as catechists to assist in religious education. Micatokla missioners also started a radio station called the "Voice of Atitlán," which offered education on literacy, health, and catechetics and provided Atitecos with news and music.[29] Eventually, the radio station was turned over to Tz'utujils, who continued its endeavor to educate and inform. In 1980, with the onset of kidnappings and murders, the station manager would be one of the first victims as the army forced the "Voice of Atitlán" off the air.

Illiteracy among the Tz'utujils was nearly universal. Enlisting the help of two native speakers, Juan Mendoza and Antonio Tzina Ratzan, Carlin soon initiated a project to have their native language put into written form. Although this task would continue over two decades, by July 25, 1968, the feast day of Santiago Apóstol, the Tz'utujil would for the first time in history hear their native language used in the Mass prayers and readings.[30] Stan Rother—the one Oklahoman who would become proficient in Tz'utujil—had arrived only weeks before.

When Stan arrived in June 1968, there were five priests, a nurse, three nuns, and two papal volunteers on Micatokla's team. The group was energized but divided on how to improve the lot of the people. Should team members immerse themselves in the culture, laboring over the long term within their traditions? Or would the more top-down methods of past missioners, who often taught that the "American way" was best, bring more immediate results? Such debates were typical at the time, with new concepts of mission coming to the fore after the Second Vatican Council.

Stan, the new team member, did not join in these often intense dinnertime conversations. By nature reserved and pragmatic and not having been exposed to the new models of theology and anthropology being discussed, he went to his room after eating. When he later participated in an intensive four-month Spanish language course and failed to achieve impressive proficiency,[31] it seemed as if his past had followed him to the mission. Monahan commented: "Some team members of Micatokla apparently had formed a prior judgment [of] him: a nice enough guy but not so bright, conservative, and basically a 'Mass priest.' There were doubts about his ability to master Spanish well enough to be effective."[32]

But Carlin realized that Rother's willingness to work would go a long way in Santiago Atitlán. In 1969, he assigned him as pastor of nearby Cerro de Oro. Then, even though Stan was still struggling with Spanish, Carlin began introducing him to Tz'utujil. Surprisingly, Rother's competence soon surpassed that of his teacher, so Carlin again sent him away to language school, this time to study Tz'utujil.[33] Carlin became the young priest's mentor, and under his guidance Stan grew in confidence. When the older priest left Micatokla in 1972 because of his health, Rother eventually took his place as pastor of Santiago Apóstol. By 1975, the only North American remaining on the mission team was the priest who some had initially thought did not have the ability to be an effective missioner.[34]

Stan adapted so well that on a 1971 archdiocesan personnel form he noted, with typical brevity, "Plan to stay here for some time." What special training did he bring to mission life? "Farming, design, construction, language."[35] His remarkable variety of abilities was not just an asset in Santiago Atitlán; it was a necessity. Here Stan could be architect, carpenter, chauffeur, repairman, mechanic, technician, purchasing agent, engineer, accountant, banker, teacher, counselor, farmer—and priest. Rother took great pride in his work. All around the mission one would encounter his handiwork—the cabinets he made, the church buildings and medical equipment he repaired, the hospital he helped build, the mission farm where he and the Ateticos experimented in raising many varieties of crops. His father later found Stan's engineering books for laying pipes and installing electricity.[36] Even his skills in bookbinding proved valuable. Stan was able to make Catholic devotions available to his parishioners in the form of a book called "Prayers for the People," written in

Stanley Rother with members of his parish

Tz'utujil. At the time of his death, a translation of the New Testament into Tz'utujil had almost been completed.[37]

Stan was creative. The weavers' co-op made Mass stoles for priests from a pattern that Rother had designed, and these stoles were sold in the United States.[38] He took pride in vestments he made for himself. Working with skilled Atitecos, he installed stained-glass windows for the historic church and revamped a massive altarpiece ("*retableau*"): "Since there were many parts and columns of old altar pieces stacked in the corner of the Church, we got the idea of putting up a big *retableau* where they apparently had one before. It will end up being about half new and half old, but an interesting mosaic of woods."[39]

One skill that profoundly helped Stan and his Tz'utujil parishioners grow in affection and respect was his ability to speak their language. Whereas Stan famously had had trouble learning Latin, he had a strong drive to communicate with all the people of Santiago Atitlán—with the Tz'utujils and the far smaller group of *ladinos*. For that he had to become proficient in Spanish and the more daunting Mayan language of Tz'utujil. Before long, he could—and did—say Mass in Spanish or Tz'utujil, achieving a proficiency in the latter that no other missioner had. Marita Rother, who often visited Santiago Atitlán for weeks at a time, commented:

> Stan did not regularly give the sermon in Tzutuhil. He gave it in Spanish and an interpreter gave it in Tzutuhil. He knew the language well enough to know that certain of his interpreters added some points on their own. Apparently this did not disturb [him] because he would laugh about it. I think Stan felt more comfortable with the Spanish and it would have been exhausting to give it in both languages himself.[40]

Stan's ability to speak their language was key to his growing rapport with the Tz'utujils. It unlocked doors for him into their history, culture, and traditions. In his letters, he called them "these beautiful people of God."[41] As their priest, but also perhaps because of their common agricultural ancestry, he often referred to himself as their shepherd.

Stan began to visit a different family every Sunday, sharing a meal with them after he celebrated Mass. He realized that the benefits were mutual: "It is quite satisfying... for the contact and interest, and revealing as to the poverty that exists so close to us here and the great faith and spirit they manifest. Maybe it does me more good than it does them."[42]

Rother embraced his parishioners' customs and traditions.[43] One unique aspect of worship was at the consecration of the Mass, when members of the congregation spontaneously began quietly voicing their individual prayers. Beginning sporadically, the murmurs spread rapidly, until the church resounded with hundreds of personal entreaties directed heavenward. Stan once said: "When I hear the cacophony of prayers going up to heaven, I know there is a God."

He was touched by the generosity of the people. Every Thursday the women of each *cantón* took turns gathering corn and bringing it to the church to be blessed; then the men would distribute the offerings among the poor and sick. Rother was especially moved by the collection one Christmas Eve. It amounted to twenty-three *quetzales* (units of Guatemalan currency), fourteen of which were entirely in *centavos* (cents). Their pastor knew that fourteen hundred families had given one *centavo* each—an offering not from their abundance but because others were more in need.

Because Tz'utujil courtship customs fascinated Stan, he hoped one day to capture them on film, but did not succeed. The girls and boys would gather around the village—girls in one cluster, boys in another—and parade around in groups. If a boy was interested in a girl, his entire group would ease over to her group, and he would yank on her shawl. The girl—and her group—might stop as she smiled and chatted with him; but, if she was not interested, she would shrug her shoulder sharply and jerk her shawl out of his grasp.

The traditions that most captivated Rother were those centering on Holy Week and Easter. It is no coincidence that in 1981, after being warned that he was on a death list and escaping to Oklahoma, he chose to return to Santiago Atitlán on the eve of Palm Sunday, to be with the people for Holy Week. Rother's fondness for these celebrations revealed a great deal about the bond that existed between him and the Indians. While most of the rituals during the most significant week of the liturgical year followed Catholic traditions, there were also key events surrounding a cigar-smoking Mayan deity named Maximón. For Rother, who was rather conservative in his religious views, to tolerate these deviations from orthodoxy showed his respect for the people and his understanding of their spirituality.

Holy Week began with a dramatic flair. There was a drumbeat in the early morning announcing the re-enactment of the triumphal entry of Jesus into Jerusalem on Palm Sunday, as the Atitecos, dressed in their colorful best, gathered in the courtyard behind the church. Waving palm branches, they surrounded Jesus on the donkey and formed a procession that wound through the narrow streets, finally entering the church for the celebration of Mass.

Monday and Tuesday of Holy Week are usually uneventful, but not so in Santiago Atitlán. On Monday night the ceremonial washing of Maximón's clothes occurred. But it was on Tuesday evening that his wooden image actually entered into the events. The customary drumbeat preceded the drama, as the people gathered at the home of the *télenel*—an official of the *cofradía*, a civil-religious indigenous brotherhood—whose role it was to carry Maximón on his shoulder during processions through town.[44] As the Tz'utujil awaited Maximón's appearance outside, excitement built to a crescendo inside the crowded hut. Maximón was carefully dressed in layers of freshly laundered clothing, including multiple colorful scarves. By the time Maximón emerged, the tension inside and out was electric. The next morning Maximón, accompanied by a crowd, paid his annual visit to the mayor's office. He was then brought to his private chapel near the entrance of the church, where he held court until his next dramatic appearance on Good Friday.

Holy Thursday ceremonies were serene. In the afternoon, people assembled in the courtyard behind the church for a re-enactment of the Last Supper. Twelve boys, dressed in colorful biblical attire, acted as the apostles, and twelve courses of food were blessed by Rother. The food was not eaten but was later given to poor families. Another procession then wound through the town, ending inside the church for Mass and the washing of the disciples' feet.

On Good Friday, an almost life-size figure of Jesus was nailed to a wooden cross and at noon the cross was raised and inserted into a hole in the church floor. Three hours later, after the Good Friday service, the statue of Christ was placed in a glass coffin. Men then lifted the coffin on their shoulders and carried it from the crowded church. Outside the entrance, the procession stopped, as the figure of Maximón was brought from his little chapel. There in the archway of the church, the Tz'utujil tradition converged with the Christian tradition as Maximón did a unique little dance before Christ in his coffin. His attitude and gestures seemed to say to Jesus: "Ha, ha, ha, you young upstart! They caught you, but they didn't catch me!" Following his encounter with Jesus, Maximón was taken away to await next year's Holy Week. Young men then carried the coffin around town throughout the night, returning at about six AM, when the coffin was reverently brought back into the church.

Easter Sunday was one occasion when the usually reserved Rother was often visibly moved. At 4:30 in the morning, a bonfire was lit in the middle of the plaza. From each of the four directions, Atitecos came in the darkness, bearing lighted candles and singing songs of joy. After they extinguished their candles, the light from the bonfire was transferred by Stan to the paschal candle, from which the other candles were relit. Inside the dark church, the only source of light was the flickering candles, until the first rays of daylight shone through the open rear door. By then, everyone in church was tense with excitement, and at that very moment, the bells would ring out, the organist would play loudly and joyfully, and a huge banner portraying the risen Christ would arise from the floor of the church.

The intrusion of Maximón into the holiest week of the year and his little dance of triumph before the dead Christ could appear to some to be a mockery of Christian ritual. However, there is an explanation for such traditions:

> [Popular] religion was fatalistic, syncretic, and paternalistic: God was like the large landowner, to be appeased and bribed; his son, Christ, who appears everywhere in Latin America as a crucified man, epitomized the suffering and death of the poor...Christ had been beaten down, tortured, and killed by a higher authority, just as they had been and their fathers before them...
>
> The Christ they know is a poor guy without influence, like themselves, not the teacher or the leader who defeated death and who inspired his people with a new vision of heaven and earth.[45]

Prior to the coming of the Oklahomans, the village had been without a resident priest for about a hundred years. An attempt to eliminate the Tz'utujil traditions could have had negative effects on the people's social structure, unity, and religious enthusiasm. Father Rother understood this.

Gradually, Rother was accepted into the inner circles of village life. The Tz'utujils and Stan exchanged many treasures. Rother presented each newlywed couple with an instant photo of themselves after the marriage ceremony, and the Tz'utujils wove vestments for him. He came to see the *cofradía* as a vehicle used by the Maya to retain their culture. He developed good rapport with the *cabecera*, head of the brotherhood, attended meetings, and even began walking in some *cofradía* processions. In time, he would be honored when the elders presented him with the symbolic *perraje*, a colorful neckstole, and accepted him as one of their own. It was the *cofradía* elders who conferred on Stan the name "A'plas"—Tz'utujil for Francis(co), his middle name.[46] Rother's participation in Mayan traditions was uncommon for Catholic priests. Regardless of whether Stan derived his enlightened outlook directly from Pope Paul VI's *Ad Gentes*, instructing missioners to inculturate themselves in the lives of indigenous peoples, his insights were in accordance with that document.[47]

In January 1976, an assistant pastor joined Stan—a native-born *ladino*, Adán García. Just weeks later, a 7.5 magnitude earthquake devastated much of Guatemala. Since Santiago Atitlán was mostly spared, Stan and his parishioners set out to help those who had been stricken. Padre Adán was in awe of Stan's strength as he rescued the injured from ravines, sometimes carrying them up steep inclines on his shoulders. The bishop soon tapped García to direct the relief effort, and Stan lost his capable assistant.[48]

Although Stan was usually alone in the rectory, he refused to lock the doors, because he wanted the people to know that they could call on him night and day—which they did. Stan was often asked to be an arbitrator in property and trespassing disputes, and he made numerous trips to Guatemala City—fifty-six miles away over awful roads—on errands for the people. "Old Nicolás," whose eating habits repulsed many, became a daily guest in the rectory for lunch; Stan cut his meat and gave him food to take home and a bed for his nap. After many years, Nicolás failed to show up one day and was found dead in his hut.

Father Stan gave his time and money for the welfare of many. Although illnesses caused by malnutrition and lack of sanitation must have overwhelmed him, he did what he could to help, often transporting seriously ill parishioners to the national hospital in Sololá—with their relatives crammed into the back of his pick-up. From a trust fund left by an uncle, Rother arranged to have a boy with cancer of the mouth treated in a private hospital in Guatemala City; the boy was eventually cured. Years before, Rother had found the boy's father dying of dysentery and rushed him to the mission hospital.[49] When an Indian repairing a well pump was overcome by fumes, Stan responded immediately and pulled the half-conscious man to safety.[50] And when he learned that an infant girl was very weak and underweight because her mother was suffering from a high fever and could not nurse, he made arrangements for the baby's adoption by a former missioner and his wife. The girl was one of newborn twins; the family had found a wet nurse for one of them, but María had been fed only sugar water for several days. Rother made several trips to Guatemala City to buy formula, and little María gained in strength before joining Jude and Julia Pansini.[51] It is no wonder that, on one visit, Stan's sister Marita noticed there were more and more children named "Francisco" after Stan.

Greeting a young parishioner

Over the years, medical professionals, friends and relatives, priests and sisters came to Micatokla from all over the U.S. Marita's religious community was particularly generous with volunteers: three sisters from Wichita, Kansas, worked at Micatokla for years, and every summer two others, often including Marita, spent weeks there helping out.[52] Volunteers remained for weeks or months, professional staff often for years. Many, if not all, felt their stay had offered them a new understanding of the world. Their experiences, when shared back home, enlightened countless individuals in the United States and had the ripple effect of an ever-increasing consciousness of the hardships suffered by the poor in Guatemala.

Rother worked closely with Project Concern, a nonprofit organization based in San Diego that provided health care and training in developing countries. Through the efforts of Jude Pansini, in 1975 Project Concern began to help staff the little hospital in Santiago Atitlán. Gradually the 50 percent infant mortality rate dropped to about 20 percent.[53] But all medical problems and diseases could not be treated by the tiny staff, and the Guatemalan government provided no medical care in Santiago Atitlán. There was a public hospital in Guatemala City, but Rother said the poor did not receive proper care there, and the Tz'utujils were afraid to venture away from home, being hampered by the language difference. They lived and died with their diseases, often dragging themselves to work in the fields. Malnutrition was so vicious that the children's skin would sometimes peel off. To alleviate some of their misery, Rother twice arranged for a team of six doctors from Guatemala City to volunteer their services in Santiago Atitlán. When a man who had been shot by a death squad returned alive and was hobbling around on crutches, Stan asked an Oklahoma doctor who was volunteering in nearby Sololá to treat the man. On the day Stan was murdered, the physician operated successfully on this man.[54]

Stan's active concern for his parishioners was evident to all, and in 1979, the death of a man named Tomás revealed just how close Stan and the Tz'utujils had become. For years the old man had counseled the young priest on Tz'utujil traditions and beliefs and was a beloved friend. Tomás, called the "Bishop" because he followed the priest in processions, was revered for his wisdom. When Stan was called to his bedside to give him the last rites and his blessing, Tomás was weak, with death a few hours away. Yet he suddenly sat straight up in bed, put his hands on Rother's head and chanted a blessing in Tz'utujil. Frankie Williams, a frequent volunteer at the mission, was present and saw that Stan had tears in his eyes and that he and Tomás were profoundly moved during this exchange. After she and Rother left the hut, she asked what Tomás had said. Stan hesitated: "I can't tell you, Frankie. I would be embarrassed. Besides, I hope it won't happen."[55]

The closer Padre A'plas grew to the Atitecos, the more austere his life became. His clothes began to acquire "more patches on patches." When he traveled, he chose poor accommodations, simple food, and cheap transportation. On one trip, Father Leven recalled, they spent the night in a hut "worse than a chicken coop" in the U.S. Their meals were so meager that Leven asked why he ate such simple fare. "Because the people are so poor," Stan answered.[56]

Yet, as Frankie Williams said, "he was not perfect," and, though many remembered his infectious laugh, "he could be angry, blunt, tenacious, and cross—a real bear at times."[57] Others agreed that he could exhibit a temper when angered. Leven remembered him scolding altar boys for their mistakes, then "agonizing over it later."[58] As Williams put it, "He was an ordinary man, who became extraordinary." As Jude Pansini, who was a former priest, noted: "Father Rother grew like I've never seen anyone grow in the priesthood."[59] And Paul Joslin, a Christian Brother working in the vicinity, said simply: "Stan was a saint even before he died."[60]

For twelve years, the life of Stanley Rother in Santiago Atitlán was essentially peaceful. He resolved to remain there, writing to Marita: "Maybe they'll let me retire here...I would stay if all support from Oklahoma were stopped. The [family] farm may have to support me one day."[61]

But the peace would be shattered in October 1980 as the town was invaded by fear and violence, a result of the brutal repression that had been spreading through Guatemala since 1974.

As the presidency of Colonel Carlos Arana moved toward an end, the armed forces had announced that only military personnel would be permitted to run in the 1974 presidential election. They then put forth General Kjell Laugerud, a close associate of Arana, as their candidate. A coalition calling itself the National Opposition Front also offered a candidate, General Efraín Ríos Montt. When the early election returns gave Ríos Montt a surprisingly large lead, the government suspended the vote count, and a few days later Laugerud was declared the victor.[62] After the military refused to permit a recount, Ríos Montt proved himself a loyal soldier and accepted its decision. Those who hungered for change now saw little value in elections.

In the 1978 presidential election, when no candidate received a majority, General Fernando Lucas García was declared the winner by Congress. This election was notable because 60 percent of the electorate, showing their disgust for the corrupt electoral system, refused to vote. Lucas García inaugurated what proved to be the most repressive period in modern Guatemalan history. Death squads recruited from the army and police killed political opponents, union members, students, Indians, and religious leaders in unprecedented numbers. By the end of Lucas García's grisly term in 1982, more than thirteen thousand people had been murdered, while countless others had been kidnapped and tortured. Rother would be one of his victims.

In May 1978 more than a hundred Q'eqchi' Indians were massacred at Panzos by the army for attempting to defy powerful landowners who had ordered them to leave an area they had lived on for ages. A few months later, thirty demonstrators were shot dead and three hundred were wounded for protesting the doubling of bus fares. On January 31, 1980, Lucas García's cruelty shocked the world. Twenty-eight peasant, university, and labor leaders had occupied the Spanish embassy to protest increased violence under his regime. When the police prepared to storm the building, the Spanish ambassador reminded them that the embassy enjoyed diplomatic immunity. The police attacked anyway and the building caught fire. As Guatemalan authorities stood by, the embassy was permitted to burn to the ground, killing twenty-seven occupiers and twelve others. The one protester who survived was kidnapped from his hospital bed and murdered by security forces. The Spanish government, incensed by this disregard for international law, broke off diplomatic relations.

International protests did nothing to temper Lucas García's brutality. Convinced that foreign missioners, rather than his own repression, were responsible for the increase in demonstrations, he vowed to rid his country of them within two years. Five priests were murdered by death squads and others barely survived by escaping detection. When Bishop Juan Gerardi of Quiché learned that police had planned to murder him on July 19 and had failed only because he had not kept a scheduled appointment, he decided to leave the diocese and ordered all priests and nuns in Quiché to do likewise. Bishop Mario Ríos Montt went into seclusion when his name was put on a death squad's assassination list because he had condemned the kidnappings of union leaders. Hand grenades were hurled at a convent staffed by Canadian nuns in Morales, Izabal, but the sisters were not injured.[63] Right-wing terrorism was then turned against the moderate Christian Democratic Party. Its October demand that all political parties be permitted to participate in the next election was answered with the assassination of seventy-six of its members.[64]

Accusations of subversion and communism directed toward anyone who called for human rights were not immediately perceived as threats to the community in Santiago Atitlán. But Rother was watching these developments carefully. In ten years his outlook had shifted from one of hope to a sense of impending evil. At Christmastime 1969 he had written: "This peace is a comfort to us who live in a world beset by unrest —political, social and religious. Happily this is not so evident here in Guatemala."[65]

By 1978, his apprehension was growing. He called his friend Harry Flynn, now the rector of Mount St. Mary's Seminary, and asked if he might visit there, saying he was tired and needed time for prayer. Flynn recalled:

> He spoke about the terrible injustices that were perpetrated against the Indian people. He spoke about his own need as a priest to speak out and yet in speaking out having some knowledge that he would either be deported or physically harmed. He spoke of many of his friends, who were priests, and who experienced some violence in one form or another because of the stand that they had taken for the Indian people.[66]

Stan was becoming frustrated with the entrenched injustices built into the Guatemalan economy. He noted in a report to the Oklahoma diocese that agro-export plantations were owned by the very few at the expense of more than a million Indians who, though they were the stimulus nationwide for tourist spending, were landless and hungry.[67] Then, in May 1979, Stan wrote that repression was hitting close to home:

> An anonymous hate sheet...made its debut a few Sundays ago. The mayor, the school director, teachers, and anybody of importance in town made the list. I was number 8...Guatemala is systematically doing away with all liberal[s] or even moderates in government, [and] labor leaders and apparently there are lots of kidnappings that never get in the papers. There are something like 15 bodies that show up every day in the country and show signs of torture...I haven't received any threats as such, but if anything happens, that is the way it is supposed to be. I don't intend to run from danger, but at the same time I don't intend to unnecessarily put myself into danger. I want to live like anyone else.[68]

By early 1980, he sensed an ominous future:

> There were the killings by police and army in the Spanish Embassy...Last Sunday the army killed four spectators at the end of a soccer game...On the Coast here, fields are being burned, strikes at sugar mills, buildings and equipment on the fincas being destroyed...The tension builds, more killings, repression. Don't know when it will all stop. It will get worse before it gets better.[69]

By 1979 Rother had backed himself into a corner. He had expressed his intention not to "unnecessarily put myself into danger." But did this mean he should close the doors of his rectory to those on death lists? Should he not help the widows and hungry children who would lose husbands and fathers, their only source of support? Rother was not political or confrontational, yet he took his priesthood and the gospel very seriously. Over the decade during which he had labored alongside his parishioners, he had witnessed their day-to-day struggle to exist. It weighed on him to see their hopes dashed at every turn. Now the Atitecos, especially their leaders, would be called "subversives" simply because they were striving for a more prosperous and dignified future. Their families would be seen as subversive. Anyone who befriended them would be called subversive, and a gringo would especially be suspect if he spoke to them in a

Mayan language few understood. Before he died, this man who had studiously avoided controversy would state: "To shake the hand of an Indian is a political act."[70]

At first in 1980, life proceeded normally. There was anticipation in the air because nine Carmelite Missionaries of St. Teresa, eight of whom were Kaqchikel Maya, were coming to work at the mission. Stan translated his excitement into intense activity, getting their house ready for them, laying linoleum and installing cabinets, a sink, and a flower box.

There were other preoccupations. The summer of 1980, which broke records for high temperatures and killed Americans in the Midwest, was also hot and dry in Guatemala, and the bean crop in Santiago Atitlán was threatened. Of major concern was Manuel Tum's accident. Tum was a Kaqchikel, a lay worker who had been hired to help out at the mission. In late summer after an evening of drinking, he took without permission a Bronco that was registered in Rother's name and set out with a companion. They veered off the road and plummeted down a steep hillside into Lake Atitlán. Manuel escaped with a few bruises, but his companion, a school teacher with a wife and baby, was killed. Manuel deserted the scene and went home to bed. The Bronco and the body were discovered the next morning and Manuel denied it all. That evening, Rother and Pedro Bocel—his new associate pastor who was also Kaqchikel—talked with Manuel and inspected his bruises. Manuel confessed and finally turned himself in to the authorities. Rother then found him a lawyer, and Tum went to prison to await trial. Stan, up until the time he was murdered, visited him every month.[71]

This episode took on a deeper meaning after Rother was killed. In several letters, Stan mentioned his visits to the prison, adding that Manuel was safer there awaiting trial than he would have been in Santiago Atitlán, for it was only a few weeks after his arrest that the army encamped on the mission farm and abductions and disappearances began. Stan believed that Manuel, a church worker, would have been targeted by the army. And Stan's association with the prisoner could also have aroused suspicion.

It was also then that the spreading repression began to touch the lives of the Tz'utujils directly. In June, while Stan was in Oklahoma, some guerrillas from the Revolutionary Organization of the People in Arms (ORPA) came at night to Santiago Atitlán attempting to recruit members. A letter from Rother written in July indicated that they seemed to have garnered some support.[72] Evidently, word of the guerrillas' visit got back to authorities, because soon thereafter armed soldiers arrived in town.

On September 22, 1980, Rother wrote a frank letter expressing how dire the situation had become not only in Santiago Atitlán but throughout Guatemala. It was hand-carried out of the country and delivered to Archbishop Salatka of Oklahoma City:

> The Diocese of Quiché...has been abandoned completely...At one place there were about sixty men of the Church lined up by the wall and they killed every fourth person.
>
> The Country here is in rebellion and the government is taking it out on the Church. The low wages that are paid, the very few who are excessively rich, the bad distribution of land—these are some of the reasons for widespread discontent. The Church seems to be the only force that is trying to do something [about] the situation, and therefore the govt. is after us. There are some that say the Diocese of Sololá, where this mission is, is the next area on the list for persecution.

Indeed, it *was* next on the list. The celebration of Santiago Atitlán's annual fiesta was marred by soldiers in camouflage carrying submachine guns. In the same letter to Salatka, Rother described the apprehension that had descended on the town:

> [The army] didn't do anything but put everyone on edge, walking around in groups of three or four, standing on the corners watching everything. Since then we have had strangers in town, asking questions about the priests, this catechist or that one, where they live, who is in charge of the Cooperative, who are the leaders, etc. Because of this intimidation, several of the leaders of the different organizations are out of town or in hiding. It has changed our style of life here in the rectory too. The doors and gates are being made more secure, the front door is now locked all the time and people just can't enter at will. These twelve years I have slept in the same room that overlooks the plaza in front of the Church, but since a rectory and convent were attacked with grenades in the Eastern part of the Country, I sleep elsewhere now where the walls are rock instead of wood.
>
> I am aware that some of our younger catechists are working with those that are preparing for a revolution. They are young men that are becoming more and more conscientious about their situation and are convinced that the only option for them is revolt...The President...[wants] to expel all those religious who were catechizing the people...

The reality is that we are in danger...All classes and group meetings have been cancelled. We are working in smaller groups. My associate and myself are seen less in the street, and almost never leave the rectory at night. The tactic of the govt. has been to kidnap those they think are leaders, torture them and then kill them. Two days ago a young man from the neighboring parish was taken..., a cousin of one of our nuns. He is not expected to be found alive.

If I get a direct threat or am told to leave, I will go. But if it is my destiny that I should give my life here, then so be it...I don't want to desert these people, and that is what will be said, even after all these years.

Stan had asserted he would leave if threatened. But what of his assistant?

It would be almost impossible for Fr. Pedro Bocel to continue here alone. Being a Guatemalan and an Indian, it is more probable that he will be dispatched first. That is the reason that I am wanting to get him a visa. I do not intend to let him [stay] here to be killed if I have to leave, or if we see he is in imminent danger, I want to get him out of the Country. He was just ordained in January and I feel that he should not have to be sacrificed so early in his ministry...I don't feel that you would deny him that chance to escape from almost certain death here if things continue to evolve as they have been. I am not in as much danger as he is, because I am a foreigner and I hope they will give me a chance of leaving if they want me out. They haven't killed an American priest yet. [73]

In late October, several hundred soldiers camped in the fields outside the town. Fear grew. Their camp was partly on the mission farm and Rother received reports that troops were stealing crops, but the cautious priest had no intention of complaining.

Within five days of the army's arrival, four Atitecos were abducted, one of whom Rother knew well. This was Gaspar Culán, director of the Voice of Atitlán radio station and a former deacon. Concerning these occurrences, Phillip Berryman commented:

The immediate motivation may have been the fact that some time previously a group of ORPA guerrillas had come into the town and held a meeting. Some said Culán had spoken favorably of what the guerrillas said. In a more general sense this

army occupation seemed to mark a new stage in which whole
towns could come under siege and in which the prior presence
[of] the guerrilla organizations could be the pretext for retalia-
tory actions against people in towns and villages. Such had been
the situation in Quiché for years, and it now became characteristic of large parts of the Indian highlands.[74]

By the end of January 1981, thirty of Rother's parishioners would be
abducted or killed.[75]

It was Rother's custom to send a Christmas letter to the Catholics of
Oklahoma that was published annually in the Catholic newspapers there.
In his letter of 1980, Rother introduced Oklahomans to what had be-
come a part of daily life at Micatokla:

> The purported reason for the presence of the army in our imme-
> diate area is to drive out and protect us from communist guerril-
> las. But there aren't any around here. A group did come into
> town in early June for about 2 hours and made some promises to
> those who were around. There seemed to be interest on the part
> of some in their presence here. So far we have ten men that have
> disappeared. The director of the radio was one of the first and
> then later the station was broken into and looted... In our town
> are a number of informers who are paid by the authorities to be
> spies... The denunciations are sometimes because of envy,
> vengeance or just downright greed. A good friend of mine just
> happened to be in the wrong place when several others were
> picked up. He left a wife and three children... Another man left
> seven children.
>
> The Sisters, the other priest and myself have not been
> threatened. My associate has felt that he has been followed etc.
> but no direct threats. We have to be careful where we go and
> what we say to anyone. A nice compliment was given to me re-
> cently when a supposed leader in the Church and town was com-
> plaining that "Father is defending the people." He wants me
> deported for my sin.

Although the Christmas letter had begun cheerfully with "Merry
Christmas! Peace in 1981!" the troubled pastor ended with these words:

> This is one of the reasons I have for staying in the face of physical
> harm. The shepherd cannot run at the first sign of danger. Pray

for us that we may be a sign of the love of Christ for our people, that our presence among them will fortify them to endure these sufferings in preparation for the coming of the Kingdom.[76]

The "informers" had touched a raw nerve. Rarely does Rother have an unkind thought to share in his letters, except in the case of friends turned into spies: "I don't know if I could offer help to one of these informers. I know quite a few of them and some had been apparent friends."[77] After Rother's murder, a parishioner observed: "Padre Francisco couldn't bear to see some pull in money by selling their brothers. He said that, and for that they killed him."[78]

Rother did not say just what the accusation "Father is defending the people" referred to, but it could have been a number of things. As fear grew, Rother opened the doors of the church for people to sleep there, and hundreds came every night for protection. Catechists sought refuge in the rectory itself, taking turns standing watch through the night. Some family members did not want to be identified as relatives of victims, fearing for their own and their children's safety, so Stan would search for the bodies of those who had been abducted. It also became well known that Padre A'plas was helping the widows and children left destitute by the disappearance of the breadwinner. He used his Christmas check to help the victims' families. He was training widows to take their husbands' places at the professional loom of the weavers' co-op and was trying to open up markets in the U.S. and Guatemala City for the sale of hand-woven Indian stoles. In Guatemala, even the simplest act of charity could be labeled "subversive"—if directed toward a family with a name on the death list.

In another incident, an army officer called a meeting to convince people that the soldiers were there to protect them against guerrillas. The officer did not understand Tz'utujil, and Stan was asked to translate the questions of the townspeople, which were critical of the kidnappings and deaths that had occurred after the army arrived. Perhaps the officer felt that Rother could have shown some support for the army but refused to do so. Shortly after this meeting, Stan's name appeared on a death list.[79]

Many who were in danger chose to leave Santiago Atitlán, yet Diego Quic, "probably the most sought-after catechist" according to Rother, chose to remain with his wife and two little boys. Diego had a key to the rectory, and for protection he ate and slept there almost daily. Frightened and puzzled over the reason his name was put on a death list, he asked Stan, "I have never stolen, have never hurt anyone, have never eaten someone else's food, why then do they want to hurt me and kill me?"[80]

The fact is that those who were kidnapped were *not* guilty of crimes; they were never accused, arrested, tried, or convicted. They were labeled "subversive," their names were put on a death list in order to spread terror in a given area, and then they were executed usually after interrogation and torture. The mutilated bodies of the disappeared that showed up in ditches or in fields testified to the gruesome treatment the abducted had had to endure before death. On January 3, 1981, it was Diego's fate to join the thousands of disappeared in Guatemala. Rother described his catechist's kidnapping in a letter hand-carried back to Oklahoma:

As [Diego] was approaching Saturday night about 7:45, he was intercepted by a group of four kidnappers... He got to within 15 feet of the door and was holding on to the bannister and yelling for help.

The other priest heard the ruckus outside and stepped out to see them trying to take him. He considered trying to help, but was scared by their height. He called me from the living room where I was listening to music but also heard the noise, and by the time I realized what was happening, grabbed a jacket and got outside, they... were putting him into a waiting car...

I just stood there wanting to jump down to help, but knowing that I would be killed or be taken along also. The car sped off with him yelling for help but no one able to do so. Then I realized that Father Pedro, Frankie Williams from Wichita and I had just witnessed a kidnapping of someone that we had gotten to know and love and were unable to do anything about it. They had his mouth covered, but I can still hear his muffled screams for help.

As I got back in the rectory I got a cramp in my back from the anger I felt that this friend was being taken off to be tortured for a day or two and then brutally murdered for wanting a better life and more justice for his pueblo...

Sunday morning we heard that all the passengers of the late bus from the City heard the kidnapped yelling for help as they met the four-door sedan led by a military jeep and followed by a military ambulance. Soon after the kidnapping that night we went out and found his hat in front of the Church and his right shoe at the bottom of the steps... He was 30 years old, left a wife and two boys, ages 3 and one. May he rest in peace!...

That makes 11 members of this community that have been kidnapped... For these 11 that are gone, there are eight widows and 32 children... These people are going to need emergency help...

Since helping these people could very easily be considered as subversive by the local government, we have asked that the money be deposited directly in the bank there, and that there be no direct communication between the donors and me... Be careful about sending letters here mentioning relief etc. We never know when the mail may be intercepted and read...

I am not ready to call it quits yet... We don't know if [Diego's] presence here with us will affect us directly... Just say a prayer on occasion that we will be safe and still be able to be of service to these people of God.[81]

Soon after the kidnapping, Williams and Rother scanned the nearby fields for Diego's body, but with no success. According to Frankie, on one of these searches Stan appeared deeply agitated remembering Diego's muffled screams—"*Ayúdame! Ayúdame!*"—and asked her, "Do you think Diego understood that I could not help him?"[82] After Rother himself was killed, Williams testified to the House Subcommittee on Human Rights and International Relations that Diego had "made the mistake of complaining to the local police" that they were lax in helping to locate kidnap victims.[83] But the answer to Diego's question "Why then do they want to kill me?" lay deeper than that.

Usually the Indians targeted for abduction and torture were those who had made some advancement in their communities. Any Indian in a leadership role, like Diego, was suspect. Victims and potential victims included teachers, catechists, cooperative leaders, and directors of radio and medical programs—those who were attempting to lead their people out of misery. With a higher standard of living, the Indians might not be as willing to migrate seasonally to the plantations of wealthy landowners as a cheap source of labor. Animosity toward the Maya was a product of centuries of racism in Guatemala, a racism so extreme that Indians were considered to be "mules," a term used to describe them.[84] Such violent racism can ultimately lead to genocide and, in fact, this word was used to describe the attacks by the army and death squads on many Indian villages where the elderly, women, and children were massacred.[85] The hostility could also be transferred to those, like Rother and others, who treated the Indians with dignity.

Four days after Diego's abduction, soldiers in a convoy, suspecting that they had been attacked by guerrillas near Santiago Atitlán, retaliated by recklessly killing anyone they could find nearby—nineteen "townspeople who were not involved in anything,"[86] wrote Rother. Then, on January 12, apparently while in Guatemala City, he received warning that he was now in immediate danger. He went into hiding in the city for sixteen days, until a visa could be obtained for his associate, Pedro Bocel. On January 28 the two priests left Guatemala and arrived in Oklahoma City the next day.

Although Stan had tried not to burden his family, they knew his life at Micatokla was in jeopardy. Stan confided to his father at this time that he would never let a death squad drag him from the rectory. He stayed mainly in Okarche for the next two months, helping his parents with chores. He traveled to New York to see his brother Jim's family; Jim had died of leukemia in 1974 and his wife, having recently remarried, had moved away with the children. Stan's brother Tom noticed a difference on this visit: "Stan would sit at Mom and Dad's and just stare for an hour at a time. His body was here, but his mind was there."[87]

Rother received numerous requests to speak but declined all but one, explaining that to talk about the violent events occurring in Guatemala could prevent him from returning there. He made one exception, and it proved to be unfortunate. He agreed to speak at St. John the Baptist in Edmund, Oklahoma, where his friend Marvin Leven was pastor. Stan told of the repression he had witnessed and said that the Guatemalan reality did not correspond to statements being issued by the U.S. government. A man in the congregation, infuriated by Rother's lack of "patriotism," fired off a "vitriolic and vicious" letter to the Guatemalan ambassador in Washington, with a copy to the archbishop, charging Rother with promoting the overthrow of the Guatemalan government.[88]

Rother, who had done everything short of renouncing his priesthood and human compassion to keep a low profile, was deeply upset by this accusation. Perhaps a fellow missioner in Guatemala, Ronald Burke, described Stan best: "He was the real low-key type, just doing his job. His real delight was upgrading the agricultural and health level of the people." He later added: "Some American government officials have suggested that missioners are killed because they become political activists. These officials should have known Stan...Stan was impatient with priests he thought were too political in their analysis of the country's problems. An unabashed conservative, he never referred to any new theology. He said that the Gospel of Jesus was enough."[89]

In March, Rother and Bocel heard it was safe to return. Bocel did return but, for his safety, not to Santiago Atitlán. Stan remained in the States for another month, agonizing over, as he described it, "the big question...should I take a chance and go back?"[90]

Stan went back. His family understood that he had to return to his people. "I've got to do it," he told Marita, who later said, "And I knew that. I could see it in his eyes...He felt like he abandoned them."[91] He returned to the Tz'utujils on April 11, the eve of Palm Sunday, in time to celebrate Holy Week and Easter. He was enthusiastically welcomed and things seemed fairly normal. No Atiteco had disappeared for certain since February, and one had actually returned, although wounded. Some were still missing, but could have been in hiding. Stan could not praise the sisters enough for the warmth and vitality they were contributing to mission life; it was these new arrivals who had kept the mission work alive while he and Bocel were away.

After Easter Rother called a general meeting of all the catechists. Most were reluctant to stir up reprisals by organizing classes again, for the army was still encamped nearby. Finally, one catechist told Rother that if it were up to the catechists nothing would ever get done and that A'plas just ought to order them back to work. Rother took this advice and was pleased at the reinvigorated spirit of his parishioners.

On the national scene mayhem continued. In 1981, Amnesty International issued *Guatemala: A Government Program of Political Murder*, charging that widespread repression was not the work of private right-wing groups, but could be traced to the army working from an annex to the presidential palace. Systematic attacks on peasant villages were commonplace. *Campesinos* were defenseless against machine guns, grenade launchers, and helicopters. In one heartbreaking instance, the people of Coyá, San Miguel Acatán, fought back with rocks; the estimated dead numbered between 150 and 300, mainly women and children.[92]

Rother visited Oklahoma once more, briefly, in mid-May to attend the ordination of his cousin Don Wolf. At that time, he gave his chalice to his parents and visited with friends. After returning to Micatokla, he revealed to Father Don McCarthy that he was considering a compromise between leaving the Indians altogether and remaining in Santiago Atitlán in constant fear:

> Maybe you can come down here on your vacation this summer? I am looking for a replacement. I am here for 13 years now and am too well known. After being on the list, I can never be real safe again...I would like to have someone to keep things going and I could be in and out on an irregular basis. I would like to have some time to help two catechists get the New Testament ready for printing [in Tz'utujil]. They are doing this work while in hiding.[93]

Rother realized he was still a death-squad target. In an interview for the *Los Angeles Times* in June he said: "I have found that I am on a list to be killed . . . I talked too much when I was in Oklahoma, and some of it got back to Guatemala."[94] Stan's concern would have intensified when on July 1 two Franciscans, Tullio Merluzzo and his Third Order lay assistant Luis Arroyo Navarro, were ambushed and murdered after they returned from teaching catechism. Merluzzo had championed peasant land claims in Izabal and had been threatened with death by the local military. His religious superiors had transferred him to another parish, but it was to no avail.[95]

By early July, Rother slept in his clothes to expedite an escape from the death squad. He joked that he was "sleeping with his boots on," and told Leven, "Don't worry, don't worry, I have my way to escape."[96] Four days before his death, Adán García, Stan's former associate pastor who worked in a nearby town, told him he had information of an imminent plan to kidnap him. He offered to drive Rother to the border so he could escape, but Stan declined, saying he had commitments to the people and the sisters: The next day, July 25, was the highly anticipated annual fiesta for Santiago Apóstol. But Stan assured Adán, "Don't worry. I will fight. They won't take me alive."[97]

Just after midnight on Tuesday, July 28, three tall men, their faces covered by masks, broke into the rectory. They could not find Rother, probably because he no longer slept in his bedroom. Instead they found Francisco Bocel, brother of Pedro Bocel, and told him to take them to Rother. So it was not the intruders who awakened Stan, but the voice of Francisco on the other side of the door. "Padre, they are looking for you," the nineteen-year-old said. This was not what he had been told to say by the kidnappers; he was supposed to trick the priest into opening the door on some pretense. Instead he had offered Rother a warning.[98] Stan could have fled. No doubt he had planned to do so. But he had not expected Francisco to be in the custody of killers. Given their brutality, Francisco could have been the one to die.

Rother opened the door. A struggle began with the masked men as they tried to drag him out. Francisco, who left the immediate area, heard Stan yell, "No, I won't go with you! You'll have to kill me here!" Stan fought alone against the thugs for perhaps two minutes more. Then two shots rang out.

When the sisters heard the shots they waited thirty minutes before they went to Stan's room. On entering, they found his body lying dead on the floor, bloody and very badly bruised, with gunshot wounds in his temple and jaw. The torn skin on his knuckles gave evidence of his desperate efforts not to be taken alive. Four of the sisters took the 3:00 AM bus to San Lucas Tolimán to report the murder.[99] Later, the people brought Rother's body to the church and gathered there throughout the morning. Embassy official Raymond Bailey arrived and saw more than a thousand Tz'utujils standing in the plaza looking in silence toward the church. "It was like their God had died. It was a sight I'll remember the rest of my life,"[100] he said. On the day he was killed, two Masses were celebrated there. Santiago Apóstol church was packed with three thousand parishioners, thirty-five priests, and two bishops. Many more Atitecos stood outside. Brother Paul Joslin, who was on the altar, said he "had never seen so many people cry" as he did that day.[101]

That same morning in Oklahoma, Franz Rother, while riding his tractor on the farm, saw two men approach in a car. One was his pastor, Charles Beckman. He knew the minute he saw them, so "pale and drawn," why they had come: "They didn't get him out of the house, did they?" No, they said. Just as he promised his dad, Stan had not been taken alive.[102]

During the funeral mass on July 29 in Santiago Atitlán, the priest's heart was buried in the floor of the church sanctuary. The Tz'utujils had been so distressed to learn that A'plas was to be buried in Oklahoma that they requested this compromise from church and government officials and the family.[103] The Rothers gave their consent.

At the funeral mass on August 3 in Oklahoma City, Archbishop Salatka called Rother "a great man and an uncommonly good priest," and said that he trusted that the government would "not rest until the truth of his death is brought to light, including the realities of life in Guatemala which conspired to harm him."[104]

Tom had read his brother's thoughts as he watched him stare into space at the farm in Okarche earlier that year. At Stan's funeral he consoled another mourner: "It's better this way than for him to have come back here and lived to be 90 years old, always knowing that he should've been there."[105] Stan was buried in Okarche. He wore the colorful *perraje* on his shoulders, the treasured stole from the elders of Santiago Atitlán. In large letters on the headstone was inscribed his Tz'utujil name, "Padre A'plas."

The archbishop's plea was ignored and a travesty of justice began in Guatemala. Three local Indians, two of them Stan's friends, were arrested and charged. Authorities stated that Sister Ana María Gonzales Arias had said the three had been surprised by Rother as they were robbing the church. Sister Ana María fled to Mexico, where a spokesperson for her religious order told the press she had never made the above statement.[106] Salatka and the Rother family protested to the U.S. State Department, and the three men were eventually released. The true murderers were never arrested, never even pursued.

In the United States, the outcries of Archbishop Salatka, the Rother family, and concerned citizens in Oklahoma, as well as the testimony of Frankie Williams at congressional hearings were not enough to prevent the Reagan administration from lifting restrictions on the sale of jeeps and trucks to the Guatemalan army. The U.S. Congress did not seriously investigate the murder, and one year later no representative from the embassy attended Stan's memorial mass in Guatemala. Sources within the embassy told reporters the matter had little priority.[107]

For three years, Santiago Atitlán was without a resident priest. The sisters continued to hold the mission together, training catechists, teaching children, helping the sick, and leading prayers on Sundays when no priest was available to say Mass.

It may never be known exactly why Rother was marked for execution. In the U.S. he had been denounced by a fellow citizen to the Guatemalan embassy. In Guatemala, he had opened up his church as a sanctuary for parishioners who found their names on a death list and he had offered a sought-after catechist the hospitality of the rectory. He had comforted the families of the murdered and the disappeared and aided the widows and children left without support. He had aroused the army's suspicion by communicating with Tz'utujils in their own language. He had criticized informers who betrayed their brothers. Any of these actions might have earned him the label "subversive." Stan's crime was that he applied the gospel to his daily life in a defenseless community under attack.

Padre A'plas's thirteen years with the Tz'utujils had established a bond that was too strong to be sundered by the fear of torture and death. In the end, Stan had left the sanctuary of the family farm in Okarche to return to the Atitecos. His family understood why, just as they understood that his heart must remain in Santiago Atitlán.

CHAPTER 2

The Tz'utujil Revolt

F rom 1980 through 1990, at least eight hundred and as many as seventeen hundred residents of Santiago Atitlán were either murdered or had disappeared. One of these was Juan Mendoza, who was instrumental in converting Tz'utujil into written form and had been working since the time of Father Ramon Carlin on a translation into Tz'utujil of the readings and prayers for the Mass lectionary along with the entire New Testament—projects held dear by the Oklahoma missioners. Mendoza knew he had been targeted and went into hiding in Guatemala City to complete the New Testament translation after the army encamped at Santiago Atitlán. He would secretly return at times to see his family. After Carlin left, Rother supervised the remaining translations and visited Juan whenever he was in Guatemala City. By May 1982, Mendoza had completed the years-long task of translating the New Testament. The next month, on one of his occasional visits to see family, Mendoza was dragged off a bus by soldiers near Santiago Atitlán, never to be seen again.

Guerrilla activity had increased in the lake region, peaking in 1982, and the military's policy of eliminating anyone it claimed was linked to the guerrillas had been successful. Often those targeted were village leaders. By 1986 the guerrilla presence in the area had all but disappeared, but kidnappings, killings, and other forms of brutality continued.[1]

In 1984 Father John Vesey, having served seven years as a missioner in Paraguay, asked to be assigned to Santiago Atitlán and permission was granted. From the start he received death threats, and Archbishop Salatka —fearing for Vesey's life—decided to replace him after a few months. One of Vesey's undertakings while at Micatokla had been to turn the room where Rother had been killed into a parish chapel. The room contained a glass case with some of Stan's belongings, including books, stole, jacket, hat, and photos. One could see a bullet hole in the floor and bloodstains where his forehead and hands had struck the wall cabinet as he had been thrown violently against it in his life-or-death struggle.

When the spiritual writer Henri Nouwen visited this chapel at the invitation of Vesey, he was overcome with an odd mixture of emotions: "I had a hard time knowing how I felt. It seemed that sadness and joy, agony and victory, despair and hope all merged in this simple room." But as he watched the Tz'utujils enter the chapel to pray, all negativity evaporated:

> It may be years, decades or even centuries before the church of-
> ficially declares Stan a saint, but the people of Santiago Atitlán
> are not waiting. They have already declared Padre Francisco—
> whom they call "A'plas" in their native language—a saint. They
> come to him daily and ask for help with their concrete, personal
> needs. He is one of them, a father, brother and friend who for 13
> years served them on earth and now intercedes for them in
> heaven. He was their shepherd, he still is their shepherd.[2]

In the future his courage would help inspire them to act with hope and valor when there seemed little cause for hope.

Father Thomas McSherry, who had been sent to Micatokla as Vesey's assistant, now became pastor. He would remain at the mission for seventeen years, from 1984 until 2001, when the Oklahoma mission was turned over to the Diocese of Sololá-Chimaltenango, which by then had enough native Guatemalan priests to run the mission.[3]

Having no prior missionary experience, McSherry embarked upon his new assignment with a humble attitude. He told a journalist from *Maryknoll* magazine, "I don't have a lot of illusions about what I can do for the people here . . . I'm more interested in what they can do for themselves."[4]

After he had been pastor of Santiago Apóstol for a few years, McSherry decided to move Stan's remains from the floor of the church sanctuary where they lay buried behind the main altar, hidden from public view. They were placed in a more accessible space just inside the entrance to the church. A shrine was erected there with a plaque dedicated to the martyred priest. On the wall of the shrine were the names, each inscribed on a small metal plate, of those from the village who had disappeared or been killed. A small candle was placed before each plate.[5]

The troubles continued. McSherry painfully recalled that on many nights he was awakened by the sound of gunshots, followed at dawn by a knock on the rectory door asking him to schedule a funeral Mass for another victim of violence. The placement of this shrine where all could see it was a bold stroke for justice. Now all who entered the church—including numerous tourists from the United States and Europe—would be aware not only of Rother's martyrdom but also of the suffering that Atitecos had to endure daily at the hands of the military. Besides commemorating the dead, the names on these plates were a stark reminder meant to make it more difficult for Guatemalan authorities to hide their crimes.[6]

Two letters written to Oklahomans in 1987—one by McSherry and another by Frankie Williams—illustrate the violence that Atitecos suffered throughout the 1980s. In the first, a Christmas letter that was reprinted in the *Sooner Catholic*, Father Tom noted with sadness that on Holy Thursday he had buried a promising young parishioner who had been a lector and choir member. He had been shot two days earlier.[7] In the second letter, Williams wrote that "oppression and violence continue to take their toll" and that two men from the Santiago Atitlán area had been assassinated during her Holy Week visit.[8]

Yet in a separate letter, also written by Williams in 1987 and published in the *Sooner Catholic*, she discerned a new optimism among the Atitecos:

> At Micatokla Mission, I found that the seed of martyrdom of Father Stan Rother and the current leadership of Father Tom McSherry have created an explosion of vitality, fervor and participation as I have not seen over 10 years and my seven visits in Santiago Atitlán...The new self-esteem of the [indigenous Carmelite] nuns and the people is like watching flowers come to full, perfect blossoms.[9]

What Williams had sensed would become evident three years later.

In 1990 a small band of guerrillas moved into the Atitlán region, which caused the army to intensify its repression.[10] Tensions were near a boiling point when late in the evening on December 1, five soldiers who had been drinking all day at local bars began firing their guns in the air and assaulting Atitecos who happened to be in the street. Two of the soldiers decided to go after an attractive young woman who lived on a street nearby with her parents. They began banging on the door, demanding that she show herself. Neighbors came to her aid and a scuffle broke out. One of the soldiers fired his pistol, shooting an eighteen-year-old boy and paralyzing him from the waist down.[11] While some Atitecos carried the wounded boy back to his house, others went to the mayor's home to inform him about what had happened. Still others went to find the president of *Acción Católica*, a prominent lay Catholic organization, to get the keys to the church.

Everyone, including the mayor, then went to the church. The bells were rung from midnight to one AM on Sunday, December 2 to call the townspeople to assemble. Many feared that McSherry had been murdered, since the bells had also been rung when Stan was assassinated nine years earlier. When about three thousand Atitecos had gathered, it was decided that they would march to the military base, a little over a mile away in the hamlet of Panabaj on the outskirts of town. Led by the mayor and the mayor-elect, the townspeople carried white flags and shouted: "*Viva Atitlán*! We want to live in peace! Get out, army!" When the mayor tried to speak to the soldiers, they fired their automatic weapons point blank into the crowd. Minutes later, eleven people lay dead, while twenty-one others were wounded. Two more died in the hospital the next day. The dead ranged in age from ten to fifty-three. None of the protesters had been armed, though some had picked up stones and sticks along the way and hurled them at the soldiers.

But the people would no longer be cowed. The men set up a cordon around the army base, not allowing anyone to leave or enter. About twenty thousand Atitecos signed or put their thumbprints on a petition that circulated, demanding that the government investigate and bring the soldiers who fired on the people to justice. But it went further. It insisted that the base be closed and all soldiers removed from Santiago Atitlán. The petition was sent to President Vinicio Cerezo, who immediately dispatched his human rights procurator, Ramiro de León Carpio, to the town. When de León arrived that same afternoon, the army defended its actions, claiming that the protesters were led by guerrilla terrorists and the soldiers had fired in self-defense.

Atiteco leaders were prepared for the lies and the usual governmental whitewash that always followed. The Voice of Atitlán Radio, which was again in operation after having been shut down by the government, broadcast news of the massacre to local listeners. No one was allowed to touch the bodies of the dead, which lay where they had been shot until two or three o'clock Sunday afternoon, when they were moved to the town hall across from the church.[12] A few men went to find a photojournalist staying in the area. When she arrived at the scene of the massacre, she took graphic photos of the dead and wrote an accompanying account. Both were sent out on the news-wire services. Word of the massacre quickly spread throughout Guatemala and the world. Fifty journalists rushed to Santiago Atitlán to be present at the funeral Mass for the eleven victims who were Catholic, which McSherry presided over on December 3.[13]

Five days later the procurator produced his report. Faced with such overwhelming evidence against the military and such national and international indignation, and with national elections taking place in a few weeks, the ruling party evidently felt it was in no position to issue a cover-up. The report blamed the army as an institution for the massacre and named three soldiers it said were responsible for the bloodshed. Never before in modern history had the government of Guatemala promulgated such a report.[14] The Archdiocesan Human Rights Office in Guatemala City followed with its own report, which labeled the massacre an act of genocide and recommended compensation for the victims' families. It also called for extensive reform of the army.[15] Next, the almost always unassertive Guatemalan Congress unanimously passed a resolution calling for the army to withdraw from Santiago Atitlán and for the soldiers responsible for the massacre to be punished.

On December 20 the military withdrew its roughly six hundred soldiers from the town and President Cerezo ordered the army to stay out forever. This marked the first time that a Guatemalan town succeeded in expelling the army. The massacre also had international significance: the U.S. State Department suspended $2,800,000 in military aid for Guatemala, citing the massacre at Santiago Atitlán as one of the reasons for its action. It noted that "reliable evidence indicates that security forces and civil patrols committed, with almost total impunity, a majority of the major human rights abuses in Guatemala."[16] A year later, a military tribunal convicted a sergeant major and sentenced him to sixteen years in prison. A second soldier received a four-year prison term for "public intoxication." As human rights organizations pointed out, one man could not have shot so many people by himself, yet this marked the first time a Guatemalan soldier had been incarcerated for a human rights violation.[17]

But the people of Santiago Atitlán were not finished. Their municipal leaders devised a plan for Atitecos to provide their own security. Neighborhood watches and night-time patrols, which already existed, were expanded. Unarmed men on patrol carried only white flags and whistles. They were directed by a Committee for Security and Development made up of Tz'utujils and *ladinos* representing all the *cantones*, churches, cooperatives, and other local organizations. If any military personnel, guerrillas, or known criminals attempted to come into the town, word would go out from the patrols, church bells would be rung, and the people would assemble. Unarmed Atitecos would then block the intruders, forcing them to retreat. If the interlopers came in a vehicle, the people would surround it until its driver turned around and left. On a few occasions the army tried to intimidate the townspeople and enter the town, but the Atitecos were successful in stopping them. Twice in May 1991, for instance, a well-armed patrol of forty-two soldiers tried to enter Santiago Atitlán in search of "aggressive elements." After they were promptly blocked by about a thousand unarmed citizens they departed.[18]

Today a replica in stone of President Cerezo's order prohibiting the army from ever entering the town again stands in a "peace park" erected by the townspeople. The park also contains crosses for each of the thirteen people who were murdered on December 2. Every year on the anniversary of the massacre, Atitecos gather in the park to remember and celebrate Mass for those who died. Following the first-year celebration, Shirley Christian, a reporter for the *New York Times*, called the response of the people of Santiago Atitlán to the massacre "a rare display of national courage."[19] She could have added that it also emboldened other indigenous communities to stand up for their rights. In July 1991 the Indians of San Lucas Tolimán, after a soldier killed a resident, followed the example of the Atitecos and forced the army and national police to withdraw.[20] Soldiers who in 1991 arrived in the village of Santa Clara to build a new base were forced by the people to leave. Before the soldiers left, however, the local priest received an unsigned, threatening note for having spoken out against the army's attempted intrusion.[21]

A 1994 interview of McSherry by John Mallon indirectly encapsulated the transformation that took place in Santiago Atitlán following the 1990 massacre. Although McSherry made no mention of the massacre, he did note that, after he arrived in Santiago Atitlán in 1984

> and until 1990 it was constant fear. And not just for me, [but] the whole town. The town would close up at night..., people abandoned their fields if they were any distance from town because they would be intercepted by army patrols or caught in a fire fight and be suspected of being with one side or another. Some people just never came back and were never heard from again. So until 1990 it was a very tense situation.

But then everything changed: "If you go to Santiago now on a Friday or Saturday night people would be out on the streets. People have reclaimed their fields they had to abandon... There have been no [violent] incidents." But, added McSherry, they only experienced such "peace and tranquility" within their town; if they had to leave, they sometimes experienced problems.[22]

Today most of the people of Santiago Atitlán still live in poverty, barely eking out enough from their small plots of land to survive. But due to their own efforts, they are at least living in peace and no longer suffering at the hands of the military or death squads. Although one cannot verify this, it seems safe to assume that the selfless example of Stan Rother was a factor in lending them courage to stand up to power even when it seemed hopeless to do so. And just as he helped inspire them in their fight for justice, their victory in December 1990 served as a powerful example for other indigenous towns and villages.

In the years since Rother was killed, the Archdiocese of Oklahoma City has sponsored a pilgrimage to Santiago Atitlán every five years. One such visit occurred on the occasion of the tenth anniversary of Stan's death. The parish staff and Father McSherry decided that the time was right for the publication of the New Testament translation completed in 1982, an event that had long been delayed because of the violence. One thousand New Testaments in the Tz'utujil language were presented, blessed, and distributed to the faithful of Santiago Atitlán on July 28, 1991, as Padre A'plas's martyrdom a decade before was commemorated.[23] And, although Juan Mendoza's body was never recovered, his life's work was brought to light at last.

Twenty-five years later, in July 2016, sixty Rother family members and friends, clergy, and religious made the journey to commemorate the thirty-fifth anniversary of Father Stan's death. On July 27 they participated in a crowded memorial vigil Mass in the mission village of Cerro de Oro, where Stan had been pastor during his first years at Micatokla. On the anniversary of his death, July 28, another memorial Mass was said in Santiago Atitlán. According to Sister Marita Rother, who made the trip, the Masses were filled with joy and solemnity, accompanied by marimba bands and guitars and the enthusiastic singing of choirs and congregants.

Because of the overflow crowd of five thousand plus, the anniversary Mass was celebrated outside in the plaza of Santiago Apóstol. Numerous clergy participated, including hierarchy—so many that some priests got temporarily lost in the huge crowd of Atitecos. Stan's assistant, Father Pedro Bocel, who in early 1981 had fled with him from the death squads to Oklahoma, was also there, his presence a joy for the family yet a poignant reminder of the sorrow of 1981. The readings were proclaimed in both Spanish and Tz'utujil by catechists, recalling the decades of effort by Fathers Carlin and Rother and translators Antonio Tzina and Juan Mendoza, who had given his life for the sake of converting an oral to a written language. The experience was "overwhelming," as Sister Marita recalled: "As I tried to absorb it all, I was visited with the thought that all of this is happening because one man had the courage, love, and the desire to continue to serve God in the people he loved until he paid the ultimate price! And—that man was my brother! How grateful I am to celebrate these moments with 'his people'!"[24]

Many Oklahoma Catholics and other Americans have journeyed to Santiago Atitlán to visit the room where Stan Rother was murdered and pray before his remains. No doubt their numbers will increase in the future due to his new status. Most of these pilgrims return to the United States with a newfound or more sophisticated understanding of the poverty that burdens the majority of Guatemalans, especially the indigenous peoples. Some may wonder why the U.S. government did next to nothing to pressure Guatemalan authorities to investigate Rother's death and bring his killers to justice or why U.S. military aid continued throughout the violent 1980s. Perhaps they will inform others in their churches and neighborhoods of the poverty and injustice that prevail in Guatemala and pressure their political leaders to work more seriously for a just world.

On December 2, 2016, Pope Francis recognized Father Stanley Rother as a martyr of the Catholic Church, thereby proclaiming him the first official U.S.-born martyr in history. He was also approved for beatification. The beatification ceremony took place on September 23, 2017, at the Cox Convention Center in Oklahoma City, where an unexpected turnout of twenty thousand meant that more than five thousand hopeful attendees had to watch nearby on closed-circuit television. In the congregation were people from all over the United States and other nations, including many Tz'utujils from Santiago Atitlán. There were prayers in Tz'utujil and Comanche, Vietnamese, Filipino, and Korean, as well as in Spanish, Latin, and English, and the congregation was encouraged to say the Lord's Prayer in his or her native tongue. It was not only an international gathering, but very much an intergenerational one, and a joyful blend of traditional and modern Catholicism.

Perhaps it is no coincidence that Father Stanley Rother was officially declared a martyr of the Catholic Church on December 2, 2016, exactly twenty-six years to the day after the people of Santiago Atitlán defied the Guatemalan army that had kept them in a state of fear for more than a decade. Perhaps this is a sign that Padre A'plas was still with his people even after his death, when the Tz'utujils stood up in a nonviolent way to the Guatemalan army and government, cried "Enough!" and demanded that they be left to live their lives in peace.

CHAPTER 3

James Miller

Christian Brother

James Miller

Brother James Alfred Miller was the last American missionary victim of the Lucas García regime in Guatemala. Like Stanley Rother, Jim had rural roots. Born on September 21, 1944, near Stevens Point, Wisconsin, he was the first-born of Lorraine and Arnold Miller, who ran a dairy farm in nearby Polonia. The practical knowledge he absorbed as a child would later infuse his life as a missioner with a farm boy's blend of cooperation, hard work, and no-nonsense pragmatism. As a youngster, he was inquisitive, outgoing, and energetic. He had the "gift of gab" as friends put it or, as his Aunt Margaret remarked, "If he found an ear open, he used it."[1]

He was self-assured and, as his father would later recall, "sensitive to people of all ages." He was close to his neighbors and often helped them on their farms. One neighbor was Wilfred Steffanus, a farmer who lived across the road. Jim offered to help Steffanus clear his fields of rocks, a rather uninspiring chore that, as Steffanus remembered, he seemed to enjoy. The young boy's generosity of time and effort that impressed his older neighbor would be a recurring theme in the comments and tributes made about Jim both throughout his life and after his death. He constantly impressed his colleagues and friends with his good-humored undertaking of boring, even menial tasks.

Jim later chose Steffanus as his sponsor in confirmation, and the two always remained close friends. Two months before he was killed,

Jim visited Wilfred's mother, who was dying. He prayed with her and his cheerful presence was a great consolation to Mrs. Steffanus, Wilfred said. Jim too was impressed by the dignity of the old woman. He told his mother: "If death is always like hers, then I don't know what people are afraid of."[2] Mrs. Steffanus's peaceful acceptance of death seemed to be a gift for which Jim was quietly grateful. Mrs. Steffanus died on the day Jim left Wisconsin for the last time to return to Guatemala, only a few weeks before he would be killed.

Jim went to Edison Elementary, a one-room public school in nearby Ellis, where one teacher taught all eight grades.[3] He walked the mile and a quarter between school and the Miller farm and when he arrived home he would give his parents and siblings—Patricia, Louise, Ralph, and William—a detailed description of all he had observed that day. Far from being bored with his garrulous rendition, they found it quite entertaining.[4]

Although some would classify Jim as an average student, he did have a notable facility for language and an interest in geography and science. When he graduated from the one-room schoolhouse in Ellis, his parents presented him with a *World Book Encyclopedia*, which he read from cover to cover in an effort to absorb everything he could.[5] Throughout his years in elementary school, Jim dreamed of one day being a priest, and, to prepare for that day, he even built a model church on the family farm. But in 1958, not long after he began his freshman year at Pacelli High School, a Christian Brothers school in Stevens Point, the impressionable fourteen-year-old changed his mind, deciding that the life of a teaching brother was more to his liking. This decision as an adolescent would have its set of life-altering consequences.

The Christian Brothers, also known as the Lasallian Brothers, are a congregation of teaching brothers founded in France by Jean-Baptiste de La Salle in the second half of the seventeenth century. As a young priest, de La Salle became so taken with a project begun in Reims by Adrien Nyel to establish free Christian schools for the poor that he embraced the mission of educating the poor as his own lifelong calling.

In order to train the teachers for these schools, Jean-Baptiste brought a group of poor schoolmasters into his own home for two years and eventually united them into a religious community called the Brothers of the Christian Schools. Though a "son of privilege," he lived simply with the brothers, at times in desperate straits, after he gave away his personal fortune. If his new community survived without his inheritance, he thought, then God must favor their endeavor. Teaching was to be the brothers' sole calling, so he directed that no brother could be ordained a priest and no priest could join the congregation—a rule that is maintained to the present day. Besides charity schools, he established teacher-training schools for secular schoolmasters, a school for illiterate young laborers, a tuition-paid boarding school for sons of the business class, and a reform school for young "delinquents"—all of which were ahead of their time. He also introduced teaching in the vernacular rather than Latin and instructing students in classes according to age, instead of the one-on-one tutoring methods used then.

Jean-Baptiste was an intensely spiritual man who, although a far-sighted organizer, was guided by Providence and the needs of the poor, leading him to take risks. He distributed his personal fortune to the poor during a famine and renounced the income and status of his priestly canonry. He also endured spiteful opposition from teachers' guilds and an archbishop who tried to banish him. He fully accepted the "doctrine of abandonment to divine providence" and imparted this to his religious community. They were to "enter practically and creatively into the world of the poor, even when it necessitated burning the bridges of clerical culture, social class, security and even family."[6] "Your zeal," instructed de La Salle, "must go so far…that you are ready to give your very life, so dear to you are the children entrusted to you."[7]

That young Jim understood all the implications of his chosen vocation at such an early age is doubtful. Yet one can assume that he was at least beginning to see himself more in the role of teacher and his vision of himself as priest was receding. Maturity, immersion in Lasallian spirituality, and a grasp of the founder's passion for educating the poor would eventually lead Brother Miller to an abandonment of self to God's providence as an educator of impoverished Indians in Guatemala. He would even one day assume the ultimate risk of putting his own life in danger for the children in his care.

Twenty years later, in an autobiographical sketch, Jim made an understated reference to the decision he had made as a fourteen-year-old freshman: "I saw my first Christian Brother when I entered Pacelli High School…in 1958. There were eleven Brothers there that year. Due to their collective good influence and," he joked, "Brother Florian Donatelli's unorthodox, strong-armed methods of recruiting, I decided to join the Junior Novitiate the following year."[8]

Before the mid-1960s, it was not uncommon for boys interested in entering religious life to embark on this vocation sometime during their high school years; girls as well might enter a convent. Thus, at the start of his sophomore year in September 1959, Jim entered the Christian Brothers' junior novitiate at Glencoe, Missouri. "In one day," he later recalled, "I left the State of Wisconsin for the first time, took my first train ride, and saw a building over four stories high." He was transferred, as part of an expansion of the juniorate, to Christian Brothers Prep in St. Paul, Minnesota, for his junior year of high school. "There were 36 of us," he wrote, "and we attended classes at Cretin High School. I believe I am the last surviving member of that historic group."[9] After returning to Glencoe for his senior year of high school, Jim graduated in 1962.

Even in those early years of formation, the young farm boy from Wisconsin impressed his teachers with his energy, simplicity, and good humor—as well as his knack for tackling jobs that others might shun. At Glencoe, Jim later wrote, "I preferred working in the chicken coop to playing field games—that got me a few points with the Visitor (Brother Philip)."[10] Brother Gerard Pihaly, who taught him at Glencoe, said: "He was a good student, but also a very generous person. He would sign up for the most challenging jobs. He liked to work with machinery very much, having come from a farm. He would take the garbage down to the farm by tractor, grade the gravel roads, dig up large flat rocks for flagstone walks."[11]

And Brother Bernard LoCoco, also on the faculty at Glencoe, recalled: "He was very outgoing, emotional, [and] offered bear hug greetings. We never discovered in him any duplicity. He was an average student, applied himself, but was always thinking about how to help others. Whatever he did, he had to be into it fully—almost like a young colt."[12] In spite of his outgoing nature, Jim did have a serious, private side—he could be a good-humored "loner" in some respects, with "his own agenda"[13] of tasks to attend to. Often he deemed these more important than group activities like sports and socializing, both of which he also relished.

Jim graduated from the junior novitiate and high school at Glencoe in 1962. At that time he wrote why he wished to enter the next stage in becoming a Christian Brother: "As I now progress from one big step to an even greater one, I think I can honestly say that I now have somewhat of a clear idea of the purpose and values of the Institute of the Brothers of the Christian Schools. I now see quite clearly, though not entirely, the value of the Religious State."[14]

After finishing his novitiate year at St. Yon's Hall on the campus of St. Mary's University in Winona, Minnesota, Jim continued with his college classes in 1963, also at St. Mary's, majoring in modern languages and earning a bachelor's degree in May 1966. Gregory Robertson taught Miller during those undergraduate years. He remembered him as an outgoing student, intelligent but not an intellectual, who would, as often as not, turn in his term papers late and who, although prayerful, would occasionally fall asleep during daily meditation.[15] Brother Theodore Drahmann, who oversaw Jim in his studies at St. Mary's, recalled: "He was an enthusiastic, cheerful sort of young man, very hard working...He was interested in Spanish all the way along, because he always seemed to have the idea that he wanted to go down to the missions in Latin America."[16]

It is to Jim's credit that he managed to graduate in the traditional four years, since one semester before graduation he was asked to substitute for an ailing brother at Cretin High School in nearby St. Paul. Although the position was supposed to be temporary, he stayed at Cretin for three and a half years. The missions would therefore have to wait. He taught Spanish, which surely gave him a stronger grounding in that language and helped prepare him for his work in Central America. But he also made time to found and coach a soccer team and took on the task of maintenance supervisor, a job that appealed to his practical nature and probably one that attracted no one else.

During these years Brother James impressed many people, but no one more than one of his students at Cretin, Don Geng:

> As a student and later as a fellow faculty member at Cretin High School, I was privileged to know this humble, committed person. He was a man who knew the true meaning of service; no task was beneath his efforts. During my high school days we admired his simple dedication; after spending his day in the classroom teaching Spanish, he would spend countless hours in the halls as a janitor and maintenance man. No work was unworthy of his dignity; he mopped the floors, scoured the toilets and cleaned the school furnaces. His students...behind his back...labeled him "Brother Fix-it" as he lumbered through the halls, tools strapped to his belt, and wielding some object needing repair.[17]

So many undertakings while teaching a full load of classes took somewhat of a toll. Before long, adherence to his own busy schedule led him to skip or be late for some of his community's daily spiritual practices. This did not go unnoticed when he applied for lifetime vows. His outstanding characteristics, a major one being the generous gift of his time to the students and to the Christian Brothers, ultimately outweighed these frequent lapses.[18]

Miller was happy throughout his stay at Cretin, but felt God was calling him to work with the Central American poor;[19] so every year he re-applied for an assignment in the missions. In 1968 he was awarded a grant for an NDEA (National Defense Education Act) summer intensive study program in Spanish at the University of Dayton, after which he spent the next year preparing for his perpetual vows and the Central American missions.[20] On June 12, 1969, he made these vows and the following month left for his new life as a missioner in Nicaragua.

He was sent to Bluefields on the Nicaraguan Atlantic Coast to teach at Cristóbal Colón High School. The U.S. Christian Brothers had first come to Bluefields in 1944 at the invitation of the Capuchin Franciscans of Detroit, who had been charged by the Vatican in 1938 with the sizable territory encompassing the east coast of Nicaragua.[21] Jim stayed in Bluefields for three and a half years, teaching mainly in the high school. Since classes were taught in Spanish, Hermano Santiago (Brother James) advanced in fluency. In addition to his teaching assignments there, he organized a soccer team, ran the bookstore, and did extensive work on the brothers' residence, including replacing almost the entire plumbing system.[22] In 1973, he returned to St. Mary's College for a year to complete a master's degree in Spanish. Although his academic record had been somewhat spotty before, by this time he excelled with all A's.[23]

Sent back to the Nicaraguan Atlantic Coast in March 1974, this time farther north to Puerto Cabezas, Brother James began to reach his full potential as a teacher and administrator. During the four years that Jim served in Puerto Cabezas, his work would involve him directly with the Somoza dictatorship, causing some to view him as a Somocista collaborator. To understand how this came to pass, some background is helpful.

The United States showed an early interest in Nicaragua. In the 1850s Commodore Cornelius Vanderbilt established a company to transport U.S. citizens anxious to get to California for the gold rush across the narrow Nicaraguan territory between the Atlantic and Pacific Oceans. Soon another American, the adventurer William Walker, was invited by the Liberal branch of the Nicaraguan elite to help overthrow the Conservative branch then in power. Walker, however, had other plans. With his army of three hundred U.S. nationals, he not only defeated the Conservatives but also proclaimed himself president, declared English the new official language of the country, legalized slavery, and gained diplomatic recognition from the United States.

Soon Liberals joined with Conservatives and with the governments of the other Central American states and drove Walker out of the country. After two additional incursions into Central America, Walker was executed in Honduras in 1860. The Walker fiasco so disgraced the Liberals that the Conservative branch of the elite was able to hold power until 1893.

When the international demand for coffee rapidly increased in the last quarter of the nineteenth century, the elite decided to expand their coffee-growing operations. Beginning in 1877, a number of laws were promulgated requiring Indians to sell off their communal lands. These laws effectively transformed the Indians into a class of dependent share-croppers. Vagrancy laws were passed which, coupled with laws sanction-ing the conscription of natives for public and agricultural work, further guaranteed the ready supply of cheap labor needed by coffee growers.

In 1893 Liberal José Santos Zelaya overthrew the Conservative regime and ruled as dictator for the next seventeen years. He allowed U.S. investors into his country in such numbers that by 1909 they con-trolled the sources of Nicaraguan wealth. Becoming alarmed by the growing U.S. control of the Nicaraguan economy, Zelaya rejected over-tures from American bankers and instead accepted a large loan from the British. This and other signs of independence persuaded the United States that Zelaya had to be replaced. With encouragement from the U.S., the Conservatives rebelled in 1909. U.S. marines quickly landed at Bluefields on the Atlantic Coast, supposedly to protect American lives and property, but in reality to prevent the Liberals from crushing the Conservatives. Realizing that he had no other choice, Zelaya resigned from office. Adolfo Díaz, a Conservative and an obscure clerk in a U.S. mining company, was then installed as president. Nicaragua soon ac-cepted loans from an American bank, which in turn was granted a con-trolling interest in the Nicaraguan national bank and railway system, as well as all customs' revenues.[24]

When some Nicaraguans tried to oust Díaz in 1912, President William Howard Taft sent in the U.S. marines, who remained in Nic-aragua for twenty years. In 1927 Augusto César Sandino began a guer-rilla war of liberation lasting for seven years that proved costly to the Americans, both monetarily and in lives. The United States eventually decided to equip and train a Nicaraguan security force, the Guardia Na-cional, to replace the marines. When the American forces withdrew, Sandino, by now a national hero, put down his arms and ceased to fight. Not long after, in 1934, on orders from the United States' handpicked commander of the Guardia, Anastasio Somoza García, Sandino was kid-napped and executed. Finally, in June 1936, Somoza García overthrew the Nicaraguan government and for forty-three years he and his two sons ruled the country as their private fiefdom. Throughout this period the Somozas had the support of the U.S. government.

In 1974, when Brother James returned to Nicaragua after receiving his master's degree, Anastasio Somoza Debayle, the younger son of So-moza García and a West Point graduate, was "elected" president. The Somoza family at this time owned five million acres of land—an area the size of El Salvador—while two hundred thousand peasants were landless. Somoza Debayle likewise owned the twenty-six largest businesses in the country and had a personal fortune of about $300 million.[25] But the dictator's fiefdom was beginning to crumble. On December 23, 1972, an earthquake destroyed much of Managua, the capital city, killing ten thousand people and leaving hundreds of thousands homeless. As international aid poured in from around the world, Somoza and his Guardia officers pocketed it. Such blatant thievery caused more and more of the middle class to join with the poor in opposition to Somoza. The Catholic Church began to speak out:

> On the first anniversary of the earthquake the Church hierarchy held a commemorative mass in the central plaza of Managua. Somoza...invited himself to the Church celebration. Meanwhile, the Christian [base] communities of Managua...made hundreds of hand-held placards and carried them secretly into the plaza. As the ceremony unfolded, Somoza and his officials were deeply offended by the statements of the bishops and angered by the display of anti-regime slogans. Abruptly he got up and walked out, while national guardsmen disconnected the loudspeakers carrying the Archbishop's speech to the audience.[26]

On December 27, 1974, not long after Brother James Miller arrived in Puerto Cabezas, a small rebel group from the Sandinista National Liberation Front (FSLN) crashed a party in Managua and took a number of important Nicaraguan officials hostage. After three days of negotiations, during which the rebels received considerable international attention, Somoza was forced to pay them $5 million in ransom money and allow them to flee the country. The audacity of the Sandinistas did much to popularize their cause, but Somoza, furious at having been humiliated, responded with increased brutality.

When Brother James Miller returned in 1974 to Nicaragua, the country was on the verge of revolution. However, Puerto Cabezas and the Atlantic Coast in general—being far removed from Managua and the other centers of political activity in the west where most of the fighting would take place—played little part in the events leading up to the overthrow of Somoza, and Miller was not unduly concerned with the political situation.

Brother James's assignment was to teach high school at the Christian Brothers' Instituto Nacional Bartolomé Colón. As soon as he arrived in his new home, he threw himself completely into his work. Just as in

Bluefields, he began single-handedly repairing the brothers' residence when he was not teaching English, mathematics, or religion. Before long he decided to resurrect the defunct volunteer fire department in Puerto Cabezas and turn it into an efficient unit. He visited many of the fire stations in Managua, where he was able to beg hoses, nozzles and—amazingly—a fire truck; he even came up with firemen's uniforms, which the volunteers proudly wore in local parades. Not surprisingly, he became the local fire chief and remained so until he left Nicaragua in July 1979.[27] Brother Bob Walsh was awed at the level of his energy: "For Santiago, I think manual work was play, was recreation. I could not even attempt nor could I ever do all the things he was doing here in Puerto Cabezas for the people—teaching, administration, parish catechetics, civic projects, and good old-fashioned manual labor. Sunday literally had to be a day of rest for his over-worked body."[28]

Brother Stephen Markham noted that Brother James contributed to the community in other ways. For example, he served on a curriculum committee at a local university, on a city library committee, and on a planning committee for an educational radio station.[29] Such community outreach linked Jim to countless townspeople in one capacity or another, leading Brother Cyril Litecky, his provincial and former teacher, to comment on Jim's rapport with the populace: "I vividly recall visiting him in Puerto Cabezas, riding in a jeep with him and stopping several times in one block so he could greet and visit with the people of the town."[30]

In Nicaragua the schools, including those of the Christian Brothers, were run by the state. In the mid-1970s, the Somoza government inaugurated a program requiring basic industrial arts at the junior high level. When the government began building small additions for this new program, Brother James proposed a more elaborate scheme for the Instituto Nacional Bartoloméo Colón. He lobbied the Ministry of Education for his proposal—a building complex for the instruction of older students, which would cost considerably more—and received approval.[31] The Instituto, with its auditorium and new structures for classrooms, science laboratories, and technical shops, was able eventually to offer courses in bilingual secretarial skills, forestry, and industrial arts. In 1977, Brother James was appointed principal of the high school, which at that time had an enrollment of 550 students. Enrollment began to climb to 800 and the faculty doubled in size. With this success, the Somoza government asked him in 1978 to supervise the construction of ten new rural elementary schools being built in the Atlantic Coast region.[32]

Although proud of his achievements, Hermano Santiago did not lose sight of the Christian Brothers' ultimate aim, which was to integrate native Nicaraguans into the administration of their schools. There were, in fact, more native Nicaraguans than American Christian Brothers teaching at these schools, and Jim, bearing in mind the Instituto's eventual autonomy, requested $1,000 from his province in Minnesota to make it possible for a Nicaraguan associate to visit the U.S. to study educational methods and practice his English. In his request to Brother Litecky, Miller wrote: "Rolando [García Gutiérrez] is an excellent candidate for higher administrative posts. Since I feel we have a moral obligation to train native personnel for the eventual takeover of the mission schools we currently operate, I . . . would like very much for him to have the chance to spend . . . time in the United States."[33]

As much as he enjoyed putting heart and soul into directing the Instituto as principal, Miller did have the challenging task of having to deal on a steady basis with the corrupt Somoza government. Brother Litecky explained this relationship: "[He got] exasperated at the red tape. In Managua . . . he would go to people and lean on them until he got things done for the school. That is why he was identified with the people in power; not because he was in concert with them, but just because he would get them to get things for him."[34]

Brother Markham saw Miller's political involvement in the same way, as purely pragmatic:

> Yes, Jim's perspective on Church, theology, politics, etc. was basically conservative. In fact he seemed to glory in projecting himself as a conservative. However, he was not a traditionalist. His conservative perspective was basically a pragmatic and utilitarian approach to life. If he set out to do something he did it and he did not hold back from exerting influence, even pressure, on those who stood in his way. Jim was not one to bother about philosophical discussions or worry about political ideologies. He focused his energies and attention on accomplishing the task at hand and it didn't matter if that task was a construction project or an educational endeavor . . .
>
> He had a way of dismissing [political] questions by saying "I don't get into that" or "it's real complicated but we are here to teach the youth to farm or read, etc."[35]

Brother James, always practical, did not spend time and energy on theoretical matters. He was unable, or perhaps unwilling, to dwell on economic dependency theories or problems caused in the developing world by multinational corporations. He would have been hesitant to accept the need for a theology of liberation within the Latin American church. In Hermano Santiago's view, the people in his mission community were poor and uneducated; a good school with quality equipment and a practical educational program would help alleviate poverty and improve people's lives. Therefore, what counted was obtaining such a school and such a program, and this was where he would concentrate all his energies.

Brother Nicholas Geimer worked and lived with Miller in Puerto Cabezas from the fall of 1977 until July 1979. He saw the relationship between Jim and the Somoza government as pragmatic, but also viewed it as a complex issue not easily defined:

> What were Jim's relationships with the Somoza government? You have to realize that in Nicaragua most directors of schools were political appointees. Many were completely unqualified—retired military officers, for example...Education was...controlled nationally. A director had to lobby for his fair share, especially if he wanted more than his fair share, as did Jim. Jim cultivated the friendship of the president of the senate (Somoza's righthand man) and a member of the lower house (also vice-minister of education). These two were from the Atlantic Coast and were concerned about improving things in this neglected part of the country. So Jim was quite successful in getting more for his school through these two. However, his relationship was on a business, not social, level.
>
> Jim told me he knew these two were personally profiting from the government money spent on the coast, through kickbacks on building contracts, high pay/low work jobs for relatives, etc., but he felt that was the way the game was played and couldn't be helped.[36]

After his appointment as supervisor for the construction of ten rural schools, Jim would go every month or so with the contractor to assess progress and make sure corners were not being cut. After one trip, he told Brother Nicholas that the contractor had said he would never again bid on a government job, since he had to kick back all his profit to the two above-mentioned politicians. This revelation of blatant corruption troubled Jim considerably, yet he realized he was in no position to do anything to stop it. Being, generally speaking, apolitical, Brother James tried to avoid direct political involvement. Being a pragmatist, however, he felt some concessions were necessary:

As director, Jim was expected to attend a reception or two...for
these two politicians when they visited Puerto Cabezas. These
receptions were really political rallies for Somoza's Liberal Party.
Many of the teachers attended also, fearing their jobs depended
upon it. Jim announced the meetings but did not force us teachers to go.

The only other political activity on Jim's part that I am
aware of is the following incident. When he returned from one
of his trips to the capital he told me that when he went to pay his
respects to his two friends in the legislature, he was called into a
"smoke-filled room" situation, and his recommendation was
asked about whom they should nominate for mayor of Puerto
Cabezas. Needless to say, the nomination was equal to election.
Jim was quite excited about this episode of backroom politics.[37]

Brother Jim even revealed his frustrations with the Somoza government to a cousin, Jane Campbell, who said: "I don't believe he was ever
intimidated by power or money. He was very impatient with them."[38]

When the Sandinistas intensified their revolutionary activities, Miller
refused to permit any political activism in their favor among the students.
Since nearly all the fighting was confined to western Nicaragua, far from
Puerto Cabezas, and, according to Brother Nicholas, the Sandinistas had
little support in this town, there were very few attempts among the students to demonstrate on behalf of the FSLN. Also, on the east coast, they
did not witness Guardia abuses, although they certainly heard about them,
but that did not produce as dramatic an impression and did not provoke
many rebellious acts. Geimer recalls only two incidents. When a student
attempted to organize a pro-Sandinista activity at school, Brother James
talked to his father, the manager of a bank. The father stopped his son,
who then became Jim's bitter enemy. On another occasion, the school's
night watchman discovered that someone had slipped a letter under each
classroom door making ridiculous accusations concerning Miller and
threatening him. Jim picked up all the copies before anyone arrived at
school. "At one time the Sandinista clandestine radio read a list of people
in Puerto Cabezas who were to be dealt with when they took over," reported Brother Nicholas. "The names must have been supplied by their
local sympathizers, and Jim's name was included."[39]

In truth, Miller was neither pro-Somocista nor pro-Sandinista. To
him the political struggle was an annoyance that interfered with the running of his school. This attitude explained why at times he was not reluctant to oppose the Somoza regime. On one occasion when the fighting

was escalating, a local militia was organized by the National Guard commander in Puerto Cabezas. All public employees, including teachers, were expected to "volunteer" and participate in scheduled drills. Members of the militia were also supposed to stand night guard duty, thereby relieving the Guardia of this odious task. The teachers at the Christian Brothers' school did not want to take part, and Jim strongly supported them, arguing that it would interfere with their school duties. Only one teacher participated and there were no reprisals against the rest by the Guardia.[40]

On another occasion, all the teachers were called by Miller to the faculty room. He informed them that he had received a notice from the Ministry of Education ordering the suspension of classes because of the expansion of violence. Since the fighting was confined to the Pacific area and Puerto Cabezas had remained peaceful, Jim suggested that the command from Managua be ignored. Many of the teachers, perhaps sensing a chance for time off with full pay, argued with him about this. Jim agreed to decide the matter by vote. When the majority voted against his position, he instructed the faculty to hold their next class and then bring their students to the assembly hall for dismissal. But shortly thereafter he called a second meeting. There the faculty were told that the local military commander had just notified him that if school were suspended teachers would have to report for "volunteer" militia duty, since it would no longer interfere with their teaching. A new vote was taken and the decision to suspend classes was reversed. "Most of the teachers thought Jim had 'suggested' this policy to the commander," noted Geimer, "and I think they were right, although Jim never said so." The events of that day resulted in some bad feelings toward Miller by the faculty, feelings that lingered.[41] Once again, Jim had demonstrated that the school was his foremost concern.

Eventually the revolution did reach the Atlantic Coast and specifically Puerto Cabezas. There was even machine-gun fire outside of the high school. When asked by a friend if he had been afraid, Jim answered: "Are you kidding? I never knew I could pray so fervently as when under my bed."[42]

The Somoza regime gradually lost whatever support it once might have had. When national guardsmen inexplicably forced ABC news reporter Bill Stewart to kneel down and then executed him while the network's cameras rolled, it was over for Somoza. His soldiers began deserting in droves and he and his political associates fled the country. On July 17, 1979, after President Carter ended military aid, the dictator fled to Miami. Two days later the Sandinistas took power.[43]

It was also in July that Miller left Nicaragua, never to return. His departure, as the supposed guardian of an elderly nun, coincided with the victory of the Sandinistas and caused many to conclude that he had been forced to flee the country clandestinely. Brother Nicholas explained that this was not the case:

> Jim had been planning a visit to the States for some time . . . The country parish where his mother's family came from was going to celebrate its centennial, and Jim planned a vacation for this time because all his relatives would be gathered for the event. As the time approached the fighting and chaos shut down regular means of transportation, and he had to beg a ride to Managua on a Red Cross flight. Getting out of Managua was even harder. All the Somocistas were trying to get out, too. He finally did get on a plane as a guardian for an old nun. But he was not *fleeing*. He had every intention of returning . . . It was his religious superiors who decided, wisely I think, that it would be better for him not to return. Had he tried, I do not think the Sandinistas would have harmed him . . . More likely they would not have let him enter the country. Had he not gotten out in the first place, I think he would have been deported.[44]

Cyril Litecky, Miller's provincial, also maintained that Jim left to visit friends in Wisconsin: "We determined it would be prudent for him not to return until things settled down." The decision was made "because we had questions about his 'safety' under the Sandinistas," since he had been principal of a Somoza-run school. After a few months, Miller asked his superiors to allow him to return to Puerto Cabezas, but a new Sandinista provision stipulating that only native Nicaraguans could henceforth be school directors caused Litecky and others to deny his request.[45]

After the family reunion, Brother James returned to Cretin High School to teach Spanish. Once more his energy impressed his colleagues; as Brother Lewis Twohig noted with admiration, he often put in sixteen-hour work days. Twohig also recalled that in his few free hours, Jim took a course in welding, because he felt it would be helpful when he went back to Central America.[46]

Upon his return to Minnesota, Miller and Geng, now himself a teacher at Cretin, renewed their close friendship, but this time Geng saw an added dimension in Miller's personality:

He was, first and foremost, a man of great simplicity. I remember in 1979 giving him a ride to his TVI welding class...He bragged that he wore the same pair of pants each week so that he would not ruin his blue jeans with some careless welding mistake. Some students even made fun of his simplicity and yet one of the most apparent changes I noticed in James...was his impatience with the high standard of material wealth in America ...He would ruffle the students' pride by criticizing the students' lack of commitment to their studies. He would say, "How can you waste your opportunities for an education—in Nicaragua less than 1% of 1% ever receive any type of education. Education is a privilege for only the most privileged. And you students don't study—you just fool around."[47]

Miller was restless in Minnesota and felt unfulfilled. He expressed this in a letter to Brother Martin Spellman in Huehuetenango, Guatemala:

I guess it's no secret that I am anxious to return to Latin America. I just don't function to my best potential up here anymore. I hope you fellows can find a spot for me in Guatemala...I have a special interest in the Indian School, but I realize that you may need my services more urgently somewhere else. I will go wherever I am most needed. I in no way attach any condition to my going to Guatemala.[48]

Brother Cyril, sensing Jim's agitation, decided to place him in a one-hundred-day spiritual renewal program at the Christian Brothers' Sangre de Cristo Retreat House near Santa Fe, New Mexico, hoping that the desert environment would induce him to do some introspective thinking. While there during the fall of 1980, Jim decided to write to the Capuchin provincial, with whom he had worked in Nicaragua, inquiring about entering the priesthood. When he was told it would take about five years to be ordained and that he could not be guaranteed an assignment in Nicaragua, he gave up any notion of a priestly call. In hindsight, Jim's interest in the Capuchins was probably the outgrowth of an attempt, perhaps subconscious, to find a way back to the Central American apostolate he loved.

In December 1980, Jim received a letter from Litecky informing him that he was being assigned, effective the following month, to the Colegio De La Salle in Huehuetenango, where he would join six other brothers—

three from the United States and three native Guatemalans—working with impoverished Indian boys. He was ecstatic.

Huehuetenango, bordering Mexico in the western highlands, is Guatemala's second largest department. About three-fourths of its population in 1980 were indigenous, coming from nine Mayan groups, the largest being the Mam. Almost all Indians resided in surrounding villages or remote rural areas, while the *ladino* minority tended to live in the city of Huehuetenango, the departmental capital. Each indigenous group had its own distinct language, and Spanish was spoken haltingly at best by the Indians. In 1943 the Vatican had assigned jurisdiction of the entire department to the Maryknoll Fathers. Prior to their arrival, there had not been a Catholic priest in the area for decades and there was little comprehension of the sacramental nature of Catholicism. Most of the Indians lived in extreme poverty and illiteracy was almost universal. The Maryknoll missioners had a daunting task before them and, therefore, in 1960 they invited the Christian Brothers to assist them, which resulted in the opening of the Colegio De La Salle. The school was a success, and within two decades its student population had increased from a hundred students to more than a thousand in three divisions: elementary through fifth grade, junior/senior high school, and the innovative Casa Indígena De La Salle—the Indian Center.[49]

When Don Geng expressed concern about his friend going into a violence-filled environment, the overweight Jim laughed: "Well, at least I have some incentive to lose weight. I can then dodge the bullets more easily."[50] His levity, however, was probably tempered by the knowledge that, following the corrupt presidential election in 1978, kidnappings, torture, and murder had become commonplace. On June 30 Eufermio López Coarchita, a parish priest in San José Pinula, was gunned down. His death was followed in 1980 by that of four more priests. The first two, Conrado de la Cruz and Walter Voordeckers, were Immaculate Heart of Mary missioners who had ministered to day laborers working on cotton plantations and in sugar mills in the department of Escuintla. The last two, José María Gran and Faustino Villanueva, Missionaries of the Sacred Heart, had worked with Indians in the diocese of Quiché. As historian Phillip Berryman noted, in 1980 "repression [had] reached a new level of intensity in the number of people killed and in the openness with which repression was carried out" and that "while the attack was directed at all sectors of society for the first time there was a systematic and virtually indiscriminate attack on church pastoral agents."[51]

The June 1980 statement by the Guatemalan bishops illustrates the terror that church personnel had to endure: catechists and prayer leaders were being kidnapped, tortured, and murdered. Pastoral agents were being continually watched and their sermons taped. Three priests had recently been killed and one had been kidnapped. Others had been expelled from the country. And priests who had been martyred for preaching the gospel had been the objects of insidious calumnies after their deaths, meant to cast a shadow on their Christian witness.[52]

Yet Miller knew that he and the brothers at Huehuetenango could offer assistance to Indians whose life expectancy was forty-five years—sixteen years fewer than that of those in the rest of the country—and whose infant mortality rate was as high as one hundred per thousand live births. His teaching and agricultural expertise was needed in a nation where 82 percent of the Indians were illiterate and virtually all Indian children suffered from malnutrition and parasites, and where in 1979 the worst land distribution ratio in all of Latin America existed, with 90 percent of rural Indian families owning either no land or less than the minimum needed to support a family at the subsistence level.[53]

Miller's assignment at the Colegio was twofold: he taught classes in religion, English, and Guatemalan culture and served as guidance counselor. He also maintained the physical plant and worked three afternoons a week as assistant director of the Casa Indígena, a relatively new addition to the Colegio and the pride of the brothers. The Indian Center had been added to the Colegio in 1974 at the suggestion of a young Guatemalan brother, Rolando López, who convinced his superiors that since the greatest social problem facing the church in his country was the poverty and mistreatment of the Indian, the brothers must aim to eradicate these evils. The Casa Indígena offered a full educational experience for about 150 Mayan boys in grades seven through twelve. It included academic classes at the Colegio, intensive agricultural training on a model farm, and religious instruction. Brother Rolando was especially concerned with leadership training and developing in the Mayan youth a deeper respect for their indigenous culture. The boys lived in a boarding house on the grounds and had been chosen from the mountain villages surrounding Huehuetenango by their teachers, principal, or parish priest on the basis of their leadership potential. They took the full curriculum of classes at the Colegio, but in the afternoon worked on the model farm learning modern scientific agriculture and soil conservation.[54] As Brother Paul Joslin, who was Brother Santiago's superior at the Colegio, explained: "[Our] hope was for the young men to return to their towns of origin and put into practice the leadership characteristics [and] updated farming techniques they had learned."[55] The young men were encouraged to pass these skills on to other Maya in their native tongue.

The assignment of Miller to the Colegio was an ideal match for his many skills, commented Joslin:

> He had a lively sense of humor, enhanced by his command of Spanish that enabled him to jab and parry with the youngsters in their own idiom. They also respected him as a hard worker who led by example more than word. But above all he shared a common denominator with the poor rural Indians... Like them, he was a farmer who loved the land.[56]

Initially, however, there were a couple of bumps in the road as Miller adapted to a very different missionary environment from the one he had experienced in Nicaragua. The nine years he spent there, first as teacher and then as principal of the high school, had intensified his predisposition to autonomous behavior. Jim had always had "his own agenda," as one brother who had overseen him in high school and college noted. Being in a position of authority as principal had honed this streak of independence, which now served to complicate his adjustment to his new assignment at the Colegio De La Salle. Thus, the old problem that Jim had had as an aspiring brother of not always adhering to the brothers' schedule of community prayers and morning Mass again cropped up.

James Miller—like the rural Indians he served—was "a farmer who loved the land"

Even though his responsibilities at the Indian Center demanded he put in a long day that often did not end until almost 11:00 PM, his frequent absences from evening prayer could not go unchallenged and were reported to LoCoco and Litecky, his superiors in the U.S.[57]

There was another issue that Jim also had to face. He initially assumed that because of his prior experience as principal he would have an administrative position in Huehuetenango with more authority, and he found his subordinate position difficult to accept. After a "rough start," Brother Paul Joslin was eventually able to report to LoCoco that "the situation has been improving" even though "not being in charge is a cross for

[Jim]." Joslin was not reticent, however, in heaping praise on Jim for his exceptional dedication to his indigenous students:

> The days were really packed. It was normal to get up at 5:30 a.m. for prayers, Mass and breakfast, before proceeding to school, which started at 7:30 a.m.... After lunch Jim accompanied a group of young Indígenas to a diocesan farm...to teach them more advanced ways of farming...Jim was finished in time for evening prayer or a community meeting and dinner. After dinner he supervised the study hall for his group until 9:00 PM. Many a night he remained in the hall quite late either tutoring or counseling someone in need. He himself mentions "18-hour days"...It was quite a workout.[58]

While adjustment issues did present challenges for Miller, he was growing daily in respect for the Maya, their culture, and especially the boys in the Casa Indígena.

Jim and the other brothers realized that the atrocities inflicted on the Maya by the military and death squads were increasing daily. It was while he was in Huehuetenango that terrified Guatemalan Maya began to pour over the Mexican border. In May 1981 about five hundred entered Chiapas, Mexico, but were forced back into Guatemala. Then in June four thousand crossed the border; they were permitted to remain. By the end of 1983, at least one hundred thousand Maya were living in squalor in Chiapas and subject to raids from Guatemalan troops crossing the border.[59]

Tens of thousands more were forced to flee military attacks on their mountain villages, thereby becoming internal refugees, causing journalist Phillip Wearne to write:

> Without identity papers, whole families live in total fear, trying to hide themselves in provincial cities or the capital. Many stay only a few weeks in the same place. Indian dress and language are quickly discarded so as to prevent being identified with a subversive area. Many are simply starving. "I know whole Indian families living on 30 cents a day," says one nun in Guatemala City.[60]

Others fled to Belize and Honduras, most arriving sick and starving after a perilous journey in which "many braved bullets along the border where the Guatemalan army allegedly created a free-fire zone."[61] Some eventually crossed into the U.S., where they were often helped by religious and other groups who chanced arrest in an attempt to hide them from immigration authorities.

In November 1981, Miller returned to the U.S. for surgery on the cartilage in both knees. While recovering from his operation, he was barraged with questions concerning the violence in Guatemala. "I asked Jim if he wasn't frightened at the thought of returning," remembered Brother Markham. Miller responded, "You don't think about that; that's not why you're there. There's too much to be done; you can't waste your energies worrying about what might happen. If it happens, it happens."[62]

Jim spent Christmas 1981 with his family, who tried to dissuade him from returning to Guatemala, but he would have none of it, saying time and again that his place was with the Indian boys. Finally, he told his sister Louise: "One of two frightening things could happen to me in Guatemala. I could be kidnapped, tortured, and killed, or I could simply be gunned down." If he had to die, he said, he prayed death would come through the second alternative.[63]

Toward the end of his recovery, Miller helped out by substituting at Cretin High. Don Geng remembered him "candidly [telling] of the dangers of speaking out on any political issue. He told the students that he had to be careful...One never knew who the spies were. He said it was very possible he could be murdered if the wrong statement was attributed to him."[64]

Miller was certainly aware of the potential danger. On February 15, Father Juan Fernández was stopped by several masked men as he drove his motorbike to celebrate Mass in the village of Cunén in Quiché. After a vicious beating, he was executed by three shots to the head. Fernández was only the first of five priests murdered in Guatemala in 1981. Carlos Gálvez Galindo, a diocesan priest, was killed in his parish house in Tecpán in the department of Chimaltenango on May 14. And on July 1 Father Tullio Merluzzo and his catechist Luis Arroyo Navarro were ambushed and murdered. Stan Rother was the next to die, and five days after his assassination Jesuit Father Carlos Pérez Alonso, a hospital chaplain, was kidnapped and never seen again. The murders of Rother and a Mennonite pastor, John Troyer, only a few months after Miller arrived would have made him realize that his U.S. citizenship was no guarantee of safety in the atmosphere of violence against religious personnel.

When Miller's knees were healed, he left the U.S. for the last time. Brother Gerard Pihaly took him to the Twin Cities Airport. On the way he asked him if the violence in Guatemala was really as bad as had been reported. Jim replied: "We never know when we rise in the morning if we will be alive by nightfall. We are teaching human rights to these poor

Indians and after they start demanding them, it leads to bloodshed." Pihaly asked him how one could bear up in such a terrifying situation. He answered: "We just don't allow ourselves to dwell on it. The need to help these poor uneducated people is so great that it is the all-consuming motive for being there."[65]

Miller's words to Pihaly are consistent with his earlier attitude as a principal in Nicaragua toward the education of his students. There, he had fought to keep the school open in trying times and had maneuvered with Somoza's officials to obtain extra funds for his school. There, Miller the pragmatist had put education above all and had consequently been considered by some to be a Somocista collaborator. Rather than dimming his overall emphasis on education, his recent experience in Guatemala had matured it. His willingness to sacrifice for the education of the underprivileged had developed to such a degree that Jim was able, in spite of personal risk, to put the education of Mayan Indians above all else. Jean-Baptiste de La Salle had challenged his Christian Brothers in the seventeenth century to achieve such zeal for teaching that they would be prepared to give their lives for their students. Brother James had apparently attained this spiritual goal by at least late 1981.

A few weeks after Jim's return, on February 10, 1982, the father of one of the Guatemalan Christian Brothers at the Colegio came to the brothers' residence to warn them that he had overheard soldiers in a nearby park scheming to murder the school's "sub-director." There were three sub-directors, Miller being one of them, but since the informant did not know which one the soldiers were talking about, it was agreed that it would be best if all the brothers tried to stay inside their residence.[66]

Yet on February 13 there was no sign of tension at the Colegio. Jim spent a good part of the morning scrubbing floors at the new convent of six Poor Clare nuns, recent arrivals in Huehuetenango from Tennessee, and around midday he took part in a picnic with students who were celebrating Friendship Day.[67] After that, ever true to his inclination never to be idle when an odd job beckoned, Miller decided to patch a wall at the Casa Indígena. It was daylight, around four o'clock on a Saturday afternoon, and since the streets were filled with people, he evidently reasoned that it was safe to venture out.

Although witness accounts of what happened next vary in details, apparently Miller, who was standing on a ladder, asked the student who was assisting him to take some equipment back into the building. When the boy left, three men in civilian clothing moved toward Jim, firing their automatic weapons. Miller, felled by six bullets, died instantly. Although the police were immediately called, they did not arrive for forty-five minutes, giving the killers ample time to flee the scene. According to witnesses, the assassins ran toward the National Police Headquarters. No longer welcome in Nicaragua, where he had been perceived as a rightist collaborator, Miller died at the hands of a Guatemalan right-wing death squad.

Bishop Victor Hugo Martínez of Huehuetenango celebrated a Mass of Resurrection for Jim on Sunday, February 14, at the Casa Indígena, after which more than a thousand Indians accompanied the body on its four-mile journey to Huehuetenango Airport. When the procession arrived at the halfway point, the casket was supposed to be transferred to a waiting car. But the young men refused to give up their burden. For the remaining two miles to the airport, Hermano Santiago's students took turns carrying the coffin on their shoulders.[68]

The body was flown to Guatemala City where Bishop Eduardo Fuentes celebrated a memorial Mass at the Christian Brothers' residence. On February 15, a third Mass was concelebrated by the papal nuncio, another bishop, and several Guatemalan and American priests.

On February 16, after Brother James's body reached the U.S., a memorial Mass was celebrated at St. Paul's Cathedral in St. Paul before six hundred mourners. Archbishop John Roach, president of the National Council of Catholic Bishops, gave the homily. After expressing his thoughts on the commitment and martyrdom of Brother James and other missioners recently killed in Central America, the archbishop paused; gripping the podium, he spoke emphatically:

> As I prepared this homily I promised myself that I would not politicize this celebration of life and death. It is impossible, however, to ignore the conditions which lie at the base of this tragedy.
>
> Last November the bishops of the United States issued a statement on Central America. We were criticized in some quarters ... with saying too much. Tonight in my mind and heart I feel we said too little.
>
> Must those who serve in Guatemala and places like it live in the constant fear that at any moment they may be the victims of violence by irresponsible people who respect neither others nor themselves? In God's name this must stop. There will be other deaths. There will be other persecutions. The tragedy will be compounded if the day comes when the world is calloused in facing the death of the James Millers of this world. We cannot allow that to happen. We must challenge the political and economic structures which not only keep people under oppression but condone deliberate violence ...

In this crisis of civilization, it is not possible to remain neutral or detached either as persons or as a nation. We are linked as brothers and sisters in Jesus Christ with those who struggle to be free. We are also linked with them as citizens of a country whose government policy affects development, and in some instances non-development, in their countries...

You and I must support those who fight the oppression of the poor, fight for the rights of those who have no rights...but we cannot afford the luxury of being spectators in that struggle. We must hold up the arms of our sisters and brothers who speak for and who work for God's poor.[69]

Don Geng was one of the mourners at St. Paul's that day:

As echoes of the final hymn...rang in my ears and moistened my eyes, my exit from the Cathedral was blocked by several activists disseminating information against our U.S. involvement in Latin America. My initial reaction was one of anger: I didn't want politics to get in the way of my grief. I wanted those activists to leave. However, I suddenly realized it was precisely politics which killed James Miller.

As I skimmed the brochures, I understood the violence... which pervades Central America. In Guatemala...80% of [the] people make less than $79.00 per year, the average city dweller can afford only $.13 a day for food (eggs are $.08 apiece, chickens are $1.79 per pound) and Amnesty International has documented over 9,000 politically motivated murders by government-supported death squads...Then I thought of the international scoffing which received Reagan's announcement that "human rights policies are improving in El Salvador." I realized how it took the brutal and shocking murder of this humble, committed Christian Brother to awaken me to the injustices that prevail in our hemisphere. I imagined for one split second the terror of not only starvation and poverty, but the brutal, inhuman fear that so many of our poor Latin American neighbors must face when confronted with powers (be they from the right, middle, or left) that do not respect human dignity...I imagined myself as a father living in squalor, without a job and unable to adequately feed, clothe or house my wife and children. I felt for a moment the stark terror of a peasant of Indian heritage in some isolated mountain village who suddenly feels a cold, automatic steel barrel jabbed into his ribs by some faceless enemy of un-known origin.[70]

Miller was no leftist. Why then was he killed? The answer may lie in the relations between the brothers at the Colegio and the Guatemalan army. The military, to meet its quota of conscripts, often rounded up In-dian boys, forcing them into the army. Even though students were sup-posedly exempt from serving, those from the Indian Center were often impressed for service in the army. When this would happen, a brother would present proof to the authorities that the particular boy in question was a student. The military would then reluctantly release him.

A few days prior to the shooting of Miller, a Mayan pupil had been forced into the army. A Christian Brother, but not James Miller, went to the authorities to obtain his release. This time the military refused to relinquish their catch. Apparently the brother, adamant in his de-mands, infuriated the soldiers. The murder of Miller was probably meant as a warning to the brothers at the Colegio to cease interfering in army affairs.[71]

Paul Joslin, as Miller's local superior, took responsibility for accom-panying the slain brother's body on the flight back to Minnesota. Prior to his departure, he met with Ray Bailey, the U.S. Consul General in Guatemala, who bluntly cautioned him that when he dealt with the media it would be unwise to suggest that anyone or any group was re-sponsible for Jim's murder. Joslin, fully comprehending the meaning of the consul's advice, issued a press release stating that at this time it would be "extremely difficult to say with any certitude who Brother Miller's murderers might be." To state otherwise would have put the other broth-ers in grave danger and Joslin was unwilling to take that risk. On the other hand, he knew that embassy officials were aware that members of the army's G-2 squad—the unit that was thought to be responsible for most assassinations in the area—had threatened another sub-director of the Colegio De La Salle just prior to the murder of Miller. The embassy had also been informed that the assassins had been seen fleeing toward the headquarters of the National Police. In fact, it should have been ob-vious to all that those responsible for Miller's assassination were the same ones who were now playing a major role in carrying out the so-called "official investigation" into the crime. Yet it seemed that this sham was going forward with few if any objections from American officials.

This became even more evident after Joslin returned to Guatemala following Miller's funeral. When he and another brother met with Fred-eric Chapin, the American ambassador to Guatemala, they were advised not to expect help in the investigation from Guatemalan authorities. A few months later, embassy personnel notified Brother Paul that the Guatemalan investigative team had found that Miller had been collaborating with local security forces in an attempt to rid the area of "subversive criminal elements," implying that leftwing forces had murdered Miller. This was patently absurd.

In August the embassy wrote to the brothers claiming that it regretted that those responsible for Miller's murder had not yet been apprehended, but that embassy officials would continue to press Guatemalan authorities for a prompt resolution. By this time the brothers in Huehuetenango had already found a "very reliable source," with no help from the Guatemalan government or American embassy, who informed them that Miller had been killed by military personnel based at the local army facility and that his killers had mistakenly murdered the wrong brother. Commenting later on his two meetings with embassy officials, Joslin was emphatic: "The consul general and the U.S. ambassador were much more interested in keeping good relations with the Guatemalan government than in bringing Br. James's killers to justice."[72]

Neither Guatemalan nor U.S. authorities were interested in determining who the assassins were. Realizing that to press them to solve Jim's murder would only put the lives of other brothers in jeopardy, all of the brothers in Guatemala at their meeting in September in Guatemala City decided by consensus not to pursue the case any further.[73] Without support from the American embassy it was simply too dangerous.

A short time before his death Brother James had written a long letter that he sent simultaneously to several friends in the U.S. In it Miller revealed his love for the Maya, a love that overcame fear and bound him to a violent land. Greg and Maura Robertson, a couple living in New Mexico, received their copy of the letter while they were grieving, having just been informed of his death. Greg read it at a memorial Mass at the College of Santa Fe. It is enlightening for its cultural and historical observations, as well as for Hermano Santiago's reflections on his life as a missioner:

> After nearly 10 years of service in Nicaragua and a year and a half in the States, I arrived in Huehuetenango, Guatemala, in early January 1981. Our community of Brothers there for 1981 consisted of three from the States and three from Guatemala. I had a double assignment from the beginning: teach in our school in Huehuetenango and help direct the Indian Center (Casa Indígena De La Salle) in the same city. Both assignments were challenging: the former, because I was assigned to teach the History

of Guatemalan Art (I had to become an "expert" overnight!) in addition to several English classes and was given the responsibility for guidance in a school of 900 pupils; the latter, because it meant living and working with 150 Indian boys (grades 7–12) in a boarding school situation with the help of two other Brothers. Besides supervision and counseling, my duties at the Indian Center also included the maintenance of a large building and the responsibility for the small farm (10–12 acres) that is one of the educational projects of the Indian Center (there is also a carpentry shop). The days were often long, and many demands were placed on my time at the Indian Center, but I thoroughly enjoyed my work with the Indian boys. Through my close daily association with them, I have come to respect and love them all and to have a deep respect for the many centuries of Mayan history and tradition that is their cultural heritage.

Guatemala is a beautiful country of mountains, valleys, lakes, lush tropical forests and fertile coastal plains. It is probably one of the most colorful countries in the world. The ancient Mayan modes of dress and customs blend with those of the Spanish conquerors to form a rich panorama of colors, sounds, and special traditions. The Indians still speak their traditional Mayan tongues (seven or eight Indian tongues are spoken among the boys at the Indian Center—Spanish has to be the common language). The Indians are industrious farmers, honest, peace-loving, simple people whose hospitality is proverbial. I always find it a joy to visit the homes of the boys from the Indian Center. The Indians of Guatemala form about 50 percent of the seven-million-plus population of the country; but they are the poor, the oppressed, the forgotten ones of Guatemala. Many of them are desperately poor, the majority is illiterate, and malnutrition and infant mortality are endemic problems.

Our apostolate at the Indian Center has for its principal purpose the formation of educated leaders among the Indian population. We have hundreds of requests each year from priests, Sisters and village leaders to accept boys from their towns and villages, but we can accept only 150, including those who are already in the six-year high school program. The selection process is difficult, but we try to accept those with the most leadership potential. We ask the families to pay $12.50 a month for their sons' room and board and schooling, but many can pay only a fraction of that (real costs are $50 per boy per month).

The rest of our funding comes from donations of the Christian Brothers in the United States, the Maryknoll Fathers and Brothers and from many generous relatives and friends in the United States and Europe. CARE provides some rice, wheat flour, cooking oil, etc., each month. God must smile on our venture with those fine lads, because somehow we always manage to receive help from someone just when we need it most.

I can't end this letter without asking for your prayers for Guatemala (and for all of Central America). The level of personal violence here is reaching appalling proportions (murders, torture, kidnappings, threats, etc.), and the church is being persecuted because of its option for the poor and the oppressed. The Indian population of Guatemala, caught defenseless between the Army and the rebel forces operating in the country, is taking the brunt of this violence. We pray and long for peace and a just solution to Guatemala's many social and economic problems (most of which date from the Conquest of 1524), but until now peace and justice elude us. Aware of the many difficulties and risks that we face in the future, we continue to work with faith and hope and trust in God's Providence. Please join your prayers with ours *every day*. Many selfish, blind and hardened hearts must be converted to the love of Christ before a lasting solution can be found. Armed force will not solve the problems; only dialogue and mutual understanding can be viable solutions. I am personally weary of violence, but I continue to feel a strong commitment to the suffering poor of Central America. "God's ways are not man's ways," says the Bible. God knows why He continues to call me to Guatemala when some friends and relatives encourage me to pull out for my own comfort and safety. I have been a Christian Brother for nearly twenty years now, and my commitment to my vocation grows steadily stronger in the context of my work in Central America. I pray to God for the grace and strength to serve Him faithfully by my presence among the poor and oppressed of Guatemala. I place my life in His Providence; I place my trust in Him. I hope you understand my position. The intensity of the past year in Guatemala has come out in these last paragraphs. Please pardon so many personal references, but I can't take the situations and experiences of the past year out of a personal context.[74]

This letter, composed a few weeks before Jim was killed, was not only eloquently written, but also illustrated that by this time, at age thirty-seven, he had come into his own as a missioner. With his years of experience as a teacher and administrator in Nicaragua and his fluency in Spanish; with his "Brother Fix-it" handyman skills, his ethic of hard work and his yearning to be useful every minute of a long day; with his knowledge of machines and equipment; and especially with his upbringing as the descendant of a farming family, he was able to offer himself body and soul to the education of Guatemalan boys, both *ladino* and Maya.

But what had his short experience of just over a year at the Colegio De La Salle and the Casa Indígena offered Hermano Santiago? This letter revealed that Jim had grown in compassion and in awareness of what it was to be "the poor, the oppressed, the forgotten ones in Guatemala," as he described the Mayan Indians. Not being caught up as he had been in Nicaragua with overseeing the renovation and building of schools, cajoling funds from powerful supporters within the greedy Somoza dictatorship, and other administrative duties, he was free to grow in spirit. He now understood more clearly the deep-rooted structures of injustice that went back centuries in Central America, a fact that he rarely alluded to during his ten years in Nicaragua.

His boyhood love of geography, his gifts for teaching and language-learning, and his devotion as a Christian Brother to de La Salle's principles of education all came together for him in the beautiful but strife-filled highlands of western Guatemala. It was sad and ironic that as he was approaching a pinnacle of personal growth his life was cut short. Hermano Santiago had developed into a man who embraced fully the Lasallian ideal of educating the poor with selfless zeal. As the founder of the Christian Brothers had foreseen three centuries earlier, this zeal might one day result in the ultimate sacrifice.

*　*　*

The death of Miller resulted in some introspection on the part of the Christian Brothers. A year after his murder Brother Litecky stated in a letter: "The Brothers tend to be rather wrapped up in their particular ministries and apostolates. Consequently, the areas of social justice, peace, and political involvement often take a back seat... [I] would like the Brothers to be 'gently challenged.'"[75]

There is now an award given yearly in Brother Jim's home diocese of La Crosse, Wisconsin, that identifies those "who have made outstanding contributions to the cause of justice and peace." And the Christian Brothers of the Midwest, his home province, have established the Brother James Miller Social Justice Fund, which provides grants to various endeavors in the United States and around the world—projects that include inner-city programs in this country, as well as missionary efforts in Latin America and Africa.[76]

After the Diocese of Huehuetenango undertook Brother James Miller's cause in 2009 for canonization, his case received the Decree of Validity in July 2010, at which time he was named a "Servant of God." At this writing, a theological commission has ruled positively on his martyrdom, which is expected to clear the way for his beatification.

The Casa Indígena is still in existence providing education, teaching new farming techniques, and training Mayan boys from the Guatemalan highlands to be leaders. The number of students is significantly reduced, however, because now there are more junior high schools near their villages for the Maya to attend. As Brother Joslin writes: "The majority of graduates are now successful teachers reaching out to the neediest; some are lawyers; some are doctors too."[77] But its name has changed: eight months after Jim was killed outside the Indian Center, it was renamed the Centro Indígena Hermano Santiago Miller.

The legacy of Brother James Miller, who gave his life for the sake of educating those who were among the most deprived and neglected in the world, continues.

CHAPTER 4

Guatemala after 1982

O n March 23, 1982, a little more than a month after Brother James was murdered, a coup d'état initiated by a group of young military officers toppled General Lucas García, replacing him with a three-man junta that included General Efraín Ríos Montt. Shortly thereafter, on June 9, Ríos Montt was able to oust his fellow junta members and have himself declared president. Reasoning that the heart of guerrilla strength lay in the indigenous rural communities, the new dictator devised a plan that was so extreme in its violence against the Mayan people and their culture that human rights organizations eventually labeled it genocide. This plan was especially intense in the department of Huehuetenango, where Miller had worked, and in Quiché.

As part of his strategy, the new president announced a "Guns and Beans" policy, stating that Indian villages that supported the government against the guerrillas would be rewarded with food subsidies, while those deemed uncooperative would be annihilated. Indians were forced to relocate to so-called model villages or strategic hamlets, which were more like concentration camps. There, Mayan males were required to serve in government-created civil defense patrols. These patrols were supposedly voluntary, but the reality was that if one did not join in all likelihood he would be killed. Members, who were provided with antiquated rifles or other even less lethal weapons, were required to patrol the area surrounding their villages and kill any guerrillas they encountered or at least report them to Guatemalan military authorities. They were to keep tabs on all community members, reporting those who seemed disloyal to the government. People could not enter or leave the hamlet without first reporting to patrol members. Patrol members were often ordered to torture or kill their fellow villagers; not to do so meant being killed themselves.

In what came to be called Ríos Montt's "scorched earth" policy more than 440 villages that were deemed uncooperative by the army were destroyed and a hundred thousand civilians—mostly Indians—were slaughtered or disappeared.[1] Up to two hundred thousand Maya survived only by fleeing across the border into Honduras or into Chiapas, Mexico, where they were forced to live in extreme poverty and misery. About fifty thousand more became internal refugees, some hiding in the slums of Guatemala City but most living in clandestine camps in the jungles, always moving to stay a step ahead of the army that was hunting them down.[2]

On May 28, 1982, the Guatemalan Catholic Bishops Conference issued a report on the massacres and placed blame for them squarely on the Ríos Montt government. Labeling what was taking place "genocide," it added that "never in the history of our nation have things gone so far." In August the president of the U.S. Conference of Catholic Bishops declared that the "massacre of numerous *campesinos* and Indian families had reached the level of genocide." Similar statements followed from the Catholic peace organization Pax Christi and the Dutch Catholic Congress. In December a Canadian-sponsored United Nations resolution condemned the Ríos Montt administration for "violence against noncombatants," demanding that it "refrain both from forcefully displacing people belonging to rural and indigenous populations and from the practice of coercive participation in civilian patrols."[3]

None of these reports, however, seemed to matter to President Reagan who, while visiting Honduras on December 4, 1982, during his tour of Latin America, met personally with Ríos Montt and announced to journalists that the Guatemalan general was "a man of great personal integrity and commitment... [who] wants to improve the quality of life for all Guatemalans and to promote social justice." He added that the Guatemalan dictator was getting "a bum rap" from international human rights groups. But Reagan was not content with words of praise for Ríos Montt. While the latter's soldiers were slaughtering tens of thousands of innocent Indians, the U.S. government was assisting these killers with more than $10 million in military aid.[4]

On August 8, 1983, Ríos Montt was overthrown by General Oscar Humberto Mejía Victores, his defense minister, but government-sponsored violence continued, and before Mejía left office Franciscan friar Augusto Ramírez Monasterio was murdered. A few weeks before he was ousted from the presidency, Ríos Montt had issued a decree of amnesty for all guerrillas who turned themselves in to government authorities. In truth, the decree was no more than a façade meant to project an image to other countries of a new "respectable" Guatemala. Ironically, it indirectly cost Ramírez, a priest in Antigua, his life. He was hearing confessions when a man entered the confessional and asked for his help in obtaining amnesty. The priest took the former guerrilla to a nearby municipal building to assist him in completing the necessary paper work. To their surprise, both he and the man he intended to aid were turned over to the National Police and tortured. The next day Ramírez was released, but not the former guerrilla. Thereafter, he received several threatening phone calls demanding that he leave Guatemala, but he would not. On November 7, 1983, he was kidnapped. The next day his battered body was discovered in the morgue.

Guatemala's economy was rapidly spiraling downward, in part because of the country's dismal human rights record. To deflect criticism from the military, Mejía decided to allow democratic elections in 1985. In the first honest election since that of Jacobo Arbenz, Vinicio Cerezo Arévalo, a civilian and leader of the Christian Democratic Party, won the presidency and his party took a majority of the seats in Congress. Although this election marks the beginning of a slow transition from military dictatorship to democracy, Cerezo proved relatively ineffective and unable to control the army. He was successful in creating an ombudsman for human rights and initiating some modest judicial reforms, but massive corruption permeated his presidency and violence continued.

In neighboring El Salvador a National Dialogue, aimed at ending that country's civil war, was established in 1988. Facilitated by Archbishop Arturo Rivera Damas, it was a promising step, and, indeed, eventually did lead to the signing of a peace accord on January 1, 1992. Taking its cue from El Salvador, in 1989 the Guatemalan Catholic Church set up a similar National Dialogue, which was presided over by Bishop Rodolfo Quezada. Peace talks were organized and held in Oslo, Norway, in 1990. The Guatemalan National Revolutionary Unity (URNG) guerrilla coalition agreed to take part, as did several political parties and other groups, but the talks made little headway and soon broke down largely because they were boycotted by the Guatemalan government, military, and business community. Nevertheless, they had some significance in that they enabled Jorge Serrano Elías to win the 1990 presidential election by promising to renew the talks. He quickly did so after his victory and this time the army and government participated.

Aside from restarting the peace talks, Serrano, like Cerezo before him, accomplished little. During his presidency, Moisés Cisneros Rodríguez, a Marist brother and Spanish national, was stabbed to death in his office on April 29, 1991. Cisneros was the director of the *Escuela Marista de San Alfonso*, a school for poor children that his congregation had founded in Guatemala City. As in the case of many other martyrs in

Guatemala, his killers were never apprehended. Serrano was toppled from the presidency in 1993 after a bizarre attempt to overthrow his own government and declare himself dictator in what became known as an *autogolpe* or "self-coup." Congress replaced him with Ramiro de León Carpio, the human rights ombudsman who had played a positive role in the aftermath of the 1990 massacre in Santiago Atitlán. In 1994 all sides agreed to have the United Nations now become the moderator of the peace process, and on December 29, 1996, during the presidency of Alvaro Arzú, a peace accord was finally signed, thereby ending thirty-six years of civil war.[5] Arzú had pushed for peace by removing some of the worst human rights abusers from the army high command and national police and by taking steps to increase civilian control over the armed forces. His presidency marks the final transition to elective—if still imperfect—democracy.

Nevertheless, during his presidency the most audacious murder of a Catholic clergyman in Guatemala took place. On April 26, 1998, Bishop Juan Gerardi Conedera was bludgeoned to death by two army officers and a sergeant two days after he released *Guatemala: Nunca Más* (*Guatemala: Never Again*) to the public.[6] This two-volume study recorded the eyewitness testimony of large numbers of Guatemalans who had survived the massacres and military sweeps that killed thousands of their fellow citizens. It also contained graphs and analysis, which led its authors to claim that the military had been responsible for almost 90 percent of the killings and the guerrillas less than 5 percent. Such an assertion was an international public relations embarrassment for the government and military.[7]

Gerardi, along with another bishop, had overseen the Recovery of Historical Memory Project (REMHI) from which this report had emanated and this presumably was the reason he was the target of an army death squad. Although the police initially arrested an innocent man in a poorly concocted attempted to cover up the military's culpability in the crime, their effort failed. With Bill Clinton now president, the Guatemalan power structure could no longer count on unconditional U.S. support. Consequently, the assassins were eventually arrested, tried and convicted in court, and sentenced to prison. Justice was grudgingly served in this case; nonetheless, Gerardi's gruesome killing demonstrated that the military remained a powerful institution in Guatemalan society still capable of extreme violence.

In 1999 the United Nations Commission for Historical Clarification issued the report, *Guatemala: Memory of Silence*, which it had been commissioned in 1994 to draw up by those involved in the peace process. Its conclusions were even more devastating for the Guatemalan government and military than the church's REMHI report had been. It stated that 93 percent of the two hundred thousand people killed or disappeared during the civil war had died at the hands of the military and their paramilitary associates. It further noted that 83 percent of those who had been slaughtered were Mayan Indians, and therefore the war could rightfully be labeled a genocide.

The report was also highly critical of U.S. conduct, noting that the United States had been actively involved in developing the Guatemalan army's counterinsurgency policies and capabilities during the 1960s. It further said that throughout the 1970s and '80s the U.S. had supported the Guatemalan government's illegal operations, had been well aware of the military's massacres and other atrocities during its "scorched-earth" operations, and had done nothing to stop them. It added that U.S. military aid to Guatemala "had significant bearing on human rights violations."[8] So devastating were the report's conclusions on the United States' conduct in Guatemala throughout its civil war that after its release President Clinton felt compelled to publicly apologize.[9]

Ironically, the termination of the civil war in Guatemala, rather than ushering in an era of peace, actually contributed, at least indirectly, to the development of an even more violent society. Almost immediately after the peace accords were signed in 1996, the Mexican Sinaloa drug cartel moved into the remote jungle areas of northern Guatemala and before long turned this region into a key location on the drug route from South America to the United States. Guatemalan army commandos known as the Kaibiles now allied with the Sinaloa cartel. The Kaibiles, who were established in the 1970s and specialized in jungle warfare, had been the principal instruments of Ríos Montt's "scorched earth" policy in the 1980s and were responsible for thousands of deaths, mostly of Indians. Many had been trained at the infamous School of the Americas at Fort Benning, Georgia, and at least one had served as an instructor there.

Soon the Kaibiles evolved into a separate Guatemalan-based drug cartel known as *Los Zetas*, which joined with various other organized crime players and local street gangs. The overland trans-shipment of cocaine, opium, and marijuana through Guatemala now increased dramatically, and the Zetas and their criminal associates soon expanded their illegal activities to include extortion, prostitution, and kidnapping. Hal Brands, writing in 2010, explained how dire the situation had gotten: "The police, the judiciary, and entire local and departmental governments are rife with criminal infiltrators; murder statistics have surpassed civil-war levels in recent years; criminal operatives brazenly assassinate government officials and troublesome members of the political class; and broad swaths of territory are now effectively under the control of criminal groups."[10]

Widespread terror has turned Guatemala into a lawless society, where those who refuse to cooperate with violent elements place themselves and their families at great risk. Consequently, seeing no viable alternative, thousands have attempted to flee their native land and enter the United States illegally. Out of desperation, others have convinced themselves that the "old days" of military-imposed "law and order" were better than the anarchy of the present. Thus, former General Otto Pérez Molina, using the symbol of an iron fist and promising to impose a firm hand (*mano dura*) on the nation, was able to win the 2011 presidential election despite his dark past as director of military intelligence during the war years.

Not surprisingly, Pérez achieved little aside from accumulating a personal fortune during his tenure in office. His presidency was cut short when, as a result of an investigation carried out by the United Nations-sponsored International Commission against Impunity in Guatemala (CICIG), he was caught in a massive corruption scandal and forced to resign on September 2, 2015. The next day he was arrested and incarcerated.[11] After his term was completed by Alejandro Maldonado, an extreme conservative formerly associated with Ríos Montt, the exasperated Guatemalan people elected as president a comedian, Jimmy Morales, who has proven to be as corrupt as his presidential predecessors.

CHAPTER 5

Dorothy Kazel

Ursuline Sister

Dorothy Kazel

D orothea Lu, arriving on June 30, 1939, was the second of two children born to Malvina and Joseph Kazel. Older brother James had been born in November 1936. "Mal and Joe," first-generation Lithuanian-Americans, had met as choir members at St. George Catholic Church on the east side of Cleveland, Ohio.[1] The Kazels lived in Joe's parents' two-family home until Dorothy was sixteen. In this ethnic environment, Lithuanian customs, traditional attire, and religious devotions were all very familiar to her. Joe was a shipping clerk, and although the Kazels were not wealthy, they had family in California, so Dorothy was able to make several trips out west. These trips may have established in her a yearning for adventure and encounters with others of diverse cultures.

Blonde and blue-eyed, Dorothy, also called "Dottie," was considered one of the prettiest girls in her class at St. George Catholic School. She was lively and unable to sit still for long. Because she took accordion lessons, she was one of the few girls in the band. She enjoyed outdoor activities; because she excelled in baseball, even the boys vied to have her on their team. Early on, she displayed a cheerful approach to life's little obstacles. Surprised in third grade by a Halloween party for which she had no costume, she rushed home for lunch and cut a dress out of newspaper. Pinning on her creation, she ran back and received first prize for most original costume. Her childhood was almost idyllic. Her father could only recall one truly unhappy moment, and that was when the dog "Lassie" was killed in a movie she saw. She cried her heart out until Joe explained that it was only a story and Lassie was still alive.

By the time she was ready to enter Notre Dame Academy, an all-girls high school run by the Sisters of Notre Dame, she was about five-foot-six, attractive, and eager to enlarge her social circle. She played varsity sports; was elected to the Student Council every year; served as junior and senior class president; joined the Mission Club, Dramatic Club, and Speech League; landed a major part in the senior play, *Cheaper by the Dozen*—this list could go on. The only way Dorothy could have been busier was if she had been a more diligent student. Friends and teachers remembered her as a more or less average, but responsible, student. Although later she would earn bachelor's and master's degrees, in high school she seemed to consider her studies secondary to extra-curricular pursuits and her social life.

Two of her passions, roller-skating and pajama parties, had begun earlier but intensified in her high school years. She took skating lessons, practiced for hours, competed, performed, and briefly considered professional roller-skating. She placed first and second in two beauty queen contests for skaters. Pajama parties were held mainly at the Kazels' new home in the suburb of Euclid, where they had moved before Dorothy's junior year. Her parents remembered well the many late nights when their living room was carpeted with noisy, wall-to-wall girls engaged in gossiping, planning for the future, and discussing boyfriends. And yes, these parties were an opportunity to experiment with cigarettes and even cigars.

For her brother Jim, Dorothy was a "great sister to grow up with." When he and his buddies organized a "swinging fifties band," she became their audience for practice sessions. Dorothy happily joined Jim's group of teenagers when she began to date his friend Russell Smith. Dorothy never missed a school dance—either her own or Russ's. She and Russ "went steady," but she wore his ring on a chain inside her uniform at school since the nuns did not approve.

No one, probably not even Dorothy, suspected that she would choose the life of a nun. Yet in the 1950s religious practices in Catholic schools were all-pervasive, and Dorothy embraced them wholeheartedly. All through elementary and high school, she went to daily Mass. Even after an all-night pajama party at her house, she and her friends would rise early on Saturday to attend Mass. As a high school student she belonged to two sodalities, one in her parish and one at school. The sodalities promoted devotion to Mary, the mother of Jesus, and required members to say the rosary daily. If she and her friends were chatting away at home and someone remembered they had not said the rosary that day, they would stop and do so. Yet Dorothy had a decidedly irreverent streak. Once, to the amusement of her girlfriends, she emerged from the bathroom clad only in towels, with one wrapped around her head and twirling another like a stripper. And in her diary she complained that on a trip to see a Passion Play with the sodality, "the nuns were buggy; all they wanted were draftees for the convent."

Dorothy graduated in June 1957, capping off her high school years by being named "Most Cheerful." Although Dorothy had been in the college preparatory track, she had not given much thought to a career beyond a brief interest in professional skating. She had taken some business courses suggested by her mother, who knew such training could land a young woman a respectable job. Dorothy did get hired as a medical secretary, but was not at all happy.

She quickly found an exciting prospect—the Cadet Program—at St. John's College, a Catholic women's institution in Cleveland (now closed) that trained teachers and nurses. Its students could earn a teaching certificate after taking classes for two years, including summers, followed by teaching fulltime at a Catholic school while continuing toward a degree. Dorothy's parents were not enthusiastic. College was expensive and they no doubt reasoned her future husband would support her and their children.

Dorothy was determined to pursue this opportunity even if it meant paying her own way. Wasting no time, she entered the program three months after graduating from high school. She soon found that the heavy course load, combined with her part-time job and ever-active social life, was much more demanding than high school. Brought to tears by her first-term grades, she adjusted to the challenges and bounced back.

During that first semester, Donald Kollenborn, a soldier from Bakersfield, California, entered her life. She met him at the department store where she worked. Stationed nearby, Don asked several times for a date, but Dorothy demurred, perhaps because she was still corresponding with Russ, now a Marine based overseas. Eventually, she agreed to a date, and when Russ came in on leave, her relationship with Don was serious enough that Dorothy decided to stop seeing Russ. This did not at first please Dorothy's mother. Russ was of Lithuanian ancestry, had been a friend of the family for years, and was Catholic. Don was not.

Dorothy chose to do her on-site observations and practice teaching at St. Robert Bellarmine School in Euclid. There she often met Don afterwards at the church, and they would talk in the back where it was quiet and private. As they grew closer, Don began the process of becoming a Catholic. One evening in church, in early 1959, Don gave Dorothy a beautiful engagement ring, and later that year Dorothy traveled to California to meet Don's family. They set the date for August 5, 1960, and began to plan their wedding.

St. Robert Bellarmine was staffed by Ursuline sisters and, while completing her on-site hours, Dorothy became friendly with two whom she admired. When she finished the Cadet Program in mid-1959, she was hired to teach at St. Robert Bellarmine for the next school year. Her third-graders loved their vivacious teacher, and, as for Dorothy, she had found a fulfilling career, one that she could throw herself into wholeheartedly.

Throughout these years, Dorothy continued her spiritual practices. Attending Mass and praying the rosary were daily activities. One day, while praying the rosary at home around the time of her engagement, she was struck by the compelling thought that she should enter the convent. It was a powerful enough experience that she mentioned it to her mother. A quiet struggle began. She loved Don, but what was her calling —marriage or religious life?

While teaching, she attended several retreats. After each Don noticed she was not herself for a while. But Dorothy did not mention her interior conflict to Don or to her closest friends, though she did confide in two priests and a fellow teacher. At some point, possibly after a retreat for engaged women in early 1960, her mother observed that Dorothy became very moody. She began to spend a lot of time in her bedroom and appeared preoccupied, very unlike herself. This behavior continued for a while, before she revealed to her parents that she was uncertain about her upcoming marriage and thought her true calling was to be a nun.

Mrs. Kazel, who was not pleased with this, did notice that once Dorothy had made this decision—an agonizing one that had required months, even a year, of prayer and soul-searching—a weight seemed to lift from her daughter's shoulders. But it still remained for her to break the news to Don, and this was a "heartbreaking" task for Dorothy, her mother recalled. Don was shocked and angry and immediately flew to Cleveland from California, where he was attending college after having been discharged from the army. He attempted to change her mind before realizing that Dorothy had already determined this was the path God wanted for her. Don, reluctantly, came to agree. Their engagement formally ended when Dorothy returned his ring to him a few weeks before they were to wed. Although they corresponded regularly until she entered the convent, she never saw him again. Don waited two years to see if Dorothy would leave the convent, then married someone else.

The summer of 1960 was a troubling one for Dorothy. There were hours spent in discussion with Don; she was distressed about returning his ring; she worried that he might not continue his newfound Catholic faith; and her mother still had reservations about her entering the convent. It was a lot to bear. Occasionally she second-guessed herself, confiding to Don her uncertainties—Would she be able to live within the rules? Was she meant to be a nun?

But the upbeat side of Dorothy could not be suppressed forever. She packed some carefree times with friends into the next weeks—taking a vacation, indulging in serious smoking of unfiltered cigarettes, and, at her insistence, spending September 7 at the race track.

The next day she entered the Ursuline Order. Barely three years out of high school, Dorothy had shown she was a strong woman who could make tough decisions, even if those she loved most were opposed to them. Her parents thought secretarial work was a good career for her—but no, she had wanted to attend college and teach. Despite her mother's initial disapproval, she had chosen Don over Russ. Most unpredictably, she decided to become a nun, though her mother and certainly her fiancé resisted. Once that decision was made, she did not waver: "The next thing we knew," said Mrs. Kazel, "she was entering the convent."

There were indications that bittersweet memories of Don followed her into religious life. In August 1961, after one year as a postulant, Dorothy was formally "clothed" as a novice and received the name "Sister Mary Laurentine." Sister Anna Margaret Gilbride recalled: "That night when I made the rounds to check on [the novices] she said to me that the guy she was engaged to—his favorite name was Laura. 'Isn't that something I would get this name? It's funny how things like that can happen to you.'" And years later, traveling by car with Sister Martha Owen from El Salvador up the California coast—not far from where Don lived—Dorothy would reveal the story of that life-altering decision back in 1960. "It was obvious that she still remembered Don with a lot of affection," said Martha.

The Order of St. Ursula that Dorothy joined has an interesting history. It was founded in 1535 by St. Angela Merici of Brescia, Italy, a Third Order (lay) Franciscan, during the turbulent time of the Protestant Reformation. Angela's companions were to pray, help the needy, and do good works—with a special emphasis on the education of girls. Their patron saint was St. Ursula, hence the name "Ursuline." (Ursula would much later be found to be a legendary figure.) As a secular association following Angela's simple rule, it was remarkably ahead of its time. The women did not reside in a convent. Remaining in their family homes, they went to churches and private homes to teach girls and young women. They wore the typical clothing of the era and did not adopt a habit nor did they take solemn vows. As Angela's society spread rapidly throughout Italy, Cardinal Charles Borromeo of Milan became uncomfortable with the loosely organized association, which existed with a degree of freedom unusual for women at that time. In 1572, the cardinal pressured the group in Milan to live in community as nuns, though they would be independent of any male order and keep their primary ministry of educating females. When the church later attempted to impose cloister, which would have prevented them from carrying out this mission, most of the communities in Italy broke up. Fortunately, groups of Angela's companions had already spread into France. When in 1612 these communities were compelled to become a cloistered order of nuns, they reached a compromise with church authorities allowing them to teach girls within the convent walls, thus continuing the original charism of St. Angela.[2]

The Ursulines in Cleveland could trace the foundation of their community in 1850 back to these French nuns. Ironically perhaps, when Dorothy became Sister Mary Laurentine, she received the name of one of thirty-five Ursulines guillotined for their faith in the Reign of Terror during the French Revolution. But Dorothy's comment was a light-hearted quip: "And if they think I'm going to be a martyr, they have another thought coming!" After the Second Vatican Council, many members of religious orders returned to their given names, so when making her final vows in 1968, Sister Laurentine became Sister Dorothy.

The Ursulines were a teaching order, and Dorothy loved teaching elementary students so she did not anticipate having to relinquish this dream. Although she already had her teaching certificate in elementary education, she did not have her bachelor's degree, and she fully expected to be allowed to complete her degree in that field. But the general superior had another plan—she would instead earn a bachelor's in secondary education. This and the fact that she was advised to major in business were big disappointments. But Dorothy acquiesced and, just a few weeks after this, professed her first vows. If she once voiced doubts about her ability to follow the rules, she had now made it past one high hurdle.

She graduated in 1965 and was assigned to teach at Sacred Heart Academy in East Cleveland, an inner-city school where she would spend seven years teaching business courses. She was not fond of these subjects and jokingly blamed her mother for having encouraged her to take them in high school. If anything, she was even more popular with high school students than with third-graders. And she was maturing into a woman of remarkable dedication and compassion.

Dorothy's highly charged energy found an outlet in the classroom and in the community. Sacred Heart was located in a transitional area of the city that middle-class whites had fled, leaving the more disadvantaged behind, mostly African-Americans. Dorothy was an integral part of two school initiatives that involved Sacred Heart's relationship with the surrounding community: "Beatitudes in Practice"—a student volunteer project—and the innovative "Thrust Program," through which students applied their studies by working in neighborhood businesses. These programs offered extra help to the struggling community while also acquainting the teenagers with various careers.

During these years, Dorothy pursued a wide range of activities that would have exhausted a less energetic woman. She went on camping trips with the Girls' Athletic Association, was an active member of an ecumenical group, and chaperoned girls on overnight retreats. She taught hearing-impaired children religion on Saturdays, after having taken lessons on how to communicate with them. And she volunteered at a hospital and at a women's correctional institution.

Dorothy's vivacious personality drew others like a magnet. A friend from her early days as a postulant, Sister Kathleen Cooney, said: "You were just drawn to Dorothy! She was very pretty, blue sparkling eyes…, high energy. Always joking…" Sister Anna Margaret observed: "She loved to get involved and jumped right into everything. She was fearless." And Dorothy was not above playing a practical joke now and then. Barbara Sever, who taught with her at Sacred Heart and later joined the Ursulines, remembered that Dorothy was pining for sunny Florida, but the rules of the order did not allow for individual vacations. So she had the brainstorm to drive to Florida, Ohio, a six-hour round trip, and roped Barb into the scheme—just so she could mail some postcards with "Florida" postmarks back to the convent, saying "lovely weather, wish you were here." But Florida, Ohio, was so tiny there was no post office and Dorothy, hugely disappointed that her brilliant idea had failed, almost missed curfew.[3]

As outgoing as she was, Dorothy did not talk excessively about herself. Though she did not deviate from set paths without ample thought and prayer, she sometimes surprised people with the apparent suddenness of a decision. This had happened when she had decided to become a nun and would happen again in 1967 when her resolution to become a missioner became known.

Pope John XXIII had called the Second Vatican Council to address the concept of *aggiornamento*—an updating of the church through renewal and modernization. Vatican II ended in 1965, and its effects were percolating through the Catholic world, when, in mid-1967, Dorothy attended a retreat that incorporated the new ideas and profoundly affected her spirituality. In her notes, Dorothy wrote: "A real Christian is dominated by the presence of the Risen Christ . . . [and is] a person with a mission to the world of 1967: loves the world; is caught up with the world; must be equipped with solid learning and mature love; makes use of natural history and philosophy of our time; listens with an open heart . . ."[4]

Dorothy's new outlook coincided with a development—not unrelated—taking place close to home. In August 1964, the diocese had launched the Cleveland Latin American Mission Team when it sent two priests to El Salvador; more religious personnel and lay workers would follow. Like many dioceses around the country, the church in Cleveland was responding to John XXIII's appeal in 1961 to send 10 percent of its personnel to Latin America. The Ursulines in 1967 agreed to send two volunteers every five years, and Dorothy quickly sent in her request:

I have always been of the nature of a person eager to be on the move—to go to new places, to meet new people, to learn to understand these people, and to help them. Before I entered [the Ursulines], I traveled to the West Coast four times. It was then that I was first impressed with the Spanish and Indian people . . . I had even "day dreamed" that my parents would disown me and leave me there . . . While at College . . . , I took a course about Latin America, and since then I have even more earnestly had the desire to go there.[5]

Since she had not yet taken final vows, two others were chosen and her request was put on hold. Undeterred, she sought out programs in the U.S. that might help her explore the life of a missioner. In the summer of 1969 she taught religion to Native Americans on a Papago reservation near Tucson, Arizona. She also attended an event where Father Paul Schindler, a member of the Cleveland Latin American Mission Team, presented a slideshow on their work in El Salvador. He met Dorothy at the end and offered words of encouragement that she would one day be accepted. "Oh, I hope so!" she replied.[6]

In 1970, she began work on a master's degree in guidance and counseling at John Carroll University. Perhaps this shift grew from her desire not to teach business any longer or perhaps it was due to her uncertainty regarding the future of Sacred Heart Academy, where she had taught since 1965. Enrollment was declining, and by the late sixties the school was fighting for its existence. The nuns went door-to-door seeking new

students, adapted the curriculum to the needs of the community, and requested grants and donations. Dorothy joined a committee to study the
issue, but despite an all-out fundraising effort and the nuns' decision to
forego their salary, Sacred Heart closed its doors in 1972.

Afterwards, Dorothy taught and counseled at Beaumont High
School in Cleveland Heights while she completed her degree. Counseling was a good match for Dorothy's listening skills and compassionate
nature. She was assisted by her innate capacity for complete acceptance
of the individual. A student who sought Dorothy's advice during her senior year recalled: "[She] was...100% present to any person she was
speaking with...She was herself—open-minded and funny. She hated
the sin, but loved the sinner. She never judged anybody at all. She had a
special feeling for people who had been kicked around."[7]

In 1974 she earned her master's degree. At around the same time she
received an offer: after a wait of seven years she had been selected for the
Cleveland Latin American Mission Team. Not long before, she had concluded that her spiritual growth had been a bit superficial: "I now need to
go deeper," she wrote in a retreat journal.[8] Little could she have guessed
then how profound an experience El Salvador would be and how much
compassion her heart could bear—nor how willing she would be to give
of herself.

Dorothy finally embarked on her missionary career when in 1974
she and Ursuline Sister Martha Owen arrived in the tiny country of El
Salvador. Only about 8,124 square miles in size, El Salvador is the smallest nation—about the size of Massachusetts—in Central America. But in
the second half of the twentieth century it was also the most densely pop-
ulated country in the Western Hemisphere, with 550 to 600 people per
square mile. At least half of its people were dependent on agriculture for
their survival. In 1971, about 3.3 percent of all landowners held 56 percent of the arable land. But between 1971 and 1975 the coffee-growing
elite decided to diversify by expanding into the coastal lowlands, where
they acquired large tracts of land for cotton production. According to
United Nations statistics, the proportion of rural families who became
landless increased from 29 to 41 percent in this five-year period. By 1975
fewer than 2 percent of the people owned 60 percent of the entire country, including nearly all the fertile soil. Salvadorans had a per capita income of only $700 a year, the second lowest in Central America.[9]

During the latter part of the nineteenth century, El Salvador's in-
digo-centered economy was replaced by an export system based on coffee. The oligarchy—often called the "Fourteen Families"—already held
most of the fertile land, so the transition was uncomplicated from its

point of view. For Indians, however, the change had serious implications, since many of them lost their communal lands to the large landholders. As profits escalated, members of the wealthy elite began to acquire whatever agricultural holdings they did not already own, thereby creating a subservient population of marginalized, landless wage laborers. With their lucrative profits, the rich landowners were able to accumulate the capital needed to establish their own commercial and banking systems. Unlike the case in other Central American countries such as Honduras and Guatemala, which had to deal with the powerful presence of the U.S. banana companies, the oligarchy in El Salvador faced few foreign competitors.

Life was comfortable for the oligarchs, but not so for most of the rest of the population:

> The rapid expansion of the coffee plantations had torn apart Indian villages and their communal lands which provided the food supply. Peasants and Indians became little more than a hungry, wandering labor force to be used at will by the oligarchy. As early as 1900 Salvadorans had sought work in Honduras with United Fruit and other U.S. companies. By the early 1920s they made up as much as 10 percent of the Honduran work force. Their numbers rapidly grew during that decade when lower coffee prices further squeezed out smaller growers and concentrated more power in the oligarchy's hands. As coffee took up more and more territory, the staple foods of maize, beans, and fruit grew scarcer. The only Salvadorans who had enough, not to mention a variety, of food, were the few who could import it from other Central American nations or the United States.[10]

Between 1922 and 1926 the suffering of the bulk of the population became desperate as the price of maize doubled and that of beans increased 225 percent. A glimmer of hope appeared when President Pío Romero Bosque refused to designate his successor and instead worked for a fair, open election in 1931. The conservative elite was caught off guard and, as a result, an outsider, reformer Arturo Araujo, was able to win. But when Araujo attempted to reform the tax laws and reduce the military budget, he was ousted from office in December 1931 by an army-sponsored coup and replaced by General Maximiliano Hernández Martínez.

Meanwhile, Augustín Farabundo Martí, a communist who had helped found the Central American Socialist Party in 1925, was secretly planning what he hoped would be a nationwide insurrection. Indians in the western coffee-producing areas, where poverty was most severe, were convinced to join the planned uprising. The revolt was to begin on January 22, 1932, but the plot was discovered and Martí and the other leaders were arrested on January 19. Yet thousands of desperate Indians rose up anyway. Leaderless and armed only with machetes, they struck out without a coherent plan. After only two days of fighting, they were easily defeated. But Hernández Martínez was not finished. Choosing to emphasize the uprising as the first communist revolution ever attempted in the Western Hemisphere, the president, supported by the oligarchy, decided to send a message to future insurrectionists. He ordered the army to pursue and exterminate as many Indians as possible. Up to thirty thousand were executed. This tragic incident, referred to even today throughout El Salvador simply as "*La Matanza*" (the Massacre), left an indelible mark on the Salvadoran psyche. As one writer pointed out: "The massacre of 1932 permanently scarred the memory of Salvadorans. Because it had been considered an 'Indian' revolt and people were killed as Indians, the survivors put away traditional clothes and customs; there are virtually no 'Indians' in El Salvador today."[11]

Although the 1932 uprising was often termed a communist revolt—and indeed many of the Indians who were involved in labor organizing on the large coffee plantations seem to have been influenced by communist ideology—such a judgment did not tell the whole story. As Berryman noted, Indian resistance also played a role:

> The Indians could still recall their communal lands and resented their expropriation by the oligarchy, whom they were forced to serve as a labor force...To what degree the 1932 uprising was a product of the efforts of leftists such as Martí and their organizations, and to what degree it was a spontaneous rebellion arising out of peasant and Indian resentment for the mistreatment of decades and centuries remains an open question. Clearly both flowed together but the proportion is unclear, and it is this writer's impression that the latter factor has been underestimated.[12]

La Matanza was exactly what Hernández Martínez needed to secure his shaky position as head of state. His readiness to punish the Indians convinced the oligarchy that they finally had a president willing to take strong action to preserve the status quo. Henceforth, the oligarchy was willing to cede the bulk of political power to the military, as long as the military continued to protect the oligarchy's wealth and status.[13] The United States had declined to recognize Hernández Martínez, but then had a change of heart and decided that since the general seemed capable of maintaining order, he should receive U.S. recognition.[14]

El Salvador was ruled up to the mid-1970s by a series of military strongmen. The 1960s saw economic growth, but growth that primarily benefited the rich. New, large industrial plants appeared throughout urban areas as manufacturing grew by 24 percent between 1961 and 1971.[15] For the first time in its history, the prosperous oligarchy welcomed wide-scale foreign investments, and forty-four multinational corporations entered El Salvador during this decade.

But the new capital-intensive industries did not absorb the available labor force, and in the late 1960s, prices dropped for Salvadoran exports, causing economic hardship for workers. Recently formed unions became more active; in 1967 and 1968 strikes occurred with increasing frequency, and with them government-sponsored repression.

Tensions mounted as the 1972 presidential election approached. The ruling class was again divided and offered two candidates, General José Alberto Medrano and Colonel Arturo Armando Molina. Sensing an opportunity, several reform-minded groups joined in a coalition to support José Napoleón Duarte, the popular mayor of the capital city of San Salvador. As votes were counted, it became clear that Duarte had won. But suddenly all election news was suspended, and three days later Molina was declared the winner.

When Dorothy and Martha arrived in El Salvador in mid-1974, it was deceptively peaceful. But for many *campesinos*, intellectuals, students, and workers, the fraudulent election of 1972 had proved that the electoral process could never bring effective reform. Older guerrilla groups and popular organizations such as FECCAS (Christian Federation of Peasants of El Salvador) began to expand and new groups and coalitions emerged. It was only a matter of time before conflicts stemming from unresolved injustices would spawn a new round of bitter strife.

The Cleveland team served parishes in Chirilagua and La Unión, both located in southeastern El Salvador, and in La Libertad, in the southwest. Each area included outlying villages or neighborhoods, called *cantones* or *caseríos*. The Cleveland team's number of staff per parish varied —usually one or two priests and two to four women (nuns or lay volunteers). Madre Dorotea and Madre Marta, as they were known, began their ministry in Chirilagua.

Neither woman spoke Spanish and initially both were disoriented.
Martha recalled some anxious moments one night when they returned
from a meeting and were stopped by soldiers:

> Suddenly the Guardia appeared out of nowhere and made us
> pull off the road. If I hadn't been so scared, I might have thought
> it was funny. There was the crazy Guardia, with rifles, helmets,
> sidearms, motorcycles, and everything, rattling off something in
> Spanish to Dorothy, who was driving. But she couldn't under-
> stand a word they were saying. Luckily we had Rosie Smith, an-
> other team member, who spoke Spanish. I figured it had
> something to do with Dorothy's Ohio driver's license, so I wasn't
> too worried at first. Then the Guardia escorted Dorothy and
> Rosie off in the car, and I found myself standing in the pitch
> dark on the side of the dirt road with two *campesinos*, not know-
> ing what was happening and not able to communicate. Then an-
> other car passed through the checkpoint and the Guardia tried
> to pull *them* over. One soldier jumped on a motorcycle and an-
> other jumped into the little sidecar attached, but they couldn't
> get the motorcycle started after numerous jumps on the starter. I
> thought I was watching a Keystone Cops movie!

A truck came by with people Martha knew and picked her up. Once
home she found that the police had "arrested" the car because of
Dorothy's driver's license, but she and Rosie were released. A fine was
paid to retrieve the car, and Dorothy and Martha realized that "we had to
learn Spanish—and fast."[16]

The next week Dorothy and Martha began their studies at a language school in San José, Costa Rica. Their first few weeks had been be-
wildering, so the two women arrived anxious to learn. The school was
run by fundamentalist Protestants who had just begun to allow a few
Catholics to study there, and Dorothy and Martha were asked not to
wear their habits. Dorothy took it in stride and fit right in, before long
joining her classmates in uninhibited, revival-style prayer. "It was typical
of Dorothy to be able to meet someone else on his or her own terms
spiritually," said Martha. "I remember when we were leaving the school,
one of the students came up to her and said, 'Dorothy, you may be a
Catholic, but in my book, you are truly saved.'" Dorothy had the gift of
true empathy, Martha added. "She could respond sincerely to whatever
emotion you were experiencing. She would cry with you when you were
sad, laugh when you were happy, pray if you wanted to pray, jog if you

wanted to jog, even climb a mountain with you if you wanted to. If there was someone around who wanted to speak in tongues, Dorothy would wind up speaking in tongues!"[17]

Martha and Dorothy returned to Chirilagua but only remained there a few months. After Easter 1975 they went to the parish of San Carlos Borromeo in La Unión. There they stayed for about two and a half years.

The mission work of the Cleveland team was always a response to the needs of the community. In the early, more peaceful, years their tasks were mainly pastoral. The priest's role was to dispense the sacraments and preside over liturgical services throughout the far-flung parish, while the sisters served as "auxiliaries." It was the nuns' role to spend time with the people, prepare them for the sacraments, and teach Catholic doctrine. But they also helped in wide-ranging ways by visiting people at home, finding out what was needed, and dispensing food or medicine when circumstances required it. These more one-on-one tasks that the priest lacked time for enabled the sisters to develop close relationships with the people and made them essential components of the missionary team.[18]

Martha and Dorothy conducted classes on baptism for prospective parents and prepared children for first communion, reconciliation, and confirmation. Since one of the team's main goals was to strengthen the family, they met with engaged couples to discuss the lifelong commitment of the sacrament of marriage and its responsibilities. But the team had another important goal: they wanted to train leaders to take over these catechetical duties in the future.

Each sister, alone, covered all outposts in her area every week. Reaching some isolated hamlets required traveling over paths that only motorcycles could navigate. The sisters trained male and female catechists, organized classes, and prepared the people for the priest's monthly visit. In addition, they gave first-aid talks, formed choirs, took parishioners to the hospital, and set up libraries. "What I remember most was the constant running around," said Martha. Without this "constant running around," not much would have been accomplished.

Martha was the more cautious. Dorothy, on the other hand, was described by several as "fearless." The unknown was not a threat and she thrived on challenge. She had an adventurous spirit: "Dorothy had a real genuineness and openness about her...She'd be the first to jump in the truck and learn how to drive a stick shift, or the first to hop on a motorcycle —just fully open and accepting to all new challenges."[19] The two Ursulines complemented each other: Dorothy would hop in the jeep and head for an isolated village at a moment's notice; Martha might pack a lunch, throw in a canteen, and worry about calamities that could befall them.[20] They would become the best of friends.

A major task that fell to the women was to oversee the distribution of food to the hungry. American bishops purchased items like flour, rice, oil, corn meal, and powdered milk from the U.S. government at discount prices and shipped it through an organization called Caritas. There were regulations to follow: the recipients were to attend talks given by

Dorothy, "the first to hop on a motorcycle"

the team on hygiene and health and how to cook the food properly. Many traveled long distances by foot or ox-cart over winding mountain paths, crossing and re-crossing rivers, to attend these lectures. At each gathering, the children were weighed to see if they were benefiting from the food and make sure that it was not being used to fatten farm animals. "They loved the rice, oil, and powdered milk," Martha recalled, "but had no idea what to do with wheat flour, since they were culturally accustomed to corn flour. So white flour often ended up being fed to the pigs."

The people had no modern conveniences. Their adobe houses were the simplest of shelters, with a table and chair, some cooking utensils, and woven mats of straw for sleeping. Rubbish was thrown in the lanes for pigs to snuffle through. Clothes were hand-stitched, and the food was simple and monotonous, mainly black beans and tortillas. Once, in a museum in San Salvador, Martha saw on display the "ancient way" tortillas had been made. "I have news for the museum director," said Martha. "Every woman in our parish still made tortillas the very same 'primitive' way."

Many suffered severely from afflictions. Because medical treatment was a luxury the poor could not afford, they simply lived with the problem or died from it. Women dying in childbirth, a pregnant woman hobbling around with a varicose vein protruding as a huge bubble in her leg, a boy who was severely burned when a lantern blew up in his face—these were everyday facts of life. The only "medical" attention that the poor received was that of the village healer, who treated their ailments with herbs, spices, and rattlesnake skins.

In spite of all these challenges, the people were hard-working. It was a common sight in La Unión to see women carrying heavy bundles on their heads and men doing strenuous manual labor, such as digging a roadbed with shovels during the heat of the day, with temperatures sometimes reaching 110 degrees. "A North American laborer would have passed out, particularly if he were malnourished like most Salvadorans," observed Martha. And everyone, old and young, did their part.

In the early years Dorothy was not immune to an occasional display of American arrogance. When she received some chickens as a gift, she put them in the same coop with another missioner's. She was not going to let them run wild like the Salvadorans did. "A typical *gringa*," Martha recalled with amusement, "she was going to teach the people how chickens *should* be raised. But, unknown to Dorothy, her chicks were diseased, and in the coop the disease spread. The chickens all developed lumps in their little throats, went blind, then keeled over one by one," bringing an end to her chicken-farming venture.

Dorothy was spontaneously compassionate, which had unexpected consequences. Barbara Sever, Dorothy's sidekick from their teaching days at Sacred Heart, would rush to meet her at the airport whenever she came for a visit and, Barbara said, Dorothy

> would have in tow a bewildered and lost-looking Colombian or somebody else coming to Cleveland for medical treatment. Of course, she would have already offered my services to him on the plane, to help him get settled in his hotel room. But first, naturally, he was to get a grand tour of Cleveland. So I'd drop Dorothy off and then continue with him in my car, trying to point out the sights of interest in English, while he would just nod and smile, since of course he only spoke Spanish.[21]

Dorothy was also extraordinarily non-judgmental. As a counselor in Cleveland, she had befriended a young woman with a drug problem. Dorothy invited her to El Salvador, hoping she might be inspired by the Salvadorans' daily struggle to improve their lives. But Dorothy had to stay up night after night with her to keep her off drugs, and the next morning would be up bright and early to face her usual responsibilities. Martha feared she was exhausting herself: "She continued to give everything she could to the young woman at night and to the Salvadoran people by day. Eventually I had to go to Guatemala for a language refresher course; when I got back I found Dorothy deathly ill with malaria—and her former student was nursing her around the clock." It was characteristic of Dorothy to be completely accepting of others, wherever they found themselves in life. She lived by this strongly held principle—it was ingrained in her personality, and an illustration of her deep compassion and spirituality.[22]

In 1976, while Dorothy and Martha were still in La Unión, the Molina regime announced a mild proposal for land reform, called the Agrarian Transformation Plan. A small group within the Salvadoran elite had come to realize that some kind of agrarian reform was necessary, for the agro-export economy of El Salvador was becoming incapable of supporting the burgeoning, landless population. If the plan were drawn up carefully, they believed it could actually benefit wealthy landowners, who would be reimbursed at market value for land that they lost and given incentives to reinvest in industry. As Berryman commented: "The Molina government was to call the land reform a 'life insurance policy for our grandchildren,' meaning, one assumes, that it would save them from losing all in a peasant revolt." However, the plan was watered down before taking effect. Most of the popular organizations criticized it for not offering true agrarian reform; and it was denounced by landowner organizations, who called Molina "a communist in uniform."[23] The only significant support for this plan came from the U.S., which was going to send El Salvador monetary aid from the Agency for International Development (USAID).

Not long after this failure to compromise occurred, tension began to build to the point of explosion in El Salvador. In February 1977 an election was held, and General Carlos Humberto Romero, the favored candidate of the wealthy, claimed the presidency in a contest that scarcely offered even a pretense of legality. In fact, hours of radio conversations were taped by the opposition in which military police and the Guardia were heard transmitting commands to stuff ballot boxes.[24] When the fraud became known, there were strikes all over the capital city, and a rally was organized by the opposition that packed the plaza with forty to sixty thousand people. Soldiers were called out and more than ninety demonstrators were killed. The opposition candidate prudently opted to flee El Salvador.[25] "This period was a watershed," wrote Berryman:

> What took place during the first half of 1977, the intensity of
> the confrontation, seems astounding even when seen in the light
> of later events. In a few months the government began to arrest,
> torture, and expel priests, two priests were murdered, two top
> government officials were kidnapped and killed by guerrillas, the
> official party won elections through widespread fraud and a mas-
> sacre, Oscar Romero became archbishop, troops launched a mil-

itary attack on Aguilares, and a terrorist organization threatened to assassinate all Jesuits in El Salvador.[26]

One of these events stands out because of its marked effect on Oscar Romero, the newly installed archbishop of San Salvador: the murder on March 12, 1977 of the Jesuit priest Rutilio Grande. Since 1973 Grande and his Jesuit team had been working with poor sugar cane workers to form Christian base communities in Aguilares. But the landowners took a dim view of their work with the *campesinos*, who were beginning to organize politically. Many joined FECCAS, the peasant federation, and were becoming involved with the BPR (Revolutionary People's Bloc), which was growing rapidly in the area.[27] And when workers went on strike against the local sugar refinery, Grande and his team supported them.

In February 1977, a week before elections, Grande gave a stirring sermon, which may have led to his murder just four weeks later; the following is a short excerpt:

> I'm afraid that if Jesus of Nazareth came back, coming down from Galilee to Judea, that is, from Chalatenango to San Salvador, I daresay he would not get as far as Apopa, with his preaching and actions. They would stop him in Guazapa and jail him there . . .
>
> They would accuse him of being a rabble-rouser, a foreign Jew, one confusing people with strange and exotic ideas . . . They would undoubtedly crucify him again. In Christianity today you have to be ready to give up your own life to serve a just order . . . to save others, for the values of the gospel.[28]

Although the then conservative Romero had long been critical of what he considered Grande's "radical politics" and had said so publicly, the two had remained friends since their seminary days. Romero had even asked Grande to serve as master of ceremonies at his installation as archbishop and the Jesuit had accepted. Not long after the installation, however, the new archbishop received word that Grande had been murdered, along with two *campesinos* who were driving with him.

Although it has been widely reported that Grande's assassination caused the new archbishop to undergo a sudden conversion from being a conservative defender of the status quo to being a champion of the poor, this is not entirely accurate. In the three years prior to his consecration as archbishop, when he was bishop of Santiago de María, he had witnessed social oppression firsthand in his diocese and responded, although somewhat timidly, by speaking out against it, while also creating diocesan projects to mitigate the physical suffering of agricultural workers.[29]

While the murder of Father Rutilio may not have caused a sudden conversion, it seems to have finalized Romero's gradual transformation from tentative advocate for the poor to their most effective spokesman. Indeed, his passion for their cause soon earned him the title of "voice of the voiceless." But the institutional church would pay dearly for his prophetic leadership. During his three years as archbishop, five diocesan priests, in addition to Grande, would be killed by government security forces, as would countless lay catechists and other lay church workers.

On May 11, 1977, Father Alfonso Navarro Oviedo, pastor of Resurrection parish on the outskirts of San Salvador, after receiving death threats, was gunned down in his rectory by four members of the White Warriors Union, along with Luis Torres, a fourteen-year-old parish assistant. The White Warriors Union, in taking "credit" for the assassinations, claimed they were in retaliation for the May 10 execution by FPL guerrillas (Popular Liberation Forces) of Foreign Minister Mauricio Borgonovo. On November 28, Father Ernesto Barrera Motto, who had worked with trade unionists and, unbeknown to archdiocesan officials, had joined a guerrilla group, was killed in a shootout with security forces. Many other priests would be kidnapped, beaten, or imprisoned, and large numbers of foreign missioners, such as Belgian Father Willibrord Denaux and U.S. Maryknoll associate Father Bernard Survil, would be expelled from the country. Yet when Archbishop Romero forcefully condemned the violence, only one Salvadoran bishop, Arturo Rivera Damas, supported him. The others, along with the papal nuncio, turned against him with a vengeance. When they claimed that his "intemperate" involvement in leftist politics was causing priests to be murdered, he responded with the following prophetic words: "It would be sad, if in a country where murder is being committed so horribly, we were not to find priests also among the victims. They are the testimony of a church incarnated in the problems of its people."[30] Such comments showed why Romero was so loved by the Salvadoran poor and his own diocesan priests, and by the Cleveland mission team as well.

At the end of 1977, the team pulled out of La Unión. Father James McCreight returned to Cleveland, leaving the parish in the charge of two native priests. Martha, Dorothy, and Christine Rody, a Vincentian Sister of Charity who had joined the team in 1976, left also. But the Salvadoran priests soon departed. One, after losing his voice from fear when his name appeared on a death list, left the country; the other fled La Unión when a close friend was tortured by army commandos and strung up by his thumbs.[31]

After leaving La Unión, the two Ursulines and Christine went to the port town of La Libertad to work with other members of the team. The three women settled outside of La Libertad in the nearby hillside village of Zaragoza, which was cooled by pleasant breezes off the Pacific, a refreshing change from the stifling heat of La Unión.

La Libertad, located on the ocean about twenty miles southwest of the capital, San Salvador, was in the 1970s a small port town of about fifteen thousand inhabitants. In the central plaza stood the church, Inmaculada Concepción, as well as buildings housing the Guardia and the National Police. The townspeople earned their livelihood mainly from fishing, venturing out in rickety boats for their daily catch. They were far from prosperous, since the fishing was not very good. The docks were busy with men hoisting up boats and mending nets and women carrying large bundles on their heads. Salted fish were laid out everywhere in the sun to dry. Everyone in the family helped out, even the children, who rarely went to school. The beaches near La Libertad were wide strips of black volcanic sand, and, before the unrest, the area had been a haven for surfers. Not far inland were large cotton and sugarcane plantations where poor *campesinos* worked as day laborers.[32]

The team divided the district of La Libertad into two zones, with Martha, Christine, and Father Kenneth Myers working the western section, and Dorothy, St. Joseph Sister Cynthia Drennan, and Father Paul Schindler the eastern section, including the plantation areas. There were about thirty-five communities in the parish, quite a large number to manage. Although Ken and Paul crisscrossed the two sections, it was impossible to celebrate Mass in every *cantón* or village each week. Therefore, it became the task of the mission team to turn some of the struggling, undereducated laborers and peasants into catechists.

To spot the natural leaders in a *cantón*, the team announced that a mission would be taking place. Three team members would work together on a mission, which would last a few days. "We called them 'missions,' although they weren't," said Paul Schindler, "because if we called them 'leadership training workshops' no one would have come. But they could sure remember the excitement and emotion of those old-style Redemptorist missions!" Leaders, male and female, emerged during these events and would be tapped for leadership training. Informal help with literacy skills might be included, but most of those chosen had a rudimentary education. The team then provided catechetical and liturgical instruction, so that the leaders could eventually have a worship service without the presence of a priest.[33]

This type of ritual is called a "Celebration of the Word." The people might or might not be able to receive communion, depending on the availability of previously consecrated hosts, but the service necessarily includes scripture readings. "Delegates of the word" were trained by the team and would eventually take over the celebrations, but one of the women from the team was often present at these services. The women would help plan the liturgy beforehand. They also organized youth groups, choirs, and women's groups, thus developing close ties with many individuals.

The Cleveland team called their leadership development program *promoción*, which can be translated as "advancement," or as Martha defined it, "empowering." There would be weekend workshops for thirty or forty potential leaders from various areas who would be taught, using games and group dynamics, how to speak in public and lead discussions, or *charlas*. Trained leaders could then prepare others for the sacraments, conduct Celebrations of the Word, and lead Christian base communities. The underlying theme of all the instruction was one which the people had never been taught and which certainly had not been part of their experience—that they were children of God, born with human dignity and basic rights.[34] It was this concept that would "empower" them, as they began to see hunger, poor health, and lack of land, education, and employment not as the will of God but as injustices to which their society subjected them.

In a country where a wealthy oligarchy depended for its continued existence upon the poverty and landlessness of the majority, this consciousness-raising of the poor was not welcome and had political ramifications. The elite feared that a growing demand by the people for their rights would topple the pillars of injustice upon which their society was based. For this reason, when tensions rose, the catechists and those who instructed them were labeled "subversives." When some of the carefully trained catechists were later visited by death squads and left mutilated and murdered, the team grieved as if a dear relative had been struck down.

At the time when Dorothy and Martha began the leadership workshops, they did not immediately see the broad implications *promoción* would have. The first few years of their ministry were rather peaceful. Occasionally, they read in the newspapers about isolated incidents, but their lives "out in the boonies," as Martha put it, were not affected. Besides the numerous visits to outlying communities, Dorothy and Martha also continued their work with Caritas, distributing food from sixteen centers. They were always busy and could have used extra pairs of hands, for as the repression grew, many native priests were forced to flee and gradually five additional *cantones* were added to the parish.[35]

There were many diversions. Having no television, team members amused themselves by reading long novels well into the night—those of Michener were favorites. Dorothy would sing, while Martha played the guitar. Dorothy, a devoted animal lover, was easily entertained by her cats, Paja and Boogers. "Dorothy didn't want a run-of-the-mill cat's name like 'Fluffy,'" said Martha, "so as a joke she picked the rather disgusting name 'Boogers.'"[36] Dorothy's love for God's creation was limitless. She would swerve the jeep erratically over bumpy dirt roads to avoid hitting a straggly dog or migrating frogs.

Dorothy's sense of humor had not dimmed. A visitor to Zaragoza recalled that Dorothy was totally unable to resist a good laugh.[37] When a newcomer was spending her first night in the little house where Martha, Dorothy, and Christine lived, Dorothy took it upon herself to explain the facts of Salvadoran life to the woman. Since there was no indoor bathroom, the visitor was shown the way to the outhouse. "But listen," Dorothy warned, "it gets really dark here at night and to scare away the roaches, rats, and dogs, you have to make a lot of noise. So on your way to the outhouse, beat the ground and bang on walls, trashcans, anything, to keep away the animals." Later, while settling into her sleeping bag, the guest would be told to zip it up tight—to keep the roaches out. If the visitor had the misfortune of needing to use the facilities at night, the whole house would know, for everyone could hear the loud clanging going on outside, as Dorothy's victim wended her way to the outhouse. And Dorothy would also warn an unsuspecting American: "This is malaria country, you know; you *have* had your shots, haven't you?" (There was no vaccine to prevent malaria, as Dorothy knew from harsh experience.) But the laughter seemed to put her guests at ease in what was for many a strange new environment.

Dorothy enjoyed traveling when she could. She went for a refresher language course to Antigua, Guatemala, a Spanish colonial city with a spectacular view dominated by a volcano—the Volcán de Agua. This visit occurred a few weeks after the earthquake of 1976 that devastated Guatemala, and Dorothy spent most of her time on that "vacation" helping the people in a nearby town dig foundations, using pitifully inadequate tools, for new shelters. The two Ursulines traveled home to Ohio via the

scenic route up the West Coast of the United States as far as British Co-
lumbia. One trip Dorothy had her heart set on was a visit to the Machu
Picchu Inca ruins in Peru, and she finally realized this dream in January
1978. The train journey was marred by an intense high-altitude headache
that beset Dorothy for several days, but Martha's photographs showed a
smiling Dorothy who refused to let a little inconvenience like a splitting
headache ruin the trip of her lifetime.

Martha and Dorothy also traveled within El Salvador, often visiting
volcanoes and other sites of particular interest to Martha, who was intrigued with geology.[38] Joseph and Malvina visited their daughter in 1977
and Dorothy gave them the grand tour. As Malvina commented: "Those
were the happiest two weeks we spent together. She showed us all the
most beautiful spots there. The Izalco volcano was one of the high-
lights—a very narrow winding road—but beautiful when you got to the
top. And flowers—she couldn't get enough of their beauty. She would get
up close to try and catch their beauty."[39]

Once, when Dorothy and Martha visited the spot where the contro-
versial Miss Universe Pageant was held in 1975,[40] Dorothy seized the opportunity to ham it up. Jumping on the rocks and parading around as if
on a pageant runway, the Ursuline nun did an unforgettable imperson-
ation of a beauty queen contestant. "She liked to clown," said Martha,
"and she was kind of cute. She just couldn't resist."[41] There was one excursion they made together which Martha later recalled with irony: "It
was back in 1976, during the Bicentennial . . . Dorothy and I were so
proud of our country's two-hundredth birthday that we climbed the
tallest mountain in El Salvador and hoisted a big American flag there.
Dorothy . . . was a flag-waver. She was terribly proud to be an American."[42] This memory later became particularly painful after her death, as
U.S. officials insinuated that Dorothy was a subversive and the Reagan
administration proved less than enthusiastic in uncovering the truth regarding her murder.

There was a certain vulnerability about Dorothy. "She had no de-
fenses whatever," Martha noted, "she was very open. She would cry when
she was hurt. But even when hurt or depressed, she would still be looking
toward the future, ready for the next challenge to come along."[43] Paul
Schindler saw Dorothy's outlook on life as essentially cheerful: "We all
drew from Dorothy's optimism. She was a communicator, a healer. We
relied on her to patch up little differences on the team. But every once in
a while she would show anger at a team meeting, and it seemed so out of
character that we at first might laugh and not believe what we were hear-

ing. So she would say, 'Look, *I am serious*; this problem has got to be taken care of!'"[44]

Dorothy's innate compassion led her to help María Rosa Rivera, who was barely able to support her nine children by selling produce in the market. Rivera was very thankful that Dorothy was able to secure employment for her as the sacristan of Inmaculada Concepción Church, but became upset when some complained that she had taken a job that traditionally belonged to men. When Dorothy heard this she told María, "There's nothing wrong about a woman being a sacristan. The people will just have to get accustomed to some new things."[45]

Dorothy, a deeply spiritual woman, prayed every night and read the scriptures every day. "She was open to the movement of the Spirit," Martha said. She would give up little pleasures—a favorite food or beverage—as a sacrifice for those who were suffering. The last of these sacrifices, her friend recalled, was to swear off chocolate, a beloved treat, for the suffering people of El Salvador.[46] The depth of Dorothy's spirituality would be revealed even more as the unrest in El Salvador descended into repression and civil war.

In 1979, the time came to rotate members of the mission team. Dorothy and Martha had both finished their five-year commitments, but the Ursuline Congregation had decided that when one of a pair of missioners would leave the other would stay on for a year to train a replacement.[47] Who should stay? The two friends spent much time praying over this. Since Cindy Drennan, who had worked with Dorothy and Paul, had returned to the United States the year before, the decision was finally made that Dorothy would stay, so that Paul would not be left without an experienced missioner.

Although Martha was gone, Dorothy now had a new companion—a young woman who had recently joined the Cleveland team. Fortified with youthful energy and enthusiasm, a sense of adventure, and a desire to help, Jean Donovan burst onto the scene in La Libertad.

CHAPTER 6

Jean Donovan

Lay Missioner

Jean Donovan

Jean was twenty-six when she arrived in El Salvador. Some of her friends had been astounded to learn of her decision to become a missioner. They thought they knew Jean well: she enjoyed the limelight at parties, rode noisy motorcycles, was generous with money, visited bars with her friends, and liked nothing better than a good laugh. There was something incongruous between her carefree lifestyle and her apparently sudden decision to join the missionary ranks of the Catholic Church.

Jean's early years[1] were hardly a dress rehearsal for the role she would play in poor and violent El Salvador. Born on April 10, 1953—two months early— Jean grew up in a world of upper-middle-class comfort. John Murphy, a first-generation Irish-American Catholic and her maternal grandfather, had married Marie Hefli, the daughter of German-speaking immigrants. He had started as a salesman and wound up as the president of Christian Dior Hosiery Company. A staunch political conservative, he had become very wealthy and was influential in Republican circles. At a ski resort in 1947, the Murphys' only daughter, Patricia, a college graduate with a degree in economics, met Raymond Donovan, son of a railroad yardmaster. A promising engineer from Cleveland, Ray was headed for a career in aeronautics. They married six months later; in 1951 their first child, Michael, was born, followed two years later by Jean Marie.

Like his father-in-law, Ray moved ahead rapidly in the corporate world, attaining the position eventually of chief of design for the Sikorsky Aircraft Division of United Technologies in Connecticut. In 1963, the family moved into a spacious home on an acre and a half of land in Westport. Following in the Murphy tradition, the Donovans were stalwart Republicans; Pat was particularly dedicated, consistently volunteering during election years.

Jean was raised in an atmosphere of financial security, success, and conservative politics. But other forces also shaped her life. The Donovans not only raised their children to strive for success and material well-being, Ray said, but also to have a healthy sense of "moral judgment." Ray, a lector at Sunday Mass, and Pat were devout Catholics and taught their faith more by example than with words. "[The children] were very active in the church," Pat said. "Michael...was an altar boy and Jeannie...thought it was terrible that they didn't have altar girls." Before the children were born, the Donovans had lived in Dallas, and Pat had worked there with Catholic social agencies, including a mission school. Later, she told Michael and Jean about her work with poor children who had been orphaned or abandoned. Jeannie—an active, boisterous youngster—was absorbing it all. For the rest of her life, Jean would struggle to reconcile the tension created when her politically conservative upbringing and quest for success would clash with her sense of compassion and her "moral judgment."

Both children were diligent students and good athletes. Jeannie was passionately devoted to equestrian sport. When she first showed an interest in horses, her parents enrolled her in the fine riding school at Fiddle Horse Farm, and horses began to occupy nearly all her free time. Jean's competitive spirit and riding skill earned her countless trophies and ribbons.

Jeannie participated in her share of pranks. For years she willingly attended religion classes in her parish for students like herself who went to public school, but decided as a teenager she had better things to do. Knowing her parents would not countenance truancy, she would arrive for class and then immediately dart out through the back door unnoticed. It was a plan with a flaw: the only escape route involved a rapid climb over a fence and a speedy getaway across the pastor's yard. Inevitably, Jeannie one day in the act of flight found herself face-to-face with the pastor. She waited for the axe to fall, but the priest instead invited her into the rectory, sat her down, and asked her to tell him why she wanted to cut religion class. They chatted, then Jeannie left, relieved by her pastor's kind way of handling her rebellion.[2]

Throughout high school, Jeannie juggled classes, after-school jobs, horseback riding, and good times remarkably well. Outgoing and intelligent, she earned good grades and was president of the junior class and co-president of the senior class. As a junior, she was one of about two dozen students in the state to win a trip to the Yale Science Symposium. To earn spending money, Jeannie worked in a discount store, but spent many more hours grooming horses, keeping the barns in order, and giving riding lessons.

It was at the riding school that Jean met Fred Taylor, three years older and a groom at Fiddle Horse Farm. At first they were "buddies," but by the time she was in high school they were dating. Fred recalled: "Jean ran all the girls at the barn. Told them what to do and how to do it...they were almost like her troops." About their relationship, he said: "She was strong-willed...but she was also shy. I think being strong-willed was to cover the shyness. I liked going out with Jeannie because ...she was so in control of everything...I could relax."

But when Jean graduated and began to make plans for Fred's future, he broke up with her. That's when a girlfriend discovered Jean's secret vulnerability: "She probably drove some people away that she might have preferred not to—I know that hurt her in her relationship with Fred. When she lost Fred, even then she responded with toughness. She didn't cry, or break down or anything. She responded by being very nonchalant...That was the first time I saw that she was really hurt."[3]

By the time Jean graduated from Staples High School in 1971, her conservative political attitudes were well forged. Her father's position as head of design for helicopters at the Sikorsky plant drew him into their production for use in the Vietnam War. The Murphy and Donovan families supported the war, and Jean, who loved nothing better than a heated discussion, did not hesitate to outline for her friends the objections she had to demonstrating against the unpopular war. The Donovans did not question what the U.S. government was telling the public about its military efforts in Asia. As Ray later conceded: "As soon as anything happened in the world, our State Department would immediately put labels like 'Left' and 'Right' on it. I knew that 'Right' was where I was. They were the good guys, and 'Left' were the bad guys."[4]

In the fall of 1971, Jean left home to enter Mary Washington College in Fredericksburg, Virginia. Its riding school was a strong draw for the young woman who had no idea as to what her major or career would be. Prior to this, Jean had faced no true misfortunes, but during her freshman year she was devastated to learn that her brother, an upperclassman at the University of Pennsylvania, had been diagnosed with

Hodgkin's lymphoma. Jean began to travel to Philadelphia every other weekend to be with Mike as he endured chemotherapy and its side effects. Michael's suffering tapped Jean's deep compassion and had a profound effect on her: "It made me realize how precious life is," she later said.[5]

Michael recovered and upon graduating landed a lucrative job as an accountant. Jean too resolved on a business career, choosing economics as her major. Like many adventurous students who can afford it, she decided to spend her junior year abroad and chose University College Cork in Ireland. Arrangements had been made for exchange students to reside with lower-middle-class families in small homes situated on the periphery of Cork. Their rent money would help the family make ends meet and the students would experience life in a typical Irish home.

The room Jean shared with two other students was overcrowded and damp, and the house was quite a distance from the college. After some initial alarm, Jean, who was used to all the conveniences of life, adapted surprisingly well. When the boarders saw that the family could not afford to put a nutritious meal on the table, they decided to contribute extra money for food, hoping that they and their hosts would benefit from a healthier diet. The meals did not improve, and after a few months the young women asked their parents' permission to look for other quarters. Leaving the family with a vacant room and all of the remaining months' rent, they established housekeeping in a small house nearer the campus, sharing all the cooking and cleaning chores. Heated only by a peat fire, the house was damp and chilly, and there was no refrigerator. But Jean began to realize that many conveniences she had accepted as necessities in America were actually not. She was growing to respect the simpler lifestyle of the Irish.

Yet there were still some challenges. Jean wrote home in dismay, saying that diet foods were simply not available in all of Ireland! What was she to do? She was a girl who was forced to count calories! Jean found a solution—a bicycle she pedaled to and from school and social engagements. Commenting much later on her experience, she noted that living in Ireland had opened her eyes to the irrelevance of the conveniences Americans held so dear.

Jean's gregariousness and sense of humor appealed to the Irish, and she made friends easily. One day a new companion, Maura Corkery, invited her to a meeting of the Legion of Mary. Jean accepted, with momentous consequences for her future, for it was at this gathering that she met Michael Crowley, a dynamic priest who would challenge Jean as no one had before.

Crowley, the college chaplain, had organized the Legion to enlist student-volunteers for weekly service projects. On Monday nights the group came to his home for a combination meeting and party. About thirty to forty students would attend, and Irish music and lively conversation flowed freely. The talk often turned to Latin American poverty, for Crowley had recently returned from a ten-year mission commitment in the barrios of Trujillo, Peru. The priest was familiar too with the poverty and affluence of the developed world, having worked in a Hispanic slum in East Harlem prior to his tenure in South America. Crowley described Jean:

> She was like a cross section of American young people . . . confused, searching for a meaning to her life. She was a conventional Catholic, if you will, but took it . . . tongue-in-cheek, in the same way as so many Christians around the world . . . She really didn't have a personalized meaning for her own life.
>
> I often had bull sessions . . ., where we discussed the world's problems and challenged these young people that when you come out now, with a nice degree and a nice job, don't become a nice comfy capitalist. Feel it as your Christian duty to change the wrong structures around you. Try and improve the world.[6]

Crowley gave the students food for thought with his stories of misery in Peru, and Jean paid attention. Convinced that rich nations have a duty to share their wealth with poorer countries, he said that Christians especially must cease misconstruing the cry of the oppressed for human dignity as part of a sinister international communist plot. If developed nations were genuinely committed to ending world poverty, he believed, communism would die on the vine. Crowley also challenged them not to ignore the plight of the underprivileged on their very doorsteps. Jean took his plea to heart and began working with Meals on Wheels and visiting patients in hospitals and mental institutions.

Jean was receptive to Crowley; he was persuasive and charismatic, but he also touched the chord of compassion and generosity within her. As a child, she had responded to her pastor's appeals to help the poor in Westport. As a young woman, she had confronted her brother's illness with tireless efforts to ease his suffering. Now, as Jean was being obliged to live a simpler life in Ireland, she was also being challenged for the first time to recognize suffering in its international dimension. An enduring legacy of her experiences abroad would be a sense of global consciousness.[7] Long talks with Crowley about his years in Peru even led Jean to wonder if she herself might have a calling to missionary life.[8]

Maura Corkery would become a lifelong friend, but Jean's love of a good time drew many others—both Irish and American students—to her as well. Their little rented house became a gathering place after the music ended and the pubs closed. But even after a Saturday night party lasting into the wee hours, Jean, half asleep, would show up at Crowley's morning Mass. Understanding that she was struggling to become more actively compassionate, Crowley became her confidant and urged her to confront suffering and poverty with a deepening spirituality.[9]

After her year abroad, Jean returned to Connecticut in mid-1974. Not long after, she met with Father Lawrence McMahon in Stratford to ask him for information on religious orders. Jean was not clear as to whether she wanted to join an order or become a lay associate, but she was insistent that her interests were in missionary work and not in nursing or teaching. Since she was still indecisive, she asked him to keep her visit confidential.[10]

Jean was pondering new ideas, but her political perspective had not evolved. Richard Nixon resigned the presidency that summer and Pat Donovan, describing her daughter as a "rock-solid Republican," recalled that she tenaciously defended Nixon well after his resignation.[11]

When she graduated the following spring, Jean could look back at her achievements with pride. She had earned an award in economics, an alumni scholarship, and a scholarship from Case Western Reserve for graduate study.[12] The next year, with her MBA in hand, she was hired as a management consultant by the Cleveland branch of Arthur Andersen and Son, then the largest accounting firm in the United States. Jean was on the road to success and she knew it. Her salary was impressive for the 1970s, and she quickly adopted a free-wheeling, free-spending lifestyle. She and her cousin Colleen Kelly rented an apartment on the Gold Coast of Lake Erie; she bought a new automobile and a large, noisy Harley-Davidson motorcycle; and she, Colleen, and Debbie Miller, a friend from Case Western, proceeded to work by day and party by night.

But Jean was not entirely the carefree, self-assured person she appeared to be. Her friends saw Jean as vulnerable, someone who masked her insecurities by grabbing the spotlight and talking too much. They watched with concern as she arranged an internship at a Cleveland hospital for a medical student she had fallen for in Cork, even paying his plane fare from Ireland. But the relationship that Jean so wanted did not develop. Her friends knew she was deeply hurt, but she never acknowledged it.[13]

After this episode, Jean may have sensed something lacking in her life. At the Christmas office party in 1976, not long after she began working at Arthur Andersen, Jean won two tickets to Spain, promptly exchanging them for a ticket to Ireland to visit Father Crowley. Did she wonder at times if she was turning into the "nice, comfy capitalist" he had warned against? Perhaps this visit inspired her to set new goals, or perhaps it confirmed her in the direction she had chosen, but when she returned, Jean was ready to make serious readjustments.

She introduced herself to Father Ralph Wiatowski, who agreed to meet weekly with her for religious counsel; she also volunteered to work with inner-city youngsters through the Cleveland diocese's youth ministry program. Soon she had gravitated to the Kaleidoscope Project, a program designed for young adults seeking opportunities to serve the church. It was through these activities that she met two young women, Rita Mikolajczyk and Mary Frances Ehlinger, who would soon become very close friends.

First impressions made by Jean could be startling. Wiatowski recalled Jean skidding on her motorcycle into the driveway of his rectory and declaring, "It's time I learned something about this God." Mary Fran's first encounter was when Jean—an unexpected volunteer—suddenly showed up at an inner-city event for children riding her noisy Harley and outfitted in a leather jacket, t-shirt, and helmet. Mary Fran, who was seven years older, thought, "Oh God, we've got a live one here." She then watched in awe as Jean herself, after rejecting help from any male present, repaired the motorcycle, which had been giving her problems.[14]

Rita's first encounter with Jean was not a positive one. She abruptly appeared in the diocesan office where Rita worked and explained that she needed a priest for a retreat she was arranging. She wanted to see Wally Hyclak, head of the diocese's youth ministry program. Somewhat annoyed that Jean had not made an appointment, Rita explained that Father Hyclak was busy and unable to see her right then. Jean said she would take a seat and wait. Later, when Hyclak entered the room, Jean sprang to her feet, ignoring Rita, and accosted him. "I'm Jean Donovan," she stated. "I'm organizing a retreat and need a priest, and I want you." Rita mused at the memory, "Jean could be pushy—it took me a long time to like Jean."

Jean's brashness was kept in check, however. "She was loving—there was no pettiness in Jean," said Rita. "She wanted to do things her way, but if you stood up to her, she backed off—she had humility. She had friends everywhere—more than acquaintances but less than best friends.

She had tremendous loyalty and loved her friends too much to intentionally hurt their feelings." Later, when Rita felt comfortable enough to tell her this, Jean said her mother had told her the same thing years earlier:

> Once, when my brother introduced me to his new girlfriend, I suggested that the three of us go out together. This was okay with him, but the girl didn't want me tagging along. I thought my brother should have insisted, but he didn't. I was furious and said I would never forgive my brother. But my mother said, "Jeannie, you're incapable of holding a grudge; you love people too much for that."[15]

Mary Fran was impressed with the way Jean related to those who wanted to volunteer for Kaleidoscope but wavered due to shyness or because they could not find a niche: "She always worked to get them involved and often brought out the best in them," adding that

> Jean was very competitive in sports, in golf, in everything—she even drove fast. I think she felt called to do something significant with her life, not necessarily on a religious level, but in whatever she attempted. She was a go-getter who loved to be in charge. You'd never know her family was well off—she wasn't the slightest bit "snooty." She was concerned with her own spiritual formation but also that of others. I remember she would take it upon herself to organize retreats; she'd get the priest, set up committees, and then give everybody a particular job to do.[16]

Jean began to delve more deeply into spirituality during her sessions with Father Ralph. Soon she asked him for information on other diocesan programs. One caught her eye—the Cleveland diocese's mission in El Salvador. Jean felt this was exactly what she had been seeking. It fit perfectly with the discussions she had had with Crowley, and before long she applied for a three-year commitment, including training and language school. She was accepted. When she told her parents about this, they were baffled and troubled by their unpredictable daughter. Her mother remembered, "She said to me, 'You know, I'm following in your footsteps,'" alluding to Pat's work with orphaned and abandoned children in Dallas years before; "I'm going to be doing the same thing, only in another country."[17] Jean did not say this just to reassure her parents. In applying for the new role, she credited her parents' example. Her father, she wrote, "has never been afraid to show love," and she described her mother as "a get-up-and-go person who always seems to have the energy to do something for someone else."[18]

Although uneasy about Jean's plans, Pat and Ray had encouraged their children to act independently and felt they could not now stand in her way. Yet, "like any other parents," they said, "we were frightened in the face of our child's courage and decision." When they grew more aware of the political climate in El Salvador, Jean's decision would sometimes become a heated topic of discussion. In the Donovan household, everyone held strong opinions on politics and religion and no one was too timid to express them.[19] Michael was bewildered by what he first thought was his sister's irresponsible yearning for adventure; then, when he examined El Salvador's recent history, he immediately feared for Jean's safety. He opposed her plans and told her so—often and bluntly. But Jean's mind was made up.[20]

Jean often chose not to reveal her motivations for this endeavor. Michael said she was a "joker," who refused to give him "a straight answer."[21] She told her friend Debbie that what she planned to do would open up future possibilities as a fundraiser for the missions. She was flippant with her cousin Colleen, saying she would be a "Maryknoll jet-setter and that they had great golf courses in South America." Known for being flirtatious, Jean joked that she would meet "cute priests" in Latin America. It was known that she found accounting unexciting, so it followed that some did believe she was in it for the adventure. But with Rita and Mary Fran, who had witnessed her recent growth in spirituality, she confided her sense that God was somehow calling her, although at times she would wonder: Why me? Why not you?[22] They knew the Jean who had divulged on a diocesan questionnaire: "I'd like to work with people, lonely people who don't realize that God loves them."[23]

Jean's future became more complicated when a new man entered her life and they started developing a close relationship. Jean and Doug Cable, a young medical school graduate, had met as he was moving into an apartment in the same building where Debbie lived. It was a hot summer day, and he had just finished carting in several loads of heavy books, when someone knocked. There stood Jean with a bottle of whiskey. "Hi, thought you might need a drink," she said with a smile. They became friends and the relationship gradually grew more serious. Doug was supportive of Jean and felt her plan was rational: she would help out as best she could in El Salvador, avoid violent areas, and hop on the next plane if the situation grew life-threatening.[24] Or so she said.

As preparation to join the Cleveland team in La Libertad, Jean spent ten days with them in October 1978 and made a positive impression on Dorothy:

> She went to Case Western Reserve ... She's quite the smart little girl and comes from a family with money, actually. Her parents live in Sarasota, Florida. They have a suite in Disneyland. So we like that! Maybe we can use it sometime! Jean's really cute—a typical twenty-five-year-old kid. She's very pleasant and friendly and seems really settled in her mind to come down here and work ... She's interested in working with the Caritas program ... , First Communion classes, or working with the youth ...[25]

Jean was leaving her promising career to become a lay missioner. "Lay missioners" volunteer for a given amount of time, but not as vowed religious. They have a long history in the Catholic Church, but with more emphasis on secular involvement after the Second Vatican Council (1962–1965), their training became more formalized. To prepare Jean, the Cleveland diocese sent her in the fall of 1978 to Maryknoll, New York, near Ossining, for orientation. In 1975, the Maryknoll Fathers and Brothers and the Maryknoll Sisters, as a logical outgrowth of their decades-long ministry in other countries, had collaborated in founding the Maryknoll Lay Missioners, and began a formal orientation program just three years before Jean arrived.

Two of her teachers, Josie and Frank Cuda, a married couple who had previously served as lay missioners, remembered her well. Josie admitted that at first she did not think Jean was all that serious:

> She spent a lot of time at Izzy's lounge in Ossining drinking with the seminarians. She was flirtatious. She saw Frank and me as authority figures, and she and her group were sort of rebellious in an adolescent way. But I saw another side of Jean on the day of the final mission-sending ceremony. I took a short-cut through the crypt to the chapel and there was Jean, obviously wrestling with some kind of a problem. She had on some very expensive jewelry, which she explained had special significance to her family; but it bothered her to be wearing this jewelry to an event that marked the beginning of her missionary work in a poverty-stricken country. And this struggle over the jewelry was making her conscious of all the things she would be leaving behind her. She was really struggling with what she was doing with her life.[26]

For all her bravado, Jean did acknowledge the possibility of danger lurking ahead with a certain "dark humor." Years later, Rita Mikolajczyk could still picture Jean at her farewell party, in the center of attention where she liked to be, drinking and laughing with her Cleveland friends. An enormous incongruity suddenly struck one of Jean's girlfriends—this same young woman now basking noisily in the limelight would soon be a missioner in Central America. She kidded Jean good-naturedly: "What are you going to El Salvador for anyway, Jean? So you can be known as 'St. Jean the Playful'?" Jean was thoroughly amused by this, and from then on would tell those who asked her why she was going to El Salvador: "Look, it's a 'can't lose' situation for me! Either I will get three years of great experiences out of it or I will die—and then *you'll* have to pray to St. Jean the Playful for the rest of your life!"[27]

The year had begun ominously in El Salvador. On January 20, 1979, Father Octavio Ortiz Luna, while leading a retreat for about thirty young men, was killed along with four retreatants by national police and the Guardia. They had smashed through the gate of the archdiocesan retreat house in an armed vehicle at six AM and stormed the building with machine guns blazing.[28] The next morning in his Sunday sermon Archbishop Romero spoke of the tragedy, read an eyewitness report of what had occurred, and denied the Guardia version that depicted the young men as engaged in a shootout. President Carlos Humberto Romero (no relation to the archbishop) had recently denounced the archbishop as "political" and had claimed there was no persecution of church people, but, the archbishop said, the five bodies proved "how great a liar he is." Guerrilla groups had added to the tension, said the archbishop, by kidnapping a Salvadoran landowner, two Englishmen, and a Japanese national, and he also condemned their actions: "Keep it in mind, you who are violent with kidnappings. Kidnapping is not civilized, any more than making people disappear...It is savagery, that's all."[29]

The final phase of Jean's transition from young executive to lay missioner was language school in Huehuetenango, Guatemala, where she would spend three months—from May to August 1979—before heading to La Libertad and a new life among the Salvadoran people. Jean was aware of the ever-increasing violence in El Salvador. Her parents, though, had no knowledge of it, and this was the way she wanted it. This changed dramatically in early May, when, prior to leaving for language school, she spent a week with them in Florida. While there, five leftist leaders of the BPR (Revolutionary People's Bloc) were arrested. The police claimed no knowledge of their whereabouts and demonstrators occupied several embassies, as well as the San Salvador cathedral and some churches. According to James Brockman,

> On May 8, while Romero was in Rome, a small demonstration stopped in front of the cathedral...Suddenly the police opened fire, as foreign journalists watched and television crews filmed. As bullets struck the crowd and glanced off the cathedral steps, people desperately tried to reach the doors. Bullets struck many in the back as they tried to reach the safety of the cathedral. For a time the police kept the Red Cross and other medical help from the cathedral, as the wounded lay bleeding inside. The total was twenty-five dead and seventy wounded...Millions around the world later watched the scene on their television screens.[30]

A CBS cameraman filmed the episode, and some Americans, including Pat and Ray Donovan, saw for the first time government-sponsored brutality against the Salvadoran people. Her parents were quite upset, wrote Jean to a friend at Maryknoll: "Their solution to the problem is that the revolutionaries should stop; that there shouldn't be any violence, and they don't understand the kind of governments...that are there. When I wanted to talk to them about it, they weren't interested. They just didn't want me to go."[31]

Ray and Pat also recalled this incident. When Jean first told them of her plans, they knew little about El Salvador and had to buy a map to see where it was located. They indeed had become distraught that their twenty-six-year-old daughter was about to leave for this dangerous country: "We knew there was violence in El Salvador; we read very graphic reports in the *Miami Herald*, and we tried desperately to talk Jean out of going to El Salvador and doing her work in a less volatile atmosphere. But she felt very strongly that she 'belonged' in El Salvador."[32]

While Jean studied Spanish in Guatemala, violence in El Salvador escalated even more, so much so that she feared she would not be permitted to join the Cleveland team. In June she took a break to visit La Libertad. When she arrived she found that Rafael Palacios, a priest from Santa Tecla, only about sixteen miles away, had just been murdered. Palacios, who had been active in forming Christian base communities, had received a written threat from the White Warriors' Union, on June 14. Six days later he was dead.[33]

The heightening tension had not yet affected the work of the Cleveland team in La Libertad. An audiocassette letter made by Dorothy and

Father Paul Schindler for Martha Owen, now back in Ohio, mentioned the customary activities of the team. But Dorothy and Paul were not deceived as to the reality of recent events and commented: "We don't want you to think we're over-optimistic—because we're not." They then related the murder on August 4 of the sixth priest to die in El Salvador in a little over two years, Alirio Napoleón Macías. He and his sacristan were cleaning the sacristy of his church when he was approached by three men. Macías, said Paul, had warned his sacristan, "Look out! These guys are police." Before he escaped, the sacristan heard Macías say, "If you're going to kill me, do it here!" And they did.

Paul then described a grisly chore that had befallen him. In a rocky seaside area nearby, eleven corpses, including decapitated bodies, had been dumped on two occasions. At first the team expected the authorities to remove them, but they had remained there rotting and attacked by vultures until Paul had asked permission of a local judge and the church to burn them. Dorothy and Paul told Martha that the Salvadoran government showed "no signs of change," but, they added, the U.S. ambassador, Frank Devine, had strongly condemned the assassination of Macías.

Saying "we're trying to think of things that are happy," Paul mentioned his plan to ask Jean to take over the mission's account books. Dorothy was skeptical, especially when Paul said Jean might set up a "whole new accounting system." Dorothy asked, "Does Jean know about that?" Paul admitted, "No. But I figure she'll look at the books and say, 'Oh, you did this wrong and that wrong,' and I'll say, 'Gee, if you can do better, Jeannie, why don't you just take them over?'" The small talk continued, with Paul looking forward to Ken Myers's return from a trip to the United States: "With Ken away, I've been doing all the Masses—I'm *so* tired of my preaching." "Ooooh, so am I!" said Dorothy.[34]

Jean arrived the next day, August 10, 1979, after having completed language school. She joined the Cleveland team members associated with Inmaculada Concepción parish in La Libertad: Dorothy, Paul, Christine Rody, and Ken. Jean rented a small apartment in the town center above the school—not far from Paul—and adopted a dog and cat. Dorothy and Chris lived in Zaragoza, a nearby hillside village, but Dorothy often spent the night at Jean's. With violence increasing, she would eventually move in with Jean.

Paul's scheme worked and Jean took over the account books. She also assisted Dorothy with her work in the Caritas program. There were more responsibilities for the team, as many native church workers had fled or been killed. But Jean was quick to learn and soon became responsible for the mission's work in several *cantones*.

The team was aware that Jean came "from a family with money," as Dorothy put it. However, Christine noted, she saw it "as a tool, a gift to use for good." One of the things that had dissatisfied her at Arthur Andersen was that the culture was all about money for its own sake. So Jean fit in well, or, as Christine said, "She met her match." Yet they found that their new missioner had some adjustments to make. Early on, they all went to a restaurant and were embarrassed when Jean made it obvious to everyone present that she believed the menu prices were raised just to "get the *gringo*." Later that evening, they discussed with Jean how uncomfortable they had felt. It was an awkward moment for all.[35]

In a letter to Gwen Vendley, a friend and teacher at Maryknoll, Jean herself recognized that she was in the throes of an adjustment period:

> I am really at times fed up with the Church and blame God for it. I find myself asking him if I can't cop out of the institution and deal with things myself—which I can—that is my personal relationship with him. But then he expects me to deal with these men running around calling themselves priests...I find Christ a lot more in a group of lay people joined in prayer, genuinely caring for one another, than in John Paul II and giant masses in Washington or wherever...I guess I just find that when my heart and soul really pour out, someone always wants to put a boundary on it. But I am sure God is calling me to something and presently I am not listening too well.[36]

Jean's desire to be in control did cause her some problems initially. "Jean was a gifted, confident young woman who had always been a success in what she did," said Christine, "but her perception of herself was sometimes bigger than reality. She was unequal to the other team members because she lacked their missionary experience and this was hard at first for her to accept." When Jean's "take-charge" tendency got out of hand, Dorothy or another team member would tell her so, as kindly as possible. To Jean's credit, she was able to accept constructive criticism; as Chris said, "She was never confrontational, never held a grudge."[37]

There was a reason why Jean was open to such comments, one that the team might not have known. While in language school Jean had taken stock of her life, she explained to Rita Mikolajczyk, and had recognized areas for future growth:

> Since I got here I've had some real ups and downs. I think everybody gets depressed a bit in language school. You have all that

theory up in your head but it doesn't seem to hit you in the mouth. So the depression at times really makes you look at all sorts of things.

I have gone through the "why am I here" syndrome. I miss Doug and everyone, etc. And the best one is: "Why would God want me? I'm so inadequate, no good, etc." But then you have a good day at school and it goes away...If I had chosen one or two different paths...I might not even believe in God let alone be a missionary. Actually, I have been having a sort of spiritual renewal—because I have been looking at my life to see what values I really have. Not always good. I have tried to write them down and then decide how and if I would like them to change... They are still a bit of a surprise to me. I don't think anything earth-shattering, but...Jean-shattering. Now I have to have God help me grow.[38]

Could it be that Jean viewed the critiques from her new friends as compelling because they forced her to be honest with herself and were God's way of helping her grow?

Yet, as a young missioner, Jean sometimes questioned the direction her life was taking. She wrote a friend soon after her arrival:

I...wonder what I am doing here as opposed to being married and living at lollipop acres...Sometimes I look back...[and] think: Oh, my God, I'm twenty-six years old, I should be married; I shouldn't be running around the way I am. And then I think, well that's true, but I've got so many things that I want to do...Besides, I haven't gotten to the point yet that I've found someone...But it is hard when my friends are getting married, my friends that have gotten married are having babies, my friends that haven't gotten married are having babies...Am I ever going to have any kids?...I talk to the Lord, and I say, "Why are you doing this to me? Why can't I just be your little suburban housewife?" And you know, he hasn't answered me yet. Sometimes I get mad at him. Sometimes I tell him I'm going to chuck the whole thing. I've had it.[39]

Jean found a compassionate mentor in Dorothy. She not only introduced her to the people and ways of El Salvador, but she was patient with the young American who was struggling to adjust to the challenges and to grow emotionally and spiritually. As Martha commented, "Dorothy had an innate ability to accept others as they were, an ability that was enhanced by her training in counseling. She believed that people were where they were at a given time in their lives because they had to be at that stage in order to survive. She never tried to push them too far or too fast and she always respected them."[40]

Thus, Dorothy accepted it if Jean partied and slept too late. And Jean had energy and a lively sense of humor to offer her new companions. Paul said, "The women would have days of recollection down at the beach or in the mountains every so often, and Jean would always join the nuns. She fit in very well with them." The fourteen-year age difference was not a barrier between Jean and Dorothy. "They kidded around with each other like a couple of teenagers," Paul remembered. "It was always a treat to pay a visit to their house; if you needed a boost they really provided a pick-me-up."[41]

The physical discomfort and inconveniences that missioners must adjust to in a developing country never bothered Jean. "She took it as an adventure," noted Christine. "It was no big deal to her." In the impoverished community of Santa Cruz, where cotton laborers lived with their families, Jean distributed food from Caritas. She also helped plan religious gatherings. Several Sundays a month she assisted the delegates who led the Celebrations of the Word; weeknights, she took part in

Jean with young people in La Libertad, El Salvador

meetings of Christian base communities. Jean befriended the young folks when she started a music group for teenagers and got to know the children—to their glee—by giving them rides on the Honda motorcycle she used to travel the dirt roads. In La Libertad she formed a youth choir at Inmaculada Concepción. This choir became rather proficient, so much so that they were invited by Archbishop Romero to sing at Sunday Mass in the cathedral.[42]

As much as she was contributing to the people, Jean still had her doubts, which she expressed in another letter to Rita:

> I've not been spending a lot of time praying...I see so many people doing so much good all the time—and it comes so easy for them. And you know, I think that sin comes so easy to me, and being good is the hard part...I just don't have that spontaneous spirituality. I believe a lot of things very deeply..., but I have many, many doubts, and I can't seem to put myself in that childlike relationship with God...I'm too independent, and I'm afraid to be dependent, even on God.[43]

By October 1979, about two months after Jean's arrival, disappearances and murders became more widespread, and the U.S. State Department issued a travel warning. It was obvious the country was on the verge of civil war. For this reason, Bishop James Hickey of Cleveland sent his diocesan mission director, Al Winters, to determine whether the project should be abandoned and the missioners withdrawn. The entire team discussed the seriousness of the situation with Winters. Dorothy followed this up with a very personal letter to Martha:

> We had a good meeting today followed by a swim and a beautiful Liturgy...I do want to say something to you—I think you will understand. We talked quite a bit today about what happens *IF* something begins. And most of us feel we would want to stay here. Now this depends on *WHAT* happens—if there is a way we can help—like run a Refugee Center or something. We wouldn't want to just run out on the people. Anyway, Al thinks people we love should understand how we feel—in case something happens...I don't want to say [this] to anyone else—because I don't think they would understand. Anyway, my beloved friend, just know how I feel and "treasure it in your heart." If a day comes when others will have to understand, please explain it for me— thanks. Love ya lots, D.[44]

Jean likewise expressed her resolve in a letter to Gwen Vendley at Maryknoll:

> I have tried to write this letter three times but it just doesn't seem to come out right...I want to write about what's happening here but it's so hard to put into words...All I can say is that things are really heating up and the tension is unbelievable...
>
> I am working with a really great lady who is an Ursuline nun. We also see two Maryknoll nuns that are really neat women. One of them...is giving Dotty and me ideas on how to run refugee camps. If war does break out I have tentatively decided to try and set up a center in Zaragoza or La Libertad. Who knows? It's strange—probably when my spiritual life is at an all-time low I know that I need more help from God than I ever had before.[45]

Soon after this, on October 15, 1979, a coup occurred in which junior military officers and civilian moderates overthrew President Romero, replacing him with a center-left junta. The new coalition government issued a reform program aimed at keeping the country from following in the footsteps of Nicaragua, where a bloody civil war had culminated in a victory for the Marxist Sandinistas. The junta's program called for agrarian reform coupled with the cessation of right-wing terrorism. While the Salvadoran left never held hope for the junta, Archbishop Romero and many political moderates initially supported it. Yet within weeks it became evident that its reform attempts were doomed when repression by security forces in the countryside actually increased in the first three weeks under the junta. Ominous also was the fact that the most conservative junta member, Colonel Jaime Abdul Gutiérrez, ignoring fellow junta members, unilaterally appointed the reactionary Colonel José Guillermo García as defense minister. This power play nullified the efforts of junta moderates to check right-wing violence. When liberal members of the junta and cabinet resigned in protest in early January, some Christian Democrats joined with the military and formed a new government. Although military members promised that repression would cease, it did not. As a result, one of the Christian Democrats resigned and José Napoleón Duarte took his place. This new junta was in reality no more than a repressive military regime with a civilian veneer.

There was a diversion for Dorothy and Jean during the Christmas season of 1979, when Jean's parents and Ursuline Sister Sheila Tobbe came for a visit. On December 26, Sheila, Dorothy, and the Donovans piled into the white Toyota microbus for a trip to Guatemala. They went shopping and sightseeing in Guatemala City and Antigua and after dinner headed for a tiny village in Quiché, where Jean had arranged for them to spend the night with an Irish priest she knew. Unfortunately, they got lost. As they drove over an endless succession of winding, mountainous roads all looking remarkably alike in the dark, they thought they would never reach their destination. Jean remained buoyant, promising every now and then that they were only "one or two villages away." It was all highly amusing to Dorothy. She later described the scene to Martha: "I was driving. We were all *so* tired and her father and mother were fit to be tied." Everyone was growing skeptical at Jean's vague reassurances, when all at once Pat demanded anxiously, "Jean, *now tell me the truth*. How many more villages *is* it?" Pat's remark broke the tension as everyone started laughing about their predicament. Finally, around 4:30 AM the band of weary travelers pulled into the sleeping village for what turned out to be a very pleasant stay.[46]

The visit with their daughter that holiday season—the last Christmas for Dorothy and Jean—was memorable for the Donovans. They had tried in the past, without success, to understand their daughter's desire to work in El Salvador. Now, seeing the satisfaction Jean was finding in her work, Pat grasped what Jean had been pointing out—that this experience was as meaningful for her daughter as her own experience with orphans in Dallas, perhaps more so.

Ray was also moved. He had never been convinced by Jean's contention that poverty and injustice, not communism, were at the root of the turmoil in El Salvador, but now his perspective began to change. He was haunted by the desperation he had witnessed in Guatemala: "One of the things I'll never forget is the sight of corn growing on a 45-degree slope. It was growing on land the oligarchs didn't want, and, at great risk to life and limb, a *campesino* must have tied a rope, lowered himself down there, and planted some corn on that little 10-by-15 patch of earth to try to get something for his family to eat."[47]

The Donovans also saw that Jean was surrounded by the warmth and laughter of other missioners, now her friends, and they saw the beauty of the land and the people. Finally, they felt a sense of relief about Jean's decision.

For Sheila Tobbe the visit was also unforgettable:

> Everywhere I went with Dorothy and Jean we were enthusiastically welcomed. It was so obvious to me that they were well loved by the people that they served.

Jean and Dorothy lived under rather primitive conditions—no hot water, not even indoor plumbing...[They] were a fun-loving pair, always teasing each other...

For all the good that these two pretty blondes accomplished as they bounced across the rough country terrain in their jeep or on their motorcycles, and despite all the dangers that they daily faced, they considered themselves very ordinary. They told me repeatedly that they weren't doing anything that everyone else wouldn't do under the circumstances.[48]

Nonetheless, not one of the visitors was reassured by the ubiquitous presence of armed soldiers. After her parents' return to Sarasota, Jean would often have to calm their fears. Pat commented later, "Jeannie used to say, 'Well last night we had this many people killed in the capital. How many people were killed in New York City?' And of course it was 3 or 4 times more. So we were shielded from the worst."[49]

The year 1980 began on a note of adventure for Jean and Dorothy, with plans being made for a short trip to Nicaragua. But Dorothy was becoming inexplicably uneasy about the future. In an audiocassette letter to Martha, Dorothy spoke of the future, for in the spring her assignment would be over (or so she then thought). After mentioning a myriad of possibilities, including a retreat, a trip to Bolivia or Brazil, and course work at Maryknoll, she commented that she really did not know what niche she would fill after leaving El Salvador. Would she work with Hispanics in the United States? With the poor in Cleveland? Maybe. Become a counselor again? Finally Dorothy admitted with frustration: "I really don't know what I want to do, Martha...I just don't know what my problem is. I just don't know. I have *no* inclination to any special area...Isn't that terrible? I've been like this for so long and I keep praying about it, but I just don't know what the Lord has in plan...to know what will really happen!"[50]

She and Martha habitually used the phrase "to know" (or in Spanish, *saber*) in jest to indicate uncertainty in the future. In the year before her death the expression might have acquired a deeper meaning. This was a period of soul-searching for Dorothy. She seemed to be unable to determine not only what she was going to *do* upon her return but also who she was going to *be*. Could she be an Ursuline in Cleveland after six years as a missioner? Missionary life had changed her. She served the poor in a dangerous country, riding a motorcycle and driving a jeep, wearing a t-shirt and jeans or knee-length culottes. Dorothy knew it was not the attire but her dedication that mattered to the people. In Cleveland she would be wearing a modified habit. She expressed her frustration to

Sheila during her Christmas visit: "How can I ever go back and put on a veil again? I just can't do it!"[51]

Could she live at the Cleveland motherhouse and conform to the rules? Though she recognized that "there is so much to do there, and...it's not that it wouldn't be interesting, but the whole house structure does worry me...I don't know if I'm going to be able to put up with this living in community business." But she expressed hope that her congregation might make some changes—in the clothing they wore, in a return to their founder's commitment to the poverty of Francis of Assisi, perhaps in a union with Canadian Ursulines.[52]

Dorothy knew several Maryknoll missioners, both in Nicaragua and El Salvador. Mentioning their mutual "camaraderie, compatibility" in her journal, she said she was being encouraged to join the Maryknoll Sisters. Or perhaps become a Maryknoll associate? "I'm really thinking about it...It might just be a passing thought except that it has very much been with me," she told Martha. Committing as an associate for a period of time meant she could remain an Ursuline *and* a missioner. "Why not stay in Salvador?" she asked herself.[53] Martha, after reading some notes Dorothy made on a retreat in late 1979, was struck by her friend's inability to get a grasp on her future—the scribblings were filled with question marks.[54] She was searching and praying, but there seemed to be no answers in her murky future.

In January 1980, Dorothy, Jean, Christine, and newly arrived Vincentian Sister of Charity Elizabeth Kochik set off for what they thought would be a four-day visit to Nicaragua. They took the ferry so that they could drive around Nicaragua, where just six months earlier the dictator Somoza had been overthrown. The trip was memorable, but not in the way they expected. Dorothy was so amused by their adventure that she sent a long, wonderfully descriptive letter to her family and friends:

> The ride over was beautiful—the heavens were full of stars and the Milky Way was close and heavy. The Southern Cross rose over us...
>
> We arrived in Potosí, Nicaragua...It was an exhilarating feeling being in Patria Libre. There were signs of reconstruction everywhere. It was good to see red and black Sandinista flags and signs around. In León [our friends] gave us the royal war tours ending with a grand visit to the Refugee Center...We also stopped at what used to be a private home of Somoza that they made into a Cultural Center.

For four days the women visited friends and toured the countryside. When they returned to Potosí to catch the ferry for El Salvador, they found that it was out of commission. They decided that Chris and Elizabeth would make the dangerous five-and-a-half-hour trip in a "dug-out canoe with a motor" over the open ocean. Dorothy and Jean stayed with the microbus, praying that their friends—neither of whom knew how to swim—would return safely.

Lavatories and drinking water were unavailable in Potosí, and each diner was "a greasier spoon than the other," so Dorothy and Jean tried to eat meager meals. But Salvadoran truck drivers who were also stranded felt sorry for the *gringas* and kept buying them food: "This of course forced us to a 3 times a day potty schedule," wrote Dorothy, "We would get up at 4:30 a.m....; at noon we visited a friend's outhouse; then again before we went to sleep we hit the beach." When the truck-drivers discovered that Dorothy and Jean were missioners, they wanted to talk with them about God—"so that we did," said Dorothy. "We even talked about forming catechists out of some of them." When they weren't discussing religion with truck drivers, three Sandinista "*muchachos*" showed them "everything one needed to know about rifles," and they talked with Nicaraguans about the war, learning that nearly everyone there had lost a loved one.

On what they thought would be their last day, Jean suggested they celebrate using her twenty-dollar bar of Estée Lauder soap to wash up in the river, where everyone bathed, including cows and horses. But the ferry was still broken down three days later, so they decided to risk crossing the Nicaraguan border into Honduras, knowing full well that the 1969 "Soccer War" between El Salvador and Honduras had never officially ended and that Honduras Immigration would give them trouble at the border. Sure enough, when the guard saw the Salvadoran plates, he told them they could not be admitted. But Dorothy appealed up the chain of command and got permission to go to Choluteca to see a certain Captain Aguilares. While Jean "babysat the micro," Dorothy enlisted a man with a pickup to take her to the base for ten dollars. Naturally, the captain had left for the day, but a kind taxi driver offered to drive Dorothy to his home—where he was nowhere to be found.

The saga went on, with many twists and turns, until Dorothy finally found herself in the presence of the *Comandante* of the Army in Choluteca:

Well, it was like a movie. I walk into this huge, warehouse-sized office with air-conditioning. There was a huge desk in the middle with this enormous gentleman with cigarette holder and cigarette. Behind him is this very red drape. To his left was a huge map of Central America. To his right was a drawing board. To the right center was his television. I could hardly believe it.

Dorothy explained their plight in graphic detail. Then—after telling Dorothy all the reasons why he could *not* let her drive through Honduras—he gave her a note and cleared her through. Apparently they hit it off, because when she left he told her: "Do come back again—but when you don't have such problems."

Accompanied by Honduran soldiers to the border with El Salvador, with their Salvadoran license plates well out of sight, Jean and Dorothy were quickly processed out of the country. After replacing their plates, they passed through the Salvadoran border and made the guards' day "because cars with Salvadoran plates NEVER pass through Honduras." They asked Dorothy, "How did you do it?" And she answered, "With GREAT difficulty!"[55] Their four-day excursion had cost them six long days to return home.

Dorothy's narrative could be important for other reasons besides its entertainment value. At this time, with Anastasio Somoza's regime having been crushed in the recent revolution, Nicaraguans were buoyant with hope. A literacy campaign was being planned and would begin a few weeks later. The landless poor were hoping for massive reforms that would shift land and property that had been appropriated by rich Somocistas back to those who had suffered neglect for decades. The cultural center Dorothy mentioned was one early example. The four visitors had toured a refugee center—a model of how they might aid *campesinos* already beginning to flee the violence in El Salvador. It would have been difficult for Dorothy *not* to compare the civil war mounting in El Salvador with the one just ended in Nicaragua. Perhaps she was infused with hope that Salvadorans would also find relief from their repressive juntas. Such thoughts could have reinforced her desire to remain in El Salvador, leading to a decision to stay well after her commitment was over, a decision that put her life in grave danger.

Upon returning from Nicaragua, Jean began to look forward to a two-week visit in early February from Doug Cable, who was now working at Los Angeles County Hospital. When Doug arrived, Paul lent them the mission jeep, and the young couple took advantage of this opportunity to visit some of the most scenic and romantic vacation spots in El Salvador. With the heightening tensions, most of these mountain and seaside resorts were all but deserted, and Doug and Jean later realized what a chance this had been for their relationship to grow. Doug felt he had finally seen the "real Jean," who was more reserved and vulnerable than the one most people saw, full of bravado. After Doug left, Jean wrote to a friend in Cleveland:

> Well, Doug came to visit. It was very good for me to have him come. Built my ego like crazy that he came all the way from Los Angeles to Salvador on his only vacation just to visit me—must be true love! But...it was harder on me than I expected it would be. I went into a little bit of depression since he left. I mean the day after he left, I was just on the floor..., I was so deeply depressed.[56]

Both Doug and Jean had obligations, and Jean was not ready to make a commitment—nor did Doug ask her to. They decided to see each other when they could—Jean was already planning a trip to Ireland in September and Doug would arrange to meet her there.

But the political situation was growing more and more ominous. The month after Doug's visit, El Salvador was rocked by the assassination of the beloved archbishop of San Salvador, Oscar Romero. Undeclared civil war now loomed in El Salvador.

Chapter 7

Dorothy and Jean

Civil War

At the risk of his life, Archbishop Oscar Romero was speaking out tirelessly against all violence in El Salvador, but particularly against the spiral of right-wing repression. To say that Romero had gained the respect and love of Salvadorans in his three years as archbishop would be an understatement. Martha and Dorothy had once seen him in Tamanique, when the whole town and countryside had turned out. The people had lined the streets with palm branches and strewn beautiful, fresh purple flowers in his path as they welcomed him to the fiesta.[1]

In his long Sunday sermons, as repression grew, Romero condemned the injustices inflicted on the people. He recounted the people's sorrow in his weekly litany of particular cases of the jailed, the murdered, and the disappeared. The people hung on his every word, and the ones who could not attend Mass in the capital listened to his sermon on the radio. His homilies became the most popular radio program in El Salvador.

By February 1980, Romero had lost hope that the October junta was capable of social and economic reform. In his sermon of February 17, Romero called upon President Carter to cease military aid to the regime and pleaded that he not exert pressure to "try to determine the destiny of the Salvadoran nation":

> At this time we are living through a grave economic-political crisis in our country. However, without question, moment by moment our nation is being conscienticized and organized. Through this process, our people have begun to make themselves capable of managing and taking responsibility for El Salvador's future. They are the only ones capable of overcoming this crisis.

It would be a deplorable injustice if, through the introduction of foreign weapons and force, the development of the Salvadoran nation was frustrated.[2]

These words attracted attention within El Salvador and internationally, but U.S. military aid did not cease. A few weeks later, Romero's fate was sealed when he spoke out against the vicious repression taking place in the countryside as the junta's agrarian reform was carried out. To the National Guard, the police, and the military, the archbishop pleaded:

Brothers: you are part of our own people. You kill your own *campesino* brothers and sisters. And before an order to kill that a man may give, God's law must prevail that says: Thou shalt not kill! No soldier is obliged to obey an order against the law of God...We want the government to understand seriously that reforms are worth nothing if they are stained with so much blood. In the name of God, and in the name of this suffering people, whose laments rise to heaven each day more tumultuous, I beg you, I beseech you, I order you in the name of God: Stop the repression![3]

The next day, March 24, 1980, the archbishop was gunned down while saying Mass in a small hospital chapel in San Salvador.

The Cleveland team was deeply affected by the death of Romero, as were the people. On an audiocassette to Martha, Dorothy described the Mass, which was packed with people, that Father Ken said when they heard the news. As she tried to repeat the words for Martha of Romero's final Sunday sermon, she broke down crying and cut off the recording.[4]

Two days after his death, a procession of five thousand people, including Dorothy, Jean, and Christine, accompanied his coffin through the streets of San Salvador to the cathedral. Christine said: "We were leading the casket...First the nuns, then the priests, then Romero, and finally the bishop [Rivera Damas]. It was one of those times that Jean claimed to be a nun so she could be right up front with the rest of us."[5] For four days, Salvadorans filed by the body in the cathedral. Jean, Dorothy, Christine, Elizabeth, and many others, took turns guarding the coffin. Dorothy sent Martha a newspaper photograph showing the coffin and the backs of several *gringa* heads in the honor guard. "How many heads do you recognize?" Dorothy wrote.[6]

The funeral was held on March 30, Palm Sunday. Bishops from twelve nations and almost three hundred priests concelebrated Mass with the papal nuncio, but Rivera Damas was the only Salvadoran prelate to attend. It was a sad commentary on events that even the funeral was not peaceful. A bomb went off at one corner of the National Palace, located near the cathedral, and immediately shooting erupted close by. A delegation of foreign visitors later issued a statement signed by eight bishops and sixteen others claiming that witnesses had seen the gunfire come from the National Palace, contradicting the government version which blamed leftists. Forty people died, most of them trampled to death in the panic that resulted.[7]

Bishop Hickey of Cleveland attended Romero's funeral and witnessed the violence. Before he returned to the U.S., a mutual decision was reached that Dorothy would stay on in El Salvador. Dorothy, having been there for six years, believed she was needed at this critical hour because the people trusted her. Hickey agreed. When she later telephoned Mother Bartholomew McCaffrey in Cleveland about extending her assignment, she did not know that Hickey had already made the same request. It is a measure of Dorothy's sense of commitment that she received the approval with joy, crying, "I can stay!" As Martha would comment: "She was supposed to come home in June 1980, but because of Romero's death she decided to stay on longer. This turned out to be about six months too long."[8]

By this time, Jean's political perspective had changed significantly. Five months earlier, when the ill-fated October coup had taken place, she had been filled with hope and spoke disparagingly about leftists who might miss out on their "glorious revolution." Even as recently as their visit to Nicaragua, Jean had revealed her conservative skepticism when she made a scornful remark about the "twerps that run Nicaragua."[9] But by February 1980, she agreed with Romero's plea to Carter not to aid the remnants of the October regime. The reason for her transformation was undoubtedly Romero himself. Before his death, Jean wrote a friend:

> I work in the La Libertad Parish...mostly because I wanted to work in the diocese of Archbishop Romero...He is the leader of Liberation Theology in practice...It is so inspiring when you see and hear a man like Archbishop Romero. He doesn't back down for nothing. He really is the voice of the people...It is like the Pope when he enters church. They stand on the pews and clap for him...At the recessional, everyone tries to shake his hand...At the same time he is a very humble person. He has been nominated for the Nobel Peace Prize.[10]

Jean rose early on Sundays to listen, along with Dorothy and Christine, to Romero's 8:00 AM Mass over the radio. Sometimes she drove with Dorothy and Chris to attend his Mass in San Salvador. But Romero alone did not change Jean's views. In her work, she saw the people's fear of army and paramilitary forces and the humiliating poverty of Salvadorans she knew to be intelligent and hard-working. And she knew catechists—friends—trained by the mission team who were being targeted by death squads.[11] Jean had been in El Salvador only about eight months when Romero was killed, under the circumstances quite enough time for a change of heart.

In La Libertad and its surrounding villages, death squad violence was increasing. During April, a death squad of armed civilians in military trucks visited Santa Cruz, where Jean had worked since her arrival. A young catechist was decapitated, and six other young men and women were mutilated in various ways, two of them beyond recognition. Christine Rody recalled how this tragedy affected Jean: "She insisted on going to Santa Cruz to participate in the next Celebration of the Word. She realized the danger, but felt her presence would give the people courage. She thought her example might help convince the villagers not to give up."[12] A few weeks later the area was struck again and three more people were tortured and killed. Jean had worked with two of the young men and was heartbroken.

By the summer of 1980, Dorothy, Jean, and Paul were being called upon more and more to bless the twisted bodies that were turning up in ditches around La Libertad. Paul had already buried or burned thirty bodies, and six of the team's catechists had been killed. Several times a week Paul would go to the headquarters of the security forces and demand that they hand over someone he knew had disappeared. If this tactic did not work, he called the U.S. embassy, which would contact a high-level Salvadoran commander and often the *desaparecido*'s release would be obtained.[13] Security and military forces knew of the team's activities to aid the living and bury the dead. Perhaps it is no coincidence that on July 6 tragedy struck close to home and to their hearts.

There were at least a couple of hundred people on the streets of La Libertad that Sunday night, said Paul. Carlos Jerez González, Paul's twenty-year-old foster son, had been playing the lottery. Armando Arévalo, twenty-four years old, had been talking with Jean and Dorothy in Jean's apartment above the parochial school in the plaza. At around 10:00 PM Carlos met Armando and the two headed over to the church to lock up for the night. Suddenly, a few feet from Jean's door, three armed men grabbed Armando and Carlos and tried to drag them off into a waiting car. But the young men struggled desperately, knowing that to go off with them was to join the ranks of *desaparecidos* who faced clandestine torture and execution. The struggle was soon over. Armando was shot first and then Carlos as he grabbed the killer. Armando died immediately, and Carlos, unconscious, was left to die nearby. Two police jeeps then drove up, took note of the young men lying in the street, and quickly drove off. No one who witnessed this seriously thought that the police had come to investigate, since hundreds died similar deaths every month, and no murderer was ever brought to justice.[14]

Dorothy and Jean were huddled together upstairs in Jean's apartment, too fearful at first to venture out. Someone on the street called an ambulance and someone else ran to get Paul, who lived nearby. But Carlos died on the way to the hospital. Carlos and Armando had shared work, tears, and laughter with the Cleveland team, and everyone grieved over this loss. Armando, an engaging young man—a baker by trade—was the parish sacristan and leader of the choral group. Paul believed he could have been pegged for his leadership role with youth and for speaking out in the group against repression. Three years younger than Jean, the two had hit it off and become good friends. They loved to clown around, but Paul remembered many a night when the "kids"—Jean, Armando, and Carlos—would stay up till the wee hours, thrashing out theological questions: If God were good, if God even existed, why was there so much evil? Why were the people of El Salvador suffering so much? Why did God permit it? Often Dorothy and Paul had joined these discussions, drawing on their own spiritual perspective.[15]

Paul was particularly devastated by the death of Carlos. Orphaned as a boy, Carlos had been taken in by an old woman who gave him odd jobs to do in return for shelter and food. After her death he had bounced around the port town; calling no place home, he befriended the surfer crowd and became involved in drugs. Paul described him affectionately as a "holy terror":

> When he started hanging around the church, even the nuns couldn't tolerate him—he was such a terrible thief. So eventually I inherited him; he moved in with me and became known as "the padre's kid." He lived with me for seven years, and he was beginning to shape up. I used bribery to keep him off drugs and away from the surfers. I even promised to bring him to Disney World. And so, sure enough, he got his trip to Disney World. He had met a girl—Sarah—who had such a good influence on him. She and her family had to leave El Salvador and were living in the

States, and I had promised Carlos that if he finished eighth grade I'd find a way to get him into the States, where he could see Sarah again and go to school. He really responded to my bribery! He would have graduated in November. But Carlos was a tough kid, a street kid, and he had spoken out many times against the government. He knew there was a chance he'd be killed; he often told me they would never drag him off—he would never be taken alive.[16]

Not long after this blow, Dorothy went to the United States. On a few occasions she revealed the intensity of life in El Salvador. At Maryknoll in New York—where she was taking courses—she spoke candidly with Sister Patricia Murray about the difficulty she expected upon returning to the U.S. after completing her mission assignment. Unlike missioners returning to Maryknoll, she said, where nearly everyone had experienced the challenges of different cultures, Dorothy feared that no one would understand how much the years had changed her. Pat commented: "I don't think she could've done what the Cleveland missionaries were doing in Salvador—finding bodies, transporting refugees, taking care of the wounded—and not change. It was a terrifying time."[17] And Dorothy mentioned to her superior in Cleveland, "When you sit in the house in Zaragoza and somebody's car backfires, you want to jump under the table." On a long car trip with her brother and his family to Florida —a vacation filled with stories, song, and laughter—the conversation at one point turned to the subject of death. Dorothy then grew serious and revealed: "I am prepared and ready to die."[18]

While Dorothy was away another tragedy struck the American community in El Salvador. During the previous few years the Cleveland team had grown quite close to the Maryknoll sisters in El Salvador— Madeline Dorsey, who worked in Santa Ana, and Teresa Alexander and Joan Petrik, who lived in La Libertad and often collaborated with the Cleveland team. In April 1980, there were two new Maryknoll arrivals, Ita Ford and Carol Piette, known as "Carla," who had chosen to serve in Chalatenango, a northern department already racked by civil war. Carla and Ita's work of transporting refugees to safer areas near the capital and obtaining food, medicine, and clothing for those forced by army sweeps to flee their villages began to draw in members of the Cleveland team. Their assistance at first was sporadic; then, while Dorothy was in the U.S., Jean and Christine began to work with them on a regular basis, arranging for or providing transportation for refugees and attempting to reunite family members.

On the rainy evening of August 23, Carla and Ita dropped off a man who had just been released from army custody in Chalatenango. On their return, they attempted to re-cross a stream near his home, but within minutes it became swollen by a flash flood. The raging water spun the jeep onto its side, trapping them both. Ita managed to escape through a half-open window, but Carla was caught in the submerged part of the vehicle and subsequently drowned. Carla's sudden death, coming so soon after the murder of Carlos and Armando, was not only a personal loss for the American missioners but also a graphic reminder that life was all too precarious in El Salvador. Paradoxically, the death of this outgoing, generous woman was also an inspiration. Terry Alexander later said that Jean had spoken on several occasions about leaving El Salvador, but that Carla's death convinced her to stay to help with the refugee work Carla had initiated.[19] Dorothy, too, wrote to Sister of Mercy Theresa Kane in the United States about Carla's death, calling it a "resurrection experience."[20]

Death was everywhere. More and more friends were being visited by the *Escuadrón de Muerte*. After Dorothy returned to El Salvador, she wrote Martha about "other sad news":

> By Hacienda Santa Lucia—there were 3 cadavers...As I pulled in to Valle Nuevo—where the Health Clinic is—there were lots of people—and I saw the candles and *caja* [coffin]. Here they also shot and killed the father of Margot (the girl catechist there who helps us). He was the *cuidandero* [caretaker] of the Centro. It seems a group of masked men came in around midnight and shot him. A 17-year-old son and 8-year-old boy were there but they hid in a bathroom that doesn't work and luckily weren't found...There was one other killed from V. N., one from Cangrejera, and one from Los Planos...
>
> Jean just came back from Zaragoza—the *Escuadrón de Muerte* is running around up there—tried to get a man out of [the sacristan's] house—but the daughter intervened. Also, supposedly the "boys" (Julio, etc.) are all on their list—so they're all in [Father] Ken's house...Hope this gives you some idea of what's happening...[21]

The work of the Cleveland team had always been a response to the needs of the people. Team members had trained hundreds of catechists, distributed tons of food, and discussed family life, first aid, and the sacraments with multitudes of parishioners. With thousands of civilians losing their lives to death squads and soldiers, with villages under siege and families uprooted, the needs of the people were rapidly changing. As these needs changed, so did the response of the Cleveland team to the challenge. Visits to outlying villages were cut back when the team saw that after they left the area the people were often harassed by the Guardia: "They want to know what the padre said," Paul explained in an interview with the *National Catholic Reporter* in September 1980; and Jean commented, "We're keeping a very low profile at this point."[22] The team was concerned that their work had caused catechists to disappear or be killed, but they concluded that their presence in La Libertad was more often a shield of protection. With a curfew in place and the streets extremely dangerous, the team became housebound after 7:00 every evening, unfortunately eliminating a time period when parishioners were usually available. In late summer, team members decided to re-evaluate their pastoral work and determine what they could best offer the people in their hour of need.

The most pronounced need now was to aid refugees. Vicar General Ricardo Urioste, head of the archdiocesan pastoral life commission, persuaded the team to expand their work in this area. Dorothy, Jean, and Christine had begun to aid Carla and Ita in relocating refugees, and Carla had gotten Christine involved in managing a refugee center, San Roque, in San Salvador. Ken now decided to turn a church building into an "Hogar del Niños," a home for orphaned refugee children. And what about Dorothy and Jean? "It seems like Jean and I will be helping Ita and Maura out in Chalatenango when needed," wrote Dorothy to Martha.[23] Thus, Dorothy and Jean became the mobile unit of the Cleveland team. From then on, their efforts would have a central focus—to aid Ita and a new missioner, Maura Clarke, in transporting to safety the victims of civil war, usually women and children.

Dorothy and Jean would be called upon at a moment's notice to drive the white Toyota microbus into zones that had recently seen bitter fighting. Sometimes it was Ita and Maura who asked them for help; sometimes it was a refugee committee or Monsignor Urioste

Jean and Dorothy in matching tops

who made the request. The team never asked those they helped if they were supporters of the guerrillas or the government.[24] Their work was no secret; in fact, they would inform the police or other authorities each time they went out into the countryside. Since their blonde hair and blue eyes eased them and their passengers through roadblocks guarded by soldiers, they were much in demand. Monsignor Urioste often said that "nobody in the country was safer than Dorothy and Jean."[25]

Christine described their work: "The Maryknoll nuns arranged to get Red Cross buses and we went into rebel territory to pick up those who didn't want to stay there, also the sick and elderly. We would take them to the San Roque refugee camp. This was a time when Jean got most serious, since we were dealing with people's lives." It was very dangerous work. Even the smallest suspicion on the part of soldiers could lead to arrest. Christine recalled one frightening incident that occurred early, while Dorothy was in the U.S.:

> We had taken some buses to pick up refugees, mostly children, to bring to the refugee camp. Jean drove a jeep. When we arrived, Jean was nearly out of gas. She left us there loading the buses and drove off to get gas. While she was gone two army jeeps filled with soldiers drove up. We were sure we would be killed, but the officer had come to see the local priest about a personal matter. When the whole harrowing adventure was over, Jean came riding up with the gas—she had missed everything.[26]

In early September, it was Jean's turn to take a vacation. Since Doug's visit in February, Jean had been planning an elaborate six-week trip, including visits with her parents in Miami and Sarasota, two weeks with Doug in Ireland, and stays at Maryknoll and in Cleveland.

Filled with parties and reminiscences of old times, the trip to Ireland was a welcome respite from the violence of Central America. At the wedding of a friend, it seemed to everyone that Doug and Jean would be the next couple to get married. But Jean was hesitant about the demands of a medical career on family life and, besides, she planned to return to El Salvador to complete her commitment. So Doug and Jean put off the decision, agreeing to settle this in Costa Rica, where they would meet in January 1981—a date that Jean did not live to keep.[27]

Jean used this opportunity to talk freely about El Salvador. She felt the story needed to be told, that too many did not know the truth behind the violence. Sometimes unburdening seemed to be a catharsis for her. But there were also many difficult moments. Because letters from El Salvador were probably read by authorities, she had not previously related to her friends the level of terror that life had reached. Now she spoke openly about the gruesome sights she had seen and the friends she had lost. Doug and Father Crowley were horrified and tried to talk her out of returning. Crowley, who had first opened Jean's heart to the suffering of the poor in Latin America and had so encouraged her, was adamant that she should not return: "I did my damnedest to dissuade her from going back…In my judgment her life was at risk and I told her that in very, very clear terms. I said, 'You're going to get it. You'll be picked, lifted, and tortured and killed. It's going to happen.'"[28]

Jean sometimes responded flippantly, brushing off the pleading of friends with one-liners like, "They don't shoot blonde, blue-eyed North Americans." But in reality their warnings deeply affected her. Despite her attempts at bravado in Ireland, the concern expressed by Jean's friends apparently caused her to regard her mission commitment from a different perspective—the viewpoint of citizens living in a safe, stable world. On the plane back to New York she wrote an eight-page letter to Crowley to justify her decision. When she arrived at Maryknoll in early October she was a "basket case," according to one nun. She stayed with Gwen and Bill Vendley, administrators of the Maryknoll lay program. Gwen recalled that Jean was "almost shell-shocked," speaking rapidly "for hours on end, trying to explain what the recent events had been like, the numbers of deaths, the kinds of oppression." It was not death she feared, but torture. "One of the last things she said was, 'I just hope I'm not found on a ditch bank with all the markings of torture.'"[29]

Jean also paid Josie and Frank Cuda a surprise visit. Josie saw that Jean had changed dramatically in the past year and a half. Before, many had wondered if the rebellious missionary recruit was truly serious. Now Josie saw Jean as a mature young woman:

> I felt that perhaps this was Jean's way of making peace with us. We had never been particularly close and it was a little trouble for her even to find us, since we had moved. But there she was in our house, sharing with us her experiences of Salvador and her fears of the future with us. I found her more open and honest. She was fearful about going back and she told us, "I don't want to go and get killed." And she said because of the danger she might not return to Salvador after Christmas.[30]

Yet Jean somehow made peace with herself. She later spoke candidly with her Cleveland friends about her "dark night of the soul." "We talked a lot about her dying," recalled Rita Mikolajczyk. "She said she spent much time in the chapel [at Maryknoll] coming to grips with the possibility of dying. She told me she yelled at God and he yelled at her. She was trying to work out going back to El Salvador—and she did."[31] She told Mary Fran Ehlinger she was not sure she could readjust to life in Cleveland after the heartbreaking injustices she had seen in El Salvador. Their last conversation was emotional: "I told her, 'I love you, Jeannie, and I want you to come home alive.' She answered, 'I love you too, but I can't make you that promise.' She had worked out her fears before she returned to El Salvador for the last time. She had put it all together before she died."[32]

While in the U.S., Jean saw that press coverage on El Salvador was distorted by fears of a communist takeover, so, as a firsthand witness, she contacted American officials to inform them of the bloody repression perpetrated by right-wing security forces of the Salvadoran government. And Jean was determined to make the same effort with her family. When she visited Michael in Connecticut, she tried to convince her brother that although the Carter administration was not perfect, a Reagan victory in the 1980 election would be a human rights disaster.[33]

By the time she arrived in Sarasota, she had cast aside the "shell-shocked" Jean. Her mother was convinced that Jean could never have merely acted the part of the "old Jeannie" on her last visit, joking and carefree. She must have "reconciled herself to what was happening and what she was to do, and...made her peace with whatever frightening thoughts that she had."[34] Jean spoke with her parents about the upcoming election. They were firmly behind Republican candidate Ronald Reagan, but Jean told them that if he were to be elected his lack of concern for rampant human rights abuses in El Salvador would be perceived as a green light for their escalation. She tried to convince them that the election of Reagan would bring about a "blood-bath" in El Salvador, but a few weeks later they cast their votes for Reagan, a decision they grew to regret.[35]

Feeling she was needed in El Salvador, Jean cut her vacation short. Soon after her return, she was confronted with a chilling reminder to put behind her any thoughts of well-being she may have carried back from Ireland and the United States. While riding her bike, she stopped to help a man and a woman huddled on the roadside. Seeing that she was an American, the man, who had been shot in the stomach and whose entrails were exposed, asked if she worked for the church; when Jean answered yes, he poured out his last confession to her. The woman had only a wound in the leg, so Jean left to go for help. She passed a truck full of soldiers heading in the direction of the couple. When she returned to the spot, Jean was shocked to find they had disappeared. Did the soldiers finish them off? Jean was furious, because the woman would have survived. Feeling helpless, Jean hurried back to the house to find Dorothy. "I can't believe this has happened," she told her. Dorothy related the story to Martha: "It was spooky," she said, "they were there, and then they were—gone...People are being killed all over."

Dorothy also told Martha about a recent trip she had made to Metapán near the Honduran border to pick up refugees. During recent fighting, their homes were destroyed, and forty-five children and ten women were stranded. Dorothy had had misgivings when Monsignor Urioste and Ita asked her to do this act of mercy. How would she get so many people out of there? They promised her a large truck and a driver. Although Dorothy made light of the journey, one can detect a current of apprehension: "It's always good to have a *gringa* face there in case something happens," she told Martha. "It seems to be about a three-and-a-half hour trip, so—to know! I just don't know where I'm going or exactly what is going to happen."

The rescue mission actually went smoothly. It was a nice day and the trip into the mountains offered beautiful views as they drove farther and farther into unfamiliar territory: "You know how it is—you never know *where* you're going, or *what* you're getting into; it's just a riot." When they finally arrived, they found that the Guardia had come into the village eight days before, opened fire on the people, and burned their houses. The women and children remained in the rubble that was once their village. Two "*muchachos*," part of some organized group, were trying to protect the people with "overgrown BB guns," Dorothy said. The whole scene was disheartening: "Martha, honestly, they're like Daniel Boone; this is worse than rinky-dink cowboys and Indians; it's like Indians against the U.S. marines of today...You just wonder *how* this is all going to turn out." As usual, Dorothy was touched by the "dear" people who had lost all their possessions. There was a newborn baby, six days old, "just an itty-bitty skinny little thing—was he ever undernourished." Dorothy added: "My heart just aches...They're really hoping to win. I just don't know how in God's name they're going to do it...[The U.S. gives] money for communication equipment and huge trucks...so the military can get up there easier to kill them...It just makes me ill when I see us doing this kind of garbage."

On this same tape, Dorothy tried to convey something of the current reality. In a low voice, almost incredulous, she said: "They massacred all these people up at Santa María en Palomar...one old man walking down the road with three cows, and one young girl, twelve years old, who had the words of a song in her hands; so they decided she was a *guerrillera* and killed her. I was so depressed [when I] saw all these cadavers and all these weeping people."[36]

This incident compelled Dorothy to write an urgent—at times indignant—letter to President Carter the next day, September 23, 1980. In it, she said that in the six years she had been a missioner in El Salvador she had seen oppression grow worse every year and U.S. aid to the Salvadoran regime was helping to foster this brutality. Now, with their "HIGH-POWERED TRUCKS" and "COMMUNICATION equipment," she emphasized, soldiers were able to travel much farther into the mountains. They had entered an isolated village and recklessly killed at least ten people, including an old man herding cows and a young girl. The soldiers brought along their spies—masked men who often pointed out "really INNOCENT people," without proof that they were subversives. "And the most appalling thing to me," she concluded, "is that...MY government gave them money for [all this] so that it's relatively easy to get into the [most isolated *cantones* to] kill innocent people ...I really would like to know..., Mr. President, whether you really realize how many innocent people we are helping to kill."[37]

When Dorothy wrote to Carter, the civil war was gaining momentum. In September, Defense Minister García had clearly shown who controlled the government when he reshuffled the military, replacing the supporters of Colonel Majano, the junta's moderate military representative, with his own uncompromising followers. On October 3, María Magdalena Henríquez, publicity secretary of the Salvadoran Human Rights office, was picked up and murdered. On October 28, Félix Ulloa, rector of the National University, was gunned down by a death squad.[38] There were military incursions into the department of Morazán, resulting in heavy casualties. By late 1980, about a thousand Salvadorans were being killed each month by government forces[39] and thousands of refugees had crossed over into Honduras. When questioned by journalists or church people as to why they had fled, they invariably claimed they were fleeing military forces who had burned their villages and killed their friends and relatives. The government's strategy in these campaigns was to destroy the infrastructure of support for the guerrillas. The fact that this "scorched earth" strategy provided future recruits for the insurgency by alienating the people in the countryside was apparently considered a risk worth taking.

Dorothy finally received a response from John D. Blacken, Director of the Office of Central American Affairs in the State Department, six weeks after she wrote to Carter. The letter neatly circumvented the issues she raised, dwelling on the left's refusal of the junta's amnesty proposal. It failed to mention the danger inherent in taking such an offer seriously as the government's armed forces were violently sweeping the countryside. Also, citing "violence…carried out by both extremes," Blacken ignored the disproportionate and indiscriminate slaughter of thousands of innocents by government forces and completely overlooked the fact that the real power behind the junta was the brutal García.[40] By September 1980, thanks to García, there simply were no reformists with power; but as Phillip Berryman commented, U.S. "spokespersons downplayed the significance out of either ignorance or lack of real concern for reform."[41]

Dorothy was not as easily deluded as the State Department. There were no reforms in El Salvador. As they transported refugees, Dorothy and Jean had a glimpse of reality that most Washington analysts did not. They came into contact with victims who had suffered almost indescribably in the bloody war. In August 1980, Mercy Sister Betty Campbell visited San Roque in San Salvador, the refugee center run by Christine Rody of the Cleveland team, where Dorothy and Jean often dropped off refugees from war-torn regions. Betty found two hundred refugees crowded into the basement under a church, sleeping on bits of paper, plastic, or clothing and sharing a single faucet and bathroom. Many children were sick with diarrhea, fevers, coughs, malnutrition, and running sores. Yet seldom did a nurse or doctor visit them, because throughout 1980 many who offered their services had been murdered or threatened for treating "subversives." Betty heard the refugees relate their stories, as Dorothy and Jean would have, too. A woman eight months pregnant told Betty:

My home is in the countryside. For many months my husband along with men in the area had been sleeping farther up in the hills because the army would come looking for men and boys to kill them. Recently, the army said that the next time they would kill women and children, too. So I started to sleep in the hills with my three children. Late one afternoon…the soldiers came…

Near a large open field, the soldiers started to shoot at us with machine guns. People were screaming and moving about. One soldier near me said, "Fall over the others and play dead." I fell over bodies and tried not to move…One soldier [said], "Let's make sure they are all dead!" My back was cut with a machete …Then the soldiers left. I got up and looked for my children, my husband. They were dead. Only five of us survived…

Another woman, also pregnant, told her story:

Many people in our Christian communities have been killed...
One afternoon I saw the National Guard and the ORDEN [a
right-wing paramilitary organization and spy network] men
coming toward my home. The ORDEN men are from our own
areas, but they are against us...They put our names on lists that
they give to the army, police, and National Guard.

When I saw these men I prayed God would help me to say
the right thing...They asked, "What kind of meetings do you
hold here? Who comes to them? What is in that loft? Where do
you have the arms?"...I thought they were going to kill me,
they were so angry. I feared for the children...

Finally, [the men] left. I waited...Sometimes I heard screams.
After what seemed a couple of hours I went to my neighbor to
see how she was. I found her stuffed into a small well. Her stomach was cut open and her baby taken out...

She could not go on. Finally, she concluded: "Our husbands were
working that day and when they returned home they found that terrible
situation. Only days later did they find us here."[42]

Jean experienced a couple of incidents she found very disconcerting.
The first concerned a Boy Scout canteen that Jean had brought back with
her from Ireland. Claiming it was "military equipment," Salvadoran customs officials confiscated it at the airport. Aggravated, Jean characteristically pursued the matter up the chain of command. Over several trips to
customs, she finally found herself in the plush office of a colonel in a military school, who took her for a tourist. Jean was taken aback to see a
colonel from the U.S. embassy poring over what seemed to be data on
U.S. military aid. The colonel looked over at Jean, surprised by the presence of another American. She left without the canteen.[43]

A couple of weeks later, while rescuing a family on a hill in the countryside, Jean was spotted by men in a helicopter who circled overhead and
tracked her movements. Although frightened, Jean got a good look at the
helicopter and was convinced it was a U.S. Huey. Since her father had
worked in the design department of another helicopter plant, Jean called
her mother and asked her to mail a picture of a Huey, which Jean recognized as the same type of aircraft that had followed her. She became incensed that U.S. aircraft were being used to track civilians and refugees.
On the day before she was killed she told Betty she intended to bring up
the issue at Ambassador Robert White's dinner party that night.[44]

Although it was often difficult to get word out to friends in the U.S.,
Dorothy did try in late October. In what was to be her final tape to

Martha, she related sadly: "Up in San Antonio de los Ranchos they chopped up women, you know, cutting off their breasts, and spearing the kid in their wombs...I mean sick, sick stuff. Oh...it just makes you ill...You wonder—it's just so diabolical, it makes you want to weep."[45]

Dorothy and Jean had seen more than enough to make them weep in the last few months of 1980. Why did they choose to stay?

One reason for Dorothy's perseverance was a deeply ingrained, cheerful attitude toward life. In her tapes to Martha, Dorothy would add humorous little stories from daily life, like one about finding a bat in her bedroom: "I thought it was a little bird; but when it hung from the ceiling, I knew it was a bat...You just never know what you're going to find in your house these days!"[46] A lover of all animals, Dorothy found a limitless source of comic relief in the antics of her cats and had assisted one of them, Paja, at the breech birth of one of her kittens. She marveled over the birth of Paja's twenty-first, twenty-second, and twenty-third kittens. "Can you *believe* her?" Dorothy asked.[47] Light-hearted get-togethers were also distractions. In October 1980, in the midst of rising fear, the Maryknoll missioners and Franciscans joined the Cleveland team for a "dress-up" Halloween party. "It's our escape from reality!" Dorothy commented.[48] Shopping expeditions with Jean or Christine for the refugees, who had escaped with "nothing, nothing," were a simple pleasure. Just before they died, using donations, Dorothy and Jean purchased clothing, underwear, and shoes for the refugees.[49]

Dorothy was a hopeful woman at heart. "Even toward the end, with all the repression and terror, she did not lose hope," said Paul Schindler. "We all, everyone, drew from Dorothy's optimism."[50] Yet despite her reference to an "escape from reality," Dorothy understood the facts. To her, El Salvador was "a country that is writhing in pain." Her hope was sustained in part by the courageous witness of catechists whom the Cleveland team had trained and befriended:

> The steadfast faith and courage our leaders have to continue preaching the Word of the Lord even though it may mean "laying down your life" in the very REAL sense is...a vivid realization that JESUS is HERE with us. Yes, we have a sense of waiting, hoping, and yearning for a complete realization of the Kingdom, and yet we know it will come because we can celebrate Him here right now.[51]

Dorothy also found hope in the conscious choice being made by some in the church to serve the poor. In September 1980 she read excerpts of

Sister of Mercy Theresa Kane's address to the Leadership Conference of Women Religious and was moved by the following:

> The intention of our predecessors was not to erect buildings solely...Today, when two-thirds of the world's population live below subsistence level, women are again being challenged by the overwhelming needs of the poor and the oppressed to respond anew. Today...women religious need to de-institutionalize ourselves...
>
> The concentration of women religious in the United States ...is not a witness to the overwhelming needs of the poor... There needs to be a distribution of woman power if we are to be in solidarity with the...marginated of our society. This call may even cause many...to eventually withdraw from traditional-based ministries such as Catholic schools and health systems.[52]

Inspired by these words, Dorothy wrote to Theresa Kane about her "challenging" address and the importance of women religious serving the poor:

> That's why I'm here in El Salvador. I should be coming back to the states next year...I hope to continue working with the poor and oppressed. Just *HOW*—is where the challenge will come in.
>
> [I want] to share a "resurrection" experience. A very good friend of mine—a Maryknoll Sister—Carla Piette—was drowned while crossing a river after taking a political prisoner home. I think her beliefs, her life, her whole being go along with what you are saying...
>
> Do continue to be Spirit-filled and challenging. Please keep the people of Salvador before the Lord as we are literally living in times of persecution...[53]

A stubborn streak of hope fortified Dorothy in her last months. But it was clear that those months had taken their toll. "Normally Dorothy was of light spirit but not those days," commented one coworker who saw Dorothy four days before she died. At the time, Dorothy was desperately seeking medical aid for a critically ill refugee, the mother of several children, even offering to drive a doctor to and from the center.[54] And just three days before her death, Martha called Dorothy to wish her Happy Thanksgiving. "She sounded so tired," her friend remembered, "and very discouraged at the end. She had seen so much violence and hatred. Perhaps if she could have foreseen that her own death would offer some way out for the Salvadorans, I think she was almost at the point where she would have offered herself voluntarily."[55]

In her last letter to Martha, Dorothy indicated that she would be willing to extend her time in El Salvador: "Right now I'm thinking about leaving here mid-March but nothing is positive. I hope to travel around and make a QUIET retreat before coming back...I *may* stay till Easter —depending on need—*saber!*"[56] Easter 1981 would have been nearly two years past the date once scheduled for her departure. But, as Dorothy often stressed, nothing was certain.

Jean too was driven by the desperate situation of the Salvadoran people. The young American who had once examined her promising career and affluent lifestyle with a critical eye and found them lacking had grown in selflessness and spiritual maturity. Having overcome her most nerve-racking fears while at Maryknoll in October, she was able to work quite effectively upon her return. She and Dorothy would respond to any request made by the refugee committees. Early on in her ministry she had commented on how much the poor were teaching her about spirituality, but she felt she was still learning. After her final trip home, she wrote her friend and spiritual advisor, Ralph Wiatowski, about the bad situation:

> Believe it or not, at times I'm actually helpful. I also was trying to deal with some very close friends that had been killed the last week in August. As a matter of fact I was with Carla so much the *National Catholic Reporter* got our photos mixed up for her obituary and had a very fine picture of me. I've already had a couple of calls about that...
>
> We are still plugging along. Sister Christine is running a center, and Dorothy and I are doing anything needed. Mostly driving and watching out for funds...
>
> I don't know how the poor survive. People in our positions really have to die unto ourselves and our wealth to gain [their] spirituality...I have a long way to go on that score. They can teach you so much with their patience and their wanting eyes. We are all so inadequate in our help. I am trying now more and more to deal with the social sin of the first world.[57]

Jean, the "rock-solid Republican," was trying to deal with the social sin of the first world. A dramatic change of perspective had occurred in her one year as a missioner.

Her thoughts of Doug and their plans to meet in Costa Rica in January occupied her spare moments. Paul had seen that Jean was becoming more comfortable with the thought of marriage and remembered that she frequently spoke of wedding plans: "She looked forward to it when her commitment was over. She talked about where and when it would take place, who would be there, whether we would all be able to come."[58] With plans for the future to sustain her, was the present reality more bearable? As the youngest member of the team, Jean also drew from the spirituality and example of her mentors. However, the overarching reason for her perseverance was the people's need. No matter how many times she was tempted to pack her bags, she simply could not walk out on the people. About two weeks before her death she wrote a friend:

> And so the Peace Corps left today, and my heart sank low. The danger is extreme and they are right to leave, but it seems that the more help is needed, the less help is available. Now I must assess my own position, because I am not up for suicide. Several times I have decided to leave—I almost could except for the children, the poor bruised victims of adult lunacy. Who would care for them? Whose heart would be so staunch as to favor the reasonable thing in a sea of their tears and loneliness? Not mine, dear friend, not mine.[59]

Many, like Gwen Vendley, Jean's teacher at Maryknoll, were drawn by her compassion and deep sense of loyalty: "She would fight for a person; that was probably what was most lovable about Jeannie. She really loved others and would go out on a limb for them."[60] The children of El Salvador were no exception.

Thus Dorothy and Jean stayed. When asked what kept them—and the rest of the team—from leaving as fear and bloodshed mounted all around, Paul Schindler answered: "Of course, we often discussed the big question, 'What if...?' But," he added, "they just could not abandon the people."[61] From Dorothy's first day as a missioner in 1974 and Jean's in 1979, their lives were dedicated to relieving the hardships of the people of El Salvador.

As suffering escalated, their selfless response spoke eloquently for their spiritual motivation. They persevered because their help was needed. And so Dorothy and Jean offered what relief and consolation they could to the victims of war in El Salvador, until they too became victims on the night of December 2, 1980.

CHAPTER 8

Carol "Carla" Piette

Maryknoll Sister

Carol "Carla" Piette

C arol Ann was born on September 29, 1939, in Appleton, Wisconsin. Her arrival may have come as a surprise to her parents, Rose and James Piette, as Rose was then forty-one, and the other children—James, Eugene, and Elizabeth—were fifteen, twelve, and ten. Carol always sensed a distance between herself and her mother, eventually linking that to Rose's age at the time of her birth, but in Carol's early life this was eased by the affectionate bond she shared with her father. As the friendly owner of Piette Family Grocery on the town's main street, James was a well-respected business leader in Appleton. For little Carol, however, he was the man she adored who toted her around in his grocery truck.[1]

When Carol was eight, her father, only fifty-one, died unexpectedly of a massive heart attack. Carol was crushed. Her grief was complicated by the fact that Rose did not permit her to go to the viewing or funeral, feeling it could have a damaging effect on one so young. Not being in attendance may have been far worse, given that Carol experienced lifelong sadness surrounding the unresolved issue of her beloved father's death.

Carol's mother was a fastidious homemaker and devoutly religious. After her husband's death, she began to spend hours in church praying daily and was not able to help Carol with her sorrow because of her own grief. At this time, Carol's brother Gene returned home to help his mother and attend college. Carol's other siblings, Jim and Betty, were by then pursuing careers. Mrs. Piette could be a critical parent; she disapproved of her daughter Betty's decisions to become an Air Force nurse and to marry Jack Frazier, a professional circus clown. Because of Mrs. Piette's disapproval, Betty did not bring Jack to Appleton often, but when she did, Carol was delighted with the juggling and clown tricks he taught her. As Jacqueline Hansen Maggiore described her lifelong friend: "Throughout her life, Carol was attracted to the clown persona. She easily amused her classmates—and, later, her fellow missioners—with her clowning, joking, and good-natured nicknames. Yet the clowning often concealed her sadness and self-doubt."

Although Carol did not challenge the very strict rules—no "ball-games, pep rallies, sleepovers, dating, and dances"—her brother and mother set, school authority was another story altogether. There, Carol, with a penchant for creative disruption, was usually involved in, if not leading, any outbreak of commotion, throwing her "zany" sense of humor into the mix. She was also blunt and had an inclination to point out hypocrisy when she saw it. Maggiore recalled "the dumbfounded expression of a young assistant priest who found himself stymied by her question: 'If you've taken a vow of poverty, how can you be driving that big, fancy new car and go on ski vacations?'"

Carol was tall, five feet eight inches, and would laugh at herself when she felt gawky and inelegant. As a teen, she often thought her petite mother was displeased with her appearance, and for that reason Carol grew more attached to Betty, who was a loving big sister and also very similar to Carol in looks. In high school, Carol pursued both the academic and business tracks, and urged her college-bound friends not to look down on her friends in the commercial classes. She babysat and worked part-time in a shop; at one of these jobs she was groped by someone older whom she had trusted, but she never divulged exactly what happened.

After graduating from high school in 1957, Carol and her friend Jackie Hansen entered Marquette University in Milwaukee. Jackie observed that Carol had several father figures in her life. She was devoted to Saint Joseph, for one, and another was the cultured head librarian at Lawrence University, where she worked while in high school. Still others were heroes. She greatly admired Pierre Mendès France, the French leader who in 1954 negotiated the extrication of France from its colonial presence in Vietnam. Carol once astounded Jackie by exclaiming that heaven would be so glorious because she would be able to meet Victor Hugo, the nineteenth-century author of *Les Miserables*, who was a most beloved hero. Above all, she maintained a very real relationship with her late father. She prayed to him and, instead of using an alarm clock, relied on him throughout her life to awaken her each morning.

Shortly after entering Marquette, a Jesuit university, Carol began to think seriously about a vocation to religious life. A classics professor, George Ganss, SJ, became her spiritual advisor. As a member of the Sodality—a campus religious group—Carol attended an event featuring a Maryknoll Sister, Maria del Rey Danforth, who had been in a Japanese internment camp in the Philippines during World War II. She had recently written the award-winning *Her Name Is Mercy*, a biography of Sister Mary Mercy Hirschboeck, a physician who had graduated from Marquette's medical school and served as a Maryknoll missioner in Korea and Bolivia. Carol was "totally on fire" with the desire to join the congregation she believed would satisfy her soul's quest for heroic adventure.

Rose Piette was not pleased with Carol's decision, often resorting to tears and begging her daughter to stay close to home. Though troubled by this, still Carol applied and was exultant when she was accepted in spite of a medical examination revealing a chronic bronchial problem. In the summer of 1958, a visit from Ganss to the Piette home, followed by a mother-daughter trip to Maryknoll, did calm the waters a bit. All that summer before entering, Carol smoked incessantly. When her friends threw a party for her, Carol, wearing a black mask and cape, showed up as Zorro, the hero of a popular television show.

In September 1958, just short of her nineteenth birthday, Carol entered the Congregation of the Maryknoll Sisters of St. Dominic. These missionary sisters traced their history to 1912, when the newly organized, all-male, Catholic Foreign Mission Society of America established its headquarters on a hilltop near Ossining, New York, which they named for the mother of Jesus, hence, "Mary-knoll." Under the inspired leadership of Smith College graduate Mary Josephine (Mollie) Rogers, a group of women—at first called simply the "Secretaries"—lent their literary, clerical, and domestic expertise to assist the Society (the Maryknoll Fathers and Brothers) in their ministry. The Secretaries' earliest responsibilities included translating mission materials from French and writing articles for *The Field Afar*, precursor of today's widely circulated *Maryknoll* magazine.

The Secretaries desired a spiritual life and were as devoted to the mission apostolate as were the Maryknoll men. Before long they sought formal religious training from Dominican nuns and in 1920 were recognized as the Foreign Mission Sisters of Saint Dominic—eventually to be known as the Maryknoll Sisters of Saint Dominic. In 1921, just three years after the Maryknoll men had sent their first missioners to China, the Maryknoll Sisters sent their own contingent. By the start of World War II, the women had several more ministries in Asia. After the war a surge in religious vocations enabled the congregation to expand into Latin America, Africa, and the Pacific islands, with ministries as well among minorities in the United States.[2]

Carol entered Maryknoll during this heyday of religious vocations, along with sixty-one other women that year, all of them embarking on a nine-month postulancy period that would determine if they were suitable candidates. The rules were not as strict as those of some religious communities, but did include censorship of mail and strictures against socializing and close friendships. Typically, about half of these women would either choose or be asked to leave—a disturbing fact of life for those who remained, since they never knew the reasons for the departures. Carol did face some difficulties. One was controlling her lively sense of humor and another may have been circumventing the censorship of mail: in one letter, just below her signature, in the tiniest lettering, she penned the sign of her champion—"Z" for Zorro.

In June 1959, she entered the two-year novitiate period and received her new name: Sister Rose Carol. In 1961, when she took her first vows and received the full habit, she was described by her novice mistress as "friendly, outgoing, jovial, big-hearted and generous, but rather naïve and tactless."[3] "Rule-breaker" could have been added: she would visit elderly nuns housed in a separate area, helping them with letter-writing and listening to their mission stories—and then miss curfew. Anticipating that this might happen, she kept a batch of acorns at the ready to aim at the window of another sister, who had agreed to unlock the door. Such behavior might have pleased their founder, Mother Mollie Rogers, who was anything but rigid and who held her followers' unique personalities in high regard.[4] Carol was a serious student, so it was a major disappointment when she was not permitted to pursue a college degree but was assigned kitchen tasks and clerical work for the next three years while studying religious subjects.

Carol's siblings and mother were able to visit occasionally, but the long trip from Appleton did make visits rare. Carol still wished for a better relationship with Rose. After one visit she wrote a friend: "Our visit was...the best I've ever had in that it was the truest. She saw me as a person, unique and different from her, and she can't quite accept this . . . Until we both face these things, our relationship will never improve."[5]

At a departure ceremony on August 9, 1964, Carol received her highly anticipated mission assignment: Chile. As excited as she was, she was also overawed by the gravity of what she was undertaking. Six weeks later, just before turning twenty-five, Carol sailed on a banana freighter from Brooklyn for the three-week passage to Chile via the Panama Canal. Her companion recalled that Carol prayed on the deck at night under the stars, and once, hoping to experience a close encounter with an approaching hurricane, the exuberant young nun had to be fetched inside by the crew.

In October, Sister Rose Carol arrived in Chile to join her new community and that very evening made her presence known. At her welcome party, Carol took center stage with her rendition of a popular comedy skit, which was greeted with hilarity. But she caused a restrained disturbance later as she pressed the sisters to discuss a Bible passage rather than say the rosary as was their practice. She even rearranged the chairs in the chapel, opened the Bible to the passage she had chosen, and assigned readers. The women acquiesced, but only for that one night.[6]

Maryknoll priests already serving in Chile and Chilean bishops had asked the sisters in 1950 to establish schools for the poor. The first step for a Maryknoll sister was language school, so soon after her arrival, Hermana Carla, who had reverted to her given name and adopted the Spanish version of "Sister Carol," was on her way to scenic Pucón in southern Chile. There she was to study Spanish in a tourist's paradise surrounded by the beauty of Lake Villarrica, the Andes, and the looming Villarrica Volcano. But the poverty of the inhabitants began to haunt her. Children walked barefoot to school, no matter how cold the weather; the people lived in one-room homes with dirt floors; food was scarce; and parents struggled to raise families on meager wages. Their living conditions contrasted sharply with the accommodations and fine shops for the affluent, and Carla grew depressed.

Carla was impatient with the slow pace of learning Spanish. She responded by ignoring her textbooks and challenging herself with the poetry of Chilean Nobel Prize winners Pablo Neruda and Gabriela Mistral. When the cold, damp weather reactivated her bronchial ailment, she visited Temuco, a town farther north, where it was sunnier. She helped the Maryknoll sisters there in their work—an early indication of her yearning to grow ever closer to the poor. Her superior finally agreed that Carla could leave language school early—something that was almost unheard of—and asked Mary Ellen Manz, the superior in Chillán, if she could "break her in."[7]

Again, Carla made her presence known immediately. The morning after Mary Ellen gave her consent, Carla turned up in a teeming rain at the convent in Chillán, a 250-mile bus ride away. Then Carla announced she was going to the office of the local newspaper and complain about the four-page paper's lack of international news, but Mary Ellen told her to wait a year. Soon Carla met the bishop and shocked everyone when she answered with the familiar "*tú*" after he had similarly addressed her. "My dear Sister Carla," he informed her kindly but in paternalistic fashion, "you do not use the familiar '*tú*' with your bishop." But Carla disarmed him and somehow endeared herself to him when she replied, "Why not? You are my father, are you not, and children speak to their parents with *tú.*"[8]

Carla did not forget Mary Ellen's admonition to wait a year to visit the local newspaper. One year to the day later, Carla and Sister Patricia Cobb showed up in the owner's office, thanked him for his "fine paper"—and helpfully apprised him of the availability of wire services for world news. Captivated by their spunk, he inquired about their work. The next day the newspaper featured a page-one photo of Carla and Pat, accompanied by a story about their delightful visit and the endeavors of the Maryknoll community in San Vicente parish.[9]

Chillán, located in the agricultural center of Chile, was then a town of about fifty thousand. The sisters ran San Vicente, an elementary school of seven hundred students from large families. Although Carla had little teacher training, she was assigned to teach second grade. When she found that many of her students, some age nine and older, could not read, she tried a novel approach. She knew of studies showing that crawling was important for early intellectual development, yet she learned that many children in her class had skipped that stage. It was discouraged by parents because crawling on the cold, muddy floor of their homes, where ground-level fires burned, was an invitation to illness and accidents. Carla devised a year-long reading program during which the children—and their teacher—would crawl around the classroom. She asked students in other classes to participate, and some did, but teachers were not happy with their absence from class. Worse, as the children filed out, other students called: "There go the stupid ones!" Carla did have a modicum of success: "We crawled together and read together and eventually made some slow progress...I was able to note some results in the final exams."[10] In spite of her lack of training,

Carla's dedication was earning her the reputation of being an excellent teacher.

Although Carla's bluntness at times clashed with other personalities, her companions enjoyed her outrageous sense of humor. Her proclivity to point out the absurd and the incongruous could lead to "embarrassing ... and later in life even dangerous" situations.[11] But for all her clowning, her soul was often troubled with bouts of depression, during which she would become withdrawn. Several factors probably contributed to this: the damp and cold that aggravated her bronchial condition; the lasting perception that her mother was displeased with her vocation; and her exceptional ability to identify with the struggling poor.

Carla's unconventional view of the tragic made her laugh at the prospect of her own death and she did not seem to aspire to a long life: "Beat me to death with a wet noodle before I am forty," she told Pat. Sister Ceci Santos recalled the version she heard as: "If I'm still alive at 40, please beat me to death! I don't want to be a grouchy old menopause lady!"[12] Carla may have been referring to her mother's late-in-life pregnancy, which she saw as a source of the emotional distance between herself and Rose.

Carla wrote about Chillán to Ben, an adolescent in Grand Rapids, Michigan, who had requested information for a school project. She clearly took time with the long, carefully worded letter. She explained the problems of an "underdeveloped" country like Chile: "The income of Chile depends on the copper mines... which in turn depend on big nations like the USA or England for the purchasing of their copper... An underdeveloped country is not free to do what it wants but [only] what it can within the circumstances that the world puts it into." This generated poverty. For one family of nine, she wrote, earning enough money for basic necessities was a daily struggle. Yet the whole family sacrificed to send one of the girls to college, and all the children had finished high school though the parents could not read or write. In another family, a widower with seven children shined shoes for a living. Carla had met his fourteen-year-old son Mariano, who had been selling roasted chestnuts on the street since the age of eight. She coaxed him into joining her class, where he towered over the second-graders, but managed to fit in two years of schooling before his father died. At the age of nineteen, he now worked twelve hours a day, earning fifty dollars a month. Carla wrote Ben that "for many people, the endings are not so happy." She wanted Ben to understand that Chileans were hard-working people who loved music and had "a wonderful spirit of making do...If a poor child sees another child with a yo-yo . . . he'll find 2 old buttons and some string and make his own yo-yo."[13]

The sisters visited their students' homes in order to understand each child's background and also to encourage the family and at times to chastise the parents if the father drank too much or if the children suffered abuse. Carla wrote her aunt that she saw, "the simple but at times desperate needs of our people for shoes, books, clothes, and sometimes food," and lauded her students: "The 42 little ones I have are the best in the whole world . . . They help me in my weak moments with Spanish and still have a beautiful spirit of optimism, not dampened by the bitter facts of life for the poor here."[14] Some of the pupils' mothers worked in a brothel and Carla and Pat paid them a visit too. The pastor was scandalized, but Carla defended their actions by explaining the reason for the home visits and pointing out the "intrinsic dignity" of these women who had no other means to feed their children. In classic Carla fashion, she also suggested that he pay the brothel a pastoral visit sometime.[15]

Carla made attempts, which she designated "Father formation programs," to nudge priests toward a firmer commitment to social justice. She called them "the Daddy-O's," and pushed them to get more in touch with the poor and show more respect for Chilean culture. Maryknoll regional superior Ray Hill later said: "The Sisters were always ahead of the priests in their thinking . . . The work they were doing was outstanding, really working with the poorest of the poor. Something we committed ourselves to but didn't do."[16]

Many were the recipients of Carla's astute assignment of nicknames. Mary Ellen Manz, whose voice carried throughout the house, was "Microphone Manz," and Carla's friend Pat was "Sport." A nun who loved to travel was christened "Pilgrim Princess." And Richard Brooker, a very reticent priest, was "Babbling Brooker," unless she was singing a duet with him at Mass, when he became "Brahms Brooker."[17]

Carla's final vows were scheduled for June 24, 1967, the beginning of winter in the Southern Hemisphere. Carla undertook a very prayerful effort to decide forever her future. She was having trouble discerning the "foggy" road ahead, she wrote to Mother Colman: "Being so weak, I know my glasses aren't even well cleaned . . . But I do ask each day to die, vowed to Him, in this life."[18]

That year, seventeen sisters had left Chile and left Maryknoll. San Vicente's parishioners were shaken by their departure, so the parish decided to make Carla's commitment a celebration by inviting students and their families. Carla, seeing the packed church and sensing the drama, changed the script and told no one. Wearing an overcoat and scarf over her habit to ward off the chill, she walked to the podium instead of approaching the altar: "She walked to the microphone, motioned to the priest that she would be with him in a moment, and asked everyone to please be seated." Mary Ellen and Pat were beside themselves wondering what she would say next. Carla then stated solemnly in Spanish: "Because I love God and Maryknoll and you, my dear, dear friends, I am able without wavering to promise to live as a Maryknoll Sister and to serve you until the day I die."[19]

Her companions recognized the depth of Carla's spirituality. One said: "She saw in the Scriptures, because of her openness to the spirit, things that I did not see."[20] Carla's poetry also revealed her spirituality and her soul's quest for justice, as in this excerpt from "Hungry Jesus":

Hungry Jesus, Spirit fed
You denied the chance to change stones to bread
Have mercy on our globe's unfed.

You've said they're blessed—let all see
Their gift of solidarity
Give them your bread of unity.

Forgive our selfish lust to own,
Forgive the bread we turn to stone
Forgive our deafness to their moan.[21]

In "Poverty" Carla humbly acknowledged her own shortcomings when interacting with the poor:

The poorest urchin approaches
   he takes one finger in his starving clasp,
   a ragged miss stands by.
She stares, not wanting to remove
   his warming glance
A vested Nun withholds, respectfully,
   full of poise,
   NO VACANCY for need.
When will I shed
   My finely woven answers
   And stand before Him, dirty, bare and poor?[22]

Carla suffered from bouts of depression. The extremes of wealth and poverty, the ubiquitous need she saw, contributed to this sadness and tested her faith. As she wrote to her sister: "I believe, Lord, help my unbelief."[23] But she also raised the spirits of those around her, and perhaps her own, with spontaneous jokes, skits, and nicknames. This "clown persona"—one she had been perfecting since childhood—was perhaps an outgrowth of Carla's spirituality.

She also dealt with depression by working hard and reaching out in prayer. According to Pat: "When she was in the doldrums, it only served to draw her closer to Him...She would throw herself into parish activities, meetings with the teachers and parents, and each evening, when she really didn't have a shred left, she would be in the chapel...giving the ups and downs of the day all back to Him."[24]

During the entire time Carla was in Chillán, the spirit of renewal initiated by the Second Vatican Council was percolating through the church. In 1968 the Sisters met in Ossining to obey a mandate that each religious congregation reassess its original charism. Many differences of opinion were expressed, but the conclusion was agreement on placing a strong emphasis on serving the poor. Soon the Maryknoll Sisters introduced a new governance structure, switching from a mother general to the election of a president and governing board. The new president, Barbara Hendricks (1970–1978), had been a missioner in Peru and knew Gustavo Gutiérrez, the father of liberation theology; she embraced the "option for the poor," the promotion of women, and building the community of God. Along with other changes occurring around this time, the habit of the Maryknoll sisters became optional, and most chose contemporary attire. All sisters kept the simple silver ring, engraved with the Greek letters "*Chi Ro*," an ancient symbol for the word "Christ."[25]

Eventually, Carla started teaching math and science to sixth-graders. She also began studies at the Universidad de Chile. In 1969, she spent four months on furlough in the U.S., which Maryknoll required for its missioners every five years, and used the opportunity to take religious studies courses at Edgewood College in Wisconsin. While Carla did earn a certificate in primary education from the Universidad de Chile, she never did earn a college degree because, as Sister Connie Pospisil said, "she had a very strong call to become poor":

She was the only one of our region who didn't have a college degree...She felt...a [diploma] would influence her [to] become richer rather than poorer. She always tried to stay away from power, be it money power or "religious" power. She never liked her physical power. But she did have a very strong moral power for herself...the morals of Christ from the vision of the poor.[26]

Carla's closest friend in Chillán was Sister Patricia Cobb. They had met when Carla would escape language school in Pucón for some sun in Temuco. When Carla arrived in Chillán, she found that Pat had recently moved there as well, and their bond strengthened. Pat was a kindred spirit—creative with a similar zany sense of humor. The two became close companions, whether it was painting daisies together all over the bathroom or supporting each other on an unconventional outing, such as a visit to students' mothers in a brothel. When others hesitated, Carla nursed Pat back to health after she was struck with both mono and typhoid simultaneously. Only "Sport" would have appreciated the nanny goat that Carla brought into the sickroom to amuse the invalid as it tiptoed daintily around as if wearing high heels.[27]

In the mid-1960s, Pat's sister was widowed and left with ten children to raise. Pat agonized over whether she should be closer by to help out. After years of inner turmoil Pat went on furlough in 1971, which was extended by a leave of absence. Carla missed Pat and suspected she might leave Maryknoll—though nothing outright had been said. Carla wrote to Pat of an odd presentiment that came over her one evening: "I felt great, rushing through the [rain]drops...and arrived at Mass in time to sing a duet with Brahms Brooker. As the Mass continued...the Lord took my heart and tried to tell me something which I wait to hear only from you...What was it, friend? Why did I arrive home in tears?...Please tell me soon."[28] Pat made the difficult decision in mid-1972 to leave Maryknoll and eventually married a widower with children.

In February 1972 Carla unexpectedly announced that she would leave Chillán and move to a Maryknoll house in Santiago, the capital of Chile. She never expressed the specific reasons for her abrupt departure. Rebecca Quinn, a motherly confidante for Carla, had recently left for another assignment. Becky and Carla had both experienced the heartbreak caused by mothers who did not fully support their vocations. Perhaps Becky's departure and the anticipated loss of Pat contributed to Carla's sudden decision to leave. But some suspected other motivations—her restless soul and her desire to be closer to the poor. She had been in Chillán seven years and her move to a struggling resettlement area for rural migrants, Población Buzeta, near a slaughterhouse in Santiago, may have been an attempt to do so. Whatever the underlying cause, it disturbed Mary Ellen, her superior, who felt Carla had been "growing by leaps and bounds" and blamed herself for not recognizing the depth of her unhappiness.[29]

Not long before Carla made her decision, San Vicente parish had embarked on a major new project: No longer would the sisters prepare children for First Communion—their mothers would do so after receiving instruction from the nuns in small group meetings. The women and their husbands balked at this. The women felt inadequate, and the men were reluctant to permit their wives to get involved. Mothers and fathers both complained that this was not the way religion had always been taught. However, the mothers reluctantly began to meet to discuss Bible readings and Catholic liturgy. When Carla was leaving and went to tell these families good-bye, she was touched when the fathers told her how much their wives and children had gained from the experience and how much they wished she would stay.

As part of her ministry in Buzeta, Carla continued this new form of First Communion preparation, working this time with well-off Chilean Air Force wives. She also team-taught religion to adolescents with a newly arrived Maryknoll seminarian. When they met, she startled him by saying, "So you're Skip Flynn, the seminarian with the beautiful blue eyes that all the sisters are talking about!"[30] Carla helped him with Spanish and saw that he was open to "Father formation," agreeing with her that some clergy were too removed from the poor and playing golf too often at country clubs.

Her bronchial problems grew more serious—aggravated by smoking and a previous bout of pneumonia—and required weekly medical attention. In her poem "Sickness," dating from this time, Carla tried to discern meaning in the eternal mystery of human suffering:

> *Phantom Knocker at our frightened flesh*
> *what is your message now?*
> *Your harsh voice of pain*
> *closes us to the message you deliver.*
> *Your clammy fingers of loneliness*
> *make us run from your visit.*
> *Now, our patience, your gift,*
> *welcomes you and waits*
> *To hear and understand*
> *the message of your call.*[31]

Carla and Ita, friends to the end

Carla remained a seeker. Only a year after her arrival in Buzeta, at age thirty-three, she jumped at the chance to relocate to La Bandera, a tougher, even more impoverished *población* across town. There Carla would be working with two Maryknoll sisters, Connie Pospisil and Mary Tracy. Soon another sister—Ita Ford—would join them. Carla and Ita's friendship would flourish as each challenged the other and herself to a deeper commitment to the poor, sharing joys and sorrows and spiritual growth, until their deaths seven years later.

CHAPTER 9

Ita Ford

Maryknoll Sister

Ita Ford

Ita Catherine Ford was born on April 23, 1940, the second of three children of Mildred and William Ford. William was older; Irene, called Rene, was the youngest. The family lived in Bay Ridge, Brooklyn, on 57th Street, where, as Bill said, "most of the people were not very rich and not very poor."[1] The population of Bay Ridge was multi-ethnic and had a large contingent of Irish-American Catholics. The Fords differed, perhaps, from their neighbors: Mildred, a public school teacher, worked outside the home. Also, the Ford family ancestry included an immigrant from Ireland, Patrick Ford, who founded the *Irish World*, an influential newspaper among Irish-Americans. Another relative, Austin Ford, had similar credentials.[2]

"Ita started answering the call to wider horizons at age three," commented her mother. She would walk out of the house with a book, pretending to "go to school" like brother Billy, but one day, unknown to Mildred, she ventured from the porch out onto the busy sidewalks of Brooklyn. After wending her way down three city blocks and crossing two busy streets, she asked a friendly woman hopefully, "Is this school?" The woman reported the child to the police and Mildred, after a long search, finally located Ita at the station.

Ita had a "secret adventure" around age nine—and this one involved an intentional act of disobedience. Instead of taking the bus, she ignored instructions and regularly took the faster subway to a YWCA summer camp. Ita even called home to report, "I'm waiting for the bus," then later, "I just got off the bus." When she confessed, her parents actually were impressed with her navigational skills. Her mother began to "push responsibility" on her, even allowing Ita to travel by subway to Manhattan with her sister in tow.[3]

Petite at five-foot-two, a graceful dancer, and "reasonably athletic," Ita also displayed considerable intellectual ability, but never immersed herself totally in academic pursuits. Thanks to a relative "who indulged her," Ita was exposed early to culture and the arts. When she graduated from Visitation Academy in eighth grade, she earned the General Excellence Medal. At Fontbonne Hall, a girls' high school in Brooklyn founded by the Sisters of Saint Joseph, she showed literary promise on the yearbook staff and as assistant editor of the newspaper. Ita always had a close relationship with nuns, her mother recalled—although she "enjoyed nothing so much as mocking them good-naturedly."[4]

Ita was very close to her father, a "beautifully spoken, very caring" man who supported Catholic traditions of social justice and loved literature and music. While she was at Fontbonne, Ita's father suffered a relapse of the tuberculosis he had had as a young adult. He spent a year at Ray Brook Sanitarium and had to retire from the insurance business on disability. Whenever he was away, Ita's friend Grace Monahan remembered, the Ford household was "missing something." Ita and her father enjoyed similar pastimes. They entertained family, friends, and themselves at the kitchen table harmonizing Irish melodies. They especially treasured the written word. Wherever Ita happened to be, she could expect long, witty letters "full of extravagant mischief" from her father, letters that she cherished.[5] Ita herself maintained lifelong friendships through frequent correspondence, often mailed from continent to continent. She carefully chose her words to clarify and analyze her thoughts, but did not mind startling her reader with offbeat comments and incisive humor.

Ita loved to roam through Manhattan and all over Brooklyn. Grace shared some of this wanderlust with her: "We'd get on our bikes, ride down to Shore Road, which is a particularly lovely and peaceful area along the water... We'd stay there for a couple of hours, sometimes talking, sometimes not saying a word." There was a protective railing, but climb it they did so they could sit on the rocks, gaze out on the bay, and daydream. At about age fifteen, Ita confided to Grace her desire to join Maryknoll—something Ita did not tell her parents until she was in college. Her mother believed Ita was "possibly looking for adventure in faraway places as well as a chance to help people."[6] The order was known to the Fords because Ita's father's cousin, Maryknoll Bishop Francis X. Ford, had died in a Chinese prison camp the year she turned twelve. Ita, aware of his Brooklyn roots and relationship to her father, would have no doubt been aware of the basic facts about his life and death.

Ita graduated from Fontbonne in 1957 and went on to Marymount Manhattan, a Catholic college for women primarily serving commuters from the metropolitan area. Ita chose English as her major, wrote for the student newspaper, and edited the *Avelan*, Marymount's yearbook.[7] While in college, Ita corresponded with Maryknoll twice about admission. In her sophomore year she mentioned her vocation to her parents, and they convinced her to finish college first.[8] In her senior year, she wrote her friend Jean Reardon that a Maryknoll sister had advised her to stop "smoking and social drinking...[and] only go out once or twice a month and not with the same boy." Ita commented: "She should know that you can't overcome temptation if it's not put in your way."[9] Late in her senior year Ita was accepted.

Spring 1961, her last term, was hectic with showers and parties to attend for friends and for her brother's fiancée, Mary Anne: "This is the sickening season of showers...Here I am spending $50.00 this weekend on something against my very nature...I'm all in favor of elopement." Bill and Mary Anne got married in a storm that dumped seventeen inches of snow on New York—requiring the bride to arrive "all wrapped up in sheets and plastic," and a bridesmaid to "ride the subway with paper bags around her legs."[10]

A surprise eighteen-day trip to Poland and Russia capped her senior year. Fordham University had chartered a plane and extended a last-minute, reduced rate to Marymount students. Ita and her sister signed on. As editor, Ita had to prepare the yearbook for the printer before leaving, and this required her to camp out for two nights in the student council office. Unfortunately, she wrote, "schoolwork has gone out the window." She had made the dean's list one time previously—but that was not to be repeated.[11]

As an American abroad for the first time, it took her a few days to grasp what she was observing in communist Eastern Europe. In Warsaw, she wrote, there was nothing to spend their *zlotys* on—"everything was junk," and the post–World War II restoration done to buildings was "lousy" and "already cracked." She praised Krakow for its fourteenth-century charm, but when the group went to Easter Sunday Mass, she experienced more than a trace of culture shock: "There was a one-hour procession. Women carried every statue in the church around on poles ...We were nearly trampled to death, since... the church is like a free for all. Only here are the people downright impolite. On the street they're lambs."

But in the Soviet Union, Ita saw things differently, and upon returning home, she realized the trip was a turning point. She wrote to Jean that she "had a new set of values":

> Being in Russia did help. I can't explain it, but at times I want to hug the whole entire world—no matter the cost...
>
>   For the first time in my life I feel really at ease. I'm not trying to hide everything with a wisecrack. And for the first time I'm positively sure about what I want to do. You can't imagine what it was like being in Russia and feeling so impotent when people needed your help. A man next to me during a Russian Orthodox service cried during the whole Credo...These people ...really believed in God—not a lip service offering as my own is—but a soul-wrenching belief...[This] has made me aware now that I really have to go to Maryknoll.[12]

She was disturbed by the lack of religious freedom for fervent Russian believers in their authoritarian society. Fear during the Cold War of "godless communism" was prevalent in Catholicism and American society in the early sixties and Ita shared in this fear, which was possibly reinforced for her by her cousin's death nine years earlier in a communist prison.

In September 1961, Ita, along with sixty-three other postulants, entered the Maryknoll Sisters Motherhouse about thirty miles north of Manhattan. The rules then were particularly frustrating for Ita. At first she felt she was becoming a "dullard," being cut off from *The New York Times* and *The New Yorker*, periodicals she had been reading since adolescence.[13] Her mother later said: "I think now the reason Ita had such problems when she entered Maryknoll was that up to that time she never had to do the goose step. She was a free soul—a responsible child—a happy student—had many friends. There were no hard and fast rules at home or at school."[14] Ita found an outlet for herself in long letters and was able to work through her thoughts and some dilemmas by unburdening herself to friends:

> For the group around me, 59 very different people, I know them all and not at all. For the next three years it's not allowed to recreate in two's...You also in the beginning anyway have to reconcile yourself to be a "number" for a while. This is sheer institution..., to the point that when I thought I'd climb a wall I

expected to see everyone else there too...When you eat, sleep, and even go to the "john" at the same time, it's a little nerve-wracking...

Well, I'm patiently waiting, no that's a lie. In fact, my whole problem, one that's plagued me my whole life, is impatience. I expect to conquer everything in one try and with one look. You don't do that with a new life...Many people find prayer a great consolation. Me, I'm just learning how to pray.[15]

A few weeks later her outlook was brighter. There were suppers outside and a roaring bonfire. She was getting acquainted with her classmates, especially Julie Miller from Savannah, who had gazed at the first snowfall with childlike wonder. But Ita, still fixated on her *New Yorker*, added: "Thursday night is confession night and every week I resist the impulse to go in and say, bless me, Father, I'm a saint. But tonight, as I was gabbing away, the priest said I could have the *New Yorker* after I've digested all of St. Paul's epistles to the point of application."[16]

Doing without, she was finding, "simplifies things—in fact I never thought a 3rd pair of shoes could be superfluous." Without possessions, she wrote: "You have to love more people...I never thought I could look at a whole roomful of people and honestly say I love them all." She had taken a critical look at her strong will and found: "I'm still rebelling... It's hard to swallow everything you've paraded as your smart self and accept the fact that...you don't want to be so glib anymore." Ita knew she was holding back: "I think I'm developing a case of 'not yet, Lord,' give me a few more minutes to relish my ill-conceived notions of freedom... It's not that the spirit is willing and the flesh is weak, so much as the will is strong and as yet won't bend."[17]

Ita was not a devotee of praying the Stations of the Cross. But as she let her possessions go and tried to detach herself from her own will, Ita became captivated by the tenth station, in which Jesus is stripped of his garments: "What could be harder than being stripped, not just of your clothes, but of all that makes you up...Somehow you have to peel off all the layers you've acquired...I could see so many things that had to go."[18]

Ita made it through her postulant year and progressed to the next phase—two years as a novice in Topsfield, Massachusetts, not far from the Atlantic Ocean. After one year as a novice, she indicated that she had had a "dizzying" peek at divine love: "I'm not a fan of much of the symbolism attached to religious life. But there is a definite relationship to be established with God, and maybe with less sentiment it could be clearer ...It's dizzying to know you're loved so."[19] She did not question her vocation: "I guess I finally committed myself: Even if it means being a mediocre clod, I've got to be one now, here. It's a little like the 'Hound of Heaven'...And in the beginning it's elation. Then you realize what it means. It's good I don't know it all now, but only a little because it would be crushing."[20]

Ita began to reap some intellectual rewards when the novices listened to taped lectures by Catholic professor Barry Ulanov. Reminiscent of the concepts of Teilhard de Chardin, wrote Ita, the lectures encompassed "how we meet the transcendent in the immanent." She now saw nature in a new way: "The psalm verses come to mind about all things praising God...Sometimes I think [these three years] would be worth it just for this new scope."[21]

Ita began to reflect on the mother of Jesus and sent Jean a medal of Mary, quipping: "I never paid her much heed...She stands out more and more. Quite a lady." She was now starting her letters with a quote in Latin from Mary's response to the angel Gabriel at the Annunciation: "*Ecce Ancilla Domine*,"—"Behold the handmaid of the Lord." Ita revealed: "I don't want to be Peter Pan for the rest of my life. Though I may not look the part, I'd like to be womanly, with what that implies, the giving, the selflessness, the strength...with the suffering used positively." She included Jean in this future of selflessness: "I hope we both give all."[22]

On June 24, 1964, Ita and her class were to take their first vows. For some time she had been experiencing nausea, which, with Julie's help, she concealed for a while. When her illness was discovered, Ita was sent for therapy. Her doctor and the Mother General concurred that she should not be "under the pressure of taking vows," as Ita put it, with the rest of her class.[23] Her parents knew nothing then of the vomiting, nor that Ita was seeing a doctor. "It was a horrendous ordeal," recalled her mother. "Finally she was allowed to see her family."[24] But then in August Ita was told she could not take her vows after all. She must leave—it would be a risk for someone with a serious, perhaps chronic, ailment to become a missioner. Ita was shattered.

Grace picked her up at the airport: "I didn't recognize her!! She came off the plane looking unlike I had ever seen her look...She was miserably sick, both in body and spirit. She spent long hours listening to Julie's piano recordings and crying...I have never seen Ita so totally devastated."[25] Many years later, Ita would call this "my '64 low-water mark"—a time when she doubted she was worthy of love, but found that there were actually many who would help her heal.[26]

Ita made the effort to bounce back. Returning from a walk around Brooklyn one day, she told her mother: "I smiled at everyone I met.

Some smiled back." She was embarking on "her greatest period of growth," according to her mother. Ita took evening classes in education at Hunter College. She began teaching religion to Puerto Rican girls—high school sophomores who had already been exposed to prostitution and drugs, but "who have a wonderful Christian attitude toward each other." After a few weeks she no longer needed a doctor. Within four weeks of leaving Maryknoll, Ita had begun a new life.[27]

She was now working full time. Through Marymount, she landed a job at William H. Sadlier Publishing Company, which published catechisms and other textbooks for Catholic schoolchildren. Ita became an editor of English and religion textbooks for high school students. The position was tailor-made for her talents and educational background—even her years at Maryknoll were advantageous. Though she may not have considered this at the time, working at a Catholic publishing company would keep her abreast of the remarkable changes emanating from the Second Vatican Council and would be exceptional preparation for her re-entry into religious life.

Those who knew Ita would agree with her friend Cathy Lavin, another editor, that she "was very well read and had one of the sharpest minds" of anyone they knew. Her professional work was exemplary, said author Joe Petulla: "She did all the editing on my books. And she was far more than the editor; co-author is more like it. I sent her a dictated draft; she would move material around, add some and send it back." Ita was popular with her colleagues—friendly and compassionate—and her sense of humor was part of her appeal.[28]

Ita's colleagues were Catholics who were excited that the post–Vatican II church, finally, was encouraging a more active role for the laity. They were well versed in periodicals such as *Commonweal*, *America*, and the *National Catholic Reporter*, which kept them apprised of the latest news and ideas circulating in the Catholic world of the sixties. These subjects would come up not only—and necessarily—at work but also in their off-hours as they gathered to socialize. It was part of the air they breathed as young Catholic professionals. As fellow editor Roger Marchand commented: "We were a bunch of 'liberal Catholics' who worked together, partied together, and protested the war in Vietnam. Ita was very much in the center of all that."[29]

The documents of the Second Vatican Council, which they discussed, called for Catholics to be active in the modern world, to "read the signs of the times," and to work for peace through justice. Ita and many of her colleagues protested and marched—for civil rights and against the war in Vietnam. Yet Ita was non-ideological, even non-partisan. She had a critical mind, Petulla asserted, and refused to jump to a conclusion without having gathered the facts. He was with her when a man asked them to sign a petition to stop the building of a nuclear power plant. Ita asked: where would New York City get its electrical power in the future if not from nuclear energy? She would not sign the petition but said she would think about it. Lavin remembered Ita inviting her to a news conference after the arrest of Daniel Berrigan, a Jesuit priest who had been pursued by the FBI for his anti-war activities. Ita warned her that the FBI would be present and might be taking photos. "Although she herself may have held strong convictions on an issue, she never tried to impose her views on others," said Cathy.[30]

Ita enjoyed happy hour and parties and—not surprising for that time—she smoked. Her no-frills pixie haircut suited her simple life-style. Her friend Ana May often saw her in the city: "There she was in the same outfit—always neat, always meticulous, but never the chic lady she could have been. She wasn't into that. She was very pretty, naturally pretty, and never used any make-up at all. She had a raincoat, her penny loafers and a few wool sweaters that she wore for years."[31] Ita dated regularly during this time; she and Ray, a Japanese-American whose family had been interred during World War II, became serious and talked of a family. Their close tie, however, ended in friendship rather than marriage.

Ita and Katherine Monahan, a friend from college, became room-mates in 1968 when Ita moved to Sheridan Square in Greenwich Village. Ita seldom watched television; in fact, they only had it in their apartment because Kathy wanted one. Instead, they found stimulation and laughter in conversations with friends. Kathy, as well as others, mentioned that Ita enjoyed nothing more than roaming through the city, enjoying whatever she happened upon. Kathy learned from Ita to take advantage of the cultural life in New York as together they strolled through museums and went to the opera and theater after purchasing the cheapest possible tickets.

Ita took vacations with Kathy and Ana. They traveled on "two dollars a day" in a Volkswagen bug down the West Coast and into Mexico. They took turns driving, but "Ita was small with short legs" and needed a pillow perfectly adjusted to reach the pedals. "I'm very glad I'm still here to talk about it because that was an experience," laughed Ana. When Ita got behind the wheel, "we would all go to sleep or close our eyes [in fear]." They stayed at the cheapest motels and swam in the pools of the most expensive hotels. Ita's father had their itinerary, and there would be a lengthy, much-anticipated letter from him waiting for her at the Hiltons along the way; Ita always read the witty letters aloud. Although on these trips the young women engaged in some embarrassing hijinks along the way, Ita "was never one to initiate an action but certainly [would] follow along...with very good sense [and] a little restraint," Kathy said. Ita was so tiny that she had trouble buying an alcoholic drink; in fact, the man in the ticket booth at Disneyland took one look at Ita's slim figure and short hair and admitted her as Ana's son.[32]

Living in New York not far from her brother, Bill, and sister, Rene, Ita was able to form long-lasting relationships with her young nieces and nephews. Bill's daughter, Miriam Ita Ford, recalled that in some of the books Ita worked on while at Sadlier she included "pictures of my brothers and sisters and me and my cousins. I was tall for my age and she was small, and she could wear my clothes...In some of those pictures in El Salvador she's wearing a shirt or something else of mine."[33]

Ita did not relinquish her dreams of Maryknoll during her seven years in the professional world: "Ita really never left Maryknoll. She continued to keep very close contact," recalled Ita's mother.[34] She apprised her novice mistress, who supported her calling, of her activities, once writing that "a good deal of me wishes I was still the over-ripe novice at Topsfield."[35] She corresponded with her friends in missions halfway around the world, and when they were in New York they often stayed at her apartment. In 1970 Ita visited Julie Miller, then a missioner in Japan. They enjoyed two weeks of sight-seeing and chatted casually about the possibility—nothing definite—of Ita returning to Maryknoll.[36] When Ita told her mother she was reapplying, Mildred questioned her, but Ita said that "the whole atmosphere was very different now...and that these were the people she wanted to spend the rest of her life with."[37] Coworker Cathy Lavin knew of Ita's decision to re-enter and that the issue of her physical stamina would soon arise. Was Ita nervous? Lavin asked. "Ita was her good-natured self...I clearly recall her smiling her impish grin and saying she would leave it in God's hands."[38]

In 1971, Ita re-entered Maryknoll. Many changes had occurred in the ten years since she first arrived as a postulant. Ita was now swimming against the nationwide tide of women leaving religious communities. Instead of scores of novices in an institutional environment, there were three women, including Ita, living in a large residence in St. Louis, Missouri, near St. Louis University. All three had been on career tracks—and another candidate later arrived from the Peace Corps. In the post–Vatican II years, the women were free to socialize and set their own schedules for prayer and study. Taking courses with them at the Jesuit Divinity School was a varied group—male and female, Catholic religious and lay persons, and non-Catholics—and Ita found her courses challenging. She wrote her friend Jean:

> My "sabbatical" year is a little more busy than I anticipated. Between Scripture courses at the Divinity School...and theology here at the house, work has been piling up...It's strange to realize that I'm back again going toward what I want, and I may have a case of arrested development, but sometimes I feel I've been through it before...In a way I feel like "I'm back home"... Well, back to the books. I'm at a slight disadvantage not knowing Greek, German, and Hebrew, but I admire it on the pages. The Greek is especially graceful.[39]

Because of her prior years in the novitiate, Ita was suddenly confronted with a decision after only a few months: whether or not to make a "promise of fidelity" (similar to the old "first vows"). She did not hesitate long. A ceremony was held in St. Louis on April 29, 1972, and in attendance, along with family and friends, was Sister Mary Galligan, the novice mistress who had always supported Ita.[40]

Ita said her good-byes and in August 1972, at age thirty-two, headed for language school in Cochabamba, Bolivia, in preparation for her mission assignment to Chile. Like many a new missioner before her, she was introduced to the extremes of wealth and poverty in stops along the way. In Lima, she got "a feel of the city, from the colonial palaces to the latest invasion site ringing the city where rural people have squatted...I was only seeing and not understanding. There's so much incongruity that it's very hard to get hold of it."[41]

Ita found Cochabamba a "very pleasant place..., large enough to have some diversion when I'm numb of tongue and brain...It also happens to have the best climate the country offers, being neither oxygen-poor mountaintop nor lowland jungle." Attending the language school were about fifty students who were mostly "church-related." Five hours a day for six months, Ita studied Spanish. She found it demanding, but her classmates provided camaraderie and her sense of humor helped see her through: "I'm looking forward to the time when I get out of the one-word-at-a-time-with-a-big-pause-in-between phase. At this stage, if the person listening to me hasn't forgotten what I started to say, I probably have."[42]

There were political tensions in Bolivia which, unknown to Ita then, were a prelude to life in Chile. Bolivia had devalued its currency, "causing quite a suffering for most of the people." Soon the country declared a state of siege characterized by martial law, suspension of civil rights, and curfews. She experienced an unpleasant jolt of surprise when two unions in La Paz called a strike to protest the economic hardships and "out rolled the tanks."[43]

Ita spent Christmas in Juli, Peru, on Lake Titicaca. Here, the *altiplano*, the world's second-highest plateau, intrigued her with its stark beauty, its tranquility, and its Aymara people eking out a living from the barren land. At Mass on a freezing Christmas morning, she was moved by the many barefoot poor. Ita understood most of the Spanish being spoken, but remarked, "I'm glad no one was holding their breath for my answer."[44]

In March 1973, Ita headed for Chile, and what she termed "a leap into the unknown." She felt she lacked fluency in Spanish and was apprehensive because she had heard that Chileans had "their own abbreviated, speed version of Spanish in which it's perfectly acceptable to only pronounce the first part of a word." In order to get a sense of where she might fit in, she traveled around Chile for several weeks, moving every three or four days, to attend Maryknoll meetings and to visit sisters working in various communities. She had no idea what the future held, yet it still seemed right to forge ahead: "If the Lord got me to Chile, I'm sure he'll provide the clues for what's next. So far it's a tease."[45]

In June, Ita went to live with a Chilean sister in Santiago. This was a relief. After weeks of roving, she could finally settle down for a month. She still felt shaky with Spanish and this immersion in the Chilean dialect would help. She had found she was attracted to Santiago —"probably because my blood is urban"—and this would give her the chance to experience life in Población Manuel Rodríguez, one of many resettlement areas around the capital. They were inhabited by poor newcomers, "squatters," who had left the countryside for the city to seek a better life. As Ita noted: "This gives me some time to get some idea of *población* work...since the movement is away from institutions and toward living with the people in their reality." Ita was looking forward to July when she would finally be able to "unpack for a while," probably at another *población* in Santiago: "There are times when the image of pilgrim church gets to be a little too real!"[46]

Traveling through Chile, Ita had noticed how hard life was for so many: "Some people say I couldn't have come at a more exciting time, while others say this is a terrible introduction...There's talk of a repeat of last October's general strike that paralyzed the country...There already are great shortages of food...It's going to be a mess."[47]

Her next stop would be more permanent than she expected. She would live in Población La Bandera for the next five years. Her work

Ita with a young child in Población La Bandera

there would plunge her into the lives and struggles of the poor for the rest of her life. It would expand her consciousness, test her stamina and courage, and deepen her spirituality and compassion. She would witness injustice and repression the magnitude of which she never before thought existed. She would meet new friends, one of whom would ultimately accompany her to a Central American country in the throes of civil war. But now she was about to become immersed in one of the most significant political events in the history of Chile, which was on the brink of political upheaval.

Chapter 10

Carla and Ita

La Bandera

C arla and Ita arrived in Población La Bandera a few months apart—
Carla in the spring of 1973 and Ita in July. Ita was only seven
months younger than Carla but Carla had years more experience
as a missioner. She had arrived in Chile in 1964, around the time that Ita
was experiencing the "low-water mark" of her life as she recovered from
her rejection by Maryknoll.

During the intervening years both had grown in their concept of
"church." They were attracted to the church's deeper emphasis on service and living in community with those suffering from society's injustices. Carla had spent these nine years gravitating from Chillán to Buzeta
to La Bandera in a steady search for a more radical Christianity in keeping with the spirit of Vatican II. Ita's immediate background for mission
life had come from a year of study in St. Louis, language school in Bolivia, several weeks of fast-paced travels to Maryknoll communities in
Chile, and one month in Población Manuel Rodríguez. Yet her earlier
work as an editor at Sadlier had grounded her in the new ideas and documents emanating from the Council. Her heart, like Carla's, was prepared
to embrace the poor.

Both women were drawn to La Bandera, one of the earliest attempts
by Chilean Presidents Frei and Allende to house the steady influx from
the countryside of people seeking work in Santiago. By 1973, such resettlement areas encircled the capital city. La Bandera's population was
more than seventy thousand, most of whom had little education beyond a
few years of grade school. They had not found the prosperous life they
sought and were poor, discouraged, and often angry that their lot in life
never improved.

Carla and Ita were drawn also by two sisters living in La Bandera. Connie Pospisil, fairly new herself, and Mary Tracy lived in a wooden house that had bare plank walls. With three small bedrooms and one room that served as living room, dining room, and kitchen, there was just enough room to accommodate the community that was about to double in size with the arrival of Carla and Ita, but it was not as simple as the surrounding homes. The sisters did have indoor plumbing, while their neighbors used outdoor spigots. The streets were unpaved and covered either with mud or wind-blown dust, depending on the season.

According to Connie, Carla's heart immediately reached out toward the "poor ole beat-up people," as Carla affectionately described them— the toughest characters, the ones who frightened others, the most needy and vulnerable—and became friends with them.[1] Ita proceeded less spontaneously and more methodically: "What we hope to be doing," she wrote, "is building community among ourselves and developing relationships with the neighbors. Exactly what form that will take for me is still not too clear. There are many neighborhood organizations and clubs as a start for contacts."[2] The bishop's hope, said Ita, was that by the missioners developing relationships with the people there would slowly evolve Christian base communities for reflection and prayer, because, due to "the history and tradition of the people there is not much of an emphasis on 'sacramentalism' or other institutional works." Worship would come later.[3]

If it is true that opposites attract, then that could be what sparked a growing friendship between Carla and Ita:

> Ita's passion for a clear and many-sided view of things left her open to receive and fairly evaluate a wide variety of opinions and attitudes—even Carla's abrasive ones...Carla's tendency to react impulsively was held in check by Ita's need to analyze, just as Ita's hesitancy to act until everything was clear was pushed along by Carla's need to move...They were opposite and alike: Carla was outgoing, boisterous, argumentative, large in size and presence; Ita was retiring, unimposing, listening, petite. They made an incongruous pair. But what they shared most deeply was a seriousness about life that...was impatient with anything less than the truth or contrary to the kingdom of God.[4]

The sisters survived on a small stipend from the archdiocese of Santiago. They lived a "very fishbowl existence" next door to the local bar; Ita explained the thin walls and close quarters: "The head of my bed is about three feet away from the head of the couple who live next door. You're into their fights, you're into the joys, you're into the disagreements, into the struggle . . . People will come to us as leaders, referees, facilitators. This is a constant all day." And they came with their needs. But the sisters had no "big magic answers." They urged the people to gather together to solve their problems: "We are there to be with, to discover with the people the coming of brotherhood and justice."[5]

Carla and Ita would hardly be settled in La Bandera when a momentous event—the overthrow of Chile's long-standing democracy—would roil the nation and shock the world.

For four decades—from 1932 to 1973—Chile had a democratic government devoid of the coups, assassinations, or revolutions that had so often plagued its neighbors. But it also suffered from severe socioeconomic problems that caused growing discontent among the urban working and middle classes as well as the rural poor.

A major hindrance to progress was that copper, Chile's primary export, was mined almost exclusively by large U.S. corporations. Although Chile benefited from taxes on the copper industry, almost all profits went to the U.S. enterprises, and the industry itself offered little economic stimulus overall. The copper industry also contributed indirectly to the inefficiency of Chilean agriculture. Because of the taxes received from copper, the government avoided taxing large estates, and rich landowners had no incentive to maximize agricultural production, so that large tracts of land went unfarmed. A nation that could have fed its own population had to import food, further contributing to the outflow of money. Agriculture remained backward and land remained in the hands of the few. As late as the 1960s, the majority of the rural labor force—more than seven hundred thousand workers—were landless, and farmers and rural workers earned on average only $100 a year.[6]

In 1922 a communist party was formed and a socialist party followed in 1933. Both soon dominated the labor movement, but rivalries between them weakened their influence and enabled coalitions of the conservative and moderate parties to hold on to power. With the advent of the Cold War in the late 1940s, the U.S., fearing the potential growth of communism, began clandestinely supporting Chile's right-wing government, which passed new laws restricting the rights of labor unions.

The Catholic Church did not stand by idle. Indeed, the Chilean church stood out in its concern for social justice long before the rest of the Catholic Church in Latin America.[7] Its commitment to the labor movement, premised on Catholic doctrine emanating from papal social encyclicals, began in the 1920s. Especially significant was the Jesuit priest

Alberto Hurtado, who in 1944 founded a movement to aid the homeless and in 1947 established a Christian workers union, which was especially prominent in rural regions. In 1951, he launched the periodical *Mensaje* (*Message*) to disseminate Catholic social teaching. Twenty years later, *Mensaje* would become an important voice in the struggle for justice during the Pinochet dictatorship.[8]

Manuel Larraín, the bishop of Talca and a colleague of Hurtado, was another early advocate of social reform and a major progressive influence in Chile and at the Second Vatican Council. He was charged by Pope Paul VI with planning the agenda for the Medellín Bishops Conference (1968), but died in an automobile accident in 1966 and was unable to see the fruit of his work.[9] Cardinal Raúl Silva Henríquez, who would himself prove to be a major force for justice during the Pinochet years, listed Hurtado and Larraín in his memoirs as "the two most influential figures in the Chilean church."[10]

The history and prominence of the Chilean church's social teachings contributed to the rise and early popularity of the Christian Democratic Party (PDC). Founded in 1957 and led by Eduardo Frei, a former student of Larraín, this new party was an outgrowth of the Catholic social teachings that had influenced Hurtado and Larraín. Critical of the capitalism of the right and the Marxism of the left, the PDC offered a middle way that was radical but more practical than that of communism and socialism. Political scientist Brian Loveman noted that Frei's call for peaceful revolutionary change was no empty rhetoric: "The Christian Democrats intended to alter dramatically the very foundations of Chilean society, to redistribute income and wealth, to improve the living standards of, and to broaden opportunities for, the nation's workers and peasants, and to democratize the country's political and social life."[11] It is no exaggeration to say that the PDC would dramatically alter Chilean politics.

Jorge Alessandri, the Conservative Party candidate, won the 1958 presidential election, but with only 31.6 percent of the vote. A leftist coalition headed by the Marxist Salvador Allende received a surprising 28.9 percent, while the PDC's Frei garnered 20.7 percent. The impressive showing of Allende shocked the Conservative Party and the PDC, but also the U.S. which, following Castro's rise to power in Cuba in 1959, began to support moderate reform candidates throughout Latin America in hopes of preventing revolution.

During his term in office, Alessandri was unable to make headway against Chile's socioeconomic problems, and his Conservative Party realized that if it and the PDC both ran candidates in the 1964 election,

Allende would probably win. Fearing the ramifications of a Marxist government, the conservatives decided not to enter a candidate and instead unenthusiastically backed Frei. This enabled Frei to win the presidency and his party to win a majority in the House of Deputies the following year. The question now was could Frei and his upstart political party deliver on what they had promised? Based on their performance over the next six years, the answer proved to be both yes and no.

Frei's accomplishments were impressive but did not go far enough in solving Chile's systemic problems. His plan to nationalize the copper industry benefited foreign companies more than Chile and his agrarian program was hampered by his reluctance to fully implement the widespread land reform the PDC had promised. While labor was disappointed that Frei's reforms were too moderate, Conservative Party leaders saw them as too radical and decided to throw caution to the wind. They entered their own candidate in the 1970 election, even though this meant that the anti-Marxist vote would be split, thereby making it probable that Allende would win. And indeed, this did occur. Salvador Allende, with only 36 percent of the vote, became the first Marxist president ever constitutionally elected in the Western Hemisphere.

Initially, Allende's programs were successful and popular—worker income rose and inflation and unemployment declined. Advances were made in housing, education, and health. But his success was short-lived. Copper prices declined, inflation became rampant, and there were severe shortages of consumer goods. Allende's expropriation of large companies (both national and foreign) made it impossible for Chile to obtain U.S. investment capital or loans from international banks. Allende's experiment with socialism did not benefit the majority of laborers who worked for smaller businesses, and they began—without his consent—to seize factories and farms. These actions, along with a worsening economy, frightened the middle class, who had initially cooperated with Allende, and turned them against his government.

By late 1972, chaos threatened, but this cannot be blamed only on the shortcomings of Allende. According to CIA Director William Colby's testimony before a U.S. Senate subcommittee, between 1962 and 1970 the CIA spent $11 million to undermine Allende's election bid, and after he became president Secretary of State Henry Kissinger authorized another $8 million to destabilize the Chilean economy.[12] With this help from the United States, a coup had become imminent.

Ita had been in La Bandera only a few weeks when she received word that her father had died. The next day, September 11, 1973, Carla and

Maryknoll Father Tom Maney drove into central Santiago to book a flight home for Ita. As they walked toward the airline office, they were stunned to see tanks in the streets and fighter planes flying low overhead. Frightened and ducking their heads, they hurried back to the truck without the ticket. The coup had begun.

General Augusto Pinochet overthrew Allende, who died in the takeover. Seventeen years of military dictatorship followed. Political activity and freedom of assembly were banned and the House of Deputies was dissolved. *Poblaciones* were raided and soldiers enforced curfew by shooting violators throughout the night. Professionals and laborers were arrested arbitrarily and thrown into detention camps. One camp, the National Stadium, held up to seven thousand political prisoners. Thousands were tortured or executed and many simply disappeared.

Since no civilians could leave Chile, a memorial liturgy for Ita's father was held at the Maryknoll Center House in Santiago. Ita read out loud from some of the cherished letters her father had sent her over the years and everyone present laughed and cried. When civilians were allowed by the new regime to leave, Ita was on one of the first flights out on September 21, too late for her father's funeral.

Ita returned to Santiago after a couple of weeks in New York, and along with the little Maryknoll community in La Bandera now had to adjust to life under the Pinochet dictatorship. There were few families in the *población* who were not affected by the repression, which not only curtailed political activity, freedom of the press, and freedom of speech but also sanctioned solitary confinement, arbitrary arrests and military trials, neighborhood spy networks, and torture and interrogation by electric shock.

Carla soon realized the sinister reach of the terror. She had been counseling Nalda, whose husband, an air force officer, had had a nervous breakdown after being ordered to kill his countrymen following the coup. With the help of Carla and a military chaplain, Nalda and her husband were finally able together to make peace with God.[13] Closer to home, Maryknoll Brother Joseph Doherty and Carla's seminarian friend Skip Flynn were arrested with what the new regime considered politically compromising reading material. They were brought to the National Stadium where they listened in terror to other prisoners being tortured and killed. Skip lost fifteen pounds during the eleven days they were imprisoned, but they were unharmed and through the advocacy of Maryknoll and others, they were freed and left Chile.[14]

Ita and Mary Tracy volunteered at a refugee center, helping those who feared arrest and wanted to emigrate to the U.S. They wrote a letter to Edward Kennedy, explaining that the form the refugees had to fill out asked for personal information that could lead to "retaliation against their loved ones."[15] Kennedy in the Senate and Robert Drinan, SJ, in the House did introduce bills to have Chilean refugees regarded the same way as those fleeing communist countries, but neither Congress nor the executive branch was interested in following through. The prevailing view was that those trying to leave Chile must have communist or social-ist sympathies. Nixon, unswayed by Pinochet's human rights violations, was a supporter of the regime and, under the auspices of "stopping com-munism," his administration was in the process of increasing aid to the dictatorship.[16] Ita and Mary's letter to Kennedy was probably an exercise in futility.

Ita's mother and sister Rene visited soon after the coup. Mildred saw the "raw poverty" of La Bandera: "the stunted children, the bleak deso-late area—the open market where people bought chicken feet as food. Children came to the door all day long asking for bread. Mary Tracy and Connie Pospisil were always sterilizing needles to give shots to sick peo-ple and children." She was touched that "the people poor as they were wanted to entertain me." Carla adopted Mrs. Ford as "Grandma," and they began corresponding afterwards. Mildred knew that Ita and Carla visited the National Stadium: "[They served] the community by going daily to the stadium . . . looking for people, carrying messages, etc.—trac-ing the disappeared." The implications were not lost on her: "Now she was ready to stand up to whatever happened."[17]

Soon after her mother and sister left, Ita wrote her friends Jean and John Baumann about life under Pinochet: "Last weekend arms were planted in a tabernacle in a small chapel in the same section of Santiago as we are. The priest was taken on charges of aiding the extremists . . . But the church is taking a stand. Within a day and a half, a pastoral letter was out, denouncing the whole incident as a put-up." Added Ita: "The report, on the other side, is my reaction to one of the searches here in the *población*."[18] This carefully crafted account, titled "Try to Imagine," was Ita's heartfelt attempt to enlighten Americans on the repression in La Bandera and was sent to several people. What follows is an abbreviated version:

Try to imagine one hundred soldiers and two dozen FBI agents surrounding a working-class neighborhood of two thousand families at dawn. All men and boys over fourteen years are sum-moned. Any man who has something, even traffic accidents or unpaid fines, recorded against him in the last ten years is taken.

Some with similar names and others for being "suspicious" are taken. It is Friday, payday. Most of these men lose the week's pay if they miss a day of work.

Try to imagine the wives and mothers milling around. Will their husband look suspicious—unshaved, not fully dressed? Is he thirsty in the sun, hungry from not eating breakfast? (There is no bread this morning. Deliveries were not allowed.) As their husbands and sons are taken to jail, put yourself in the women's place, asking if they might send along something to eat. The soldiers refuse because the men are delinquents. "He's not a delinquent," one mother answers, "he's my son."

Try to imagine the children frightened by the soldiers with machine guns. Some begin to cry, "Daddy, don't let the soldiers take you away."

Try to imagine yourself in your own living-room with five FBI agents and a soldier at the door with a machine gun. Now explain who you are, why you live where you live, what you do. Make sure you produce the necessary documents to back you up. Are you nervous? Why? You haven't done anything wrong. Everything is in order except the order of a society that takes this visit in stride.

Try to imagine each of these things and make it as personal as possible because it is real. It has happened to us. How would you react?

Would there be camaraderie among the men in your neighborhood, sharing cigarettes and jokes to keep up each other's spirits? Would the women be equally, if not more, solicitous? Would their faith be that of the poor who have no "connections" but who must rely solely on the mercy and love of God?

We hope so. The only way you and your neighbors could overcome arbitrary "fishing expeditions" and organized terror is by being very concerned for each other and by having a deep faith, not in man's justice, but in a God who cares for his people. Of course, experiences like this among the poor and powerless run through the Old Testament up to today's headlines. Yet until you experience it, or somehow make someone else's experience your own, it never is truly real. We are privileged to have shared this, to know and feel a little of the suffering of the powerless, of those without voice. And we want to share it with you because our neighbors are your neighbors (Luke 10: 29–37).[19]

At one of these round-ups, Carla confronted the armed soldiers, claiming that the men and boys they were arresting were innocent. Miguel Cruz, a community leader in La Bandera who worked closely with the sisters, broke down thirty years later as he recalled the soldiers roughly pushing Carla to the ground when she intervened. She continued to insist on their innocence, believing that since she was a nun the soldiers would respect her word. Miguel and others had to hold her back to protect her from more harm.[20]

Militaristic terror invaded the sisters' home three times when it was searched by the army, air force, and security police. The last was the most frightening, for hidden away on a closet shelf were some textbooks on Marxism. The books had followed a circuitous route to the closet. They had belonged to a priest in the neighborhood who was teaching a political science course on Marxism at the Catholic university when the coup occurred. Not knowing what to do with them, he buried the texts in his yard before he was forced to leave Chile. The people who moved into the house feared the books would be discovered and asked the sisters for advice. The sisters took the texts. But instead of destroying the expensive books, they hid them in a suitcase they placed way back on the top shelf of a closet, a decision that Connie later acknowledged was "crazy," since to possess such reading material was considered a crime.

When six plainclothes security police barged in one day, three of them forced the missioners who were present—Ita, Carla, and Mary—up against the wall and held them at gunpoint, while the others searched the premises, emptying drawers and bookcases and upending everything. When a policeman found a book he thought looked suspicious (not one of the hidden textbooks), Ita answered, truthfully, that it was written by a theologian outlining the evils of Marxism. Ita explained in a shaky voice: "My mother sent it to us," which momentarily amused Carla. As the panic-stricken women watched, the policemen got dangerously close to the "subversive" books, even emptying out a suitcase full of clothes directly in front of the one containing the texts. The six men finally left, taking Mrs. Ford's gift with them.[21]

In January 1974, Ita spoke at a regional Maryknoll Assembly in Talca, Chile, striving to discern the sisters' "Common Call" in light of the Chilean reality. She recognized that each was only living a small piece of that reality, yet all of them were working, with their variety of gifts, toward the "establishment of the Kingdom of God." She cautioned:

> We are a people who not only live in time but in an age of accelerated change, and we must always be aware of the pitfalls or

temptations to fix ourselves in one historically or culturally conditioned expression of our common call. Those are all relative and subject to change. Understanding the true meaning of our call and reading the signs of the times will enable us to adapt to the word of God in a new and changing age, and to do so in peace and in union with each other.[22]

Ita and Carla were trying to read the "signs of the times," and one sign they saw was that children were malnourished. Hunger had dramatically increased under Pinochet. Carla was justifiably proud of one group of mothers and wrote to her sister that they regularly visit "the poorer people, those who have no food, no decent clothes or shoes, and together we see how best these poor can be helped. The project at hand is a soup kitchen for the undernourished kids."[23] The mothers courageously began requesting food donations from local merchants, even though anyone involved in food redistribution risked harassment by police. Every week Carla and Ita also sought donations for the five free *comedores* (soup kitchens) in their locality.[24]

Overseeing the kitchens was a challenge to Carla's spirituality, forcing her to be brutally honest with herself. In "What have I learned?" she wrote about Señora Rosa, who inadvertently had driven her toward true empathy. Rosa and her five hungry children were coming regularly to

Carla (second from left) and Ita (fourth from left) in Población La Bandera

the *comedor*, but she had never registered them with the government after their births as required. With Rosa ignoring the law, Carla foresaw serious problems for the children, and perhaps for the *comedor*, and pressured her to take care of this. Finally Carla gave the woman an ultimatum: they could not eat in the soup kitchen unless she registered her children.

What Carla had not realized was that Rosa's lethargy was a result of malnourishment. Other mothers explained Rosa's situation and admonished Carla: "You are always saying that the right to eat comes from God. How can you take that right away just because someone doesn't do what you want them to do?" Ashamed, Carla confessed: "[This] profound truth...taught me volumes...I'm only one person who has a lot of blind spots and I need the whole church to help me to see." Rosa returned to the *comedor*. One day she called out "Madre!" and approached Carla to tell her proudly that she had registered all her children.[25]

Carla continued to grow spiritually as she met so many suffering mothers and children in the *comedores*. Weak from hunger, ill-clothed, and timid, one mother led Carla to reflect:

> Her gentleness and patience have showed me more of the beatitudes than many sermons. Her hunger and thirst have cried out for justice more strongly than the whole United Nations. Her single-hearted struggle for her children speaks more for love than many commandments...I need her faith to help me believe. After all, I know that all the rights she has been denied— food, work, education, decent housing—exist for some people —and sometimes they forget the "least of my brethren."[26]

After the coup, the challenges were many, but Carla wrote to her sister and brother-in-law that she was thriving: "I love the work I'm doing here. For the first time I feel like I am living with the poor as I should be, that I'm preaching the Good News to them as I should be, and that I'm open to what the Lord sends today and trust tomorrow in His Hands."[27]

The harsh conditions complicated tragedies that would have occurred anyway. There were two major fires near the sisters' house. In May 1975, one broke out three blocks away from where the sisters lived, destroying or damaging six houses and their contents. It was frustrating, said Carla, that the nearest telephone was a twenty-minute walk away, but a relief when finally a "fire truck of 1930 vintage putt-putted down the street." Thankfully, everyone got out in time.

Two days later, Ita and Connie went for help to Bishops' Relief and Caritas, and Carla, with a group of mothers, went door-to-door to collect clothes and money. Carla was profoundly moved at the generosity of even the poorest people: "Since it was Thursday and the men here get paid on Friday, we set out pessimistically. However, the response was unanimous. 'Today for you, tomorrow for me' as the saying is here." Most had no money, but contributed a little food, a cup, a jacket. Carla compared her own values to those of the *población*:

> [They] work for barely enough for the day, due to the yoke of oppression that lies heavily on the shoulders of the poor. If they lived with our values, they'd soon drown under the tides of despair. It seems to me that the Christian way of sharing can only become a reality with and in the surroundings of the poor. What little bit one family may have obtained today is constantly being used or needed by another who doesn't have today but who shared yesterday.[28]

There was "another big fire—this time right in front of us," started by a little boy lighting a kerosene stove. It flared up and he ran out of the house: "The church, the cantina—11 houses burned in 10 minutes." The sisters' house had to be hosed down "because the boards were steaming." This fire had one positive outcome: it provided men who had long been out of work a job digging new outhouses. "And thank God," Ita wrote, "no one was hurt."[29]

On Easter Sunday 1975, Ita and Carla met a British doctor, Sheila Cassidy, who was working in an emergency hospital in Santiago. About the same age, the three women quickly became friends and for six months gathered often for prayer at Sheila's or in La Bandera:

> These were not pious foreign missionaries coming in to preach a message of brotherly love [in the *población*] and then returning to their comfortable American-style house, but educated young women who lived in a little wooden house like [the people] did, who travelled on foot and by bus as they did and who shared their bread and their friendship and their talents...
>
> The coup had been a great proving time, for the nuns had stayed in their home and their house had been searched along with those of their neighbours. They had shared the terror... when the *población* had been surrounded and the tanks had driven between the little houses and over some of them.[30]

On a retreat, Sheila surrendered herself to God's will, wondering where that would lead. Soon after, a priest asked her to treat a man with a bullet wound. Sheila consented, although she knew the man was a guerrilla in the MIR (Revolutionary Left Movement), which had been attacked by security forces. As a doctor and a Christian, she could not refuse to treat a wounded man, even if, as she then thought, she might be expelled from Chile.

On October 31, 1975, agents from the secret police took her into custody. Dr. Cassidy was stripped, interrogated, and tortured. Torture by electric shock was so severe that she blurted out the names of religious who had protected the revolutionaries. A wave of repressive action against the church resulted. Some religious were deported or escaped, others were imprisoned, and two lay church workers were tortured. Held incommunicado for two weeks, Sheila was unaware of the debate raging in the Chilean media as to the ethics of doctors treating fugitives and religious protecting them. When visitors were allowed, Ita and Carla showed up at the camp where hundreds of political prisoners were jailed. They brought her books, treats, and a breviary, and defied the guards by smuggling in the Eucharist. Unlike the Chilean prisoners, Sheila was lucky: Great Britain obtained her release after two months and she left Chile immediately. When her story was revealed, there was an outcry from the international community.[31]

Reports of the Cassidy incident and other troubles in Chile worried Ita's family:

> The news was getting so interesting that Bill and Mary Anne came down for a week's visit. They left this past Saturday much more at ease, now able to situate me in my habitat... We milked every hour discussing what they saw until 3:00 a.m. By the end of the week we were exhausted but very full from the sharing. They left very impressed with the Chilean church's direction, which they said was light years ahead of the States.[32]

What no doubt had so impressed Bill and Mary Anne was the Catholic Church's response to Pinochet's repression. The subjugation of society had become so pervasive under the military dictatorship that the church soon became its only effective critic.[33] This was not because other organizations or faiths did not make the attempt; it was simply that the Catholic Church was the only institution in Chile with the prestige and power to successfully challenge the general. Not long after the 1973 coup, the Committee of Cooperation for Peace had been founded by

Protestant, Jewish, and Catholic leaders. Its goal was to locate and defend political prisoners who were in detention camps or had disappeared. In October 1975, the Pinochet government refused to allow the Committee's co-chairman, Lutheran Bishop Helmut Frenz, to reenter Chile after a visit to Europe to seek funding. Pinochet then pressured Cardinal Raúl Silva of Santiago to dissolve the Committee, which he did on December 31, 1975. But the next day, Silva countered by founding the Vicariate of Solidarity, which was placed under the direct protection of Pope Paul VI. The Vicariate not only provided legal aid to political prisoners and their families, but also set up a free school lunch program and system of food collection that saved thousands of malnourished children. When adults and teens also turned up hungry, the program was expanded to include them.[34]

By replacing the ecumenical Committee of Cooperation with the Catholic Vicariate, Silva was not coopting Protestant efforts within the former. On the contrary, he was relieving the pressure on Protestant members who, because they lacked the historical power and prestige of the Catholic Church, were more vulnerable to retaliation. But the Vicariate had another attribute that other Chilean institutions lacked. The Chilean church had an integral relationship with Catholic churches and agencies across Latin America and worldwide. The transnational nature of these Catholic groups, and their readiness to express solidarity with a branch being persecuted, gave the Vicariate a power that transcended the borders of Chile. With negative attention worldwide focused on Pinochet, the Vicariate was a public relations disaster for the dictator.[35]

Ita later described how the church's efforts affected La Bandera: "We've watched a situation go from bad to worse and we've tried to respond. In collaboration with the hierarchy and with outside financial support..., programs have been created..., dining rooms, health programs, cooperatives, cottage industries, legal help, programs for the families of political and disappeared prisoners." Yet these "are temporary measures that don't touch the source of the problem. At best, they serve as a means of denouncing a situation of sin and injustice."[36]

In January 1976, Carla went on retreat. A single line of Psalm 23 inspired her to compose "Near restful waters He leads me, to revive my drooping Spirit":

Waters of mountains, rivers of God,
Cleanse us, renew us, so shabbily shod.
Rios de Chile, streams of burnt snow,
Melt us, tow us, beyond friend or foe.

Currents so fast, pools deep and clear,
Tune us, quiet our hearts to still hear.
Lord of the river, God of the stream,
Teach us your song, our dryness redeem.[37]

With the troubles in Chile weighing on her, it is not surprising that Carla would write about her "drooping Spirit." She often sought therapy to cope with her depression. She was planning to go to the U.S. on furlough in April and perhaps she viewed this with trepidation. Being geographically far away from family had aggravated an already distant emotional relationship, which she had attempted to address in a letter to her sister, in the hope of bringing about some healing:

> It's been so long since I've heard from you. I wonder how are you?...Mama writes about once a month now with very little in her letters...You guys could all be moved, sick, sad, in the poor house or on 5th Avenue for all I know...Altho I'm far away, I still think about you and remember you to the Lord. It's not much I ask—just a letter to say how you really are! I feel badly that our family is so dispersed—myself perhaps the most removed—yet here I really know...what it means to be close to people...Why can't it [also] be among brothers and sisters who do have a bond in blood and beliefs? Maybe I look for too much from the family that always went its own way. You, Betty, are the only one that I see, visit and try to keep up some kind of ties...I guess that's why I feel close enough to rant and rave like this. Don't worry about me—I haven't flipped—I just thought I'd express what runs through my mind and heart once in a while.[38]

Carla's infrequent communication with her family would have painful consequences during her six-month furlough. Her siblings had not informed her of her mother's increasing dementia nor had she told her family exactly when she would arrive in Appleton. Mrs. Piette was confused by Carla's presence in the home and woke her up on her first night by pointing a flashlight in her face and shouting: "Who are you? What are you doing here? Get out of my house!" Startled and afraid, Carla hurried through the darkness to the convent near her parish church, where she spent the nights for the rest of her visit. What was particularly unfortunate was that Carla, through therapy, had begun to understand the causes of her mother's aloofness and had envisioned this trip home as a happy reunion. Another sad complication was that Carla was unaware that her mother had spoken with pride to others of her missioner daughter's vocation and had even provided some of Carla's letters to the local newspaper for an article about her experiences with the Chilean poor.[39]

Carla did realize that her mother's behavior resulted from dementia, but the visit was painful, causing her to feel like "a little less than a basket case."[40] She left Appleton earlier than planned and headed for Maryknoll, where she attended the ordination of Skip Flynn.

In July Carla spent thirty days on a much-needed retreat at a Jesuit house in Wisconsin. By chance she ran across George Ganss, her spiritual advisor from college, who "saw anew her genuine religious spirit and her love of her vocation to Maryknoll."[41] She met Sister Bernice Fenske at the retreat, who recalled that Carla once "broke" during a liturgy:

> But always she went on. She shared with me her breakdowns in Chile, her rebirths, too. Her concern for her "beat-up-ole ladies" was a regular theme in the many times she [later] wrote me. One could tell how she gave of herself so utterly and completely until she was so down that there was nothing left to give. She had a very sensitive soul, a very artistic spirit, and a jolly (she used that word so often) quality that sparkled in her eyes...She said [the people in Chile] called the Sisters "*compañeras*"...because they were one of them.[42]

Carla had a way of showing up unexpectedly. Sometimes this was a delightful surprise, as when she turned up at the Maggiores' home in June instead of in August as planned. The couple felt privileged to hear Carla's take on the situation in Chile, much of which was being ignored by the U.S. press. But when Carla showed up at her brother Jim's doorstep, clutching her tote-sack and "looking like a bag lady," she felt the awkwardness between them and cut the visit short. Her stay with Betty and her brother-in-law in Michigan, thankfully, was pleasant.

As her furlough was ending, Carla tried to prepare herself emotionally for the ten-day final visit to Appleton. She was anxious to return to Chile and again found it impossible to relate to her family. But "just as she felt that her family did not understand her mission work," wrote her friend and biographer Maggiore, "perhaps Carla could not understand or accept their lives." Distressed by her visit, she promised never to return to Appleton. Carla also bluntly told her friend, former Maryknoll sister Patricia Cobb McKenny, now married and living on Long Island, that her lifestyle was extravagant, putting an end to their friendship.[43] Carla simply could not tolerate the rift between the poverty of La Bandera and the consumerism of the U.S.

After her return to Chile, Carla reentered therapy. She was reunited with Ita, but now Connie was at Maryknoll discerning whether to return to Chile. Both Ita and Carla wrote to her, saying that they wanted her back with them. Carla wrote: "I believe you... have a certain call to work with the poor and the native church...I support whatever decision you make. Know you are wanted and needed... [although] I'm no prize to live with."[44]

Characteristically, Ita, listed her thoughts precisely. The fact that she found seven points in favor of Connie's return to La Bandera, while listing four in favor of accepting a new assignment, stacked the deck in favor of Connie's return. The first point Ita made perhaps gave Connie pause: "The region needs the 'moral assurance' of sisters returning after being in the States."[45] Connie did return and remained in Chile for six more years.

While Carla was in the U.S. she had missed the July Assembly of Maryknoll's Regional Governing Board (RGB), so she summarized her twelve years as a Maryknoll missioner in a very honest and humble letter of gratitude, briefly excerpted here:

> I recognize myself as far from the well-rounded mature religious I'd have a "vision" of being... Because of my personal problem [the RGB] helped me see a bit my own weaknesses and suggested I get professional help, and encouraged me when I didn't always see the best results... Since I've been in Bandera, the RGB has been a big help when there were situations with which I could not cope... They've given me support when I felt pretty beaten-up.
>
> Why do I say all this? Maybe just to say that my vision of the RGB is one of a weaker member of the region who needs someone to help them along the *camino*...I owe [the RGB] recognition and support... for the caring that is given.[46]

Ita and Carla often prayed together, sometimes late into the night, and leaned on each other as they pondered the mystery of suffering and resurrection. They could see that Chile was going through its Good Friday of the soul and reflected on that theme, Ita in her prose and Carla in her poetry. In *Orientation*, a newsletter circulated internally by the sisters, Ita wrote:

I see Chile deeply experiencing the paschal mystery, with the light of Easter still to come. We can't wish away the suffering. Like Christ, how many times have we asked with the people, "Father, if it's possible, let this pass." Yet it seems the cup cannot pass without our drinking it.

The challenge that we live daily is to enter into this mystery with faith. Am I willing to suffer with the people here, the suffering of the powerless, the feeling impotent? Can I say to my neighbors—I have no solutions to this situation; I don't know the answers, but I will walk with you, search with you, be with you. Can I let myself be evangelized by this opportunity? Can I look at and accept my own poorness as I learn it from other poor ones?[47]

In these stanzas from "Paschal Mystery in Third World," Carla saw the suffering of Good Friday finally giving way to the light of Easter and the beginning of a new hope-filled struggle:

Sleeping eyes open,
Watching eyes understand,
Understanding eyes sparkle;
The Easter Sun dawns.

Humility speaks truth,
Meekness defends rights,
Oppressed listen to oppressed;
The Easter Earthquake begins.

Bleeding feet walk,
Wounded hands join,
Hungry voices sing;
The Easter Message appears.

Solitaries form groups,
Groups develop strength, but
Strength encounters force;
The Paschal Moon rises.[48]

After almost five years in a poor *población*, Ita had evolved in her understanding of mission and shared her insights in a letter to several sisters, noting that the switch from an outdated "doing for" to "working

with" the poor presented frustrating challenges. She wrote: "Our concepts of time, efficiency, providing for the morrow, a certain 'calculating'
side of us doesn't jibe with the culture of the poor."

> Working with the poor calls for a great restraint and modesty on
> all levels so as not to overpower, overcome, or take over the situ-
> ation...Working with the poor means promoting [empowering]
> and then allowing the person to be subject of his own destiny,
> instead of forming him in our own image...Being with the poor
> means overcoming our distaste of getting dirty literally and
> metaphorically: the literal dirt, mud, excrement; caring for and
> supporting the sinner, the underdog, and unpopular causes; en-
> tering into messed-up lives; running the risk of being misunder-
> stood, misinterpreted, of being accused as subversives, etc....
>   Our experience of trying to live simply...has allowed the
> possibility of being "just a neighbor" with whom one exchanges
> recipes [and] cuttings of plants, borrows extra dishes or chairs
> when visitors arrive, invites to family events.[49]

In August 1977, Ita was due to return to Maryknoll for her year of
Renewal and Reflection and final vows. She got a postponement till the
following spring because she did not want to leave Chile. She believed a
year to be a "very long time to reflect about something I'm already convinced of."[50] She was also concerned that Carla, who often became
downhearted, might need her for stability.[51] In the end it was the fragile
Carla who realized that Ita—the usually perceptive, clearer thinker—was
emotionally drained, and she gave her the push she needed to leave.

When Ita arrived in New York, her family saw what Carla had seen.
This "gentle and vivacious" woman, as her brother, Bill, described her,
was in need of a lengthy respite.[52] As Mildred Ford described Ita's home-
coming:

> We all went to meet her at the airport and I had lots of food I
> remembered she especially liked...We all talked and ate but Ita
> didn't talk all that much and ate only bread. I'm sure the variety
> and quantity seemed extravagant. For some weeks she was de-
> pressed...She was also physically drained. Like many others she
> had those microbes in her digestive track.[53]

Maryknoll Sister Rachel Lauze remembered Ita at this time as a
"seething volcano," haunted by the ignorance she perceived in her own

country concerning Chile and its people.[54] Other friends observed that for the first time in her life, she finally looked her age: "The suffering was there, the acuteness of it, and the tragedies...She was a scarred person..., physically worn."[55]

It took some time, but Ita finally perceived what others already knew—she needed professional help to deal with her anger and depression. She began to see a psychiatrist. Realizing that she had to address her prayer life also, she asked John Patrick Meehan, president of Maryknoll Seminary, to be her spiritual advisor: "From the first she was very open and honest about herself...She found prayer cold, empty, dark and useless but kept trying. In what proved to be a short time the Spirit began to touch her...From that point on she began to experience true contemplative prayer and the peace, love and joy that accompany it."[56]

As her retreat notes revealed, reaching the "peace, love and joy" was a process:

> The Lord is bigger than my...hang-ups...Of course you have weaknesses, defects...Yet all around, spring is bursting forth... Let go and experience all the love that is in and surrounds you...
>
> If the new creation is on its way or here, I don't want a malnourished, deformed, neglected self—but one that's alive—that hands on the good news, that lives it...What seems to be slowly happening is an acceptance of the truth of who I am... how I've been gifted for others.

About midway in her notes, Ita thought it was possible she was being "loved and led for larger purposes":

> Maybe this year is to tune into where the Spirit is leading you— you with your own history and future..., as the individual loved and led for larger purposes...It all adds up to something...see the mistakes, your own detours...Let it all be lighted up to see what comes next.

At the end of her notes, Ita recorded an intimate dialogue she had with Jesus, which ended with a nudge from him: "Come on, Ita—the hurdles are clear—I've done that for you too. I've been waiting for you and I'm glad you've come. We have a lot to talk about."[57]

During this year of renewal, Ita, as a Maryknoll sister having served abroad for several years, was expected to inform others about what she had learned from her experience. When an interviewer asked about the people in La Bandera, Ita described them: "They are very unsophisticated but very open...You go to someone's house and they [put] a chair on the dirt floor..., take a rag and dust the seat of the chair and say, 'Sit down'...And it's like a throne...You never go into anybody's house where they do not want to serve you something and it offends them not to serve." She also contrasted the individualism of Americans to the solidarity she saw in Chile: "The poor say, 'We, the poor.' Even if a man has a job...he stands with [his] people...I've come to understand what solidarity means...The focus is on the group, because individuals are never going to make it."

When the interviewer asked her how her expectations had changed from when she entered Maryknoll, Ita mused:

> In 1961 I think I went in...with the feeling that I had received a great deal and wanted to say thank you. What it means now— What's more important to me now is building the Kingdom [of God], trying to understand just what the future might be, if there really were bread for all the people, if there really were justice. There're a lot of things that are very uncomfortable about being there, but it's... the right place to be...I can't say it's my place forever and ever.[58]

In another interview, Ita gave a little history of her experience in La Bandera: When the sisters had moved into the *población*, one man had exclaimed, "The church has changed!" "How?" Ita asked, and he replied: "Before, we had to go up to the church. Now the church has come to us." She told her listeners about the unemployment and repression following the 1973 coup and described the solidarity that flourished in its wake, as the people pulled together to help those families whose children were hungry because the breadwinner was unemployed. Out of this had emerged the *comedores infantiles*—the children's dining rooms—so that the hungry would at least have one meal a day.

Another reason that children were so hungry was that many fathers had "disappeared," explained Ita, and the family's problems would multiply. If the wife of a *desaparecido* looked for work she would be unlikely to succeed if it was known that her husband had been picked up by the police, even if unjustly. Yet her children were hungry: Should she shame her husband by saying he had left her? But "this would go against her soul as a victim."

Sometimes those in authority would destroy records, arguing that a person had never existed, Ita told her listeners. So the church and other groups created lists of the disappeared and collected evidence from witnesses who had seen the person being taken away. "It's the church's natural role to be the voice of those who have no voice," said Ita: "The church has an innate role in . . . serving the most abandoned and right now there is the opportunity in Chile to really focus on this. Especially, I would say, in insisting on the truth. When something happens . . . , often the church's role is to investigate what is really taking place, telling the truth so that society does not [become like] the monkeys who don't want to see anything, hear anything, or say anything, out of fear."[59]

When Ita had arrived for her year of renewal, she had not been quite herself with her family; she felt it and so did they. But the year-long period of reflection had allowed them all time to overcome this. Her mother wrote: "Before she returned to Chile for the last time she was apologizing to us all for the bad time she gave us on her arrival."[60]

Before Ita was to return to Chile, her girlfriends treated her to a night out in nearby Tarrytown. Kathy and Ana wondered if Ita was comparing the grim problems of Chile to their trivial complaints about home repairs and high mortgage rates but "she listened in tolerance." When the bill came to fifty dollars a person, they were embarrassed about how many poor could be fed with that. Then, as often occurred when these three got together, the evening turned raucous: "We laughed and laughed and laughed and we got thrown out of the place because we laughed so much and we went across the street . . . to Howard Johnson's where we laughed even more because I being quite fat [and] active on the women's softball team—I was one of the thinnest ones—got up in the middle of Howard Johnson's and explained how I hit home runs and whatever and we got thrown out of there. We laughed and laughed so hard."[61] One can only imagine what a gift Kathy and Ana had given Ita, who was able to let go completely that night and just "laugh and laugh and laugh."

Ita's reflection year had been fruitful emotionally, spiritually, and intellectually. She had given interviews to inform Americans on the church, the people, and the struggles of Chile and edited the committee papers of the sisters' 1978 General Assembly. But one thing she was not in a hurry to do was renew her vows, viewing this merely as a "canonical requirement": "By the time I made my commitment in 1972, I had been through an eleven-year period of clarifying what my call was . . . Being reasonably sure myself and more confident in God's faithfulness, my commitment was for life . . . " Ita decided to postpone her vows.[62]

Ita wrote those words in May 1979 at a retreat house in Watch Hill, Rhode Island, during the final retreat of her reflection year. The day after it ended, she joined three friends who were headed for Massachusetts for a short vacation. On the highway just beyond Watch Hill, a freakish hit-and-run accident occurred in which Ita alone was injured. It was night-time, and none of the four saw exactly what happened, but they believed that the car that hit theirs had been traveling toward them when it inexplicably swerved sharply and rammed the left rear door where Ita was sitting. So, instead of departing for Chile, Ita found herself recovering for six months from a broken pelvis and torn knee.

Ita's attitude during the month-long stay in the hospital and her convalescence at the Watch Hill retreat house surprised many—particularly her spiritual advisor, who expected that the long recovery period would cause a relapse of depression. Instead, Ita was cheerful and exercised tirelessly to hurry along the day when she could return to Chile. Meehan noticed that she grew spiritually then, perhaps seeing this setback as "preparation for something."[63]

While Ita recuperated during mid-1979, the explosive events in Central America captured her thoughts. The struggle in Nicaragua against the dictator Somoza had intensified that spring, and the Maryknoll sisters worried about the safety of their missioner friends running a refugee center in León in the midst of the fighting. In July 1979, Somoza fled the country and the war ended. Ita admired the nuns who had stayed to help the people while civil war raged around them.

The tiny country of El Salvador was also increasingly in the news. One voice was heard beyond its borders speaking out for the poor in a way that Ita found compelling. The man with the charismatic words was Archbishop Oscar Romero. In the summer of 1979 he appealed to Spanish-speaking church personnel to come help his people. His call merged with the pledge of the Maryknoll Sisters, who had stated at their recent Assembly: "Solidarity with the poor is not an option but a sign of the Kingdom that must be made explicit in our day. We commit ourselves to the cause of the poor through the witness of our lives, our words, and our ministry."[64] Ita began to consider serving in El Salvador as a possible future for herself. It is possible that reflecting on a new purpose in life propelled her along the road to full recovery.

She kept these thoughts under wraps, however. By November, she was walking with no trace of a limp. Her doctor pronounced her fit, but jokingly advised her "to avoid countries where she might have to run."[65] Along the way back to Chile she planned to stop in Nicaragua to visit the Maryknoll sisters there, including her friend Julie Miller. Before she left the U.S., Ita told Julie by telephone that she was thinking about volunteering for El Salvador. Julie was dismayed: "No, not you, Ita. Not El

Salvador after the Chile coup and now this accident."[66] But high on Ita's agenda in Nicaragua was to discuss with friends a move to El Salvador.

Back in La Bandera, Carla had been working closely with community leader Miguel Cruz, who had overseen the building of a little chapel. He recalled Carla fondly as "the Sergeant," assigning chores to everyone from her lists and plans.[67] "Next to your beautiful church it looks like a shack," Carla wrote to Betty and Jack, "but to me it's a sacrament of the effort of these people." They had no priest, so Carla directed the first celebration:

> One of the ladies [began with] a prayer asking pardon for all the ills that affect us—the hunger, the violence, the oppression ... Instead of the Gloria, all the people said what they praised God for... [For the creed], one of the women said what she believed in and why, which was very powerful... Then for the offertory I had asked each family to bring a piece of bread [which they broke into pieces]. We all thought about what our commitment to one another is... I went around with a basket and each one as they dropped their piece of bread in said what their commitment was that week. The men said, "I commit myself to work for the daily bread of my family"... The women committed themselves to... working in the dining rooms for the undernourished kids, and the kids committed themselves to their studies. Instead of communion I asked the men to give out the bread, [the] sign of our commitment to one another..., the ole beat-up men saying as they gave out the bread: "This is the bread of my commitment and yours."[68]

Although not keen on traveling, Betty made the long trip to Santiago in November 1978 for several reasons: She missed Carla and knew her sister wished for more frequent and detailed news from home. There was also the necessity to discuss a nursing home for their mother, and Carla seemed reluctant to take that step. Not understanding Spanish, poor Betty had a terrifying experience with authorities at the Santiago airport over paperwork, and seeing armed men everywhere made it worse. Although very fearful during the entire visit, she won the hearts of all she met in La Bandera, probably, Carla said, because "you're so gentle... and I'm so wicked and mean you were a welcome relief!"[69]

Mrs. Piette did go into a home soon thereafter. Carla happily passed on some good news to her sister: Her friend Jackie and her mother had visited Mrs. Piette and found that she had friends there at the home—one was a friend of their father's from World War I—and was even able to recognize her visitors. Carla was thankful the troubling situation had been resolved: "Little by little I believe more and more that the Lord's ways certainly aren't our ways but that He manifests His love for us in the circumstances of our life the way it is."[70]

Carla had been looking forward to Ita's return in May 1979, and when that was delayed due to Ita's accident, she became dejected. Carla was getting restless again—she had been in Santiago for seven years and in Chile for fifteen. "She felt her faith slipping out from under her feet," Connie said. "She felt there was too much evil [in Chile] and she didn't believe that good would triumph over evil."[71] Her friend Rebecca Quinn was alone in Coelemu, a country town south of Santiago. Becky invited Carla for a stay and in October 1979 Carla left for Coelemu.

Becky Quinn, eight years older than Carla, was a motherly woman, who related to Carla much the way Betty did. They had worked together for several years in Chillán and had established a lasting friendship. Now Carla's spirit was revived in Coelemu. It was Becky, it was being in the country, it was the kindness of the people. Friends recalled Carla as saying that she "had died in Bandera," but after being in Coelemu for two months, Carla was cheerful and more creative than ever. According to Becky, the most surprising things happened to Carla during her short stay. She went to nearby Chillán one day and ran into Mariano, the young man who had joined Carla's second-grade class at age fourteen and now, seven years later, was working in Argentina. He too happened to be visiting Chillán that day. Carla also discovered that three girls she had taught had entered religious life because of her influence. There were so many happy moments and coincidences that Becky jokingly told Carla she must have a direct pipeline to God.

Carla was full of gratitude and joy in Coelemu: "I didn't even have a room but rather slept in the hall, and...we had to eat with the priests, which I can't say I enjoy. However, I came to love the work so much that even the priests weren't hard to take and...I enjoyed them as good brothers with whom I could joke and fight and really learn from."[72] This peaceful sojourn was just what she needed after seven years in grim *poblaciones* and six years of repression under the dictator Pinochet, but Carla did not view it as a potential next assignment.

After a year and a half on different continents, Ita and Carla were reunited in Coelemu and enjoyed a rustic, peaceful Christmas there with the people. It was to be their last Christmas. Ita had stopped off in Nicaragua on her way to Chile and discussed with her Maryknoll friends whether to volunteer for El Salvador. These sisters had just been through one civil war and were not ready to face another long, bitter conflict; rather, they felt they should stay and work with Nicaraguans to rebuild their country. Yet, since only two Maryknoll sisters were serving in El Salvador, the need was pronounced. Despite her friend Julie's misgivings, this visit no doubt contributed a "pro" to the mental list of pros and cons Ita was gathering on whether El Salvador would be her next mission destination. Carla, however, was leaning strongly toward Nicaragua.

By early January, Carla and Ita were back in Santiago. The Maryknoll sisters of Chile gathered for a retreat and reflected prayerfully on the call for more religious personnel to go to Central America. Ita and Carla listened to the reservations expressed by some as to the advisability of such a move for them, especially considering Ita's recent accident and Carla's bouts with depression.[73] But Ita continued reflecting on the possibility of El Salvador, while Carla went ahead with her plan to leave for Nicaragua by mid-January.

As that day neared, there were beautiful farewell testimonies for Carla. She would be very much missed, but it was obvious she was leaving behind "a lot of solid work" in La Bandera.[74] Before leaving Chile, Carla visited Pedro Pérez, a spiritual advisor she had often consulted while in La Bandera: "It is not often that I have known a person as restless and admiring of Jesus as Carla . . . A simple woman, with humor, conflictive in matters of justice and humble." Padre Pérez thought that Carla seemed very tired and recommended she not go to Central America, but "she was very firm about her ideas and plans [and] she never wavered."[75]

Stopping over in Lima and Panama, Carla delighted in being "a Pilgrim again." She wrote of rainbows and tears of joy, but sometimes reflected on her years in Chile with "attacks of nostalgia." In a letter to Becky, Carla referred to her lifelong clown persona: "My praying habits are changing as I've come to favor the night time since it's cooler and the stars link me to the past. Also night is quite sacramental in so far as it's still unknown where I'll hang up my clown."[76] Carla playfully characterized God as "*el dueño del circo*," the ringmaster directing the circus whose generosity and love would continue "wherever I end up."[77]

Carla spent a few weeks in Ocotal, Nicaragua, and when the sisters of the area gathered to discuss the need for missioners in El Salvador, Carla, the itinerant Pilgrim, volunteered to check it out. But it was difficult to enter El Salvador, where an undeclared civil war was heating up. Referring to the country by its English translation—the Savior—Carla had to wait for "the Lord of complicated cases" to solve the problems she was encountering entering "Saviorland" from revolutionary Nicaragua.[78]

Once in El Salvador, Carla saw firsthand the need for the experienced, Spanish-speaking missioners Archbishop Romero had requested for his troubled country. Maryknoll Sister Madeline Dorsey—alone—was managing a health clinic for four thousand shantytown dwellers, and Sister Joan Petrik was running a rural parish without a resident priest. Carla heard Romero's Sunday homilies on the radio and was inspired by the love the people had for their outspoken archbishop. She returned to Ocotal, now viewing El Salvador as a distinct possibility for "hanging up her clown." Shortly thereafter, César Jerez, Jesuit provincial for Central America, visited Ocotal and may have clinched her decision. Carla asked him which would give greater glory to God—serving in Nicaragua or El Salvador? His honest answer? El Salvador.[79]

Meanwhile, in Chile, Ita wrote her mother, carefully introducing her, probably for the first time, to the idea that her daughter might be going to El Salvador:

> Around the time of the operation, I began to get interested in El Salvador...After meetings in different countries, it's now been decided that Nicaragua and Salvador—for different reasons—are both [Maryknoll] priorities for Latin America...In a couple of weeks, I should...see if I fit into what they want...What even makes Salvador a question is the Congregation seeing that it's very important to support Archbishop Romero. [80]

After conferring with the sisters in Chile, asking others for their prayers, and scrupulously examining her motives for wanting to work in El Salvador, Ita finally made her decision. She attempted to break the news gently to her mother by letter:

> The last week or two—on my part—have been mostly spent letting the El Salvador possibility roll around inside me. Then I went to the new House of Prayer...[and] went through the old Ignatian process of the pros and cons, besides reading my guts. What I came to and feel good with is a decision to go...I think within a week or two it should be finalized...I realize this isn't the greatest news I've ever given you and, in fact, one of the cons was that the family would not be overjoyed, but I think it's a good decision.

And to ease the blow, Ita cheerfully observed, "I'll also be a continent nearer!"[81]

In the end, Carla's and Ita's different trains of reasoning and their exploration of various future paths had converged on El Salvador. Why? The example of the Maryknoll sisters who had stayed in Nicaragua despite the danger during the recent civil war was inspirational—as was the courage of Romero to defy authorities within the Salvadoran power structure. Romero's call for missioners to "accompany" him was urgent and compelling. The years that Carla and Ita had spent in Chile had strengthened their character and deepened their compassion. And they were fortified with the profound belief that they had a role to play in bringing about the Kingdom of God.

At the same time, another Maryknoll sister, Maura Clarke, was going through a similar discernment process. After three years in the United States, should she return to Nicaragua to help with the rebuilding effort? Or should she volunteer for El Salvador? Where was the greater need? All three sisters would ultimately offer themselves to the suffering people of El Salvador.

Chapter 11

Maura Clarke

Maryknoll Sister

Maura Clarke

Maura Clarke was born in New York City on January 13, 1931, the first child of John and Mary McCloskey Clarke. Although she was baptized Mary Elizabeth, her Irish-born parents Gaelicized her name and affectionately called her Maura. The Clarkes had two more children, James and Julia, nicknamed Bud and Judy. After the birth of Bud, the family moved from the Bronx to Rockaway, Queens. Because Rockaway was a popular summer resort for New York urban dwellers, rents rose each year with the approach of hot weather. The Clarkes could not afford the escalating prices, so they would often move away in the summer, only to return in the fall when rents were more reasonable.

Like most Irish immigrants, the Clarkes were willing to struggle and sacrifice so they could give their children a Catholic education. Maura attended Saint Francis de Sales Elementary School and Stella Maris Academy (high school), where she applied herself diligently to her studies and received good grades. She made friends easily and in high school participated in several extracurricular activities including the yearbook, sodality, Glee Club, and the Catholic Students' Mission Crusade, where she first heard about the Maryknoll Sisters and their work in "exotic, far-away lands."

Maura entered Saint Joseph College for Women, a small liberal arts school in Brooklyn, where she majored in elementary education and worked after school to earn money for her education. "Typically, though," commented Sister Judith Noone, "she did not save a dime but bought presents for her parents and siblings." This reckless, Saint Francis-like generosity was a trait that would always remain an endearing quality. As Sister Margarita Jamias, who worked with Maura in both Nicaragua and the U.S., noted: "She would give whatever she had to the poor... We were laughing the other day remembering how in Nicaragua she was always drawing advances on her monthly allowance (about $15), because as soon as she got it, she gave it away."[1]

Sister Kay Kelly, who was working at the time in the countryside outside of Siuna, Nicaragua, but would return to the town at the end of each week, remembered once confronting Maura with being an easy mark:

> Maura could never say NO to anyone so there was a constant line at the door asking her for money. She would give her whole allowance. One day... our cook told me that those who came would tell their friends that Maura was a soft touch. I remember telling Maura this and her being so angry with me because, as she said, "You're not here every day and don't have to answer the door and tell the people 'I don't have money' when you know we have it."[2]

In one of her last letters to her parents from El Salvador she asked for a pair of shoes—the pair she owned she had given away to a poor peasant woman. Sister Peggy Healy, who had delivered the new shoes from the Clarkes, commented after Maura's death that she just did not know how to say no.[3]

During her freshman year at St. Joseph's, Maura began to think seriously about entering Maryknoll. After discussions with her parish priest and parents, she applied and was accepted into the novitiate. But before she left for the convent, her mother took her and Judy on their first trip to Ireland, so they could see the birthplace of their parents and meet their Irish relations. Several of Maura's relatives had fought for Irish independence, and her father, inspired by the famous 1916 Easter Monday Rising, had even taken an oath of allegiance to the Irish Republican Brotherhood. Indeed, from her earliest years, Maura had listened countless times to her father and his Irish friends in Rockaway as they romanticized over a few glasses of whiskey about the "glorious" struggle against English oppression. In Ireland she now heard similar stories from her uncles and aunts. She loved listening to these tales and they made a lasting impression, creating within her a strong sense of identification with oppressed people the world over.

In September 1950 Maura began her novitiate. She progressed smoothly and in 1954 received her bachelor's degree from Maryknoll Teachers' College. She hoped to be assigned to the African missions and was slightly disappointed when she was sent instead to teach first grade at Saint Anthony of Padua School in the Bronx. Although the Bronx lacked the romance of faraway places, its impoverished Puerto Rican and black students could surely use her teaching skills. Besides, her new assignment was not far from the Rockaways, so Maura could see her parents and siblings often.

Located in an area with one of the highest crime and unemployment rates in all of New York City, the school did provide a beacon of hope. But teaching first-graders at Saint Anthony's was no "soft job," and Maura would soon become acquainted with the dismal results of poverty:

> Beyond the red brick walls [of St. Anthony's], drugs, prostitution, related crimes, and the accompanying violence—though camouflaged by day—raged undisguised at night. The sounds of shattering glass, screeching tires, drunken cries, a shot in the night were so common that a certain insensitivity towards tragedy seemed to hang in the air. Maura never grew accustomed to hearing the children's stories about their mothers being beaten, their fathers slashed, their brothers shot, their sisters raped. At first she was incredulous and then saddened when she realized...how many children were apparently deprived of the love with which she had been lavished.
>
> "Sister," a surprisingly obstinate little boy called out in class one day, "if God's a father, Sister, I don't want nothing to do with him and I sure don't want him messing around with me!"[4]

An entry from the sisters' "Bronx Diaries" graphically described "normal" life in the neighborhood where St. Anthony's was located:

> A two year old baby fell out of a 5th floor tenement window. There was a very quiet commotion for about 10 minutes while the ambulance took the hysterical mother and dead child to the hospital. Then things returned to normal. People continued their conversations on the steps of houses, teenagers went back to their dice on the corner, the children finished their ice sticks and life resumed its shouting, tumultuous pace.[5]

Sister Richard Marie McKinney, who worked with Maura at St. Anthony's, recalled a murder that took place directly across from the convent. A woman screamed as she hung by her hands from a windowsill outside her tenement and her husband beat her fingers until she fell to her death.[6] Sister Pat Redmond remembered a child coming to school late and explaining that she was afraid to enter St. Anthony's because "there were stiffs right outside our door. They had taken an overdose or something." Several others, Redmond recalled, were murdered right next door.[7]

But for Sister Pat the constant noise was also very disturbing. "The thing that really got to me was all of the noise outside all the time, with the traffic and the children screaming and the people yelling at each other." Life in the Bronx was depressing and sometimes terrifying for the sisters, but they conquered their fear and did their job well. Maura, who came from such a loving family, was no exception. "Maura never said an unkind word about anybody," said Sister Richard Marie. "When kids came to school who didn't have breakfast, she would take them down [to the kitchen] to get them something to eat, but without making a fuss."[8] Sister Rita Owczarek remembered her as generous to a fault. She could never say no to beggars and when the shoeshine boy came to the convent on Sundays, she always paid him seventy-five cents even though the standard rate was fifty cents.[9] Maura went through a "baptism of fire" at St. Anthony's, but it no doubt prepared her for even more shocking experiences in Nicaragua and El Salvador.

In late 1959, Maura received a new assignment. She was to teach second grade in Siuna, Nicaragua, a small gold-mining town near the east coast. Another sister, Kay Kelly, was also assigned to Siuna; before long the two became best friends and remained so for life.[10] On October 9, the two enthusiastic—if somewhat nervous—young women bid farewell to Maura's parents at the airport. Kay remembered that while they awaited the arrival of their plane, an airline pilot, recognizing their religious habit, introduced himself as the father of a Maryknoll sister they both knew. As they prepared to board, the pilot turned to Mr. and Mrs. Clarke and said: "Thank you for giving your daughter to Maryknoll." These words came back to haunt Kay after Maura's murder: "Little did we realize the extent of the 'giving,'" she later thought to herself.[11]

The day the two newcomers arrived at their mission home was a day to remember. They were greeted not only by the missioners but by the school's fife-and-drum marching band as well. Siuna was a small town of about five thousand inhabitants near a similar pueblo, La Luz, where a Canadian multinational company had operated a gold mine since 1938.

Both towns provided laborers for the mines. Siuna was situated in a depression surrounded by mountainous jungle thick with green vegetation; to Maura and Kay, both from large urban areas, it was a wondrous and beautiful sight. Kay once mentioned this to a student only to be enlightened by her very different view: "We're trapped in a hole and there's no way out."[12] For most of the poor this was true. There were no roads into or out of Siuna—the town was accessible only by plane or by a long, arduous horseback ride through the jungle. The plane trip took only forty-five minutes to Managua, the capital, but that flight could be terrifying, said Kay:

> When the plane hit air pockets, it was really scary. I remember us going over on one occasion, when it was really turbulent. Maura and I were hanging on to each other and praying like mad. Meanwhile we tried to reassure the passengers as they looked to us for protection. They always felt safe somehow when a priest or sister accompanied them. But they didn't know we were just as petrified as they were...I remember on [our] first trip [Sister] Marie Lamond pointing out a wreckage of a plane that crashed on the mountain on the takeoff from Siuna. That was really encouraging news![13]

Maura and Kay needed to learn Spanish quickly if they were going to be of much benefit to their students. Soon they left for Colegio Monte María in Guatemala City for language studies. They remained there for six months, but did not attend formal classes. Instead, lay teachers were assigned to them and two other nuns on a daily tutorial basis. That arrangement did not turn out as planned. Two of the sisters on permanent assignment with the Colegio community contracted hepatitis. Short-handed, the other sisters called on Maura and Kay to fill in during their convalescence. This proved frustrating because the two spent so much time doing communal tasks that they were unable to concentrate on their studies. "We could see [their] needs," Kay later noted, "but also the urgency for us to learn the language since we had to go immediately to the classroom after language study." They debated whether or not they should bring up the dilemma to the convent superiors, but Maura was too timid to do so, promising Kay that "God would provide." The two felt their progress in Spanish was so inadequate that when Holy Week approached they made excuses to remain in Guatemala City rather than return to the Siuna community where their ignorance would be transparent to those relying on them to be prepared for the next school term. In time, Maura and Kay did become proficient in Spanish and would perform very effectively as grade-school teachers.[14]

The Siuna that the two Irish-American nuns returned to in mid-1960 was, like many towns in Central America, a social tragedy. The men toiled long hours for very low wages in the Canadian-operated mine. Most of the workers would eventually develop lung disease and then would be left to fend for themselves, with no disability or health insurance or worker's compensation. The miners and their families lived in long rows of dilapidated, unpainted, company houses. Because there was no running water, sanitary conditions were appalling. The shanties were infested with mosquitoes, vermin, and rats, and the children suffered continually from parasitic infections. Mortality rates, especially for infants and young children, were high. In one of Maura's most touching letters to her parents, she mentioned this sad fact of life:

> One dear little farm boy, Natividad, came the other day for his religion class; he stood there all ragged but happily smiling with his gift of a little bag of bread that he bought in the pueblo for the Madres. Today he came with big tears to ask for a coffin and clothes for his baby brother who died this morning. When I told him that he had a little saint in heaven, he answered, "I have four."[15]

Above the "hole," high on the mountain was "the Zone," the exclusive area where officials of La Luz Mining Company and their families lived in North American, suburban-style homes with beautifully landscaped flower gardens and green lawns. The Zone had its own golf course, private club, and swimming pool, a cruel contrast to the extreme poverty below. No one was permitted to enter the Zone except the Canadians, their guests, and of course their servants—the hired help from Siuna and La Luz. Armed Nicaraguan soldiers guarded this private domain from any potential interlopers.[16]

The wife of the director of the Zone was always very kind to the sisters. Sometimes she helped out at their clinic and on occasion gave small sums of money and material goods to some in the town who were especially impoverished. She and her husband once invited Maura and the other sisters to the Zone for Christmas dinner. Kay Kelly felt she was back in the U.S. again:

> Surrounded by beautiful, rolling green lawns, one house was more beautiful than the other with lots of space. The Zone was

located up on a hilly area so that you looked down upon the village below. We gazed out the window and felt as if we were in another world (we were!!!) . . . We nearly gagged on the *filet mignon* that was served by one of our villagers, who worked as the maid for the . . . family. [The director's wife] offered us one of the empty houses in the Zone if we wanted to get away for a day. I think we used it once or twice for a community meeting. Somehow we felt it a betrayal to our friends in the village to spend time in the Zone.[17]

In the early 1950s, the miners of Siuna and La Luz tried to better their dismal condition by organizing a union, but the leaders were fired by the company and blackballed so they could never get another job anywhere. The miners "got the message" and abandoned their attempts at unionization.[18]

Maryknoll sisters had first arrived in Siuna in 1944—upon news of their coming the people of the town built a school-convent complex for the *madres*. By 1959, when Maura arrived, a clinic had been added that treated, on average, a thousand people per month. While the convent was modest by U.S. standards, it was a palace compared to the hovels of the people. Each sister had her own small room, with a bed and desk, though at times they had to share quarters.

Since the residents of Siuna had little to do for recreation aside from frequenting the bars, Father Roderick Brennan, the Capuchin pastor, decided to have movies flown in from Managua for viewing each weekend in the parish auditorium-theater. Most of the films were quite dated, but they nevertheless proved a hit, especially with the young people. But sometimes the movies provided humorous, if slightly embarrassing, moments, for the sisters. Every time they would enter the auditorium, someone would call out in a loud voice, "*Alabado sea Jesús Cristo!*" ("Praised be Jesus Christ!") and all would come to attention. This was the way the children always greeted them as the nuns would enter the classroom. Only when the sisters answered "*Por los siglos de los siglos!*" ("Forever and ever!") did the audience again relax. To be the object of such reverence on social occasions was always disconcerting to the sisters but never more so than one evening when they entered the darkened theater late. Since all the ground floor seats were taken, they went up to the balcony, which to their embarrassment was filled with teenage couples hugging and kissing. "It was a riot," recalled one of the sisters. "Someone called out in a high voice '*Alabado sea Jesús Cristo!*' and all the young fellows who had been hugging their girls separated and came to attention." Another time, when there was a romantic scene Maura felt was risqué, she insisted that the nuns all get up together and immediately leave the auditorium, lest they give bad example. Some sisters tried to tell her she was being too prudish, but she insisted. So in the middle of the movie the sisters, dressed in their habits, all rose in unison and deliberately walked out.[19]

Although she loved to paint, because of her heavy workload Maura had little time for artistic creation. She would usually find a few moments, however, to paint a religious message on a rock or small piece of wood for the nuns' birthdays. On one occasion, a few of the sisters went to Poneloya on the Pacific coast for a few days of rest. Maura walked along the beach busily collecting seashells. Later she glued them in the shape of a cross to a wooden board and printed in beautiful lettering: "There is no greater love than this: to lay down one's life for one's friends." She gave her creation to Kay, who was upset over the recent murder of Félix Padro González, organizer of a *campesino* union. Kay treasured the plaque and later regarded it as a testimonial to Maura's own "no greater love" for the Central American poor.[20]

In 1962, Maura received news from Maryknoll headquarters in New York that surprised and disturbed her, but that also provided her with a new avenue for spiritual growth and deeper commitment to the poor. She had been appointed school principal and superior of the community of sisters at Siuna. Maura, one of the youngest sisters at the convent and with less mission experience than most of them, never saw herself as leadership material. She could not understand why she was chosen and was reluctant to accept the positions. She resigned herself to her new role, but only after telling the other sisters that her gifts did not include analysis and decision-making, so everyone would have to make special efforts to help her.[21]

Maura remained superior and principal for six years. During this time, due to the influence of the Second Vatican Council, the community —as well as the Maryknoll congregation as a whole—began to examine its entire way of life and decide if changes should be made. As Sister Laura Glynn would later explain, prior to the 1960s the nuns in Siuna had little sophistication when it came to matters of social justice:

> A consciousness of the social reality with its contradictions and exploitation was a slow process [for us]. The shocking poverty of the people brought more a response of compassion than of a realization of injustice...
>
> We didn't question American policy in Nicaragua, nor its complicity with the Somozas [Nicaragua's ruling family]...We

did not see the real importance of promoting people's organizations, not even that of the gold miners, whose working conditions were quite terrible. It's as if we thought that if we educated their children, they might escape the fate of having to work in the mines.[22]

Sister Bea Zaragoza's recollections were similar to those of Laura Glynn. Prior to Vatican II, she said, the sisters believed their purpose was to educate the youth of Siuna to prepare them for high school. The nuns were aware that the miners were not receiving a fair wage and that their working conditions were far from good, but they excused this by reasoning that the company's labor policies were fully in accordance with Nicaraguan law.[23]

But this simplistic thinking was about to be challenged during Maura's tenure as local superior. Inspired by Pope John XXIII's *aggiornamento*, some in Siuna's Maryknoll community insisted it was essential that the sisters develop a closer identification with the poor they had come to serve. They argued that their house with its plumbing, phonograph, furnishings, and stockpile of tasty foods from the U.S. branded them as outsiders and distanced them from the *campesinos*. They felt that their material well-being caused the poor to identify them with the upper class and that their relationship with the peasants was not one of equality but of paternalism. Maura, the "soft touch," had always given money and goods to needy families. But these sisters contended that such charity only maintained the unjust status quo. It would be better, they reasoned, for the missioners to address the causes of the people's misery, and this would mean a more active involvement in efforts to terminate institutionalized injustice. Some of them even questioned whether they should continue to run their school. Could others not be found to replace them as teachers, leaving them to pursue a more active ministry? A few even asked to be relieved of their teaching duties and sought permission to go out to the remote villages where they could immerse themselves more fully in the people's way of life.

Yet there were also more traditional nuns who, along with the bishop of the diocese, felt such views were too radical. They believed the sisters should continue to live as they always had. They were not overly disturbed about the comforts from home they enjoyed and felt that traveling on foot and by horseback to remote villages— to say nothing of sharing in the impoverished lifestyle of *campesinos*—was too rigorous and unacceptable for females.

Maura agonized over these alternatives. As community superior, she, more than the others, had to decide which course to follow. The weight she carried was greatly reduced though when she—along with all other local Maryknoll superiors worldwide—received a copy of Leo Joseph Cardinal Suenens's influential new book, *The Nun in the World*, from Maryknoll Mother General Mary Colman. Suenens urged nuns to examine their way of life in light of the original charism (mission) of their religious community and stated that they should not be restricted by an outdated semi-cloistered lifestyle that had for too long impeded them from reaching their full potential. They could play a more positive role in the world, he added, by immersing themselves more actively in the lives of the people they worked with, so as to better understand their needs.

Suenens's book made a deep impression on Maura and helped her decide that the sisters in Siuna had to move in a more activist direction. Two of the nuns were released from their teaching duties and allowed to accompany the Capuchin fathers on their mission trips to the small villages between Siuna and Managua. Lay teachers were gradually hired to free other sisters who then also joined the Capuchin fathers in their new ministry of empowering the poor.

The sisters began traveling to remote areas where they taught the basics of the faith, not by the old method—the expert teacher instructing students who listened passively—but by engaging the people in active dialogue. Villagers would be provided with Bibles published in basic Spanish and with short books of Bible stories in comic book form. They were encouraged to discuss what they read in terms of how the stories related to their own lives. Those who displayed leadership potential would be sought out and trained, and they in turn would instruct and train others in their villages. Eventually Christian base communities would be set up so that the people could continue to analyze and dialogue on the Bible when the priests and sisters were not present. This method of active learning was originally developed by the Brazilian educator, Paulo Freire, in the early 1960s and is described in his book, *Pedagogy of the Oppressed*. Its aim was to raise the consciousness of marginalized people—in Spanish this process was called *concientización*—so they could move beyond the fatalism that had permeated their outlook for centuries and now take charge of their own liberation from injustice.

While the sisters were making the transition from school teachers to pastoral associates, the community searched for a congregation of Nicaraguan nuns to take over their school. The Divina Pastora sisters, who were from Nicaragua and Spain, agreed to replace them,[24] so in December 1968 the Maryknoll women left Siuna permanently, some of them to pursue an apostolate living among the poor in the barrios of Managua.

Maura, however, returned to the United States where she made a retreat at Maryknoll and visited her family. When her mother took sick, she received permission to extend her visit to help her. Altogether, she spent about a year in New York before returning to Nicaragua. As her sister, Judy, later noted, during this time the family detected a change in Maura. She had come to believe that the "Band-Aid" approach to mission work—that is, treating the wounds that festered from poverty without attempting to change the unjust structures that had caused those wounds—was no longer enough. Missioners must toil alongside the people to bring change. To do otherwise was little more than meaningless.[25] Maura had undergone a radical transformation, and her traditional Catholic family did not at first know what to make of it.

Maura returned to her mission work, and this time she joined Sisters Bea Zaragoza and Rita Owczarek in the barrio of Miralagos on Lake Managua. The three nuns had taught together in Siuna; now they would work with three Jesuits to develop Christian base communities.

The Miralagos barrio was filled with thousands of poor families that had been displaced from their rural homes by rich landowners expanding agro-export businesses. With no fields to plant, *campesinos* had come to the city in hope of finding employment. Few would be successful. Those who were would be forced to work for extremely low pay; if they objected, they could easily be replaced by others from the endless stream of the unemployed. Soon after her arrival, Maura wrote her parents that Father Valentín Martínez had asked her to begin a new apostolate working in a poor area where she had been making home visits:

> Some of these poor people live in a one-room hovel—very dark and miserable. They sell in the market and just live hand to mouth. I am trying to get to know them and after a while we hope to form the Family of God, which is a way of trying to unite them to solve their own problems and to be formed in their faith through discussions at night.[26]

Just as they had during their last years in Siuna, Maura and the other sisters spent considerable time visiting homes, talking to the people, and listening to what they had to say. In this way the sisters learned about their struggles: the humiliations they faced daily; the grief they experienced when their babies got sick, often dying because of inadequate food or lack of money for medical treatment; the physical abuse women often endured at the hands of their frustrated spouses, who used alcohol and *machismo* to escape their sense of worthlessness. By listening to the people, the sisters came to understand what they had not fully realized when they taught school and lived a semi-cloistered life in Siuna, namely, how devastating the Somoza dictatorship was for the poor of Nicaragua.[27] As missioners, Maura no longer saw their goal as solely helping people reach heaven; she now believed it equally important to strive for justice so that the Kingdom of God would become a reality on earth.

While in Miralagos, Maura taught part-time in the public elementary school. In a letter to her brother and his family, who were finding it difficult to understand her nascent radicalism, she gently tried to explain the extreme poverty she encountered daily. Since Bud's wife, Carol, was an elementary school teacher, Maura addressed her directly:

> Carol, you would be saddened by the terrible conditions of the public schools where I teach Religion in the afternoons. They are dark, crowded and hot with miserable desks and so noisy— but I find the children wonderful. The sad thing is that the smoking of marijuana has begun here and a number of the boys I teach are trying it. It is sold so freely around here.[28]

Maura with residents of Miralagos, Nicaragua

Yet, as Maura explained in a letter to her parents, although living conditions were miserable, all was not negative in Miralagos. In the afternoons, the sisters met with a youth group they had formed and at night they were busy with Family of God meetings. These groups were flourishing and slowly but surely creating a sense of self-worth and empowerment among their members. But success could be exhausting: "Everything goes on all night here and so sometimes we don't get finished until about ten-thirty."[29]

On September 19, 1970, Somoza's security forces arrested several university students and teachers. When the government refused to release them, six priests and ninety students, led by Jesuit Father Fernando Cardenal, occupied the National Cathedral in Managua in protest. Word of their action quickly spread through the city, leading other young people to show solidarity by taking over other churches in the capital and in various parts of the country.

Maura enthusiastically supported the occupations, and in a letter to her parents noted that the student protesters reminded her of her father's younger years in Ireland, when he had struggled courageously against British oppression.[30] But her appeal to her father's "glory days" did little to diminish her parents' worries. Evidently they sent her a letter warning her to stay clear of any riots resulting from the occupations, because her next letter attempted to alleviate their uneasiness:

> Actually there really weren't any riots when they took over the churches and the cathedral...It was a very peaceful and disciplined protest and showed that the Church represented by the six priests who stayed with the students was fighting for the poor and suffering in contrast to the former image of a Church tied to the apron strings of a corrupt government. Don't worry, dear Hearts, I'll be careful and stay out of the riots and fights but we must do what we can to lend support to those who have the courage to give themselves for...change.

Maura touched on how the occupations highlighted the divisions in the Nicaraguan church; she also made clear to her concerned family which side she was on:

> A sad thing happened shortly after the incident of the churches. Four of our Bishops who are quite conservative denounced the action of the priests and students, thus showing themselves as siding with the government against most of the People of God who stood with the protesters. It was too bad they just didn't keep silent but we believe that they were pressured by the papal nuncio who is a representative from Rome.[31]

If she had intended to allay her family's worries, she had probably done the opposite, so she tried again in a second letter: "There was a protest on the part of a good number of priests. We did stay out. Don't worry Dad, we will be careful and pray more." She then added: "We have to be careful as the Guatemala affair did much harm to Maryknoll."[32] Although it might not seem so at first glance, this last sentence is significant.

"The Guatemala affair" Maura referred to was an attempt in 1967 by six Maryknoll priests and sisters to form a so-called "Christian guerrilla movement" in Guatemala. The six were immediately expelled from the country by their Maryknoll regional superior, once he learned of their actions, and all but one soon left the vowed religious life. Their conduct had inadvertently opened Maryknoll to a scandal that would taint its reputation—and by extension that of all U.S. Catholic missioners in Guatemala—almost beyond repair. On January 16, 1968, Guatemalan guerrillas, who had no connection with the six expelled missionaries, assassinated two U.S. military attachés in Guatemala City. The next day newspapers throughout the country attempted, falsely, to link the expelled Maryknoll missioners to the assassinations with bold front-page headlines about "Maryknoll guerrilla priests." Soon similar articles appeared in periodicals in the United States and elsewhere.

The so-called "Guatemalan affair" had been a devastating blow to Maryknoll, so much so that the Society made sure that all of its missioners understood the potential negative results for the entire Maryknoll community that could come from "overzealous behavior" by even a single member. Maura's mention of this "affair" indicated that she realized this and had no intention of involving herself in actions that could be construed as "imprudent." She did take part in a few demonstrations and on at least one occasion visited political prisoners. Yet, as her biographer, Eileen Markey, points out, she was always careful to avoid more dramatic actions that had the potential to draw attention to herself and the Maryknoll Society.[33]

In October 1970 Maura, her two coworkers, and about three hundred residents of the barrio were forced to relocate when an exceptionally rainy season caused the waters of Lake Managua to flood their homes. They were sent to an area about seven and a half miles from Managua called OPEN (Operación Permanente de Emergencia Nacional) Number Three. There, twenty-four hundred lots had been set aside for landless families with promises that eventually they would be granted ownership titles. However, once those lots were occupied, new families simply moved in along the periphery of the project, expanding the shantytown by several miles and increasing its population by the thousands. Maura still worked in Miralagos and was now forced to spend three hours traveling to and from OPEN Three to her job each day. She was therefore doubly thrilled to receive word that Kay Kelly was returning to Nicaragua to join the staff of the Instituto Promoción Humana, a lay organization in Managua. This meant not only that Maura would again enjoy the companionship of her close friend, but also that she could leave Bea and Rita at the distant OPEN community and rent a shack in the capital city with Kay and a third nun, Melba Bantay.[34] After about a year, the three were offered the third floor of a newly constructed parish center. They were reluctant to accept, since the residence was large and comfortable and therefore superior to the houses of the barrio. After much prayer and discussion, however, they decided to make the move, since the parish center would be rent-free and they could use the money saved on much-needed projects.

Shortly after midnight, on the morning of December 23, 1972, the three nuns were awakened by the tremors of a devastating earthquake, only to find themselves trapped within their home. A few days later Maura wrote to her parents describing the chilling event:

> We were violently awakened by a terrible shaking. The house seemed to be pulled completely off from its foundations and flying. I thought that it was our end but then the three of us called out to each other and ran down the three flights, barefooted and in our nightgowns and kimonas. We were very frightened when with all [the] efforts of the priests we couldn't get out of any door of the house. Another tremor [took place] and we thought the house would crush us. We climbed out the window of the second floor after breaking the glass. We had to tie sheets together to slide down and with the help of the priests and a small ladder we got down to the ground. Our whole city came down in a few seconds. Many, many people were crushed to death. Everyone ran all over trying to rescue people from below the cement walls crushing them.[35]

Kay Kelly took the story further:

> Maura's first concern was for all the people she knew in the parish. We heard that Carolina and her husband [Sergio, two friends who lived in the barrio] were trapped under the rubble about a couple blocks from where we lived. When we arrived at the site, Maura immediately jumped on top of the rubble to where someone said they had talked to Sergio trapped beneath.

She began to pray in English with him (in her excitement) until he said to her "Please pray in Spanish, I don't understand English." The men were able to free both of them finally but their baby girl died. Melba and I returned to OPEN to sleep the next night but Maura said she couldn't leave the people. The tremors continued for two or three more days. When I returned the next day to Managua, there was Maura walking down the street with [Father] Marciano, S.J., who was distributing communion to the people housed on the sidewalks in front of their belongings. Melba and Maura lived in Tent City with the people who were relocated there from Managua, which is another story of Maura's total identification with the poor.[36]

The tent city mentioned by Kay was called Campamento Esperanza (Camp Hope). It was one of several temporary camps built by the U.S. Army Corps of Engineers. Two priests lived there also and, together with Maura and Melba, they tried to alleviate the suffering of the homeless thousands. This task was made especially difficult by the Nicaraguan military, who forbade religious personnel to assist in the relief effort or to form prayer and discussion groups for the displaced.[37] The dictator Anastasio Somoza was pocketing the relief money sent from around the world. Evidently he feared that religious workers would refuse to "look the other way," and hoped that such restrictions on their activities would diminish criticism of his chicanery.

Just a few months after they had settled in Camp Hope, the problems of the homeless were further compounded, as Maura explained to her parents:

Our people from the tent camp just received the word that they will all be moved to a temporary housing project. It is a project of 5,000 small wooden houses, very poor with dirt floors which they will rent for about $6.00 a month. They will have a hard time paying this. We would like so much to go with our people and they keep asking us if we'll be with them. Right now we can't say because where they are being moved is a way out of our area ... They were sad about receiving the word so abruptly.[38]

In another letter sent to her brother a few days later, Maura explained why the Camp Hope residents were being moved on such short notice. The American embassy had just finished constructing a new facility on the adjoining property and embassy personnel did not want an eyesore filled with poor people next door. Maura ended her letter by expressing hope that the displaced people would feel confident enough to unite in a peaceful but strong protest against their unjust removal.[39]

If such a protest ever took place, it was evidently ineffective, because Camp Hope was promptly shut down and its inhabitants were displaced to a distant camp near Lake Managua. Maura and Melba did not accompany them. Instead, they returned to the community at OPEN, where Maura would serve for the next three years. She had plenty to do; so many of the homeless had relocated in OPEN that the barrio now held twenty-five thousand people.[40]

During this period of her apostolate, tensions mounted as opposition to Somoza and his Guardia increased. Toward the end of her last year in Nicaragua, an incident occurred which raised the usually diffident Maura to new heights of courage. The water company, in which the Somoza family had financial interest, decided to hike up the cost of water in the barrio to twice that for Managua. The people held emergency meetings, resolving not to pay the unfair increase. A committee of leaders was formed, leaflets were circulated throughout the barrio, and peaceful marches were held. Increased pressure, including violence, was brought to bear on the barrio people, but the protest went on for four months. At one point, the Guardia broke up a demonstration and attempted to arrest some of the protesters. Seeing what was happening, Maura stepped in front of a military vehicle and began smashing her fist on the hood, demanding that the soldiers release their prisoners. Not used to such aggressive behavior and afraid to antagonize an American citizen, they released the demonstrators. Maura's action may have prevented their torture or even saved their lives.[41]

In a June 1974 letter to her family, Maura described the violence and despair that the powerless women of Somoza's Nicaragua had to contend with almost daily:

> There has been a great deal of turmoil over a very tragic case of a *campesina* woman named Amada, who was taken into custody unjustly by the *guardia* (military) under suspicion for belonging to a union of farmers or something. She was raped by fifteen soldiers—a few of them officers—for about three or four days. This is one case but there are so many like it. The other women are afraid to reveal such a thing. This woman is beautiful and has a striking natural dignity. We went to the court to support her. Katie [Kelly] has especially been helping her.[42]

In a second letter written four months later, Maura kept her mother updated:

> [Amada's] case is coming up again and needs your prayers. This Sunday there will be an assembly and procession in silent support of her cause. We will be going with some of the women of the barrio... [Kay] has been very instrumental in fighting to unite people, priests, religious, and the bishop in Amada's cause. It is very hard for this reason for Kay to leave [for a new assignment in the U.S.] at this time.[43]

Although Maura in her many letters does not disclose the outcome of Amada's case, it is virtually certain that no soldier was indicted for the crime. Poor Nicaraguan women had to face every day knowing that they could suffer a fate similar to Amada's. Maura's letters do reveal, however, how valuable a role the U.S. sisters played in walking with the poor in their quest for dignity and justice. They also show how hard it was for the Maryknoll sisters to leave those Central Americans, with whom they had developed such close relationships, when they were reassigned to the United States.

But all was not so grim at OPEN Three. The team of Jesuit fathers and Maryknoll sisters was making progress in faith formation and *concientización*. In fact, in one of her frequent letters home Maura brimmed with pride when she mentioned that her team had formed a parish council with six men "who have shown real promise" and "a desire to serve the Church and to work towards liberation, as they see it quite clearly a part of their Christian Commitment." She must have pleased her father when she added, "[just] as you did in Ireland, Dad dear."[44]

In an August 1973 letter from Maura to her family, she mentioned that she and her religious coworkers had attended "a very important meeting" at OPEN where people from her barrio had discussed transportation issues. She added this significant comment: "So many men have lost their jobs because they can never reach their work on time. [But] the problem of this meeting was that we were afraid it was becoming political and they were trying to use us and the people—a strong Communistic group exists here in the pueblo."[45] After the December 1980 murders of Maura and her three fellow martyrs, members of the Reagan administration would callously accuse the sisters of being Marxist guerrillas. Maura's short comment above illustrated the absurdity of such a claim, showing that Maura and the other religious saw themselves as distinct from any communist group and were well aware of the pitfalls that could result if they unwittingly allowed themselves to be coopted.

In the fall of 1976, Maura received word that she was being reassigned to the U.S., where she was to work for the next three years. She had known for some time that such an assignment was coming, but, as often happened to missioners returning to the comfortable society of the industrialized world, she was thrust into deep depression soon after her arrival. "I entered into a time of sadness and deep loneliness and wept over my separation from the people I love, the Sisters, the Fathers, all. I saw the tortured people who fight for justice today in the place of Christ, and I pictured the rulers and the military as the high priests. I envisioned the poor... as the tortured Jesus."[46]

Maura knew all too well that justice for the poor in Central America must be won, in part, in the United States. The American people had to be made aware of their suffering and demand that their politicians alter U.S. policy to be more supportive of the poor against dictatorial military governments. Maura shook off her depression. For the next three years she partnered with Sister Jennie Burke and dedicated herself to what Maryknoll called "reverse mission." Together they conducted "World Awareness Programs" at churches and schools throughout the northeast. These workshops challenged the preconceived notions of middle-class Americans, who had always assumed that U.S. foreign policy was grounded in moral values and selfless generosity. When the sisters related the facts about what they had seen and experienced on their mission assignments, the workshops sometimes became tense and some participants expressed anger at what they considered the sisters' lack of patriotism. Maura, however, had the perfect temperament for such work and her calm demeanor and gentle nature often defused tensions.

Though far from Central America, Maura never ceased to follow closely the struggle of the Nicaraguan people against the Somoza dictatorship and lend moral support whenever possible. In July 1977, she joined Maryknoll Father Miguel d'Escoto and several others in an occupation of the Nicaraguan consulate to the United Nations, in hope that their action would publicize Somoza's misrule. When the New York police were called by embassy officials to arrest the protesters, Maura stepped forward and informed the officers that the consulate was outside their jurisdiction, since it was legally considered the property of the Nicaraguan people. The baffled officers, perhaps uncomfortable at being confronted by a nun, concluded that the best course to take was to allow the protesters to leave peacefully under their own volition.[47]

Although she found it difficult to speak in public, Maura was called on to do so in September 1978 at an anti-Somoza protest rally in Boston. When a college professor who was scheduled to speak had to cancel at the last minute, Maura was asked to take his place. Conquering her nervousness, she told of the poverty and atrocities she had witnessed during her missionary tenure, concluding with an eloquent appeal to President Carter and Congress to terminate support for the dictator.[48]

Like most Americans, she was horrified when on June 20, 1979, Somoza's soldiers, unaware they were being filmed by ABC news, dragged correspondent Bill Stewart from his automobile, forced him to kneel in the street, and executed him. Unlike most of her fellow citizens, she expressed her indignation with action. On July 15 she joined several other Christians at Riverside Church in New York in a prayer vigil and fast expressing solidarity with the Nicaraguan people.[49] Two days later, Somoza fled Nicaragua. Finally, Maura was able to join—if only in spirit—with her friends in Siuna and the barrios of Managua in celebrating their liberation from the Somoza family after forty-five years of U.S.-supported dictatorship.

As she read the joyful letters from the nine Maryknoll sisters who had remained in Nicaragua during the insurgency that toppled Somoza, Maura found that she had confusing emotions. She tried to explain this to her former mission colleagues in Managua:

> My dear hearts, I feel so proud of you—so full of awe and wonder at what you have suffered and witnessed. It is incredible... pure miracle... Somehow you have all taken on a new strangeness —special heroic [*sic*], and I fear not being able to relate to you— that you are different—changed—not the same sisters of mine ...after all you've been through and endured and learned to believe. Maybe I am sad in a way to have been left out of all that you have experienced—and yet for some reason the Lord wanted it this way.[50]

Maura's three years of mission awareness work were coming to an end. For a long time she had anxiously awaited the day she would return to Nicaragua. But, as she tried to articulate in her note, she felt a strange mix of emotions now that Somoza had finally been toppled without her being there to participate in the "pure miracle." On the one hand, she felt great joy as she read the letters from her jubilant former companions in the barrios of Managua and longed to be with them again. On the other, she sensed that she no longer belonged in the country where she had toiled with them for so many years. Perhaps, she wondered, God might be calling her to something new.

Around the time of Somoza's fall, she received word from the Maryknoll congregation calling for volunteers to serve in El Salvador in response to a plea from Archbishop Romero. As soon as Maura heard this, she began to ask herself if this was where God wanted her to work.

A few months after a "never-to-be-forgotten" August visit to Ireland with her parents and niece, Maura composed a Christmas letter to family and friends. In it, she waxed eloquent about the "new Nicaragua," but also hinted that it might no longer be the place for her:

> This past year will never be forgotten by the Nicaraguans and all those who love them because they have come to the beginning of a new freedom and suffered so much pain and death in order to bring forth this new life and hope...Our nine sisters, who lived through this revolution with the people..., tell us in their letters of the exhilarating hope and faith that the poor have for a better future in spite of the devastation and hunger that continues. They are striving to create something new in government that will truly be for the wellbeing of all the people of Nicaragua....
>
> In just a couple of weeks, I'll be finishing my three year commitment here in the [S]tates...[During] the months of January through May, I will be participating in a Mission Renewal Program, which is a time of study, prayer and reflection before returning to Nicaragua or Salvador in June.[51]

By mid-January she had almost concluded that God was calling her to El Salvador, but, as she expressed to Jennie Burke, a small degree of uncertainty still lingered: "Since El Salvador has been made a priority for Sisters with some Latin American experience I may be going there. This I must pray about and discern so that I will not be naïve and go on superficial motivation, but by what the Lord wishes only."[52]

The assassination of Archbishop Romero of San Salvador on March 24, 1980, caused great concern on the part of her family and friends, nearly all of whom pleaded with her to stay out of harm's way and return to Nicaragua. But far from discouraging Maura, the death of the charismatic archbishop only strengthened her belief that this troubled country was where she should be. Later, after Maura's death, Mary Clarke would remember that as she watched her daughter struggling with the decision about her future, she saw, with some sadness, that El Salvador would be Maura's new mission home.[53]

Perhaps at least partly in deference to the pleas of her loved ones, Maura resolved to visit her friends in Nicaragua before making her final decision. She did this in July 1980, and at the end of the month, she wrote two letters on the same day, one to "family and friends" and the other to her parents. In the first she wrote how exhilarating it was to be back finally in OPEN Three, now called Ciudad Sandino, where she had joined the thousands who gathered in the plaza to celebrate "the first anniversary of liberation." She enthusiastically relayed how "thousands of young students and teachers" were going to the isolated countryside to teach those who never before had the opportunity to learn how to read and write. She proudly proclaimed that the fledgling Nicaraguan government was increasing food production, constructing new roads, and creating housing for the poor, while the poor, with the government's blessing, were forming grassroots neighborhood organizations that would enable them to have a voice in the new government. She closed by noting how "very hopeful" she felt about the role the church was playing in standing with the poor during this transition.[54]

It would seem that Maura had decided to remain in Nicaragua. But her second letter, the one to her parents, revealed another possibility: "I would really love to stay here in Nicaragua where there is so much to do, but I know I must go to El Salvador to see if it is right for me to be there ... Don't worry about me. The Lord takes care of us all. If I see that it isn't the place for me I'll return to work in Nicaragua very soon." She reminded them—and herself: "We must not be afraid. No matter what happens we are one with God and with one another."[55]

A few days later, on August 5, 1980, Maura boarded a plane for El Salvador.

CHAPTER 12

Carla, Ita, and Maura

Chalatenango

arla arrived first in El Salvador. She traveled by bus from Nicaragua to San Salvador, where Sisters Madeline Dorsey and Joan
Petrik met her on March 24, 1980. They drove from there
northwest to the city of Santa Ana. By the time they reached Colonia Lamatepec, a shantytown on the outskirts of Santa Ana where Maddie lived
and ran a health clinic, it was about nine o'clock.

Things did not seem quite normal in the *colonia* to Maddie, and the
Maryknoll sisters soon discovered why. The neighbors told Maddie that
Archbishop Oscar Romero had been gunned down at 6:25 PM—only a
few minutes after Carla's bus had arrived in the capital. He was shot in
the chest, just after his homily, while saying Mass in the chapel of the
Hospital of Divine Providence, where he lived in a small residence.
Though this was an assassination that shook the nation and the international community, the sisters found that there was no news coverage
about the event on Salvadoran radio and television stations.

This violent incident did not dissuade Carla from her plan to work in
El Salvador. Four days later she wrote a lengthy letter[1] to her friend Rebecca Quinn in Coelemu, Chile:

> Here I am in the land of my dreams and desires . . . I feel I've ar-
> rived to cry with the *pueblo* . . . Yesterday . . . I . . . unworthily was
> privileged to be in the guard of honor for this saintly man who
> gave his life for the poor. As I stood before his body I prayed
> that I may be converted also from my pride and egoism to be of
> the people. As I watched [them] file by and cry with me—I be-
> lieve I am being healed—I believe that this country is being
> healed at the high price of blood and lives—just as *Semana*

Santa [Holy Week] brings to mind. Now I am entering into a new history and I want to follow the Lord of History as He wants.

Carla's years in Chile had awakened her to the complicit role the CIA played in Augusto Pinochet's overthrow of Salvador Allende's democratically elected government. She also had heard from Maryknoll friends in Nicaragua how the United States had supported the decades-long regimes of the Somoza family there. She was aware of Romero's plea, only a month before his murder, that President Carter stop sending military aid to the Salvadoran army that was killing its citizens—a plea that was rejected. This explains the description that follows of her visit to the U.S. embassy to apply for a new passport after hers was stolen:

> The American Embassy here…is full of buzzers, searchers, guards, bars and gloom, and there was the beautiful Archbishop, a man in love with life, so simple, so for the poor and truth with no guards and the Lord blessed him with the greatest likeness to Jesus—giving his life for the poor. Now I'm into praying for the conversion of the U.S.A.…. At least we gringos never have to look for something to be sorry about—we belong to a nationality that has committed so many atrocities against the little people that I believe we'll always be able to say "Have mercy on us, Lord, we are sinners!"

Back at Maddie's house all was not calm. The *colonia* where Maddie lived and worked was similar to the grim *poblaciones* in Chile. At 2 AM on her fourth night there Carla was awakened "by Maddie telling the man who was trying to break into the house to go away or she'd ring the bells. He didn't go away so she rang the bells—neighbors came and finally we were able to go back to sleep. And this is the beginning of the surprises in Saviorland."

With all the troubles, Carla retained a sense of humor: "Today all the buses are on strike in protest of Monseñor Romero's death so I've been riding trucks. It's practically pornographic how we have to hold on to one another since there are no ropes or anything. Yet in it all—the great Circus Master directs the show."

By April 2, Wednesday of Holy Week, Ita was en route to Nicaragua to meet with all the sisters of the region, including Carla, who would be gathering during Easter week. Ita wrote her mother of the shock resulting from Romero's murder:

The Archbishop's death started a continental examination of conscience about how each local Church was or wasn't being faithful to the Gospel...I have all sorts of reactions—from feeling robbed of...having the opportunity to know Mons. Romero ...to horror at the paranoia and fear of the right and their brutality, to wonder at the gospel message...to feeling with the poor of Salvador and their loss.

But we believe that his death will bear fruit. It's part of the Christian mystery we celebrate this week; in that same Christian tradition, we'll go to Salvador.[2]

Ten Maryknoll sisters at the meeting, including Carla, had been at the archbishop's funeral and were shaken when a bomb had gone off, followed by shooting and a stampede of panicked mourners. At least forty people had died. "The past 2 weeks...were a rather dramatic entrance into the country with Bishop Romero's death and the whole Cathedral massacre," wrote Carla to Becky: "And yet I'm still glad to be here and at peace. Close and frequent encounters with death make one aware of the Lord's love and the frivolities that one can leave behind...So far I can take the violent and adventurous life of Salvador—I believe taking a nap each day helps."[3]

Ita was troubled after hearing of the "Cathedral massacre" and wrote to friends: "My timing couldn't be worse...I am still reeling from Romero's death because we were prepared to work with him...I feel that part of my future was robbed. Then...I heard about the funeral scene ...So my free-floating anxiety has been intense."[4] Though frightened, Ita knew that for her there was no turning back. The next day she wrote: "I think I'm pretty grounded now and with fear and faith I get on the bus tomorrow for Salvador."[5]

Carla and Ita's plan to work wherever the archbishop needed their help had died with him. They would have to discover for themselves what their role would be. They arrived in El Salvador on April 15 and immediately drew up a plan for the first month. They would share community with Maddie in Colonia Lamatepec. This would help with expenses, and the pastoral activities they assisted in would help Maddie out and help them better understand the people's needs. Typically, Ita was intent on grasping the nuances of the dialect as she steadily made contacts; Carla, on the other hand, forged ahead, quickly mingling with the people. They would also get acquainted with the other Maryknoll sisters in El Salvador—Joan Petrik and Teresa Alexander (a recent arrival from Panama), both of whom worked in La Libertad.[6]

In late April, as part of this plan, Carla and Ita attended a "mini-workshop" of catechists and delegates of the word—about sixty men in all, mainly *campesinos*. They possessed "an extraordinary faith and simplicity," wrote Ita to her mother. "It was awe-inspiring to listen to them talk of their experiences."[7] Carla was equally moved: "So many said—'I know that *entrega* [surrender] to the Lord may mean death—but I believe I will not die forever, but will rise as Mons. Romero lives on in our [devotion to] the truth.' Wow, I really received a lot from them." This experience seemed to deepen Carla's relationship with Jesus. She added:

> I guess I've always believed in Christ but more as a kind of *compañero en el camino*. Now that I'm hanging with really very little security and with a situation of violence, I've come to believe in Christ as . . . dynamic life which can cast out the fear that every now and then dollys into my feeling. I've seen the difference in myself . . . not because I'm me but because Christ does live in me.[8]

While Ita still felt that part of her future had been "robbed" by the bullets that killed Romero, she had begun to enjoy a brighter outlook: "Having the chance to meet and talk with a number of people, I feel differently. It's a privilege to come to a church of martyrs and people with a strong committed faith. Though I'm only here two and a half weeks, I have a strong conviction that I'm where I should be, though the particulars of the future are not very clear yet."[9]

Carla and Ita decided that they would still work through Romero's archdiocese. An important part of the plan was to attend archdiocesan meetings of religious personnel and become informed on the political, sociological, and economic situation, while investigating possibilities for serving. César Jerez, Jesuit superior of Central America, Fabian Amaya, vicar of Chalatenango, as well as Monsignor Ricardo Urioste, vicar general of the archdiocese, and Bishop Arturo Rivera Damas, apostolic administrator, all pointed to one department as most in need of aid: Chalatenango.[10] By the middle of May, Carla and Ita had made their decision.

It was not one they made lightly. Chalatenango, a northwestern department with a population of about two hundred thousand, was a province of landless or nearly landless *campesinos*. Landlessness had increased dramatically throughout El Salvador—12 percent of rural families had no land in 1961 compared to 29 percent in 1971 and 41 percent in 1975. As successive regimes and the oligarchy dragged the tiny country closer to chaos by refusing to alleviate the desperate need of their people for agrarian reform, guerrilla organizations won the support of many peasants. A bitter commentary on their hopeless situation was a popular saying of the rural poor, "Better to die of a bullet than die of hunger."[11]

By early 1980, the popularity of guerrilla groups in Chalatenango had drawn the attention of the military to this department. That May, while Ita and Carla were considering the possibility of aiding the people there, the high command declared Chalatenango a "military emergency zone." The area thus became the object of "clean-up" sweeps that terrorized peasants in the villages and countryside while rooting out guerrillas. Anyone, including women, children, infants, and elderly men, was a potential target. Those sought out included teachers, leaders of cooperatives, and catechists. The army was aided by the Guardia Nacional and by members of ORDEN. Headed by former army officers, ORDEN's ranks included many peasants who collaborated with those in power to obtain a job, to plunder the homes of other peasants, or simply for personal security in a violent country. Members of ORDEN were not paid salaries, but were allowed to carry weapons.

Sometimes ORDEN took control of an entire town. Carla wrote to Becky that she and Ita had gone to Arcatao, a town in Chalatenango where all forty-two catechists and delegates of the word had been tortured and killed, and where nuns had had to leave because of threats on their lives. The town was now mostly ORDEN, explained Carla: "They are the same humble poor *campesinos* as those they kill and call *extremistas* and *Comunistas*." At Mass they were the ones with "pistols and pencils" who jotted down the names of anyone who talked with the Padre.[12]

On May 14, 1980, National Guard forces combined with the Salvadoran Air Force and ORDEN to slaughter from three to six hundred civilians—virtually all women and children—near the hamlet of Las Arades in Chalatenango. The terror-stricken refugees were caught between two militias. Fleeing the bullets that rained down from Salvadoran helicopter gunships, they tried to cross the Río Sumpul into Honduras, only to be welcomed by Honduran soldiers firing on them and driving them back to El Salvador. Earl Gallagher, a U.S. Capuchin missioner in Honduras and eyewitness to the massacre, claimed that those shooting from the helicopters could not have mistaken their victims for guerrillas, since all were clearly women and children. Some survivors said that ORDEN men tossed babies and young children into the air, "slashing them with machetes, cutting off their heads, and slitting them in two." One soldier was heard to say, "We are killing the children of subversion." Political science professor Terry L. Karl later emphasized the extent of the carnage when, before an immigration court in Miami, Florida, she testified that "this massacre was unparalleled in recent Salvadoran history."[13]

Ita and Carla would learn of the massacre and realize they had entered a situation of mayhem. But on the day it occurred, Carla was in an upbeat mood as she wrote a newsy letter to a friend in Chile about her experiences in "this little concentrated bouillon cube of a country":

> I like this place with its spunky people. If this country would have had the democratic gov't that Chile had for so long, El Salvador would be the most developed country in the world. I've never seen such an energetic crowd; even road gangs really work. I call them little ants, always on the run...I can't keep up with them.
>
> But, given their history and the *sin vergüenzas* [shameless ones] who have had power, they just make ends meet and now the top is about to blow off...[14]

Three days later, probably after hearing of the Río Sumpul massacre, Ita wrote: "Historically this is not the ideal time to arrive on the scene—but the Lord got us here for some reason."[15]

In the wake of Río Sumpul and other sweeps, archdiocesan personnel and church workers saw that the most obvious need was to aid refugees—those who had fled their homes because of fighting and persecution. Thus the Emergency Refugee Committee in Chalatenango was born. It would provide refugees with clothing, food, and medicine—and, critically, with transportation to safety. "Since we were the two without full-time work, we got...the job," Ita wrote. Others would help with planning and making contacts.[16]

These refugees were considered subversive by government and security forces because they happened to live in an area where guerrillas were active. It would not take long before those who helped the refugees, including Carla and Ita, became suspect. Things were heating up in Chalatenango, wrote Ita to her sister, Rene:

> I'm super saturated with horror stories and daily body count to the point that I thought I'd hit the next person who told me someone else was killed. I'm not sure how you get "acclimated" to a country that has an undeclared civil war going...

Carla and I now have a job. We're the full time workers of the emergency committee in the Vicariate of Chalatenango... The Church of San Salvador is facing reality and getting ready to help with food, medicines, and refugee centers...I don't think we could have dreamed this job before we came...

There're a lot of bizarre things that go on in this country including the help from Uncle Sam. It's pathetic that there're millions for army equipment, but nothing for humanitarian help until war is declared. Groups like the International Red Cross cannot or do not respond until the point is catastrophic. Carla keeps asking how many dead make a war? What's the magic number?...

There's going to be a food shortage because a lot of farmers feel caught between groups that are training in the mountains, etc. and need food so come to ask for it or rob it if it is not given. The armed forces retaliate because the farmers are collaborating with "extremist" or "subversive" groups...After awhile a lot of people just leave...because they can't take it anymore.

And in all this turmoil, commented Ita, she was trying her best to understand the people and the culture: "It's like forming friendships in a psychiatric hospital. It's real, but crazy."[17]

Carla, too, was trying to figure out the Salvadorans. She was in awe that the people remained strong "in the midst of insane violence" but was even more impressed by their faith:

These people have a spunky faith in Jesus as Savior which isn't just words. The presence of evil is quite tangible...but the presence of real dynamic goodness is very tangible too. It kind of is like the epistles of St. Paul where over and over he reminds the readers of Jesus' sacrifice as enough to get them going to be the people that God wants...I have gotten scared a couple of times and I pray that I can be faithful to the call when the crunch comes.[18]

She wrote Connie Pospisil and other Maryknoll sisters in Chile of a nasty experience she and Ita had on a trip into the countryside, when they—along with two seminarians, a Salvadoran priest, and another woman—had been roughly searched by soldiers. Carla, always the clown, added her sense of the incongruous: "They could have popped us off right there where so many *campesinos* have been killed...However, my one preoccupation was that the elastic on my pants was broken and with hands on wall and legs apart and ransacking of body, it could have been deleterious, to say the least. Thanks be to God and a safety pin that held, nothing funny happened."

This was possibly the first time Carla and Ita experienced personally just how intense was the hatred on the part of government forces for the church. Carla wrote: "Even to be a catechist is dangerous." She underscored the "incredible" repression with a single unexaggerated comment: "The newspapers here look like anatomy books with pictures of the mutilated bodies found hither and yon." Yet, whenever she heard a popular greeting—"*Primero Dios*" ["First of all, God"]—she understood where the poor placed their hope.[19]

There were also "surprises" in Maddie's *colonia*. Ita tried to keep her sense of humor: "My baptism into the violence was spontaneously arranged by some local thugs (I'd guess thirteen or fourteen years old) ... Coming up behind me, one put a knife to my ribs, another a machete to my neck. Being New York City trained, I said, 'I'm a nun. I won't hurt you'...I really prefer being pickpocketed."[20] When Carla wrote to Becky Quinn about this incident, she too saw humor in it: "This is the 3rd time since I've come that I've been robbed. It kind of loses its drama after a while."[21]

Carla wrote quite frequently to Becky, eight years her senior. Unburdening herself of her fears was one objective, but Carla also bared her soul as she recognized in herself a deepening spirituality. Becky seemed to fill a void in Carla's life and became her spiritual confidante:

> I was re-reading your letter about 3 AM and as I reflected on it I ...heard the shots in the night that mean I am here in this violent mess. I'm glad I'm here...I've been scared but have always felt the Lord's peace and His presence.
>
> I was glad to get your letter today of May 7 where you say you are proud that we can suffer with and support the people at this time...Not that I'm anyone to be proud of, but I am here "for others" and that's the work of the Church. So since [Ita and I] are of the Church and for the Church I believe we are involved the way the Lord wants us to be...
>
> Ita and I were out in Chalatenango where we'll no doubt be working. It's a *campo* area, beautiful scenery and very poor and wild. If you knew how the soldiers search us and treat us you'd worry. But I take it as the power of evil really getting back at the good. When we came back with the priest last week, we were

stopped... and really treated rough in words and deeds. About 5 of them had us at gun point and we could have easily been shot right there since the hatred of the Church is so tangible and *fuerte* [strong]... We were on our way after Father looked under the hood of the car to see if the boys had planted a bomb there...

However, weak, limited and aware that this is quite raw and real, I'm for sticking it out. I believe that Good will win over evil, that Creativity will win over destruction and that Peace will win over war... God has never abandoned me... and He is present even in this mess.[22]

Carla had met Ita's mother when she visited them in Chile and had adopted her as "Grandma." For years the two had corresponded regularly. In one letter, Carla compared the "tepid priests" she had met that day to the "dedicated" ones: "We have just come back from the poorest part of Salvador... We saw the beautiful poor people, the dedicated priests, the ruthless repression, the faith of a valiant people." Yet Carla had also observed "the simony like devotion of some people, the tepid priests who make you want to vomit." With characteristic humor, Carla signed off: "We got 1000 bites of all the species of insects. Needless to say, we'll go back for more, which is the crazy absurd life we've been chosen for and choose."[23]

On May 22, Carla and Ita were introduced to Sisters Dorothy Kazel and Christine Rody, who were working in La Libertad. Dorothy described the encounter on an audiocassette for her parents: "We went out to visit Madeline and Carla and Ita—one of them is named Ita Ford... She's real cute. She's tiny and very Irish, and her name 'Ita' is an Irish name." They had all gone up to the Izalco volcano for a picnic lunch together.[24]

Not long after this connection with the Cleveland team had been made, a friend from Chile, Sister Jane Kenrick, made her way to La Libertad searching for Carla and Ita. Dorothy and Jean brought them to her, and the three women enjoyed an emotional reunion. They told Jane how difficult it had been to find their role, that they had decided to aid refugees in spite of the army's antagonism toward the church in Chalatenango, and that this decision was final. Dorothy told Jane: "Carla and Ita will be doing very dangerous work—I'm very afraid for them."

Carla and Ita said goodbye to Jane the next day, and Jane recalled them saying: "If anything happens to one of us, we pray that we both go—don't know how we'd do without the other." Jane had experienced the terror under Pinochet, but she felt El Salvador was absolutely lawless.

She had seen at least a façade of justice in Chile but only all-pervasive fear and chaos in El Salvador.[25]

One of the first actions Carla and Ita took on behalf of the displaced was an attempt to alert organizations outside of El Salvador about the "lived reality" of refugees. Since the war was undeclared, the international norms of behavior for wartime were not being respected. Carla and Ita, at the request of the Salvadoran Ecumenical Humanitarian Aid Committee (CEAH), petitioned Maryknoll leaders in the United States to present the refugees' case to the International Red Cross and the U.S. church. What was needed most was: "An international declaration and recognition of the lived reality here. Hospitals are being invaded—with patients being kidnapped or killed; no guarantees have been given for existing refugee centers. The internal refugee problem is growing."[26]

Following their first six weeks in El Salvador, as they prepared to immerse themselves full time in refugee work, Ita meditated on the readings of the Easter Season from the Acts of the Apostles. She saw a parallel between the early church and the church in El Salvador: The apostles had lost their leader, Jesus, just as the Salvadorans had lost theirs—Archbishop Romero:

> I arrived in El Salvador during the liturgical reading of Acts which seemed so appropriate: coming into a church that had just lost its leader; listening not only to testimonies of him, but also to the personal testimonies of the delegates of the word and catechists...who have risked and have been threatened because of their association with the church...Priests and sisters have had to leave the country...People are making choices and are being killed for those choices...
>
> Now it's the cycle of Pentecost...the time of my own empowering to participate. The gift of the spirit is very real and important to me, especially his teaching, enlightening, leading me/us into the truth.
>
> "Each one of you has received some spiritual gift, use it for the good of all; activate the different gifts that God has distributed among you" (1 Pet. 4:10)...To believe that we are gifted in and for Salvador now, that the answer to the questions will come when they are needed, to walk in faith one day at a time with Salvadorans along a road filled with obstacles, detours and sometimes washouts. This seems to be what it means for us to be in El Salvador. And it is good for us to be here (Lk. 9:33).[27]

Ironically, there was indeed to be a "washout" in Carla and Ita's future.

Although she did not always elaborate on the violence, Ita did write her mother regularly. In one letter, Ita explained their nomadic existence. After two months in El Salvador they did not have a permanent home. They had been promised two rooms in the town of Chalatenango, but these were not yet habitable. In the meantime, three Asunción nuns living there made room for them whenever they needed it. Other sisters, "who have a shower," housed them when they stayed in San Salvador, which was frequently. The refugee problem was "not at the scale of the recent year's film footage of Vietnam, Cambodia, etc.," but kept them busy providing "food, medicine, clothes, shelter, plus financing." Sometimes they stayed with Maryknoll colleagues Joan and Terry in La Libertad and with Maddie at least once a week.[28] But, as Carla said—and as Ita refrained from writing her mother: "If war comes—who can be worried about where to live?"[29]

In a letter to Becky, Carla wrote that the perils of their new mission were enhancing their spiritual lives: "Our job of running around is very good for promoting a mobile faith...My faith in Jesus is tried every day and in the fire of testing, grows. I've come to see the difference between panic, fear and courage...The Lord has never abandoned me in life and I believe He never will." She noted that she finally had a Christian base community to mentor, adding that this was a serious responsibility, for her words could have life-or-death implications for others: "Words must be measured here and real wisdom is the need of the moment. In a country where people are killed for going to meetings or associating with key people, this is a heavy load...I just pray that my words are truth and if death comes to me or to others, it was in alliance with truth."[30]

Carla and Ita were not only aiding victims of army and right-wing repression. They also helped another type of refugee—the *campesino* fleeing guerrilla groups. In one report to Maryknoll, they conveyed the fear and distrust suffered by both types of refugees, and one item indicated that they drove food supplies to contacts for refugees hiding from guerrilla forces.[31]

However, groups monitoring human rights in El Salvador had determined that most murders (about 85 percent) were committed by right-wing forces. Carla and Ita, then, generally did aid *campesinos* fleeing government forces—and their sympathy lay with them as well. Not only were there far more of them than there were victims of guerrillas, but they also knew that many catechists and members of Christian base communities were being targeted. Moreover, they and other humanitarian aid workers felt that U.S. citizens were mostly ignorant of their country's contribution, through its financial and military aid, to the mayhem in El Salvador. This would explain Ita's words to Melinda Roper, president of the Maryknoll Sisters:

> Since the death of Monseñor Romero [U.S.] news coverage on Salvador has declined to almost nothing. [CEAH fears] that decisive action will be taken by [the U.S.] under the guise of "stopping subversives" and "containing communism"—and that all of Central America will be involved if this happens. If we have a preferential option for the poor as well as a commitment for justice as a basis for the coming Kingdom, we're going to have to take sides in Salvador—correction—we have.[32]

After providing emergency relief for several weeks, Carla and Ita wrote to the Maryknoll sisters in Central America and Chile explaining the history of the conflict and the difficulties the church had been experiencing since Romero's death. Without Romero, the church was rudderless and there was "no other voice of equal credibility." More than two thousand families in the area, whatever their political loyalty, had had to flee their homes. Carla and Ita outlined their numerous duties as part of the Emergency Committee, including collaboration with humanitarian groups, driving priests to outlying districts, procuring food for those in hiding, and transporting refugees.

In their letter, Carla and Ita described how the situation had affected them emotionally—revelations that caused a stir among their Maryknoll sisters. The two nuns were frustrated. For three months they had been living as nomads. They felt "isolated and alone" because visitors and mail were rare as a result of the war situation and they needed "more palpable solidarity." Although they wished there was more support for themselves, they thought it best at this time *not* to send someone until their mission in Chalatenango had more structure. But they did request, again, that another sister come to help Maddie. They admitted that neither of them were "emotional or psychological giants in this crazy situation." Ending on an upbeat note, they did feel they had learned much from this experience, including, "a total dependence and trust in God," and "an awareness of the ability to adapt to incredible situations."[33]

When tension built up, Ita had a "safety valve." She wrote Ana May, "I fantasize and forget everything...Today I think I'll visit Bermuda."[34] Yet her work with refugees was giving her life meaning, and she urged her niece Jennifer, who was turning sixteen, to find her own purpose-filled existence:

What I want to say—some of it isn't too jolly birthday talk, but it's real. Yesterday, I stood looking down at a 16-year-old boy who had been killed a few hours earlier. I know a lot of kids even younger who are dead. This is a terrible time in El Salvador for youth. A lot of idealism and commitment is getting snuffed out here now.

The reasons why so many people are being killed are quite complicated...One is that many people have found a meaning to life, to sacrifice, to struggle and even to death! And whether their life spans 16 years or 60 or 90, for them their life has had a purpose. In many ways, they are fortunate people.

Brooklyn is not passing through the drama of El Salvador, but some things hold true wherever one is, and at whatever age...I hope you come to find that which gives life a deep meaning for you. Something worth living for, maybe even worth dying for, something that energizes you, enthuses you... [This is] for you to find...I just encourage you to start looking...

Maybe...no one else will talk to you like this, but then, too, I'm seeing and living things that others around you aren't...I hope this doesn't sound like...a sermon. In fact, it's my birthday present to you. If it doesn't make sense right at this moment, keep this and read it some time from now...Or ask me about it, okay?[35]

In mid-July, Carla and Ita acquired a used jeep to facilitate their refugee work. Carla called it *La Tonquita*—Miss Piggy—because it took to the road like a pig to a puddle. And in early August, Carla and Ita moved into their own rooms—plain and separated by thin plywood—in the parish house in Chalatenango. About a dozen residents lived there, a number that fluctuated from day to day depending on who needed a place to stay while looking for refuge. The refugees seemed to be trusting them more, hence Carla and Ita grew more confident in their ability to help. They also were getting assistance from Jean Donovan and two visitors to El Salvador, Carmelite Father Peter Hinde and a nurse, Mercy Sister Betty Campbell.[36] And Maryknoll Sister Maura Clarke had just arrived to help Maddie in Santa Ana. Things were looking up.

Carla wrote to Becky saying that she was getting "more immersed" in her work with the people. "We're moving refugees, zipping food around, comforting survivors of bombing and taking hot priests [under suspicion by security forces] to hot places. I love this circus...I leave the future in the Circus Master's hands."[37] To Father Ganss, her former spiritual advisor, she confided: "The great privilege of serving this suffering Church is one of the greatest graces of my vocation."[38]

The two friends continued a practice they had started in Chile— praying at night together. Once, they found themselves crying "because it was so unclear to us why we were here, although we felt strongly we should be." Because of the "very violent things" occurring, they often discussed dying, but believed it would be too hard to bear if one of them were "left behind," said Ita.[39]

However, Carla felt protective of Ita, so, though Ita protested, Carla carried the heaviest loads of food and accepted the riskiest missions. She told Ita's mother: "In this insane situation, who's to know what is risky, and actually all we're doing is very humanitarian...There is a certain freedom for me since contact with my family is so minimal. I always say to Ita that if anything happens to me—she has only to advise Maryknoll, but should she be harmed, I dread having to advise the Ford Foundation."[40] Carla's lighthearted words masked the pain she felt after those missions of mercy. Often she turned to artwork for relief; she drew birds crying, their tears forming streams of water, and wounded doves of peace. She wrote a song or two in El Salvador—but no poetry.[41]

In late August, Carla made a private retreat in San Salvador. Troubled, she fasted and prayed for the sorrows of Salvadorans to be lifted. She felt tainted by the role her country was playing in their misery, but her spirits lifted as she reflected on her work, perceiving that her efforts on behalf of refugees was her way of counteracting American policy. Before leaving, she filled La Tonquita with medicine for refugees, then returned to Chalatenango.[42]

The next day, Saturday, August 23, Carla went off to deliver food, and Ita went to the nearby army base to discuss some missing persons. The commander told her to return later and finally, around six, he gave her a prisoner. She brought the man to the parish house, where refugees staying there told Ita they thought he was an informer. She and Carla decided for everyone's safety to take him to his village. Two seminarians offered to go with them.

By then it was about seven and the weather was menacing. They would have to cross a meandering stream five times. It began to rain hard, and after the fourth crossing, Carla, who was driving, refused to go on. Ita told the prisoner he would have to get out and walk. Carla turned the jeep around but in the span of five minutes the stream had become a torrent and she lost control. The seminarians escaped and tried to help, but the current turned the jeep on its side. The passenger door with its half-closed window was topside, and the women were trapped as a wall of water rushed in. One seminarian still had a loose hold on Ita and when Carla gave her a push, she made it through the tiny window opening. The current took Ita downstream, bobbing her around helplessly and battering her on rocks. Unable to breathe, Ita prayed, "Receive me, Lord." Finally, grabbing onto some sturdy roots, she dragged herself out of the river, up a steep slope, and into a field. Exhausted, she lay under some bushes—wet, cold, and plagued by mosquitoes—till the next morning when she met people who brought her back to Chalatenango. Ita then realized how many townspeople had been searching for her and Carla all night long.[43]

The seminarians had made it to safety, but later that day Carla's body was found ten miles downstream. The river had stripped her naked and she was badly bruised with a broken neck. She would have to be buried the next day—but in San Salvador or Chalatenango? Ita chose Chalatenango, with the "people she belonged to." Though depleted of nutrients and strength, Ita planned the funeral. There were tributes by *campesinos* and townspeople, who called her "*fogosa*,"—a fiery spirit. Following Carla downhill in the procession to the town cemetery, Ita had to brake the descent of the coffin. She told her mother, "I...had to sort of laugh." As the heavy coffin pulled her forward, she realized this was the last time she would have to "hold Carla back." She and Carla had often tugged on each other—Ita pulling her friend back from the brink of trouble, and Carla prodding cautious Ita to make up her mind, and at the end giving her a push to save her.[44]

In a way, Carla's death seemed fitting: Joking that she didn't want to live past forty, she died just before age forty-one, and the "Lord of the river, God of the stream" had redeemed her, as depicted in her poetry. Two days before she died, Ita remembered, they had read a Bible verse that had deeply moved her, and Carla had said, "Now you can dismiss your servant in peace, O Lord." Did she have a premonition? Ita wondered.[45]

Ita insisted on remaining in Chalatenango. She felt that her experience the night of the accident—wet and shivering all night in a farmer's field—now tied her inextricably to refugees fleeing their homes and sleeping in the hills.[46]

Maura Clarke attended the services for Carla and was moved by her life of sacrifice and the people's testimony. When she saw that Ita wanted to continue the refugee work, Maura, who had been in El Salvador only about three weeks, volunteered to join her in Chalatenango.

*   *   *

Maura had arrived in El Salvador in early August. Maddie and Terry had picked her up at the airport, then driven to the port town of La Libertad, where that evening Maura met Jean Donovan and Fathers Paul Schindler and Ken Myers of the Cleveland team. The next day Maura was introduced to Carla and Ita when they came to La Libertad to confer with Ellen McDonald, who had been sent by the Maryknoll governing board. The board, shocked by the high murder rate in El Salvador and perhaps concerned over the emotions expressed in Carla and Ita's three-month report, wanted to discuss the dangerous nature of the sisters' mission work. Ellen informed all five that they had full approval to leave if they thought it necessary. Everything she was hearing and seeing underscored for Maura that the violence in El Salvador exceeded anything she had witnessed in Nicaragua. She described it to her friend Mary Manning:

> We had a community meeting all day...The point kept coming up—you don't have to stay...The answers from the four who have been here a little while—one five years and the others only three or four months—was that they believed deeply that God wants them to be here..., although why God wants them here is what they are searching out.
>
> The above strangely enough reflects where I'm at...I said I was at peace about being here and trying to find out if this is where I'm supposed to be. The deep pain or fear hasn't touched me really yet. I hear about it and have witnessed it somewhat as we saw five [dead] men thrown by the roadside on Saturday and one in the town where we went with Father Paul for the Mass yesterday.

But when she had gone with Sister Teresa to observe a Christian base community, Maura added, the *campesinos* helped her face her fears and feeling of unease:

> These are the most rugged...and faith-filled men and women who are religious leaders of their various pueblos. It takes courage for them to continue any celebration of the Word or meetings because anyone suspected of being in an organization or attached to the church is in serious danger. I was so impressed, Mary, by this little group...The poor really strip you, pull you, challenge you, evangelize you, show you God. [47]

After two weeks of discerning, she was about to decide her future: "Being here in this tragic situation of El Salvador there are moments when I question very much why I'm here." She often thought of Ciudad Sandino in Nicaragua: "I would love to be there now as there is so much hope and much that can be done but somehow I believe the Lord wants me here and He will show me what He wishes little by little."[48] The next day she wrote that the little children had affected her deeply:

> You would especially love the precious little children with their big dark eyes and black hair. A couple of days ago I visited a crippled woman whose precious grandson was cooking, washing the clothes and putting wet soaks on her legs. He is just seven years old. Surely the Lord has a plan of hope and joy for this little one and so many others.[49]

Maura made her decision and settled in to work at Colonia Lamatepec in Santa Ana. Finally, Maddie would have some help—but only for a few days.

Maura quickly teamed up with Ita when Carla died. Even in her sorrow, Ita perceived that the refugee ministry would be enhanced by Maura, whose warmth and loving heart would be "God's gift" to the traumatized people.[50] Maura understood that Ita was still grieving and Ita understood that Maura was new to the Emergency Committee. And both recognized that they were "overstretched" and often knew nothing about situations demanding an urgent response.[51]

Maura would become as immersed in aiding refugees as Carla had been. Soon they were called upon to bring food to *campesinos* living in the hills. Betty Campbell and Peter Hinde went with Ita and Maura to help unload powdered milk and corn and saw the hungry people gather up even the few kernels that fell from the sacks.

The Americans listened to the story of these sixteen adults and forty or so children. For eight months they had been sleeping in the hills in the cold and rain to avoid nighttime raids by death squads and early morning sweeps by the army. They would return by day to their village to tend their fields. Their houses had been burned or stripped of possessions by soldiers and ORDEN spies. The vil-

Ita and Maura in El Salvador

lagers had finally fled one morning because the soldiers had threatened that the next time they would "finish off the women and children." After a five-hour trek, the *campesinos* had arrived at a priest's house, where one woman immediately gave birth to twins. Ita promised to arrange safe transport for the group to San Salvador the next day.[52]

One result of indiscriminate attacks and killings was that relatives of victims would often join the guerrillas as their last hope. Even youngsters were heading for the hills. Betty told Maura and Ita about a girl she had met as she gave first-aid talks in the villages of Chalatenango. An elderly woman had begged Betty to speak with her granddaughter, Esperanza. "She says that she is joining the resistance in the hills tomorrow. She is only thirteen years old. My husband doesn't approve." Betty discovered that the girl's parents had been killed by the National Guard. Esperanza was vivacious and bright; when Betty asked her about joining the resistance, she said: "I want to defend my grandparents, my village…If we don't defend ourselves we will all be killed." Her grandfather asked: "Doesn't it say in the bible, you shall not kill?" The girl answered, "I am not going to the camp because I want to kill. I am going because I want to defend my people…It is not [even] safe for us to go to school. One of our teachers was killed last week."[53]

There had been continual tension in Chalatenango between the members of the parish team and the local army commander, Colonel Ricardo Peña Arbaiza, since the spring of 1980. With the slaying of Archbishop Romero in March and the army sweeps of the department in May, Colonel Peña had adopted an openly hostile attitude toward the efforts of the parish team, including Ita and Carla and later Maura, to aid the refugees. In the late summer and fall of that year, around the time of Maura's arrival, tensions were mounting ominously.

In an attempt to keep rumors about their activities from flourishing, Ita and Maura were always open about their work and quite visible on their missions. They would speak directly to local officials about the refugees who came to them for help, outlining what transportation or relief the team intended to offer. Frustrated by the unrelenting hostility of Colonel Peña, the Chalatenango parish team even went to his headquarters across the street from the church and asked him to pay a visit to the parish house. They wanted him to see for himself the refugees, food, and supplies that were there and realize that reports of the church's "subversive" activities were lies. However, Colonel Peña did not respond to their request.[54]

The attacks on San Antonio de los Ranchos, a town that Maura often visited after she joined Ita in the refugee ministry, illustrated the increasingly hostile atmosphere in which church personnel had to operate.

Many *campesinos* in the area had joined the BPR (Revolutionary People's Bloc), a political organization comprising labor and peasant groups who had united to exert pressure for land reform. In 1980, the army—claiming it was defending the people—began sweeps in the vicinity to root out guerrilla forces, using troops, tanks, artillery, helicopters, and planes and causing heavy civilian casualties. When the army offered Los Ranchos a contingent of National Guardsmen to "protect" the town from guerrillas, the people turned them down in a town meeting. This infuriated Colonel Peña, who fumed to a reporter, "The priest [Padre Salazar] of Los Ranchos has ruined the people of this town."

The first attack on Los Ranchos was launched on August 15, 1980. A helicopter circled the fields, its guns mowing down three men and a woman. Two *campesinos* were taken prisoner and brought back to the Chalatenango garrison. Salazar and another priest interceded, saying that they were "responsible catechists." The men were freed—one of them was on the brink of death even as the priests were speaking with the colonel. He later told church workers he had been kneeling in front of the troops, waiting to die, when the order came to return him to his cell. This and similar incidents caused the army to cease bringing prisoners back to the garrison, for, as one soldier told Ita, "the priests or sisters free them and all our work is for nothing."

This was only the beginning for San Antonio de los Ranchos. In October, as soldiers overran the town, shooting indiscriminately at people and plundering homes, a tank bombarded buildings. A convent and church were raided and consecrated hosts were profaned. Two young mothers were dragged off behind their houses and were viciously tortured and decapitated. The next week, Los Ranchos was again marauded. This time the soldiers invaded the sacristy of the church and fouled the altar linens.[55]

Throughout the fall of 1980 rumors spread in the department of Chalatenango that the Catholic Church was engaged in subversive activities. Nevertheless, Maura and Ita, as well as other members of the parish team, continued to aid the victims of civil war. This took courage. When the Guardia stopped a bus Ita was riding to check everyone for identification, the soldiers pulled a young man aside, waving the bus on. Ita confronted the Guardia: "If you take him you take me," she said, and the soldiers released him.[56]

Their refugee work in the department of Chalatenango did not endear Maura and Ita, or other church personnel, to the suspicious Colonel Peña Araiza. He and his men continued deriding the activities of the church in Chalatenango, and their attacks on San Antonio de los Ranchos were obscene assaults on Catholic sacraments and ritual. Around this time, Peña questioned two boys who claimed they had been shot by guerrillas. Then, insisting that the boys had told him of contacts between church workers and guerrillas, he summoned individuals from the parish team to his office and harangued them about the church's alleged "subversive" activities. The Colonel was quite serious about these accusations; he even made several trips to San Salvador to relay his concerns to army officers. It was apparently due to his influence that a ten-year-old boy from Chalatenango—a dubious authority—testified to high government officials in the capital regarding church contacts with guerrilla groups. At this meeting Defense Minister García singled out church workers in Chalatenango for special criticism.[57]

Knowing that Ita was going through a difficult period, Maura tried to relieve her of some of the most taxing aspects of their work. Ita handled requests for aid, called relief agencies, and did the paper work. She found keeping busy therapeutic, writing her mother, "Being busy is fine for me now—especially on some days when I just don't feel like myself. I guess it's the blahs that come after someone close to you dies...It will pass with time, and in the meantime I'm running Maura ragged."[58] Her sense of humor was returning, a good sign. One task—purchasing large quantities of food—was required because, with so many refugees fleeing their farms, no grain was being planted, which led Ita to observe: "I feel like a Chicago merchant specializing in grain futures—or maybe Joseph in Egypt—storing grains against the coming shortage. There's nothing more absurd than two Brooklynites judging the quality of red beans and corn!"[59]

Ita did accompany Maura into the countryside to deliver supplies or transport refugees, for both felt their presence would help ensure that *campesinos* and supplies got through checkpoints. The Cleveland team also helped out regularly. Ita wrote her mother: "They have a fleet of cars at their disposal and are quite ready to show up in a microbus, pickup truck or jeep...Their biggest asset is being blonde, which makes roadblock passing easier. Carla kept threatening to bleach her hair when she saw how they got through."[60]

Maura was finding her new life in Chalatenango an adjustment; she wrote to Kay Kelly:

> I am beginning to see death in a new way, dearest Katie. We have been meditating a lot on death and the accepting of it...It is an atmosphere of death. The work is really what Bishop Romero called "acompañamiento" [accompanying the people]

...This seems what the Lord is asking of me, I think, at this moment. We are on the road continually, bringing women and children to refugee centers. Keep us in your heart and prayers, especially the poor forsaken people.[61]

Since Paul Schindler would be carrying the letter out of the country, Maura wrote very candidly to her parents, saying that even though this was "bad news," she thought it best to tell the truth:

I know that you would like to hear a little bit more of the reality here and what we are doing. Ordinarily, by mail or phone call, one cannot really say the truth because of the extreme vigilance. There is a great deal of tension and violence. The situation is very tragic. People are fleeing from their homes looking for some kind of safety as the so-called death squadron strikes anywhere and everywhere. The squad is made up of the military rightists who are the most ruthless. The cutting up of bodies by machete is one of the tactics to terrorize the organized groups from continuing their efforts. There are crimes on both sides, but the military and the rich oligarchy have committed extreme crimes, and many more.

The effort of the oligarchy is to wipe out the farmers and the workers who have organized for change, and they do this in the name of fighting communism. It is a much more vengeful, confusing and frightening case than that of [Somoza's] Nicaragua ...The organized groups do not trust or accept the present Revolutionary Junta as it continues to permit such outrageous slaughter of human lives, so they feel they must fight, even with their little, almost toy pistols.

Each day we trust the Lord to guide our ways as to what he wishes of us...At times one wonders if one should remain in such a crazy incredible mess. I only know that I am trying to follow where the Lord leads, and in spite of fear and uncertainty at times, I feel at peace and hopeful.[62]

In early November 1980, an ominous threat appeared on the door of the parish house where they lived. On the sign tacked to the entrance was drawn a knife and a head, dripping with blood. A verbal threat was attached: "Everyone working here is a communist, and anyone entering here will be killed." And Colonel Peña told Ita personally that he believed the Catholic Church was "indirectly subversive because it's on the side of the weak." By late November, hostility toward the church had reached the point where soldiers from an army barracks and Guardia headquarters only a block from the parish house came and went freely in the church buildings and had all but taken complete charge there. Even to ring the bells, church personnel had to ask permission.[63] Feeling there was some safety in numbers, the three Asunción sisters who lived across the street from the church began sleeping in the parish house.

A climate of fear had settled over Chalatenango. Yet, like Dorothy and Jean in La Libertad, Ita and Maura persevered. "We keep plugging along here, because life is threatened by other evils worse than death—hatred, manipulation, vengeance, selfishness," Ita wrote her old friend Jean Baumann.[64] And Maura wrote to friends:

> The way innocent people, families, children are cut up with ma-chetes and blessed temples of the Lord thrown and left for the buzzards to feed on them seems unbelievable but it happens every day. The other day passing a small lake in the jeep I saw a buzzard standing on top of a floating body. We did nothing but pray and feel. The pain goes on and there are many hungry peo-ple hiding and struggling. Being here with Ita and working for the refugees has its sweetness, consolation, special grace and is certainly a gift. The courage and suffering of these people never ceases to call me.[65]

There was also conflict occurring in other areas of El Salvador. In mid-September, the FDR (Revolutionary Democratic Front)—estab-lished in April 1980 to unite various political parties, unions, and grass-roots organizations—occupied churches throughout the country to protest rampant repression. In the following weeks, government forces attacked several occupied churches, killing at least fifteen protesters and capturing scores of others, many of whose corpses were later found with notes attached that read: "Thus die subversives who go around occupy-ing churches."[66] Also, the seminary in San Salvador was bombed, causing extensive damage to the building and adjoining archdiocesan offices.

On November 27 five leaders of the FDR were kidnapped by sol-diers and police from a Jesuit high school in San Salvador, where they were holding a strategy session. Their tortured bodies were recovered the next day. The shock and international condemnation that followed caused little governmental concern.[67]

While El Salvador was suffering through this latest crisis, Maura and Ita, as well as Madeline Dorsey and Teresa Alexander, were attending the annual regional assembly of Maryknoll sisters in Managua. Sister Maria Rieckelman, a psychiatrist who had flown in from the United States, observed the psychological state of Maura and Ita at this time. Maria found Maura to be coping with her new life in El Salvador surprisingly well:

> Maura had arrived in better shape than Ita, principally because she was not grieving as heavily for Carla, but also because— though she could not understand it herself—she was dealing with the horror quite well. She spoke of the mutilated bodies and the little children but it was as if she were walking through it with the sense that God was going to bring good out of that tremendous evil, and she was very conscious of her faith.

Rieckelman reported that Maura told friends at the assembly that she felt strong "not in myself but in the sense that the Lord will be faithful to me and his great love will take care of it."[68]

In Maura's last letter to her parents, mailed while she was en route to the meeting in Nicaragua, she expressed this inner peace, but also hinted that she was aware of the uncertain direction her life was taking: "It was so good to get your letter, Pop, telling me about Mom resting on the couch after supper. I can see you so well with the eyes of my heart and have so many precious memories of you always. Here we are all well and trusting very much in the Lord's strength." Then, explaining that it had "a lot of meaning for me these days," Maura included a prayer from the Trappist mystic Thomas Merton, which included these lines: "My Lord God, I have no idea of where I am going. I do not see the road ahead of me ... Though I may seem to be lost, and in the shadow of death, I will not fear for you are ever with me, and you will never leave me to face my perils alone."[69]

Ita, however, was not faring so well. At the Thanksgiving dinner that began the sisters' assembly in Managua, Ita told Maria she really did not feel very thankful—Carla was dead and El Salvador was in the throes of civil war. Maria suggested to Ita that perhaps she should spend some time in Chile or in the United States, and Ita promised to think about it.

To everyone's delight, Ita seemed to recover from her depression as the meeting progressed. On the second day, after a healthy bout of tears, Ita regained some of her old cheer, became more relaxed, and was able to participate effectively in several of the sessions. In fact, Ita was looking forward to a time when there would be more Maryknoll missioners serving in El Salvador, and it was partly due to her influence that the sisters agreed to compose a letter to hurry that day along. When the week-long series of meetings was over, Ita told Maria she did not want to go to Chile or the States but was ready to continue her work in El Salvador.[70]

Toward the end of the assembly, Ita received news from home that a baby had been born to her brother, Bill, and his wife, Mary Anne. Apparently the message had been garbled, for Ita wrote the following postcard to the Fords back home: "*Felicidades*, as they say here. With you I celebrate birth and new life—because at this point that's all I know. The message I received was that 'a child has been born,' and that's good enough for me! When I get near a phone that works, I'll get filled in on the particulars. Love to all, Ita."[71] She never made that phone call.

The Maryknoll sisters at the assembly were all aware of the dangers to which their friends Maddie, Terry, Maura, and Ita were returning. To conclude the assembly on the evening of December 1, they expressed their faith and their fears in prayer. Maddie read these prescient verses from Psalm 18: "The waves of death rose about me, the torrents of destruction assailed me. The snares of the grave entangled me. The traps of death confronted me. For the poor who are oppressed and the needy who groan, I myself will arise, says the Lord."[72]

Ita had translated a passage for the prayer service from a sermon of Oscar Romero on the beautitudes, part of which read: "Christ invites us not to fear persecution because, believe me, brothers and sisters, one who is committed to the poor must risk the same fate as the poor. And in El Salvador we know what the fate of the poor signifies: to disappear, to be tortured, to be captive and to be found dead."[73]

The assembly ended on a happy note. A little party was held during which Ita, almost her old self again, joined in one of the skits and amused everyone with her rendition of the "barnyard shuffle" as the group sang "Old MacDonald Had a Farm." And Maura, who could never resist an opportunity to dance and entertain, performed an Irish jig.

The following day, December 2, Maddie, Terry, Ita, and Maura left Managua for San Salvador in two shifts, with Maddie and Terry on board the early afternoon LANICA flight and Maura and Ita waiting for the later COPA flight. Arrangements had already been made with Dorothy and Jean to make two trips to the airport to pick them up. They arrived first for the flight bringing Maddie and Terry and drove them safely home to La Libertad. Then they returned to the San Salvador airport to pick up Maura and Ita, who, since they would be arriving near dark, had decided to spend the night in La Libertad and return to Chalatenango the next day.

But these plans were never realized. Unknown to any of the women, the arrivals of first Maddie and Terry and then Maura and Ita at the airport were being closely monitored by the Guardia Nacional. It was apparently either Ita or Maura or both of them that the Guardsmen were after, for the white Toyota microbus carrying Dorothy, Jean, Maddie, and Terry had been allowed to leave the airport unmolested after the first flight arrived from Managua.

After the arrival of the second flight, however, as the white microbus was leaving the airport and proceeding down the main road, it was halted by the Guardia Nacional. Dorothy, Jean, Ita, and Maura were never seen alive again.

CHAPTER 13

Execution, Cover-Up, and U.S. Complicity

On Thanksgiving Day 1980, Ambassador Robert White and his wife, Marianne, attended an ecumenical service held by the U.S. community in San Salvador. White had been appointed to El Salvador by President Carter in early 1980, and at the reception following the service met Dorothy and Jean for the first time. After chatting a bit, the Whites invited the Cleveland mission team to their home for dinner the following Monday. The mission team accepted the invitation.

At the dinner party on December 1, the volatile political situation in El Salvador was the primary topic of conversation. The Whites had insisted that their guests bring a change of clothes for an overnight stay, so they would not have to venture out late at night—El Salvador's roads were far too dangerous. So the next morning Dorothy and Jean said good-bye to their hosts. They climbed into their white Toyota minivan for a few hours of shopping in the city before they were to drive to the airport to pick up the four Maryknoll sisters who were returning from a regional meeting in Managua. Before they left the ambassador's house, Jean leaned out of the van window and called to Father Schindler who was also leaving the Whites: "Don't forget...get back to Libertad early—we'll have a party tonight with the Maryknollers when they arrive."[1]

The next time White saw Jean and Dorothy was Thursday, December 4, as they, along with Maura and Ita, were lifted by ropes from their common grave in a cow pasture in Santiago Nonualco, about an hour's drive from the airport. Their bodies were bruised and bullet-ridden; the ambassador could see from the evidence that some of them had been raped. Sickened by what he was witnessing, White cried over and over, "They're not going to get away with this."

Gradually, the sequence of events that had led to the deaths on the night of December 2 began to unfold. In Chalatenango, ominous incidents of intimidation and outright threats against church personnel had occurred. On the very day the women were murdered, the pastor in Chalatenango, Efraín López, had received an anonymous threatening letter. That night, on a street in Chalatenango, the parish sacristan was approached by a stranger and shown a death list containing the names of nearly everyone on the parish staff, including Sisters Ita Ford and Maura Clarke. The unidentified man shook the list in the sacristan's face and said, "The killings will begin tonight."[2]

All four women were aware that their work with the victims of the civil war had fueled the hatreds of the ruling class, the armed forces and police, and the paramilitary death squads. Each woman had had to face this reality within the past year, and each had made the voluntary commitment to continue her work with the Salvadoran poor anyway. The women also had enjoyed a certain immunity to the evils that surrounded them. Although Archbishop Romero and many Salvadoran priests had been murdered, no nun had been injured or killed. As Americans, too, they felt protected. Salvadoran Monsignor Ricardo Urioste used to joke that he felt secure driving through the countryside with Dorothy and Jean, "because no one in the country was safer" than these blonde, blue-eyed women.[3] All four women had experienced situations in which they felt protected by their *gringa* looks.

On the afternoon of December 2, Dorothy and Jean headed for San Salvador's international airport to pick up two of the four Maryknoll sisters returning from Managua. Sisters Teresa Alexander, Madeline Dorsey, Maura Clarke, and Ita Ford were arriving on different flights: Teresa and Madeline in the afternoon and Maura and Ita at around 6 PM.

On their afternoon trip to the airport, unknown to the women, Margarito Pérez Nieto, a National Guardsman on patrol at the airport, was watching Dorothy and Jean and called his detachment commander, Subsergeant Luis Colindres Alemán, to report that he suspected that the women had weapons concealed in a bag that one of them had carried from their van.[4] According to journalist John Dinges, Pérez soon placed a second call in which he was overheard saying: "No, she's not on this flight. We'll wait for the next one."[5] Around six o'clock Dorothy and Jean returned to the airport only to find that Maura and Ita's flight would be delayed an hour. The airport was crowded with foreigners who were arriving to attend the funeral the next day of Enrique Alvarez Córdoba, president of the Revolutionary Democratic Front (FDR), and five of its directors. The six had been kidnapped by members of the General Maximiliano Hernández Martínez Brigade, a right-wing death squad, and later been found slain along a roadside.

After Maura and Ita arrived, the four set off for La Libertad in the white minivan; again, their actions were being closely monitored by the Guardia. Judge Harold R. Tyler, Jr., in a report commissioned by the Reagan administration in 1983, described what then happened:

> At the airport traffic checkpoint, Guardsman Perez Nieto, following instructions, allowed the van to pass through. He detained all other traffic for about ten minutes, and then returned to the National Guard headquarters.
>
> Passing the checkpoint, the churchwomen arrived at Subsergeant Colindres Aleman's position. They were stopped and ordered to vacate the van. The guardsmen searched the van and questioned the women. Thereupon, Colindres Aleman ordered them back into the van together with Guardsmen Contreros Recinos, Canales Ramirez and Moreno Canjura. Contreras Recinos drove the van and, with Colindres Aleman and Guardsman Contreras Palacios and Rivera Franco following in the National Guard jeep, the small convoy started its journey fifteen miles into the hills of El Salvador.
>
> Shortly thereafter the jeep developed engine trouble. After a brief stop for temporary repair, the two vehicles made it to the National Guard command post at the town of El Rosario La Paz. There, Subsergeant Colindres Aleman telephoned the airport and instructed his second in command . . . to send another vehicle to El Rosario to retrieve them. The jeep was then left at the Guard post, with Guardsman Rivera Franco to guard it.
>
> The five other guardsmen crowded into the small van with the four churchwomen and proceeded in the direction of Zacatecoluca. At the intersection of the road to San Pedro Nonualco, the van left the main road and drove for another six kilometers, finally turning off onto a dirt lane. At a deserted site along the lane, Subsergeant Colindres Aleman directed Guardsman Contreras Recinos to bring the van to a halt, and ordered the women out of the van. The guardsmen sexually assaulted the women. Then, at Colindres Aleman's orders, they shot the women dead with their service rifles, leaving the bodies along the roadside as they fell. The guardsmen, upon completion of their grisly mission, then returned to El Rosario La Paz . . .

[Later] after the guardsmen had removed several items from the van, ... Guardsman Contreras Recinos opened the middle door of the van and, with the help of Contreras Palacios and Moreno Canjura, poured aviation fuel on the inside and outside of the van and set it afire ... Early in the morning on December 3, 1980, villagers from Santiago Nonualco, a remote village fifteen miles northeast of the airport, found the bodies of the four churchwomen sprawled along the roadside. One of the villagers contacted the local Militia Commander, Jose Dolores Melendez, to report the discovery. Shortly thereafter, two National Guardsmen and three Civil Guardsmen arrived at the scene, and ordered the preparation of a common grave. The local Justice of the Peace, Juan Santos Ceron, was summoned by the Militia Commander, and authorized the immediate burial of the women as "unknowns," an unfortunate practice that had become common in El Salvador ...

Word began to circulate in the community that four female Caucasian "unknowns" had been found dead and buried in Santiago Nonualco. A local parish priest heard the news and informed the Vicar of the San Vicente diocese. In turn, the Vicar notified the United States Embassy that the bodies of the American churchwomen had been found.

Upon learning the news, United States Ambassador Robert White went immediately to the murder site, where he found Father Schindler, who also had been notified by the parish priest of the discovery of the bodies. The Secretary of the Justice of the Peace arrived and gave permission for the removal of the bodies from the grave. All four women had been shot in the head; the face of one had been destroyed. The underwear of three of the women was found separately, along with bloody bandanas.[6]

Maryknoll sister Madeline Dorsey watched in anguish as the bodies were extracted: "Jean was first, her lovely face destroyed. Dorothy had a tranquil look. Maura's face was serene but seemed to utter a silent cry, and last little Ita." Maddie stepped forward to place Ita's contorted arm at her side.[7] The missioners and *campesinos* present then reverently wrapped the bodies in sheets.

Several years later, White recalled that as the women's bodies were being lifted by ropes out of their shallow grave, he asked the local town clerk if he knew who was responsible for the crime. To his surprise, the clerk informed him that "it was the military," adding that soldiers frequently used this isolated area to dump their victims' bodies.[8] Many years later, Clara Margarita Cortes, who lived close to where the women were killed, recalled that on the night of the killings, she and her husband heard a vehicle on the remote road near their home. They next heard loud screaming and then gunshots, followed by the vehicle speeding away with its radio blasting. Once the soldiers had left the area, her husband went to where the commotion had taken place and saw the lifeless bodies of the women.[9]

On Friday, December 5, the day after the missing bodies had been unearthed—scenes of which had been televised to millions of shocked Americans—President Carter suspended all assistance to El Salvador. He also commissioned a special fact-finding team headed by former assistant Secretaries of State William Rogers and William Bowdler to investigate the crime. After spending less than a week in El Salvador, the commission reported that although there was "circumstantial" evidence that security forces may have been involved in the killings, it found "no direct evidence" linking Salvadoran government officials or "high echelons" of the security forces to the crime. Over the strong objections of Ambassador White, the commission added that "positive steps were being made by Salvadoran authorities in their attempt to solve the crime." Based on this shaky evidence, on January 14, Carter announced the resumption of aid, citing "progress" being made in the case.[10] In all, the suspension had lasted little more than a month.

If seekers of justice were dismayed with the Carter administration, they were stunned by statements made by appointees of the newly elected Reagan administration. On December 16, just two weeks after the murders, Jeane Kirkpatrick, future United Nations ambassador, stated in an interview with the *Tampa Tribune*: "The nuns were not just nuns. The nuns were also political activists. We ought to be a little more clear about this than we actually are. They were political activists on behalf of the *frente* [Farabundo Martí National Liberation Front] and somebody who is using violence to oppose the *frente* killed these nuns." She then added: "I don't think the government [of El Salvador] was responsible [for their murders]."[11] Kirkpatrick gave no evidence to back up her assertions.

In February 1981, in a radio interview with CBS News, Reagan's appointee for human rights commissioner, Ernest Lefever (who was later rejected by Congress), made an even more startling allegation about "nuns hiding machine guns for the insurgents."[12] Like Kirkpatrick, he presented no evidence to support his claim. But the most salacious words were reserved for Alexander Haig. Testifying before the House Foreign Affairs Committee in March, the Secretary of State stated:

I would like to suggest to you that some of the investigations would lead one to believe that perhaps the vehicle that the nuns were riding in may have tried to run a roadblock or may have accidentally been perceived to have been doing so, and there had been an exchange of [gun] fire, and perhaps those who inflicted the casualties sought to cover it up.[13]

Prior to Haig's appearance before this committee, the FBI had completed an investigation of the crime scene. It had concluded that the churchwomen had been beaten and raped, blindfolded, and killed—execution style—each with a single shot to the back of the head. The FBI found nothing to indicate that the women had been armed, had run a road block, or that "an exchange of fire" had taken place. The van had no bullet holes in it, which certainly would not have been the case had the women been in a shootout. Since it is safe to assume that the FBI would have informed the State Department of its investigative findings, one can only conclude that Haig had to know that what he was saying to the House committee was false. Indeed, so outlandish and cruel was Haig's testimony that it prompted outrage and condemnation from journalists throughout the country. But even in the face of such national outrage, the efforts of Ita's brother, Bill Ford, and Michael Donovan, Jean's brother, to obtain a public retraction and apology from the secretary were to no avail.[14]

When Ambassador White traveled to Washington for the presidential inauguration of Reagan, he was summoned by Haig to meet him at the State Department. There, the new Secretary of State ordered him, upon his return to El Salvador, to send a cable to Washington noting that the Salvadoran government was making progress in its investigation of the murders. White replied that he was unable to do so "because the Salvadoran military killed those women, and the idea that they're going to investigate in a serious way their own crimes is simply an illusion."[15]

White's refusal to follow Haig's order to lie cost him his career. On March 20, 1984, in testimony under oath before the Senate Subcommittee on Western Hemisphere Affairs, White stated:

On January 22, 1981 . . . I received a telephone call from Acting Assistant Secretary [of State] John Bushnell. His statement shocked me to the point that I immediately dictated a memorandum of the conversation and sent a copy to the office of Central American Affairs, Bureau of Inter-American Affairs (ARA), Department of State. The memorandum reads

"John Bushnell called to tell me that ARA had finally succeeded in getting something which would pass for a policy statement on El Salvador from the people working with Secretary Haig. According to Bushnell, Haig stated that El Salvador was a government under stress and that he therefore was not going to be a party to any criticism of this government. This statement attributed to the Secretary was in response to ARA's concern about how it should handle the problem of how to characterize the Salvadoran government's investigation into the murders of the American churchwomen.

"Bushnell said that the Secretary's statement obviously created a problem for all of us. I responded that I could certainly see how it created a problem for ARA but that I did not believe that it created a problem for me at all...My assertion that no serious investigation was under way was in my opinion accurate and that I did not intend to change it.

"Bushnell stated that it could be a problem for me ... He went on to say that ARA had only said that there was 'progress in the investigation' and that this did not necessarily mean that there was a 'serious investigation.' I responded that to me this was playing with words and that either there was an investigation or there was not and if there was not, we should say so... "

Three days later I received a call from the personnel officer of the ARA bureau in the Department of State who informed me that he was calling at the [insistence] of Acting Assistant Secretary John Bushnell to point out to me that now was a particularly advantageous time to retire from the foreign service.

White concluded: "I regard the continuing cover up on this case as one of the most shameful chapters in the history of United States diplomacy."[16]

On February 1, Haig removed White as ambassador and forced him from the Foreign Service. As journalist Raymond Bonner later attested in an article on the churchwomen's case, such an action against a career diplomat was quite rare.[17]

Thus, in the short space of three months after their rape and slaying, Dorothy, Maura, Ita, and Jean were derided as "political activists" and were depicted as having concealed guns and being engaged in an "exchange of fire" while running a roadblock. Excuses had been made by the American Secretary of State for the "panic" of right-wing security forces of El Salvador. It would seem that high-ranking members of the Reagan administration agreed with the view of Subsergeant Colindres—their accused killer—that the women were "subversives." As Joseph Kazel, Dorothy's father, told the authors in an August 23, 1985, interview, "The Reagan people were looking for something to throw suspicion on my daughter and the other women... But they couldn't find a thing—because there was nothing to find." How different would be the eulogies and lamentations of the Reagan administration when four U.S. Marines were gunned down by leftists in a Salvadoran café in June 1985. The American public would not then hear a strained rationale for this terrorism or an intimation that the Marines had somehow sealed their own fate.

But in fairness to the Reagan administration, it must be remembered that the cover-up of the churchwomen's murders actually began while Jimmy Carter was still president. Indeed, it seems that the lame-duck Carter administration's strategy was to "make no waves" and pass the Salvadoran problem on to the Republicans. In the weeks following the killings, Ambassador White sent several cables to the State Department showing that the investigation by the Salvadoran government was a sham. Included were ballistics tests, fingerprints on the van, and other evidence linking the Guardia to the murders. The Carter administration, however, refused to make this information public. Moreover, although the families of the women were promised that the State Department would relate to them all pertinent data it received concerning the case, when Carter left office the families had learned nothing.

Reagan took office on January 20, 1981. The next day White decided to go public, reporting to the *New York Times* that the Salvadoran government had failed to conduct a serious investigation and that he had strongly protested to the State Department when it reported that authorities of that government had taken "positive steps." He concluded with the startling words, "I am not going to be involved in a cover-up."[18]

As has been noted above, a few days later, on February 1, White was removed as ambassador to El Salvador. Taking this as a sign that the Reagan administration was "in its corner," the Salvadoran Special Investigative Commission was terminated by the junta on February 27 without having filed a report.[19] On March 2, White House officials announced their decision to send an additional $25 million in military aid to El Salvador, along with twenty new military advisers who were to set up a training program for the Salvadoran armed forces. When the Senate Foreign Relations Committee questioned this action, the administration inferred that it had no intention of linking aid to human rights improvement.[20] Around this time the State Department also announced that a six-man U.S. Navy training team had been assigned to El Salvador to help maintain naval patrol craft equipment.[21] Disturbed by such actions, Senators Edward Kennedy and Paul Tsongas told reporters that they intended to present legislation to the Senate calling for the termination of all military aid to El Salvador until a thorough investigation of the churchwomen's murders had been completed.[22] Jeane Kirkpatrick, however, immediately spoke in defense of the Salvadoran government, calling it, in a debate with Robert White, "the best Government available for El Salvador."[23] Then, on March 14, the *New York Times* reported that the White House now planned to send fifty-four military advisers to El Salvador and to ask Congress for approval of an additional $60 million in military aid.[24]

Realizing that Congress might be reluctant to sanction such an escalation of involvement, the Reagan administration felt it essential to do whatever was necessary to convince not only the legislators but also the American people that the process of justice was moving forward in that tiny country. And since the public was particularly disturbed by the rape and murder of the churchwomen, the State Department was willing to go so far as to lie to Congress in this case. An incident related by former Ambassador White in 1984 illustrates this point:

> On March 18, 1981, before the Senate Committee on Foreign Relations, Mr. Francis M. Muller, Executive Assistant Director of Investigations, Federal Bureau of Investigations, volunteered the information that the legal attaché in El Salvador believes "a conscientious effort is being made to solve this crime [churchwomen's murders]." Yet on January 20, 1981, the legal attaché in San Salvador [had] submitted a report to Washington which made clear that the ongoing investigation was a hoax.[25]

The administration's efforts to influence public opinion did little to stem the growing opposition to increased involvement in El Salvador. Grassroots reactions began all over the country. On March 24, 1981, demonstrations, vigils, and hunger strikes took place in most major cities. Bumper stickers appeared on automobiles saying "U.S. Out of El Salvador" and "El Salvador is Spanish for Vietnam." At the end of March, the American Lutheran Church issued a statement opposing the U.S.'s Salvadoran policy. This was followed by similar statements from leaders of a dozen major Protestant denominations, as well as from Catholic and Episcopal bishops. Even the bishop of San Salvador, Arturo Rivera

Damas, risked his life by saying publicly that U.S. military aid to his country was helping to expand violence.

The Reagan policy soon received a powerful blow. At the end of April, the House Foreign Affairs Committee voted 26 to 7 to require the president to provide assurance every six months that "indiscriminate torture and murder" by security forces were being brought under control; if he could not do so, aid should then be terminated. On May 1 eleven House Democrats filed suit in U.S. District Court to force the administration to end military aid to El Salvador and withdraw all U.S. military advisers on the grounds that the White House had violated the Constitution and the War Powers Act. Finally, the administration was faced with newspaper editorials asking similar questions to that of the *New York Times* on May 3: "Why are there no Administration voices demanding an end to the torture and murder by El Salvador's 'security forces'?"

In light of such mounting criticism, it became apparent, even to the Salvadoran generals, that some dramatic gesture was necessary to prevent an eventual cut-off of aid. Thus, on May 9, 1981, Defense Minister García announced that six members of the Guardia had been arrested for the churchwomen's murders. That this was merely an attempt to sway U.S. public opinion was demonstrated on March 11, 1983, when the Salvadoran Appeals Court later ruled there was "insufficient evidence" to try them, despite the fact that one of the accused had already confessed and implicated four others.

The arrests of the guardsmen did little to weaken congressional opposition. A few days after they were taken into custody, the Senate Foreign Relations Committee passed an amendment similar to that of the House. Eleven of twelve senators voted to require Reagan to certify that "substantial progress" was being made by the Salvadoran government in implementing human rights. Even though junta leader José Napoleón Duarte accused the Senate of interfering in "an internal political problem" of El Salvador and Secretary Haig charged that such a vote only served to encourage leftist guerrillas, the full Senate approved the amendment on September 23, 1981. Henceforth, Reagan would have to certify every six months that "significant progress" was being made in El Salvador. If he could not do so, aid would be suspended. The amendment also stipulated specifically that progress in the investigation of the four churchwomen had to be demonstrated. [26]

It soon became clear that the congressional decree would prove no obstacle for Reagan. Despite obvious evidence to the contrary, he simply certified semiannually that "significant progress" was taking place. As White later remarked in 1984 before a Senate subcommittee, Reagan's conduct sent a message to the Salvadoran military: "These officers believe the Reagan administration is protecting them from the insistence of Congress that justice be done."[27]

It seemed clearer each day to large numbers of the American people that U.S. policy toward El Salvador was morally bankrupt. Consequently, thousands expressed their feelings on December 2, 1981, the first anniversary of the deaths of Ita, Maura, Dorothy, and Jean. Candlelight vigils and memorial services were held across the nation; in town squares, streets, and churches speaker after speaker eulogized the four women and denounced the Salvadoran policy of the White House. Such widespread condemnation of U.S. foreign policy by leaders and congregants alike of so many Christian churches was unprecedented in modern American history.

Reagan officials were aware that they were losing the support of the American people when it came not only to El Salvador but to all of Central America. A dramatic action was needed to turn public opinion around and, therefore, on January 26, 1982, Defense Minister García, now a general, announced that his government was ready to bring the previously arrested guardsmen to trial "within a very few days."[28] This enabled Reagan to "certify" that progress in ending human rights abuses in El Salvador was going forward. The scam succeeded and a placated Congress released a $135 million aid package.[29]

On February 14, Salvadoran authorities announced that one of the detained guardsmen had confessed to the churchwomen's murder and implicated four low-ranking associates. There followed a television appearance by Duarte in which he noted that lie detector tests taken by the accused satisfied him that no higher authorities had been involved in the crime.[30] Others were not so sure.

In his Sunday homily Archbishop Rivera Damas told his Salvadoran congregation: "But there is one thing that worries me. And that is how a sergeant could give orders unless beforehand . . . someone had not opened the way for decisions of this nature to be taken."[31] Five months earlier, Ambassador White had expressed similar doubts to a House subcommittee.[32] Bill Ford also noted at a hearing of the House Inter-American Committee in February that two of the three judges assigned to his sister's case had resigned, supposedly in fear for their lives. If only five low-level soldiers were involved in the murders, he asked, then why should the judges be so fearful?[33] Several months later, on June 30, newspapers revealed that the families of the churchwomen had found it necessary to file a suit against the U.S. government, charging that the State Department had violated the Freedom of Information Act by refusing to give them access to files on the case.[34]

In July Reagan again certified progress on human rights in El Salvador. A month later, Catholic Church officials in San Salvador publicly noted that following his certification, political murders had sharply increased. Surprisingly though, this time the U.S. embassy in San Salvador concurred. Two months later, on October 29, the embassy went further when Ambassador Hinton, addressing the local Chamber of Commerce, called the Salvadoran legal system "rotten" and threatened to end U.S. aid if security forces continued to murder civilians. When similar critical statements followed from Hinton, he was replaced as ambassador in May 1983 by Thomas Pickering.

But Hinton was not alone. Assistant Secretary of State for Inter-American Affairs Thomas Enders was likewise becoming disillusioned, especially concerning the unwillingness of the administration to push for negotiations between the Salvadoran government and the popular forces. Consequently, he too was removed from office and replaced by Langhorne Motley.[35]

The peak of frustration reached by Hinton and Enders was understandable in light of the ever worsening situation in El Salvador in the six months prior to their termination. On March 13, Marianella García Villas, president of El Salvador's Human Rights Commission, was murdered; the army reported that she had been killed while fighting along with guerrillas. Her colleagues at the Human Rights Commission denied the charge.[36] A few days later, after Archbishop Rivera Damas criticized the Salvadoran government's refusal to set a specific date for the trial of the churchwomen's killers, Republican Senator Nancy Kassebaum joined Democrats Christopher Dodd and Daniel Inouye in calling for sharp reductions in the administration's latest request for Salvadoran military aid. White House policy was clearly in jeopardy and it was evident that dramatic gestures were needed to salvage Reagan's aid program. Thus, in July 1983 the administration announced the formation of a commission headed by former judge Harold Tyler to investigate the churchwomen's case.

But congressional frustration continued. Although Deputy Secretary of State Kenneth Dam tried to dissuade him, Republican Senator Arlen Specter spearheaded a move by the Senate Appropriations Committee to hold back 30 percent of its Salvadoran military aid package until a satisfactory verdict had been reached in the churchwomen's case. A House subcommittee adopted a similar proposal.[37] In November both houses approved the measure; Reagan's request for $86.3 million was cut to $64.8 million, and $19 million of that was to be conditioned on a verdict in the trial of the killers of Ita, Maura, Dorothy, and Jean. A signal had been given: if a trial were not held and completed soon, Congress could be expected to take even sterner measures for the following fiscal year.

Reagan's problems intensified on December 2, 1983—the third anniversary of the deaths of the churchwomen—when Judge Tyler submitted his report to Secretary of State George Shultz. Far from lending credibility to U.S. Salvadoran policy, its contents proved devastating—so much so that the State Department immediately classified the report "Secret," even though Tyler himself had told several people that he had deliberately withheld from it anything that could not be made public. The administration's tactic actually backfired, for the essential thrust of the report was quickly leaked to journalists. Anthony Lewis of the *New York Times* expressed the thoughts of many in his profession when he asked in his column: "Is there no decency in the Reagan administration?"[38]

What was so devastating in the Tyler Report to cause the Reagan administration to withhold it from the public? Tyler's revelation that "the evidence . . . shows irrefutably that the five defendants . . . raped and murdered the women" was not enough to warrant its classification as "secret." His comments that Salvador is "a society that seems to have lost its will to bring to justice those who commit serious crimes against it" and that its "criminal justice system . . . is in a state of disrepair"[39] would perhaps have brought the State Department some discomfort, but certainly not enough to cause it to withhold the document. It was probably Tyler's conclusion that high-ranking Salvadoran officials could well have been involved in a cover-up of the crime that caused the administration to fear the report might provide Congress with a "smoking gun," which could justify a repudiation of current U.S. Salvadoran policy. More important, the White House was in the final stages of preparing to submit legislation to Congress in February 1984 requesting a four-fold increase in Salvadoran military aid, while also asking that further aid no longer be conditional on certification of progress in ending human rights abuses. In fact, on November 30, 1983, Reagan had vetoed a bill that would have extended the requirement for certification.[40] Obviously, Congress would have faced serious difficulties in complying with Reagan's request had remarks from the Tyler Report such as the following become public knowledge:

> The first reaction of the Salvadoran authorities to the murder was, tragically, to conceal the perpetrators from justice. Evidence available to the United States, including the special Embassy evidence, shows beyond question that Colindres Aleman confessed his involvement in the crime to ranking members of the National Guard within days of the murder. They responded by concealing this fact from the outside world, and the switching of their weapons to make detection more difficult.
>
> At a minimum, then Major Lizandro Zepeda Velasco, the National Guard officer in charge of the Guard's internal investigation, was aware of the identity of the killers and participated in

these acts. Sergeant Dagoberto Martinez, Colindres Aleman's immediate superior, has admitted that he also knew Colindres Aleman's guilt. We believe it is probable that Colonel Roberto Monterrosa, head of the government's official investigation of the crime, was aware of the identity of the killers and, further, that he participated in the cover-up by purposely failing to provide Colindres Aleman's fingerprints to the United States for analysis. We believe as well that it is quite possible that Colonel Carlos Eugenio Vides Casanova, then head of the National Guard and now a General and Minister of Defense, was aware of, and for a time acquiesced in, the cover-up.[41]

On the question of Salvadoran officials being involved in the actual murders, Tyler's report was inconclusive:

> The question whether Colindres Aleman was ordered to commit this crime by higher-ups is a troubling one. To the extent the Salvadoran authorities have investigated this matter, their inquiry is not nearly as complete as we would have liked. There is some evidence suggesting the involvement of higher-ups; most importantly, two low ranking guardsmen have testified that, in ordering them to participate, Colindres Aleman told them he was acting on higher orders.
>
> On the other hand, there is evidence to the contrary... Although it is unlikely that a dispositive answer will ever be known, we record here our best judgment: *on the basis of the evidence available to us*, we believe that Colindres Aleman acted on his own initiative.[42]

Had Tyler waited a few months longer before issuing his report, he would have been able to obtain important new evidence which might have changed some of his conclusions, for in March 1984 the news media revealed that a former high-ranking Salvadoran official had provided Senator Paul Tsongas and Representative James Shannon, and later the *New York Times* and Walter Cronkite of CBS News, with detailed information on the inner workings of Salvadoran death squads. Although the senator and congressman refused to name their source, it was later learned that he was Colonel Roberto Santiváñez, former chief of the intelligence unit of the Salvadoran army.[43] Santiváñez revealed that Colonel Oscar Edgardo Casanova had ordered the women "eliminated." Santiváñez further stated that Oscar's cousin, National Guard head and later Defense Minister

Vides Casanova took charge of the cover-up. In other words, the Minister of Defense, an official who had an important say in determining how U.S. military aid would be used, had played the major role in protecting the killers of the churchwomen. If such a disclosure placed Reagan's Salvadoran policy in jeopardy, it was dealt an additional blow three weeks later, when Walter Cronkite and the *New York Times* revealed that Colonel Nicolás Carranza—also implicated by Santiváñez in death squad involvement—had been secretly receiving more than $90,000 annually for five or six years from the CIA.[44]

With prospects for continued congressional support for the administration's Salvadoran policy growing dimmer each day, the White House moved to a new tactic, one which would prove quite successful. Administration officials finally convinced the power structure in El Salvador that it would have to allow a presidential election for aid to continue. Reagan officials then touted the upcoming election as a turning point in Salvadoran history. When leftist parties announced that they would boycott the election—an understandable decision since their candidates would have been targets for the death squads—the State Department accused them of refusing to participate because they had no popular support. When U.S.-backed Duarte led Roberto d'Aubuisson by a comfortable plurality and prepared for a run-off election, U.S. public opinion on Salvador began to shift back toward the Reagan position.

Following Duarte's run-off victory in May, Salvadoran judicial officials announced that they had finally completed arrangements for the long-awaited trial of the five guardsmen accused of murdering the U.S. churchwomen. By curious coincidence, the trial would begin on the day the U.S. House of Representatives was to vote on a Reagan request for an additional $62 million in emergency Salvadoran military aid.

Armed with news of the upcoming trial, Duarte journeyed to Washington, where in a dramatic speech he pleaded that Congress pass the emergency aid request. He had put his life on the line, he said, and now congressional help was needed if Salvador was to be saved. His speech, along with the news of the forthcoming trial, won the day. Former congressional opponents of continued military aid assured Duarte that he could now count on their support. Even liberal *New York Times* columnist Tom Wicker urged those on Capitol Hill to pass the aid package, but to make it clear that they were only doing so because of Duarte.[45]

On May 24, 1984, three and a half years after the slayings of Ita, Maura, Jean, and Dorothy, the trial of their murderers took place in the town of Zacatecoluca. In keeping with Salvadoran judicial procedure, a narrative of the crime was presented and the testimony of the accused guardsmen and witnesses was read. Arguments by both prosecuting and defense lawyers were then made.

None of the lawyers—neither prosecuting nor defense—or the judge brought up the possibility that higher officials might have ordered the murders. A year after the trial, Salvador Ibarra shed some light on the probable reason they had not. Ibarra had been the lawyer for Carlos Contreras Palacios, one of the accused guardsmen. On May 5, 1985, Ibarra, then living in Texas and applying for political asylum, told a *New York Times* reporter that in 1983 his client's wife had told him that Contreras and the other guardsmen had only been "carrying out orders from above." At first Ibarra refused to pursue this line of defense because he had been ordered not to do so by authorities. Later, however, he became less compliant. After ignoring a warning "not to pursue the case on his own," he was kidnapped and taken to National Guard headquarters where he was tortured. When he was finally released, he immediately fled to Texas. He concluded his story by telling the *Times* reporter that the Salvadoran government's claim—that a possible cover-up of high official involvement in the slayings had been thoroughly investigated—was "an outright lie."[46]

After the prosecution and defense attorneys presented their arguments, the jury members left the room for deliberation. Fifty-five minutes later they returned with a verdict of guilty. Members of the churchwomen's families were pleased with the convictions but agreed with William Ford when he noted that several questions remained unsolved: "Who ordered, who directed, who covered up, [and] who paid for these crimes?"

Once the defendants were found guilty, the U.S. House of Representatives voted 267 to 154 in favor of Reagan's $61.75 million emergency military request. A few days later, President Duarte remarked that he would not actively investigate whether high-ranking military officials were implicated in the crime: "If there is a case that I know absolutely, it is the case of the nuns. I don't need to investigate anything. I know it all." He added that he had taken it upon himself to investigate the crime personally and was thoroughly convinced that no officials were involved. He denied reports that on his recent trip to Washington he had told several congresspersons that he believed the cousin of General Vides Casanova (Colonel Edgardo Casanova) had been involved in the killings.[47]

In June 1984 all five guardsmen were sentenced to thirty years in prison. A Maryknoll spokeswoman then read a statement to the press: "True justice in this case will not be attained until the intellectual authors of this crime and those involved in the cover-up have also been prosecuted."[48]

On November 22, 1984, David Fernández Espino, head of the Salvadoran Lutheran Church, was kidnapped, mutilated, and killed by security forces. His "crime" seems to have been that he provided refugees with food and medical care.[49] On January 6, 1985, Pedro René Yanes, head of a Salvadoran investigative commission on official corruption, was gunned down.[50] On February 8, the Salvadoran human rights office of the Catholic Church reported that after a lull of almost a year, death squad murders were again on the rise.

But none of this mattered anymore; Duarte had been elected president and the murderers of Dorothy, Jean, Ita, and Maura had been convicted. In January 1985 Congress overwhelmingly approved $326 million in economic and $128 million in military aid for El Salvador for fiscal year 1985, but the Reagan administration claimed that was not enough; $200 million was needed for the military and at least $426 million in economic aid. A few months later, when leftist suspects were arrested for the June 19 murder of four U.S. marines, Reagan congratulated Salvadoran authorities for their "speed and professionalism" in apprehending the killers. He saw no reason to question why such "speed and professionalism" had been lacking in the case of the four churchwomen or in the forty to fifty thousand unsolved murders committed by the right. And the U.S. public no longer cared.

Gravesite of Carla, Ita, and Maura in Chalatenango, El Salvador

CHAPTER 14

El Salvador after 1982

After José Napoleón Duarte's victory in the much-touted 1984 presidential election, U.S. conservatives and many liberals thought that he and his Christian Democrats would be able to significantly reduce military violence, revive the failing Salvadoran economy, and defeat the FMLN (Farabundo Martí National Liberation Front) guerrillas. During his five years in office, however, he failed miserably in all of these goals. Moreover, widespread corruption of Christian Democratic Party (PDC) officeholders caused Duarte and his party to lose credibility with most Salvadorans who had voted for him in 1984.

Duarte deserved a modicum of praise, however, for his efforts in the area of peace negotiations. In July 1982, at the urging of Bishop Rivera Damas, the Salvadoran bishops' conference had for the first time issued a call for the creation of peace talks aimed at ending the civil war. The following October, the FMLN and FDR (Revolutionary Democratic Front) sent a letter to Rivera stating its willingness to enter into dialogue with the government. Nothing came from this since the junta and the Reagan administration felt a guerrilla defeat in the civil war was imminent and therefore preferable to peace talks. When Duarte was elected president, however, he announced that he was willing to enter into dialogue with the opposition. On October 15 both sides met, the first time at La Palma, Chalatenango, with Rivera serving as mediator, and then again in August at Ayagualo, near San Salvador.

The possibility of another meeting broke down when on September 10, 1985, FMLN guerrillas kidnapped Duarte's daughter, Inés, and a friend. Although Archbishop Rivera, with the help of Ignacio Ellacuría, the Jesuit rector of the Central American University, was able to obtain the two women's release by brokering a prisoner exchange, the damage was done. No more peace negotiations would be held in the remaining two years of Duarte's presidency. In August 1987, however, without consulting the U.S., Duarte, in a futile attempt to revive his crumbling political fortunes, did join with the other Central American presidents in signing the Central American Peace Accord that had been formulated under the direction of Costa Rican president Oscar Arias. Hopes for an end to the civil war were again raised, but no attempts were made to follow up on the Arias plan. The Reagan administration refused to lend support and, with its coffers being filled with ever-increasing American dollars, Salvadoran military leaders had no incentive to take negotiations seriously. At any rate, the assassination on October 26, 1987, of Herbert Anaya Sanabria, president of the nongovernmental Salvadoran Human Rights Commission, ended even the most remote possibility that negotiations might be revived. Anaya was the seventh member of the commission and its fourth president to be assassinated by the right.[1]

The failures of Duarte and the PDC, which had split into rival factions, opened the door for the National Republican Alliance (ARENA). Founded in 1981 by former Major Roberto d'Aubisson, who masterminded the assassination of Archbishop Romero, ARENA was closely linked to the death squads that for years had operated with impunity. ARENA's leaders realized that if their party was to have a chance in the 1988–89 elections, it would have to undergo a massive makeover. Consequently, d'Aubisson resigned from the party and was replaced by the U.S.-educated coffee planter and industrialist, Alfredo Cristiani. D'Aubisson's influence in ARENA continued, however, behind the scenes until his death in 1992. In the March 1988 elections, ARENA won 178 of the 257 mayoral offices and thirty-one of the sixty seats in Congress. The following year Cristiani took the presidency with 53.8 percent of the vote.

Following the elections, assassinations not only by right-wing security forces but also by left-wing guerrillas increased. On the positive side, however, on June 1, the day Cristiani took office as president, he announced that he would begin talks with the FMLN-FDR and, true to his word, two promising meetings were held in September and October, with representatives from the United Nations and the Organization of American States present. A scheduled third meeting was abruptly cancelled by the FMLN-FDR, however, following the bombing on October 31 of the headquarters of the National Federation of Salvadoran Workers (FENASTRAS) that killed eight to ten union leaders, including "Febe" Elizabeth Velásquez, the federation's charismatic director.[2]

On November 11 the FMLN responded to the bombing by launching a major offensive, which it had prepared for over the last two years, but had put on hold due to the peace negotiations. Five days after the offensive began, on November 16, 1989, Salvadoran soldiers entered the José Simeón Cañas Central American University (UCA) at about 1:00 AM and executed six Jesuit priests, along with their cook, Julia Elba Ramos, and her daughter Celina.

The reaction of the international community was an unequivocal denunciation of the heinous killings. In 1993, the United Nations Truth Commission on the Salvadoran civil war issued a report describing the events surrounding the November 16 killings. On November 15, the General Staff of the Salvadoran armed forces met with high-ranking military officers to discuss how to deal with the guerrilla uprising, which had proven to be stronger than expected. The military chief of staff, Colonel René Ponce "authorized the elimination of ringleaders, trade unionists and known leaders of the FMLN." Following the meeting, Ponce ordered Colonel Guillermo Benavides "to eliminate Father Ellacuría and to leave no witnesses." Father Ignacio Ellacuría, the UCA rector and a long-time critic of government-sponsored violence, had in recent years played a valuable role by serving as mediator between the FMLN-FDR and the Salvadoran government in an attempt to foster peace negotiations. Because of his efforts, he was despised by the army high command, which considered him a Marxist guerrilla.

To carry out Ellacuría's assassination, Benavides was assigned a unit of the U.S.-trained Atlacatl Battalion. Four lieutenants were charged with taking care of the physical execution of the Jesuit rector and any witnesses. Just after midnight, the four officers led a contingent of soldiers into the UCA Pastoral Center, where the priests lived. The soldiers "searched the building and ordered the priests to go out into the back garden and lie face down on the ground." Fathers Ellacuría, Ignacio Martín-Baró, Segundo Montes, Amando López, and Juan Ramón Moreno were then executed. Father Joaquín López y López and the two women were discovered in their rooms and also murdered. Before leaving the soldiers stole $5,000 and wrote on a piece of cardboard: "FMLN executed those who informed on it. Victory or death, FMLN."

As the U.N. Truth Commission Report made clear, several Salvadoran officers had prior knowledge of the planned assassination of the Jesuits, while others were involved in the attempted cover-up. The military placed Lieutenant Colonel Manuel Rivas Mejía in charge of the government's investigation and Colonel Benavides informed him of exactly what had occurred at the UCA. Rivas then promised to assist him in a cover-up.[3]

Although it might seem inconceivable that members of the new Bush administration would publicly defend the Salvadoran government and military, some did. Secretary of Defense Richard Cheney, for instance, told reporters that "there's no indication at all that the government of El Salvador had any involvement" in the crime, while a senior official of the State Department, who asked not to be named, claimed that "leftist rebels could have been responsible," since the FMLN "absolutely" had a motive for shooting the priests.[4]

Perhaps most disconcerting were the unusual measures resorted to by U.S. embassy officials and the Federal Bureau of Investigation (FBI) when it came to the only two people who claimed to have eyewitness testimony concerning the murders. On the night the crime was committed, Lucía Barrera de Cerna, the Jesuits' housekeeper, was sleeping with her husband, Jorge, and their four-year-old daughter in a normally unoccupied dormitory room on the periphery of the UCA campus. Like Julia Ramos and her daughter, the Cernas had asked if they could stay overnight on the university grounds because of heavy fighting in their neighborhood.

At about 1:00 AM the couple, awakened by gunfire, peeked out the window and, although they did not see the actual executions, saw five soldiers dressed in Salvadoran military uniforms.[5] After relating this to María Julia Hernández, head of *Tutela Legal*, the archdiocesan legal aid office, Lucía gave testimony under oath to a judge assigned to the case. Since her life could be in danger if she stayed in El Salvador, arrangements were made by the French and Spanish ambassadors to fly her on a French military plane to Miami, where they reasoned, as did Salvadoran church authorities, she would be safe.

When U.S. Ambassador William Walker heard of what was happening, he immediately called the French ambassador with a request to allow FBI agents and Richard Chidester, the legal officer at the American embassy, to fly with the Cerna family to "facilitate a smooth entry into the U.S.," since the family had no visas or passports.[6] Then, without informing any of the other parties involved, Walker arranged to have the plane met in Miami by State Department officials who took the Cerna family into custody. For the next week they were kept illegally in a hotel room and subjected to daily twelve-hour interrogation sessions by two FBI agents and Lieutenant Colonel Rivas, the same Salvadoran officer who had been assigned to investigate the murders and was already well aware of who the killers were.[7]

Rivas was particularly brutal in his interrogation and eventually terrified the Cernas into recanting their testimony, telling them if they did not he would have them sent back to El Salvador to face certain death. Following their recantation, the FBI agents gave the couple several lie detector tests, all of which they failed since they now said they had seen nothing.[8] Both Cristiani and the U.S. embassy in San Salvador, bolstered by the FBI "findings," issued press releases claiming the witnesses had admitted lying.

Following the Cernas' release, the outraged Jesuits arranged for the couple to be interrogated by teams from the Lawyers Committee for Human Rights and Scotland Yard, both of which concluded that they had been telling the truth.

Archbishop Rivera Damas accused the State Department of "brainwashing" Lucía and subjecting her to "aggressive and violent interrogation," while Jesuits in both the U.S. and El Salvador issued similar statements to the press.[9] But the damage was done; the testimony that Lucía had previously given to the Salvadoran judge was declared tainted and therefore null and void in a court of law.

Yet evidence had been accumulating that made it harder to perpetuate the cover-up of the Jesuit murders—so much so that Colonel Ponce evidently reasoned that some officers would have to be sacrificed to save the rest of the high command. Consequently, on January 7, 1990, President Cristiani finally admitted at a press conference what virtually everyone already knew—that members of the army had been responsible for the UCA killings.[10] Criminal charges were filed shortly thereafter against Colonel Benavides and four other officers. They were tried and—although countless army officers and lower-ranking soldiers had been either directly or indirectly involved in the murders or the cover-up—only Benavides and one other officer were convicted. They were sentenced to thirty years in prison, but were given amnesty and released on April 1, 1993.[11]

The Jesuit murders and the attempted cover-up of the crime outraged people throughout the world, including in the U.S. Despite the vehement objections of the Bush administration, majorities in the U.S. House and Senate jointly voted to suspend $42.5 million in Salvadoran aid that it had previously authorized. On January 15, 1991, however, following the FMLN's downing of a U.S. helicopter and the execution of the two surviving crew members, President Bush used his executive prerogatives to counteract Congress and release the aid. To justify his decision, he sent a certification to Congress regarding human rights in El Salvador, in which he falsely ascribed the majority of political killings in that country to the FMLN.[12] Seemingly, like Reagan and, to a lesser extent, Carter before him, defeating a supposed communist threat in El Salvador justified the giving of billions of dollars in military aid to a government that murdered tens of thousands of its own people, including its archbishop, four U.S. churchwomen, several priests, and now six Jesuit intellectuals at the Central American University. U.S. government officials appeared to have learned nothing from more than a decade of atrocities committed by the Salvadoran military.

On January 16, 1992, peace accords were signed by the FMLN and the Salvadoran government, thereby ending a bloody civil war that had taken the lives of at least seventy thousand Salvadorans, while displacing as refugees more than 25 percent of the population.[13] During the war, four billion U.S. dollars had been squandered in support of a ruthless government and military which, according to the U.N. Truth Commission, were responsible for almost 85 percent of those who were killed.[14] In a section of its report titled "Patterns of violence by agents of the State and their collaborators," the Truth Commission revealed the chilling mentality of the killers enabled by U.S. tax dollars:

> This violence originated in a political mind-set that viewed political opponents as subversives and enemies. Anyone who expressed views that differed from the Government line ran the risk of being eliminated as if they were armed enemies on the field of battle...
>
> Any organization in a position to promote opposing ideas that questioned official policy was automatically labelled as working for the guerrillas. To belong to such an organization meant being branded a subversive.
>
> Counter-insurgency policy found its most extreme expression in a general practice of "cutting the guerrillas' lifeline." The inhabitants of areas where the guerrillas were active were automatically suspected of belonging to the guerrilla movement or collaborating with it and thus ran the risk of being eliminated.[15]

Over the next few years, under the guiding hand of a United Nations commission, the Treasury police and National Guard were abolished and internal policing now became the responsibility of a newly created civilian police force. The size of the armed forces was reduced nearly in half, while by 1993 a purge of military officers accused of human rights abuses was completed. Furthermore, guerrilla forces were disarmed and the FMLN began its transformation into a political party. But on the negative side, five days after the United Nations Truth Commission issued its scathing report, the ARENA-dominated National Assembly passed an amnesty law guaranteeing protection from prosecution to all human rights violators, including those who had committed "genocides and crimes against humanity."

On November 26, 1994, Archbishop Rivera died of a massive heart attack. He had been the only Salvadoran bishop to support Romero during his tumultuous three years as archbishop. Like Romero, he had been an outspoken, if less charismatic, advocate for social justice and in this vein he especially stood out for his indefatigable pursuit of peace negotiations. Also like Romero, he faced opposition from all but one of his fellow bishops, at least in the early years of his episcopacy. Only Gregorio Rosa Chávez, who became his auxiliary bishop in July 1982, vigorously supported him in his attempt to follow in the footsteps of his predecessor. In 1984 the Vatican appointed Rodrigo Cabrera Cuéllar bishop of Santiago de María, while also naming Eduardo Alas Alfare bishop of Chalatenango in 1988 and José Mojica Morales bishop of Sonsonate in 1989. All three were moderates and their appointments reduced the power of the ultraconservative faction in the episcopal conference.[16] With the death of Rivera, social justice advocates hoped that the Vatican would choose Rosa Chávez as his successor. Rome, however, seemed more intent on reducing tensions between church and state and therefore passed over Rosa, naming instead Fernando Sáenz Lacalle archbishop. Sáenz, a conservative Opus Dei prelate, had been auxiliary bishop of Santa María and apostolic administrator of the Salvadoran military. His elevation as archbishop was a harsh blow to those in the Salvadoran church who hoped for a church more in line with the vision of Romero and Rivera.

Following the end of the civil war in 1992, the ARENA Party held both the presidency and control of the National Assembly until 2009. ARENA's neoliberal policies did little to revive a sluggish economy. Internal squabbles coupled with corruption also hurt the party. Indeed, the last two ARENA presidents were both eventually indicted for pocketing millions of dollars designated for earthquake relief.

El Salvador also faced a new problem in the post-civil war years—gang violence. Military sweeps into poverty-stricken rural departments, coupled with death-squad brutality in urban barrios in the 1980s and early 90s, had driven hundreds of thousands of Salvadoran peasants and low-income urban workers to flee the country. Thousands settled in Los Angeles, California, where they had little chance of obtaining decent employment. Faced with such hopelessness, some survived by immersing themselves in the Los Angeles gang culture. In 1996 the U.S. Congress passed the Illegal Immigration Reform and Immigrant Responsibility Act, which among other things called for the deportation of immigrants with criminal records. Thousands of gang members were now forced to return to El Salvador. Gangs that had originated in Los Angeles, most notably the *Mara Salvatrucha* (MS13) and its rival, the *Calle 18*, reestablished themselves in the land that they or their parents had earlier been forced to flee. Specializing in drug trafficking, extortion, and human trafficking, the returnees jacked up El Salvador's crime rate, which soon soared, and terrified its population—especially in the barrios of the poor. Ironically, with the signing of the peace accord, poor Salvadorans had survived the terror of the military and security forces, with their death-squad associates, only to face the new terror of gang violence.

On March 15, 2009, the FMLN finally came to power when Mauricio Funes was elected president. The FMLN also won the majority of mayoral elections and a plurality in the National Assembly. But Funes fared little better than his ARENA predecessors. Toward the end of his presidency, he too was indicted for embezzlement and escaped prosecution only by fleeing to neighboring Nicaragua, which offered him political asylum.

In 2014, Salvador Sánchez Cerén, a former guerrilla commander, became the second FMLN president in an extremely close contest in which he received 50.11 percent of the vote. After attempts to negotiate with the gangs (*maras*) failed, Sánchez moved to what he termed an "iron fist" policy. In August 2015 the Salvadoran Supreme Court declared the gangs terrorist organizations and the military was brought in to assist police in an effort to break their strength. Scores of gang members were arrested, but the *maras* viciously fought back. As a result, by early 2016 El Salvador had gained the dubious distinction of being the murder capital of the world, with a murder rate twenty-two times higher than that of the United States. Since the Salvadoran gangs have active members in forty-six states in the U.S., they have been able to create a lucrative business in transnational crime. [17] It is indeed ironic that a U.S. policy that financed a brutal Salvadoran military during the civil war and indirectly spawned the Salvadoran *maras* has now resulted in tens of thousands of boys and young men entering the U.S. illegally in order to flee gang violence at home.

But despite all the negatives, there is still hope in El Salvador. Images of Archbishop Oscar Romero appeared everywhere and thousands took to the streets in San Salvador on May 23, 2015, to celebrate his beatification. Moreover, in July 2016 the Salvadoran Supreme Court declared the nation's amnesty law unconstitutional, thereby finally making it possible to bring to justice those military officers and death-squad members who were responsible for so many thousands of murders—including those of Ita, Maura, Jean, and Dorothy.

Two weeks prior to his assassination, when he knew he would probably soon be murdered, Archbishop Romero told a Mexican journalist: "If I am killed, I shall arise in the Salvadoran people...If the threats are carried out, from this moment I offer my blood to God for the redemption and for the resurrection of El Salvador."[18] With Romero's canonization in Rome in October 2018, it seems that the martyred archbishop's prophecy may be on the verge of becoming a reality.

Conclusion

T he seven missioners in this book corresponded the old fashioned way—they wrote letters. Only a few decades later, this seems archaic, but it is a blessing for researchers who tell the missioners' life histories and want to understand their willingness to sacrifice on behalf of those they served. Whereas today's communication via texts, emails, and social media is instantaneous, it is also quickly written, brief, and often ephemeral. Our missioners, on the other hand, painstakingly kept family and friends informed with long letters—sometimes oral letters by audiocassette—expressing their hopes and fears, observations and sometimes analysis of events they witnessed, witty commentary, poetry, and artwork. They often reflected on their spiritual lives. Fortunately, much of their correspondence was retained and is today catalogued and stored in archives of religious communities. Otherwise, it would be almost impossible to delve into the reasons why these seven otherwise ordinary men and women became so extraordinary.

The letters are especially valuable because—when read over the progression of time—they project a remarkable roadmap of spiritual transformation. Like other Catholic missioners of their era, these seven began their mission commitment with pastoral and humanitarian goals. While trying to alleviate the hardships of the people they served, they would also catechize them, teaching them about the sacraments and liturgical rituals of the Catholic Church. A basic knowledge of traditional Catholic theology, it was hoped, would help those they instructed not only to save their souls but also to withstand the dual challenges of communism and Protestantism.

As time went on, in response to the directives of the Second Vatican Council, the missioners began to incarnate themselves more fully into the lives of the poor. This enabled them to develop a more complex understanding of the problems of Latin America. They came to realize that, although the spread of communism was a concern, far more important was the structural socioeconomic injustice that relegated the masses to a life of misery. Like so many other Catholic missioners, these women and men made a "preferential option for the poor," and in so doing came to know personally the fear experienced by the oppressed underclasses when they demanded justice and dignity. Unlike earlier generations of American missioners who could count on the good will of the governments and business elites in the countries where they worked, these two men and five women came to understand that taking the side of the marginalized was viewed as a "subversive" attempt to upend the long-standing unjust power structure. This is what put their lives in jeopardy.

Remarkably, these missioners became evangelized themselves by those they had come to evangelize. They began to question their own consumerism: they pared down their possessions to a minimum, wore simple clothing, and ate less. What money and possessions they did keep, they often gave away to those in need. And, as their letters and lives make clear, they also questioned their own country's support for the violent and repressive power structures of the countries where they served.

Like many church workers in Guatemala and El Salvador—both lay and religious—who committed themselves to the marginalized, our seven missioners eventually realized the potential consequences of their ministry. They knew they could be tortured and killed; all worked in situations of extreme danger and violence and most had received death threats. But none sought martyrdom. When they visited family and friends in the U.S., their loved ones begged them not to return to their mission assignments. Their religious superiors gave them the option to leave. They anguished over what to do, but in the end, they opted to stay despite the danger. They could not leave the suffering people that they had grown to understand and love. Fear of torture and death remained and haunted them. In facing their fear, in their weakness and inability to control their own fate, they came to know firsthand the God of those with no power. They learned to trust this God unconditionally, just as the poor did—they began to pray the prayers of the poor. They were no longer ordinary people. This spiritual transformation made them extraordinary.

Although poverty, injustice, and violence still repress the marginalized of Central America, it would be a discredit to our seven missioners to end the story of their lives on a note of sorrow. Not only did they offer much-needed hope during their lifetimes to thousands of victimized Central Americans, but this hope, like a relentless breeze, has crossed international borders to refresh and enlighten North Americans as well. Thousands can trace their interest in the people and politics of Central

America to the day they first questioned why a missioner had been shot to death and why the U.S. government was supporting the powers behind the execution. Many began to question why our country trained—and still trains—soldiers from Latin America at the School of the Americas[1] when so many of its graduates return home only to continue brutalizing the poor and impeding the development of true democracy. Others began to ask why the United States so often provides military aid to right-wing dictators throughout the world who use that aid to oppress their own citizens. And such questions have caused more than a few to conclude that a foreign policy replete with imperialistic notions and seemingly perpetual war is morally bankrupt and has to be changed.

These missioners injected a new vitality into North American Christianity. Documentaries were made and books were written about their lives and their sacrifices. Memorial services were held on the anniversaries of their deaths, where their stories were retold. Their portraits were hung in convents, rectories, schools, and private homes. Their names are still invoked at peace rallies, such as that held every November at the gates of Fort Benning, where the School of the Americas is located. And after the mention of each name, the marchers respond with a simple Spanish word, pregnant with symbolic meaning: *"Presente."* Indeed, it is no exaggeration to say that, as a result of the selfless witness of these missioners, countless religious congregations and individual Christians have determined to follow their example by reexamining their own commitment to the marginalized people of God.

Notes

Preface

1. Gerard O'Connell, "Pope Francis Recognizes Fourth Path to Sainthood," *America* (July 11, 2017), www.americamagazine.org.

Introduction

1. Samuel Eliot Morison, *Christopher Columbus, Mariner* (New York: Meridian Books, 1955), 43.

2. Bartolomé de Las Casas, *History of the Indies*, book 3, chapter 5, in *Witness: Writings of Bartolomé de Las Casas*, ed. George Sanderlin (Maryknoll, NY: Orbis Books, 1992), 67.

3. The best study of Las Casas is probably Gustavo Gutiérrez, *Las Casas: In Search of the Poor of Jesus Christ* (Maryknoll, NY: Orbis Books, 1993).

4. Enrique Dussel, *A History of the Church in Latin America: Colonialism to Liberation* (Grand Rapids, MI: Eerdmans Publishing Co., 1981), 52–53.

5. Quoted in Anne Chapman, *Los Lencas de Honduras en el siglo XVI* (Tegucigalpa, Honduras: *Instituto Hondureño de Antropología e Historia*, 1978), 3.

6. Robert Chamberlain, *The Conquest and Colonization of Honduras, 1502–1550* (New York: Octagon Books, 1966), 133, 239.

7. Dussel, *History of the Church*, 55.

8. Benjamin Keen and Mark Wasserman, *A Short History of Latin America* (Boston: Houghton Mifflin, 1984), 74.

9. George Pendle, *A History of Latin America* (Harmondsworth, England: Pelican Books, 1983), 58–59.

10. Dussel, *History of the Church*, 91.

11. José María Tojeira, *Los Hicaques de Yoro* (Tegucigalpa, Honduras: *Edición Guaymuras*, 1982), 22–34.

12. John Coulson, ed., *The Saints: A Concise Biographical Dictionary* (New York: Guild Press, 1958), 614.

13. Quoted in Keen and Wasserman, *Short History*, 101.

14. Edward L. Cleary, *Crisis and Change: The Church in Latin America Today* (Maryknoll, NY: Orbis Books, 1985), 59–60.

15. Ibid., 60–61.

16. Ibid., 42.

17. Ibid., 115.

18. See Gerald M. Costello, *Mission to Latin America: The Successes and Failures of a Twentieth-Century Crusade* (Maryknoll, NY: Orbis Books, 1979).

19. Ronald Burke, "Cry from Guatemala: 'They Killed Stan,'" *Maryknoll* (January 1982), 51.

Chapter 1. Stanley Rother: Diocesan Priest

1. Stanley Rother, letter to Archbishop Charles Salatka, September 22, 1980, in Stanley Rother, *The Shepherd Cannot Run: Letters of Stanley Rother, Missionary and Martyr*, ed. David Monahan (Oklahoma City: Archdiocese of Oklahoma City, 1984), 31. Hereafter cited as Monahan, *Shepherd*.

2. Rother, letter to Frankie Williams, November 16, 1980, Monahan, *Shepherd*, 39.

3. Bob Rivard and Tanya Barrientos, "Murdered Priest's Family Prays for Justice," *The Plain Dealer* (August 8, 1982): 3-AA.

4. Thomas McSherry, email to the authors, March 12, 2017; Monahan, *Shepherd*, 91.

5. Monahan, *Shepherd*, 4–5.

6. David Monahan, "Rotherville: A Place of Pioneers and Strong Faith," *Sooner Catholic* (August 16, 1981): 5.

7. Christopher M. Riggs, "Kansas nun shares memories of her brother," *The Catholic Spirit*, Archdiocese of St. Paul and Minneapolis, September, 2017, http://thecatholicspirit.com/news/nation-and-world/kansas-nun-shares-memories-brother-path-sainthood/.

8. Marita Rother, ASC, "Reflections: Sr. Marita Rother," *Sooner Catholic: Father Stanley Rother* (September 23, 2017): 26, special beatification edition.

9. "Yearbook: 'Noise is not his specialty. Cooperation marks his personality,'" *Sooner Catholic* (August 16, 1981): 4.

10. Rother, letter to Mary and Joe Tinker, July 12, 1981, Monahan, *Shepherd*, 81.

11. Riggs, "Kansas nun shares memories."

12. Martha Mary McGaw, "Father Stanley Rother: 'My People Need Me,'" *Sooner Catholic* (August 16, 1981): 20.

13. Marita Rother, letter to the authors, November 25, 1984.

14. Marvin Leven, audiocassette sent to the authors, July 27, 1985; McGaw, "Father Stanley Rother," 20.

15. Harry J. Flynn, "I Remember Stanley Rother," *Sooner Catholic* (January 3, 1982): 6.

16. McGaw, "Father Stanley Rother," 20.

17. María Ruiz Scaperlanda, *The Shepherd Who Didn't Run: Father Stanley Rother, Martyr from Oklahoma* (Huntington, IN: Our Sunday Visitor Publishing Division, 2015), 68.

18. *National Catholic Reporter* (November 19, 1982): 8.

19. Martha Mary McGaw, "Memories of happy laughter, old clothes and night watches," *Sooner Catholic* (August 16, 1981): 6.

20. Leven, audiocassette.

21. George Rigazzi, Archivist, Archdiocese of Oklahoma City, email to the authors, May 19, 2017.

22. Walter LaFeber, *Inevitable Revolutions: The United States in Central America*, 2nd ed. (New York: W. W. Norton, 1993), 8.

23. Phillip Berryman, *The Religious Roots of Rebellion: Christians in Central American Revolutions* (Maryknoll, NY: Orbis Books, 1984), 170–73; Benjamin Keen and Mark Wasserman, *A Short History of Latin America* (Boston: Houghton Mifflin, 1984), 441–42.

24. Monahan, *Shepherd*, 6.

25. Gerald M. Costello, *Mission to Latin America: The Successes and Failures of a Twentieth Century Crusade* (Maryknoll, NY: Orbis Books, 1979), 44.

26. David Monahan, "Santiago Atitlán was a place only for the patient," *Sooner Catholic* (August 16, 1981): 13.

27. The description that follows, unless otherwise noted, is based on Frankie Williams, audiocassette for the Religious Task Force, Washington, DC, June 1982, which Williams sent to the authors, and on visits by the authors.

28. Monahan, *Shepherd*, 2.

29. Scaperlanda, *The Shepherd*, 95.

30. Ibid., 96.

31. Ibid., 97–101, 103–104.

32. Monahan, *Shepherd*, 3.

33. McGaw, "Father Stanley Rother," 20; Scaperlanda, *The Shepherd*, 104.

34. Monahan, *Shepherd*, 3, 6.

35. "Yearbook," *Sooner Catholic*, 4.

36. Martha Mary McGaw, "Guatemala visit brings sorrow and joy," *Sooner Catholic* (August 28, 1983): 3.

37. Rother, letter to Frankie Williams, July 9, 1980, Monahan, *Shepherd*, 15.

38. Marita Rother, letter to the authors, April 6, 1985.

39. Stanley Rother, letter to Marita Rother, Christmas 1979.

40. Marita Rother, letter to the authors, April 6, 1985.

41. Rother, letter to Joe and Mary Tinker, September 14, 1980, Monahan, *Shepherd*, 28.

42. Rother, letter of 1973, Monahan, *Shepherd*, 8.

43. The descriptions that follow, unless otherwise noted, are from Williams, audiocassette; Williams, telephone interview, May 9, 1985; McSherry, email to the authors.

44. Robert S. Carlsen, *The War for the Heart and Soul of a Highland Maya Town*, rev. ed. (Austin, TX: University of Texas Press, 2011), 152.

45. Penny Lernoux, *Cry of the People: The Struggle for Human Rights in Latin America—The Catholic Church in Conflict with U.S. Policy* (New York: Penguin Books, 1982), 375–77.

46. Williams, audiocassette.

47. Scaperlanda, *The Shepherd*, 116.

48. Ibid., 144–47.

49. Rother, letter to Williams, July 9, 1980; Monahan, *Shepherd*, 15.

50. Rother, letter to Marita Rother, Christmas 1979; Leven, audiocassette.

51. McGaw, "Memories," 6.

52. Marita Rother, letter to the authors, March 10, 2017.

53. Rother, letter to Marita Rother, Christmas 1978; Monahan, *Shepherd*, 9.

54. Rother, letter to Gertrude and Franz Rother, July 9, 1980, Monahan, *Shepherd*, 87–89.

55. Williams, audiocassette.

56. Leven, audiocassette.

57. Williams, audiocassette and telephone interview.

58. Patty Edmonds, "Oklahoma priest murdered in Guatemala," *National Catholic Reporter* (August 14, 1981): 7.

59. McGaw, "Father Stanley Rother," 20.

60. Paul Joslin, telephone interview with the authors, February 2, 2017.

61. Scaperlanda, *The Shepherd*, 118–19.

62. LaFeber, *Inevitable Revolutions*, 257.

63. Ibid., 189-93, 196-205.

64. John D. Cozean, *Latin America 1982* (Washington, DC: Stryker-Post, 1982), 65.

65. Rother, letter to Oklahoma Catholics, Christmas 1969, Monahan, *Shepherd*, 10.

66. Flynn, "I Remember," 6.

67. Scaperlanda, *The Shepherd*, 156–57.

68. Rother, letter, May 21, 1979, Monahan, *Shepherd*, 10.

69. Rother, letter, early 1980, Monahan, *Shepherd*, 10.

70. Ronald Burke, "Cry from Guatemala: 'They Killed Stan,'" *Maryknoll* (January 1982): 51.

71. Rother, letter to Marita Rother, September 14, 1980, Monahan, *Shepherd*, 24–25.

72. Rother, letter to Williams, July 9, 1980, Monahan, *Shepherd*, 14–15.

73. Rother, letter to Archbishop Salatka, September 22, 1980, Monahan, *Shepherd*, 29–31.

74. Berryman, *Religious Roots*, 206.

75. Rother, Christmas letter 1980 to Oklahoma Catholics, Monahan, *Shepherd*, 54; "A Letter from Father Rother," January 5–7, 1981, *Sooner Catholic* (September 13, 1981): 7.

76. Rother, Christmas letter 1980, Monahan, *Shepherd*, 54–55.

77. Rother, letter to John Steichen, January 5, 1981, Monahan, *Shepherd*, 61–64.

78. Burke, "Cry," 52.

79. McSherry, email to the authors; Christopher P. Winner, "Guatemala Aid Issue Debated in Congress," *National Catholic Reporter* (August 14, 1981): 6.

80. Rother, "A Letter from Father Rother," January 5–7, 1981; Williams, telephone interview.

81. Rother, "A Letter from Father Rother," January 5–7, 1981.

82. Williams, audiocassette.

83. Winner, "Guatemala Aid," 6.

84. Phillip Wearne, "Guatemala," *Central American Indians*, Minority Rights Group Report No. 62 (London: 1984): 11.

85. Patricia Scharber Lefevre, "Pax Christi Study: Guatemalan Genocide," *National Catholic Reporter* (February 26, 1982): 20.

86. Rother, "A Letter from Father Rother," January 5–7, 1981.

87. Edmonds, "Oklahoma Priest," 7.

88. Monahan, *Shepherd*, 69; Leven, audiocassette.

89. Ronald Burke, "Guatemala: Requiem for a Missionary," *Time* (August 10, 1981): 41, and "Cry," 51–52.

90. Rother, letter to Mark Gruenke, March 3, 1981, Monahan, *Shepherd*, 70.

91. Riggs, "Kansas nun shares memories."

92. Amnesty International, "Guatemala: A Government Program of Political Murder" (London: 1981): 3; Berryman, *Religious Roots*, 208–10.

93. Rother, letter to Don McCarthy, June 1, 1981.

94. Dial Torgerson, "U.S. Priest Reportedly Killed by Guatemalan Kidnappers, Not Thieves," *Los Angeles Times* (August 25, 1981): Part 1, 15.

95. Junno Arocho Esteves, "Pope Recognizes Martyrdom of Franciscans Killed in Guatemala," *Crux* (October 10, 2017), https://cruxnow.com/cns/2017/10/10/pope-recognizes-martyrdom-franciscans-killed-guatemala/.

96. Leven, audiocassette.

97. Scaperlanda, *The Shepherd*, 213.

98. Williams, audiocassette.

99. Ibid.; Monahan, *Shepherd*, 91; Torgerson, "U.S. Priest," 15.

100. Monahan, *Shepherd*, 91–92.

101. Paul Joslin, email to the authors, February 7, 2017.

102. "Oklahoma Martyr," *Back in Time*, Episode 604, Oklahoma Educational Television/PBS video, 2016.

103. Williams, telephone interview; Martha Mary McGaw, "His Indian friends kept his heart in Guatemala," *Sooner Catholic* (August 16, 1981): 3.

104. Edmonds, "Oklahoma Priest," 8.

105. Ibid.

106. Torgerson, "U.S. Priest," 15.

107. Rivard and Barrientos, "Murdered Priest's Family," 3-AA.

Chapter 2. The Tz'utujil Revolt

1. David Monahan, ed.,"Notes and Identifications," in *The Shepherd Cannot Run: Letters of Stanley Rother, Missionary and Martyr* (Oklahoma City: Archdiocese of Oklahoma City, 1984), 80; Thomas McSherry, email to the authors, March 29, 2017; *Americas Watch*, "Guatemala, Getting Away with Murder: An Americas Watch and Physicians for Human Rights Report" (NY and MA: Americas Watch, August 1991), 52–64. James Loucky and Robert Carlsen, "Massacre in Santiago

Atitlán: A Turning Point in the Maya Struggle?" *Cultural Survival Quarterly* (September 1991), https://www.culturalsurvival.org/publications/cultural-survival-quarterly/massacre-santiago-atitlan-turning-point-maya-struggle.

2. Henri J. M. Nouwen, *Love in a Fearful Land: A Guatemalan Story* (Notre Dame, IN: Ave Maria Press, 1985), 18, 24–25, 116.

3. McSherry stated that "eight or nine" Guatemalans had been ordained in Sololá in his last years there, adding that the memory of Father Stan was a factor in explaining the rise in native vocations; McSherry, telephone interview with the authors, February 27, 2017.

4. Stephen T. De Mott, MM, "A Martyr's Legacy," *Maryknoll* (May 1985): 38.

5. McSherry, email to the authors, March 12, 2017.The list of those from Santiago Atitlán who disappeared or were killed from 1980 through 1990 is also in the introduction of the Tz'utujil New Testament, published on July 28, 1991, the tenth anniversary of Rother's martyrdom.

6. McSherry, telephone interview.

7. Thomas McSherry, "Christmas 1987: A Letter from Santiago Atitlán," *Sooner Catholic* (December 27, 1987): 6.

8. Frankie Williams, undated letter, copy mailed in 1987 to the authors.

9. Frankie Williams, letter to *Sooner Catholic* (May 31, 1987): 12.

10. The description of the 1990 Santiago Atitlán massacre that follows is taken from Loucky and Carlsen, "Massacre"; *Americas Watch*, "Guatemala"; Report of the Archdiocesan Office of Human Rights (*La Oficina de Derechos Humanos, Arzobispado de Guatemala*), ordered by Archbishop Próspero Penados of Guatemala City, 1990; unpublished, undated notes of Frank Kendrick, PhD, University of Akron, who went to Santiago Atitlán, probably in 1991, and interviewed witnesses.

11. Through the auspices of Micatokla, the young man, Diego Ixbalan Reanda, was flown to Oklahoma for specialized treatment in a hospital.

12. McSherry, telephone interview.

13. Loucky and Carlsen, "Massacre"; Kendrick, notes; McSherry, telephone interview; McSherry, email, March 12, 2017.

14. Loucky and Carlsen, "Massacre."

15. Report of Archdiocesan Office of Human Rights.

16. Loucky and Carlsen, "Massacre."

17. Kendrick, notes; Loucky and Carlsen, "Massacre."

18. Loucky and Carlsen, "Massacre." These incidents were brought to the authors' attention by historian Susan Fitzpatrick–Behrens.

19. Shirley Christian, "Santiago Atitlán Journal; Routed by Village's Rage, a Feared Army Retreats," *New York Times* (December 12, 1991), https://www.nytimes.com/1991/12/12/world/santiago-atitlan-journal-routed-by-village-s-rage-a-feared-army-retreats.html.

20. Loucky and Carlsen, "Massacre."

21. Author Edward Brett visited Santa Clara the week after this happened and learned the details from the priest and the Christian Brothers, who ran a school in nearby Santa María Visitación.

22. John Mallon, "An Interview with Father Tom McSherry," *Sooner Catholic* (July 3, 1994): 4–5. Much of what McSherry said in this article was confirmed in the authors' interview with him on February 28, 2017.

23. McSherry, email to the authors, March 29, 2017.

24. Marita Rother, "Return to Santiago Atitlán, Guatemala: Reflections," July 2016; copy sent to the authors.

Chapter 3. James Miller: Christian Brother

1. Theodore Drahmann, *Hermano Santiago: The Life and Times of Brother James Miller, FSC, a De La Salle Christian Brother and Missionary* (Memphis, TN: Christian Brothers Archives of the Midwest, 2002), 17–18.

2. Stephen Markham, "Brother James Miller, FSC, 1944–1982," *Memorial to James Alfred Miller, FSC, of the Winona Province* (Winona, MN: St. Mary's Press, n.d.): 1.

3. James Miller, "Autobiography," June 1, 1978, in Markham, "Brother James," 7.

4. Ibid., 2.

5. Ibid., 1–2

6. Carl Koch, Jeffrey Calligan, and Jeffrey Gros, eds., *John Baptist de la Salle: The Spirituality of Christian Education*, Classics of Western Spirituality Series (Mahwah, NJ: Paulist Press, 2004), 5–20.

7. John Baptist de la Salle, "6th Meditation for the Time of Retreat, Point #2," in ibid., 51.

8. Miller, "Autobiography," 7.

9. Ibid. Miller meant he was the only one of the group to remain a Christian Brother.

10. Ibid.

11. Gerard Pihaly, FSC, "Notes on Brother James Miller," written at request of the authors, March 26, 1985.

12. Patty Edmonds, "Brother slain in Guatemala 'gave his life for students,'" *National Catholic Reporter* (February 26, 1982): 19.

13. Drahmann, *Hermano*, 19.

14. Ibid., 21–22.

15. Gregory Robertson, interview with the authors, 1982.

16. Mordecai Specktor, "Murder in Guatemala: The War Comes Home," *Twin Cities Reader* (February 25, 1982): 7.

17. Don Geng, "A Humble Servant: Brother James Murdered in Guatemala," *Cretin Quarterly Bulletin* (Spring 1982): 1.

18. Drahmann, *Hermano*, 28–29.

19. Geng, "Humble Servant," 1.

20. Miller, "Autobiography," 7.

21. Drahmann, *Hermano*, 35.

22. Markham, "Brother James," 3; Miller, "Autobiography," 7.

23. Drahmann, *Hermano*, 26.

24. Benjamin Keen and Mark Wasserman, *A Short History of Latin America* (Boston: Houghton Mifflin, 1984), 443.

25. Phillip Berryman, *Religious Roots of Rebellion: Christians in Central American Revolutions* (Maryknoll, NY: Orbis Books, 1984), 66.

26. Michael Dodson and Tommie Sue Montgomery, "The Churches in the Nicaraguan Revolution," in *Nicaragua in Revolution*, ed. Thomas Walker (New York: Praeger, 1982), 168.

27. Markham, "Brother James," 4; Miller, "Autobiography," 7–8.

28. Markham, "Brother James," 2.

29. Ibid., 4.

30. From a bulletin sent to the Christian Brothers of the Winona Province after Miller's death.

31. Nicholas Geimer, letter to the authors, March 17, 1985.

32. Drahmann, *Hermano*, 36–37; Miller, "Autobiography," 78.

33. Drahmann, *Hermano*, 37.

34. Edmonds, "Brother Slain," 19.

35. Stephen Markham, letter to the authors, March 19, 1985.

36. Geimer, letter to the authors.

37. Ibid.

38. Jane Campbell, letter to Don Geng, March 8, 1982.

39. Geimer, letter to the authors.

40. Ibid.

41. Ibid.

42. Geng, "Humble Servant," 1.

43. John A. Booth, Christine J. Wade, and Thomas W. Walker, *Understanding Central America: Global Forces, Rebellion, and Change*, 6th ed. (Boulder, CO: Westview Press, 2015), 104.

44. Geimer, letter to the authors.

45. Edmonds, "Brother Slain," 19.

46. H. Lewis Twohig, letter to the authors, March 1985.

47. Geng, "Humble Servant," unedited, unpublished draft, 2–3.

48. Miller to Martin Spellman, 1980, in Drahmann, *Hermano*, 43–44.

49. Drahmann, *Hermano*, 47.

50. Geng, "Humble Servant," 1.

51. Berryman, *Religious Roots*, 200.

52. Ibid., 201–2.

53. Phillip Wearne, "Guatemala," in D. Stephen, P. Wearne and R. Stavenhagen, *Central America's Indians*, Minority Rights Group, Report No. 62 (London: 1984): 12.

54. Stephen Markham, "Memorial Reflection," *Memorial to James Alfred Miller, FSC, of the Winona Province* (Winona, MN: St. Mary's Press, no date), 15–16.

55. Paul Joslin, email to the authors, February 27, 2017.

56. Paul Joslin, "I Know What God Has in Store," *Maryknoll* (July 1982): 14.

57. Drahmann, *Hermano*, 19, 50–51.

58. Ibid., 51–52.

59. Wearne, "Guatemala," 18; Victor Perera, "Pawns in the Political Game," *The Nation* (November 12, 1983): 455–59.

60. Wearne, "Guatemala," 18.

61. Ibid.

62. Markham, "Brother James," 4.

63. Ibid., 5; Edmonds, "Brother Slain," 19.

64. Geng, "Humble Servant," 1.

65. Pihaly, "Notes."

66. Drahmann, *Hermano*, 55.

67. Joslin, "I Know," 14.

68. Ibid.,13.

69. Archbishop John Roach, "Pray that God Will Change Oppressors' Hearts," St. Paul, Minnesota, *The Catholic Bulletin* (February 1982).

70. Geng, "Humble Servant," 1, 5.

71. This speculation is based on comments made to the authors by Joslin and other Christian Brothers in 1987 and February 2017.

72. Joslin, email to the authors, March 1, 2017.

73. Drahmann, *Hermano*, 57–59.

74. Miller, letter to Gregory and Maura Robertson and others, Christmas 1981.

75. Cyril Litecky, letter to Reverend Bryan Hehir, Director of the International Office of Peace and Justice at the United States Catholic Conference in Washington, DC, 1983.

76. Drahmann, *Hermano*, 62.

77. Joslin, email to the authors, February 27, 2017.

Chapter 4. Guatemala after 1982

1. Susanne Jonas, *The Battle for Guatemala: Rebels, Death Squads, and U.S. Power* (Boulder, CO: Westview Press, 1991), 149. Hal Brands postulates that half of the two hundred thousand who died in the Guatemalan civil war were killed in the two-year period between 1981 and 1983. See Hal Brands, *Crime, Violence and the Crisis in Guatemala: A Case Study in the Erosion of the State* (May 2010), 11–12, http://publications.armywarcollege.edu/pubs/2070.pdf.

2. Jim Handy, *Gift of the Devil: A History of Guatemala* (Boston: South End Press, 1984), 257–58; Phillip Berryman, *Stubborn Hope: Religion, Politics, and Revolution in Central America* (Maryknoll, NY: Orbis Books, 1994), 119.

3. Handy, *Gift*, 259–60; Berryman, *Stubborn Hope*, 121.

4. Jennifer Schirmer, *The Guatemalan Military Project: A Violence Called Democracy* (Philadelphia: University of Pennsylvania Press, 1998), 33; William M. LeoGrande, *Our Own Back Yard: The United States in Central America, 1977–1992* (Chapel Hill: The University of North Carolina Press, 1998), 180.

5. Susanne Jonas, *Of Centaurs and Doves: Guatemala's Peace Process* (Boulder, CO: Westview Press, 2000), 39–40. For a meticulous treatment of the peace process, see Jonas, ibid., 39–161.

6. Mike Lanchin, "Death Squad Claims Responsibility for Bishop's Death," *National Catholic Reporter* (May 22, 1998): 2, 12; Francisco Goldman, *The Art of Political Murder: Who Killed the Bishop?* (New York: Grove Press, 2007).

7. An English summary of the report is *Guatemala: Never Again! REMHI, Recovery of Historical Memory Project, The Official Report of the Human Rights Office, Archdiocese of Guatemala* (Maryknoll, NY: Orbis Books, 1999).

8. *Comisión para el Esclarecimento Histórico, Guatemala Memoria del Silencio* (Guatemala City: UN Office for Project Services, 1999).

9. Charles Babington, "Clinton: Support for Guatemalan War Wrong," *Washington Post* (March 11, 1999), https://www.washingtonpost.com/wp-srv/inatl/daily/march99/clinton11.htm.

10. Brands, *Crime*, 5. See also Tim Padgett, "Guatemala's Kaibiles: A Notorious Commando Unit Wrapped Up in Central America's Drug War," *Time* (July 14, 2011) http://world.time.com/2011/07/14/guatemalas-kaibil-terror-from-dictators-to-drug-cartels/.

11. Michael E. Miller, "Guatemalan President Resigns after Judge Orders Him to Face Corruption Charges," *Washington Post* (September 3, 2015).

Chapter 5. Dorothy Kazel: Ursuline Sister

1. Unless otherwise noted, the early biographical information that follows is from: Joseph and Malvina Kazel, interview with the authors, August 23, 1985; Martha Owen, OSU, personal interview with the authors, August 23, 1985; Cynthia Glavac, OSU, *In the Fullness of Life: A Biography of Dorothy Kazel, O.S.U.* (Denville, NJ: Dimension Books, 1996), 26–64; "Life of Love," a script and slide show prepared by Cheryl Kazel and Susan Mary Rathbun, OSU, 1983.

2. George C. Stewart, Jr., "Ursulines (O.S.U.)," in *The Encyclopedia of American Catholic History*, ed. Michael Glazier and Thomas J. Shelley (Collegeville, MN: The Liturgical Press, 1997), 1411–12.

3. Barbara Sever, OSU, personal interview with the authors, August 23, 1985.

4. Glavac, *Fullness*, 155.

5. Ibid., 169–70.

6. Paul Schindler, telephone interview with the authors, May 2, 1986.

7. "Life of Love," 7.

8. Glavac, *Fullness*, 130.

9. Walter LaFeber, *Inevitable Revolutions: The United States in Central America*, 2nd ed. (New York: Norton, 1993), 10; Ana Carrigan, *Salvador Witness: The Life and Calling of Jean Donovan* (New York: Simon and Schuster, 1984), 77.

10. LaFeber, *Inevitable Revolutions*, 72.

11. Phillip Berryman, *Religious Roots of Rebellion: Christians in Central American Revolutions* (Maryknoll, NY: Orbis Books, 1984), 95.

12. Ibid., 93.

13. Thomas P. Anderson, *Politics in Central America* (New York: Praeger, 1983), 64.

14. LaFeber, *Inevitable Revolutions*, 75.

15. Berryman, *Religious Roots*, 98.

16. Owen, interview; email to the authors, September 25, 2017. Rosemary Smith was a lay volunteer for the Cleveland team from its beginning in 1964 through 1980.

17. Owen, interview.

18. Angelyn Dries, *The Missionary Movement in American Catholic History* (Maryknoll, NY: Orbis Books, 1998), 264–67.

19. "Life of Love," 7.

20. Owen, interview. The next five paragraphs are also from this interview.

21. Sever, interview.

22. Owen, interview.

23. Berryman, *Religious Roots*, 115–16.

24. LaFeber, *Inevitable Revolutions*, 245.

25. Ibid.; James R. Brockman, *Romero: A Life* (Maryknoll, NY: Orbis Books, 1989), 4–6.

26. Berryman, *Religious Roots*, 117.

27. Ibid., 106–9, 114.

28. Ibid., 120–21.

29. Zacarías Díez and Juan Macho, *"En Santiago de María me tope con la Miseria": Dos años de la vida de Mons. Romero (1975–1976)* (San José: no publisher listed, 1994), 67–81, 182–89; and María López Vigil, *Monseñor Romero: Memories in Mosaic* (Maryknoll, NY: Orbis Books, 2013), 43–45.

30. *Mons. Oscar Romero: Su Pensamiento*, VII (San Salvador: *Publicaciones Pastorales del Arzobispado*, 1988), 35–37.

31. Martha Owen, audiocassette to the authors, 1985.

32. Ibid.

33. Schindler, telephone interview; Owen, interview; Owen, email to the authors.

34. Owen, interview.

35. Ibid.

36. Ibid.

37. Ibid. These stories were originally told by Sister Mary Ann Flannery (formerly Sister Mary Regis), Vincentian superior.

38. Owen, interview.

39. "Life of Love," 8.

40. During the Miss Universe Pageant of 1975, there were marches in El Salvador to protest the government's sizable pageant expenses while so many Salvadorans were living in extreme poverty.

41. Owen, interview.

42. T. D. Allman, "An American Tragedy," *Penthouse* (January 1984).

43. Owen, interview.

44. Schindler, telephone interview.

45. Glavac, *Fullness*, 182.

46. Owen, interview.

47. Glavac, *Fullness*, 63.

Chapter 6. Jean Donovan: Lay Missioner

1. The early biographical information that follows, unless otherwise noted, is from Raymond and Patricia Donovan, letter to the authors, September 1987; Joe Lynch, "Footsteps of Faith: Jean Donovan's Legacy to Her Parents," *Sojourners* (June 1987): 21–22; Ana Carrigan, *Salvador Witness: The Life and Calling of Jean Donovan* (Simon and Schuster: 1984), 31–45.

2. Rita Mikolajczyk, telephone interview with the authors, October 3, 1987.

3. Carrigan, *Witness*, 41-43.

4. Lynch, "Legacy," 21.

5. "Special Report: Way of the Cross in El Salvador," *Maryknoll* (March 1981): 24.

6. Carrigan, *Witness*, 52.

7. "Way of Cross," 24.

8. Carrigan, *Witness*, 50–52, 55.

9. Ibid., 54–56.

10. Lawrence McMahon, telephone interview with the authors, September 26, 1987.

11. Lynch, "Legacy," 22.

12. Donovans, letter to the authors.

13. Carrigan, *Witness*, 58–61.

14. Ibid., 62-63.

15. Mikolajczyk, telephone interview.

16. Mary Frances Ehlinger, telephone interview with the authors, September 19, 1987.

17. Lynch, "Legacy," 22.

18. "Way of Cross," 24.

19. Donovans, letter to the authors.

20. Carrigan, *Witness*, 65.

21. Stephen T. DeMott, "Mission Inherited: 'Our Own Blood Spilled in El Salvador,'" *Maryknoll* (December 1983): 52.

22. Carrigan, *Witness*, 70, 72.

23. Stephanie Russell, "Donovan Called the First Jet-Setter Missionary," *National Catholic Reporter* (December 19, 1980): 29.

24. Carrigan, *Witness*, 72–73.

25. Cynthia Glavac, OSU, *In the Fullness of Life: A Biography of Dorothy Kazel, O.S.U.* (Denville, NJ: Dimension Books, 1996), 62.

26. Josie Cuda, telephone interview with the authors, May 21, 1986.

27. Mikolajczyk, telephone interview.

28. James R. Brockman, *Romero: A Life* (Maryknoll, NY: Orbis Books, 1989), 154–56.

29. Phillip Berryman, *Religious Roots of Rebellion: Christians in Central American Revolutions* (Maryknoll, NY: Orbis Books, 1984), 137.

30. Brockman, *Romero*, 171.

31. Lynch, "Legacy," 22.

32. Donovans, letter to the authors.

33. Brockman, *Romero*, 175–77, 135–36.

34. Dorothy Kazel and Paul Schindler, audiocassette to Martha Owen, August 9, 1979.

35. Christine Rody, telephone interview with the authors, September 23, 1987.

36. Carrigan, *Witness*, 109.

37. Rody, telephone interview.

38. Carrigan, *Witness*, 97.

39. Ibid., 99.

40. Owen, personal interview with the authors, 1985.

41. Paul Schindler, telephone interview with the authors, May 2, 1986.

42. Ibid.; Rody, telephone interview; Carrigan, *Witness*, 102–5, 135.

43. Carrigan, *Witness*, 105.

44. Dorothy Kazel, letter to Martha Owen, October 3, 1979.

45. Carrigan, *Witness*, 108–9.

46. Dorothy Kazel, audiocassette to Martha Owen, December 1979–January 10, 1980; Donovans, letter to the authors.

47. Lynch, "Legacy," 23.

48. Sheila Tobbe, "Witness to Sister Dorothy and Jean Donovan," liturgical reflection delivered December 14, 1980, St. Catherine Church, Cleveland, Ohio.

49. Lynch, "Legacy," 23.

50. Dorothy Kazel, audiocassette to Martha Owen, December 1979–January 10, 1980.

51. Glavac, *Fullness*, 136.

52. Ibid., 136–37. The founder of the Ursulines, St. Angela Merici, was a Third Order Franciscan.

53. Ibid., 135–36.

54. Martha Owen, audiocassette to the authors, 1985.

55. Kazel, letter to friends and family, January 20–30, 1980, sent by Sheila Tobbe to the authors.

56. Carrigan, *Witness*, 142.

Chapter 7. Dorothy and Jean: Civil War

1. Martha Owen, personal interview with the authors, August 23, 1985.

2. Oscar Romero, *A Martyr's Message of Hope*, trans. Felipe Ortega et al. (Kansas City, MO: Celebration Books, 1981), 105.

3. James R. Brockman, *Romero: A Life* (Maryknoll, NY: Orbis Books, 1989), 241–42.

4. Cynthis Glavac, OSU, *In the Fullness of Life: A Biography of Dorothy Kazel, O.S.U.* (Dimension Books, Denville, NJ: 1996), 82–83.

5. Ana Carrigan, *Salvador Witness: The Life and Calling of Jean Donovan* (New York: Simon and Schuster, 1984), 159–60.

6. Martha Owen, audiocassette to the authors, 1985.

7. Brockman, *Romero*, 246–47.

8. Owen, audiocassette.

9. Carrigan, *Witness*, 125, 129.

10. Ibid., 110–11.

11. Ibid., 136, 147–48; Christine Rody, letter to the authors, December 10, 1987.

12. Christine Rody, telephone interview with the authors, September 23, 1987.

13. Carrigan, *Witness*, 179–80, 184.

14. Paul Schindler, telephone interview with the authors, May 2, 1986.

15. Ibid.

16. Ibid.

17. Glavac, *Fullness*, 131.

18. Dorothy Chapon Kazel, *Alleluia Woman: Sister Dorothy Kazel, OSU* (Cleveland, OH: Chapel Publications, 1987), 35–36.

19. Carrigan, *Witness*, 200.

20. Dorothy Kazel, letter to Theresa Kane, October 6, 1980.

21. Dorothy Kazel, letter to Owen, September 5, 1980.

22. June Carolyn Erlick, "Cleveland Team: 'We'll Stay,'" *National Catholic Reporter* (September 5, 1980): 28.

23. Kazel, letter to Owen, September 5, 1980.

24. Rody, telephone interview.

25. Schindler, telephone interview.

26. Rody, telephone interview.

27. Donovans, letter to the authors, including comments from Doug Cable.

28. Carrigan, *Witness*, 214–15.

29. Ibid., 216–17.

30. Josie Cuda, telephone interview with the authors, May 21, 1986.

31. Rita Mikolajczyk, telephone interview with the authors, October 3, 1987.

32. Mary Frances Ehlinger, telephone interview with the authors, September 1987.

33. Carrigan, *Witness*, 218.

34. Ibid., 219.

35. Stephen T. DeMott, "Mission Inherited: 'Our Own Blood Spilled in El Salvador,'" *Maryknoll* (December 1983): 52.

36. Kazel, audiocassette to Owen, October 21, 1980.

37. Chapon Kazel, *Alleluia Woman*, 37–38.

38. Thomas P. Anderson, *Politics in Central America: Guatemala, El Salvador, Honduras, and Nicaragua* (New York: Praeger Publishers, 1982), 91.

39. William Stanley, *The Protection Racket State: Elite Politics, Military Extortion, and Civil War in El Salvador* (Philadelphia, PA: Temple University Press, 1996), 2.

40. John D. Blacken, U.S. Department of State, letter to Dorothy Kazel, November 7, 1980, photocopy in authors' possession. For the key role that García played in the massacres of thousands of civilians from October 1979 to April 1983, see the report submitted by Professor Terry Karl that provided crucial evidence in the general's deportation trial. In 2015 the court ruled against García,

who had been living for several years in the U.S. despite his violent past. He lost his appeal the following year. Karl, "United States Department of Justice for Immigration Review...In the Matter of Garcia-Merino."

41. Phillip Berryman, *Religious Roots of Rebellion: Christians in Central American Revolutions* (Maryknoll, NY: Orbis Books, 1984), 157.

42. Betty Campbell, RSM, and Peter Hinde, O.Carm., *Following the Star: The Liberation Process of the People*, ed. Gary MacEoin (Washington, DC: Religious Task Force on Latin America, n.d.): 5–6.

43. Kazel, audiocassette to Owen, October 1980; Campbell and Hinde, *The Star*, 24.

44. Campbell and Hinde, *The Star*, 8.

45. Kazel, audiocassette to Owen, October 1980.

46. Kazel, audiocassette to Owen, August 1979.

47. Kazel, audiocassette to Owen, October 1980.

48. Kazel, letter to Owen, November 5, 1980.

49. Owen, audiocassette.

50. Schindler, telephone interview.

51. Kazel, letter to Ursuline community, November 1980.

52. Mary Bader Papa, "'Fight Sexism, Paternalism in Church'—Kane," *National Catholic Reporter* (September 5, 1980): 23.

53. Kazel, letter to Kane.

54. Campbell and Hinde, *The Star*, 8.

55. Owen, personal interview.

56. Kazel, letter to Owen, November 28, 1980.

57. Carrigan, *Witness*, 226–27.

58. Schindler, telephone interview.

59. Patricia Donovan, "Families Respond to Murders and Disappearances," Campbell and Hinde, *The Star*, 27.

60. Carrigan, *Witness*, 69.

61. Schindler, telephone interview.

Chapter 8. Carol "Carla" Piette: Maryknoll Sister

1. The early biographical information that follows, unless otherwise noted, is from Jacqueline Hansen Maggiore, with Catherine McDermott Vint, *Vessel of Clay: The Inspirational Journey of Sister Carla* (Scranton, PA: University of Scranton Press, 2010).

2. Janet Carroll, MM, "Maryknoll," *The Encyclopedia of American Catholic History*, ed. Michael Glazier and Thomas J. Shelley (Collegeville, MN: The Liturgical Press, 1997), 850–51; Barbara Hendricks, MM, "Mary Rogers (1882–1955)," ibid., 1214–15.

3. Judith M. Noone, MM, *The Same Fate as the Poor* (Maryknoll, NY: Orbis Books, 1995), 4.

4. Penny Lernoux, with Arthur Jones and Robert Ellsberg, *Hearts on Fire: The Story of the Maryknoll Sisters* (Maryknoll, NY: Orbis Books, 1993), 39–40.

5. Maggiore, *Vessel*, 14.

6. Noone, *Same Fate*, 5.

7. Maggiore, *Vessel*, 20–21.

8. Noone, *Same Fate*, 10.

9. Ibid., 6–7.

10. Carla Piette, "The Crawling Experiment," 1974, Maryknoll Sisters Archives (MSA), Creative Works: 40-45.

11. Noone, *Same Fate*, 4, 7.

12. Ibid., 6; Maggiore, *Vessel*, 25.

13. Piette, "Dear Ben," March 26, 1972, MSA, Same Fate as the Poor (SFATP): 8-17.

14. Piette, letter to Laudert family, July 27, 1966, MSA, SFATP: 8-16.

15. Maggiore, *Vessel*, 27.

16. Ibid., 29.

17. Ibid., 22, 27, 29. Piette, letter to Patricia Cobb, August 11, 1971, MSA, SFATP: 8-17.

18. Piette, letter to Mother Mary Colman, October 2, 1966, MSA, SFATP: 8-17.

19. Noone, *Same Fate*, 11.

20. Maggiore, *Vessel*, 28.

21. Piette, "Hungry Jesus, Spirit Fed," no date, MSA, Creative Works: 40-17.

22. Piette, "Poverty," September 1966, MSA, Creative Works: 40-13.

23. Piette, letter to Elizabeth Frazier, October 7, 1967, MSA, SFATP: 8-17.

24. Maggiore, *Vessel*, 28.

25. Carroll, "Maryknoll," 851; Lernoux, *Hearts on Fire*, 174–75.

26. Maggiore, *Vessel*, 42.

27. Ibid., 27.

28. Piette, letter to Cobb.

29. Maggiore, *Vessel*, 38.

30. Ibid., 40.

31. Piette, "Sickness," April 30, 1972, MSA, Creative Works: 40-46.

Chapter 9. Ita Ford: Maryknoll Sister

1. Timothy M. Phelps, "For Two Nuns, Needs of Poor Hid the Danger," *New York Times* (December 7, 1980): 9.

2. "Anniversary Marks Tragic Loss of Sister Ita Ford '61," December 1, 2010, Marymount Manhattan College announcement, https://www.mmm.edu/live/news/239-anniversary-marks-tragic-loss-of-sister-ita-ford.

3. Mildred Ford, letter to Judith Noone, MM, Summer 1981, Maryknoll Sisters Archives (MSA), Same Fate as the Poor (SFATP): 6-9.

4. Mildred Ford, letter to Noone, January 28, 1982, MSA, SFATP: 6-9.

5. Grace Monahan Niemeyer, letter to Judith Noone, May 1, 1981, MSA, SFATP: 6-9; Mildred Ford, letter to Noone, Summer 1981.

6. Niemeyer, letter to Noone; Mildred Ford, letter to Noone, January 28, 1982.

7. "Anniversary Marks Loss."

8. Mildred Ford, letter to Noone, January 28, 1982.

9. Ita Ford, letter to Reardon, February 25, 1961, MSA, SFATP Collection, 7-5. Most of Ita's letters cited here are found in Ita Ford, *"Here I Am, Lord": The Letters and Writings of Ita Ford*, ed. Jeanne Evans (Maryknoll, NY: Orbis Books, 2005).

10. Ford, letters to Reardon, November 15, 1960 and February 7, 1961, MSA, SFATP: 7-5.

11. Ford, letters to Reardon, March 17, 1961 and February 7, 1961, MSA, SFATP: 7-5.

12. Ford, letters to Reardon, Easter Sunday, 1961 and April 19, 1961, MSA, SFATP: 7-5.

13. Ford, letter to Reardon, November 8, 1961, MSA, SFATP: 7-5.

14. Mildred Ford, letter to Noone, January 28, 1982.

15. Ford, letter to Reardon, November 8, 1961. Some postulants had already left.

16. Ford, letter to Reardon, December 28, 1961, MSA, SFATP: 7-5.

17. Ford, letters to Reardon, January 7 and 25, 1962, and August 27, 1962, MSA, SFATP: 7-5.

18. Ford, letter to Reardon, August 27, 1962, MSA, SFATP: 7-5.

19. Ford, letter to Reardon, August 18, 1963, MSA, SFATP: 7-6.

20. Ford, letter to Reardon, December 30, 1963, MSA, SFATP: 7-6.

21. Ford, letter to Reardon, November 17, 1963, MSA, SFATP: 7-6.

22. Ford, letters to Reardon, August 18, 1963, and November 17, 1963, MSA, SFATP: 7-6.

23. Ford, letter to Reardon, June 12, 1964, MSA, SFATP: 7-6.

24. Mildred Ford, letter to Noone, January 28, 1982.

25. Niemeyer, letter to Noone.

26. Ford, letter to Jean Reardon Baumann, October 26, 1972, MSA, SFATP: 7-6.

27. Mildred Ford, letter to Noone, January 28, 1982; Ita Ford, letters to Sister Paul Miriam [later Sister Mary] Galligan, September 10 and December 2, 1964, MSA, SFATP: 7-6.

28. Jeanne Evans, "New York: 1964–1971," in Ford, *"Here I Am, Lord,"* 41–42.

29. Ibid., 41–43.

30. Ibid.

31. Katherine Monahan Gregg and Ana May, transcript of audiocassette interview with Noone, April 24, 1981, MSA, SFATP: 6-9.

32. Ibid.

33. Michael Gallagher, "Kirkpatrick's Views Invite College Protests," *National Catholic Reporter* (April 29, 1983): 15.

34. Mildred Ford, letter to Noone, January 28, 1982.

35. Ford, letter to Galligan, December 2, 1964.

36. Julie Miller, letter to Noone, February 14, 1982, MSA, SFATP: 6-9.

37. Mildred Ford, letter to Noone, January 28, 1982.

38. Evans, "New York: 1964–1971," 47.

39. Ford, letter to Baumann, October 6, 1971, MSA, SFATP: 7-6.

40. Evans, "Maryknoll to Chile: 1971–1978," in Ford, *"Here I Am, Lord,"* 55.

41. Ford, letter to Baumann, September 24, 1972, MSA, SFATP: 7-6.

42. Ibid.

43. Ford, letter to Baumann, November 28, 1972, MSA, SFATP: 7-6.

44. Ford, letter to Niemeyer, January 15, 1973, in Niemeyer letter, MSA, SFATP: 6-9.

45. Ford, letter to Niemeyer, April 4, 1973, in Niemeyer letter, MSA, SFATP: 6-9.

46. Ford, letter to Katherine Monahan Gregg, June 9, 1973, MSA, SFATP: 7-6.

47. Ford, letter to Baumann, May 23, 1973, MSA, SFATP: 7-6.

Chapter 10. Carla and Ita: La Bandera

1. Jacqueline Hansen Maggiore, with Catherine McDermott Vint, *Vessel of Clay: The Inspirational Journey of Sister Carla* (Scranton: University of Scranton Press, 2010), 42.

2. Ita Ford, letter to Kathy and Mike Gregg, August 12, 1973, Maryknoll Sisters Archives (MSA), Same Fate as the Poor (SFATP): 7-6. Most of Ita's letters cited here are found in Ita Ford, *"Here I Am, Lord:" The Letters and Writings of Ita Ford*, ed. Jeanne Evans (Maryknoll, NY: Orbis Books, 2005).

3. Ford, letter to Jean Reardon Baumann, August 12, 1973, MSA, SFATP: 7-6.

4. Judith Noone, MM, *Same Fate as the Poor* (Maryknoll, NY: Orbis Books, 1995), 30.

5. Ford, interview with Maureen Flanagan, MM, 1978, in Ford, *"Here I Am, Lord,"* 114–16.

6. Benjamin Keen and Mark Wasserman, *A Short History of Latin America* (Boston: Houghton Mifflin, 1984), 322–23.

7. Jeffrey Klaiber, *The Church, Dictatorships, and Democracy in Latin America* (Maryknoll, NY: Orbis Books, 1998), 42.

8. Brian Loveman, *Chile: The Legacy of Hispanic Capitalism* (New York and Oxford: Oxford University Press, 2001), 2, 234; Klaiber, *Church,* 44–45, 56. Hurtado was canonized a saint in 2005.

9. Klaiber, *Church,* 45.

10. Ascanio Cavallo, ed., *Memorias: Cardenal Raúl Silva Henríquez,* II (Santiago: Ediciones Copygraph, 1991), 84.

11. Loveman, *Chile,* 237.

12. Keen and Wasserman, *Short History,* 337.

13. Carla Piette, MM, "There is a housing project...," probably 1973, MSA, SFATP: 8-15.

14. Brother Kevin Dargan, MM, *The Maryknoll Brothers: The Catholic Church in the United States and a New Way of Mission* (Maryknoll, NY: [no publisher listed], 2010), http://www.maryknollbrothers.org/Brothers_History.pdf, 52; Maggiore, *Vessel of Clay*, 47–48.

15. Ford and Mary Tracy, letter to Senator Edward Kennedy, November 25, 1973, MSA, SFATP: 7-6.

16. Gil Loescher, *Calculated Kindness: Refugees and America's Half-Open Door, 1945–Present* (New York: Simon and Schuster, 1998), 97.

17. Mildred Ford, letter to Judith Noone, January 28, 1982, MSA, SFATP: 6-9.

18. Ford, letter to Jean and John Baumann, January 27, 1974, MSA, SFATP: 7-6.

19. Ford, "Try to Imagine," reflection sent to friends and relatives, January 1974, MSA, SFATP: 7-4.

20. Maggiore, *Vessel of Clay*, 50–51.

21. Noone, *Same Fate*, 35–36.

22. Ford, "Thinking about Our Common Call," January 1974, MSA, SFATP: 7-4.

23. Piette, letter to Betty and Jack Frazier, August 3, 1974, MSA, SFATP: 8-17.

24. Penny Lernoux, *Cry of the People* (New York: Penguin Books, 1982), 401; Noone, *Same Fate*, 32–33.

25. Piette, "What have I learned?" 1974, MSA, Creative Works: 40-6.

26. Piette, "Reflections Inspired by Pictures," June 1977, MSA, Creative Works: 40-13.

27. Piette, letter to Fraziers, August 3, 1974.

28. Piette, "Población La Bandera," letter to friends, May 1975, MSA, SFATP: 8-15.

29. Ford, letter to Mildred Ford, October 26 [no year], MSA, SFATP: 7-7.

30. Sheila Cassidy, *Audacity to Believe* (Cleveland: Collins World, 1978), 112–15. Because Carla and Ita were still working in Chile at the time of publication, Cassidy gave Carla and Ita the pseudonyms "Anna" and "Frances."

31. Ibid., 122–23, 156–58, 172–94, 243–46, 284–90, 328–33.

32. Ford, letter to Jean Baumann, January 27, 1976, MSA, SFATP: 7-6.

33. Klaiber, *Church*, 54–63; Loveman, *Chile*, 5, 264–68.

34. Klaiber, *Church*, 52.

35. Thomas E. Quigley, "The Chilean Coup, the Church and the Human Rights Movement," *America* (February 11, 2002), https://www.americamagazine.org/issue/360/article/chilean-coup-church-and-human-rights-movement.

36. Ford, "Reflections on Mission Phase," *Orientation*, vol. 3, Maryknoll Sisters' newsletter (May 1977), MSA, SFATP: 7-4.

37. Piette, "Near Restful Waters," Retreat, January 1976, MSA, Creative Works: 40-6.

38. Piette, letter to Fraziers, August 3, 1974.

39. Maggiore, *Vessel*, 62–63, 71–72.

40. Piette, letter to Connie Pospisil, MM, September 20, 1976, MSA, SFATP: 8-17.

41. George E. Ganss, SJ, letter to Camilla Kennedy, MM, August 25, 1980, MSA, Creative Works: 40-3.

42. Sister Bernice Fenske, letter to Sisters of Maryknoll, September 28, 1980, MSA, Creative Works: 40-3.

43. Maggiore, *Vessel*, 72–73, 77–78.

44. Piette, letter to Pospisil.

45. Ford, letter to Connie Pospisil, November 22, 1976, MSA, SFATP: 7-6.

46. Piette, letter to Maryknoll Regional Governing Board of Chile, Fall 1976, Creative Works: 40-1.

47. Ford, *Orientation*, Maryknoll Sisters, May 1977, MSA, SFATP: 7-4.

48. Piette, "Paschal Mystery in Third World," [n.d.], MSA, Creative Works: 40-4.

49. Ford, letter to Jane Buellesbach and others, March 3, 1978, MSA, SFATP: 7-7.

50. Ford, letter to Jean Baumann, November 28, 1977, MSA, SFATP: 7-7.

51. Maggiore, *Vessel*, 87.

52. Timothy M. Phelps, "For Two Nuns, Needs of Poor Hid the Danger," *New York Times* (December 7, 1980): 9.

53. Mildred Ford, letter to Noone.

54. Noone, *Same Fate*, 42.

55. Katherine Monahan Gregg and Ana May, transcript of audiocassette interview with Judith Noone, April 24, 1981, MSA, SFATP: 6-9.

56. Noone, *Same Fate*, 43.

57. Ford, "Retreat Notes, August 1978-August 1979," in Evans, "*Here I Am*," 119–31.

58. Ford, interview with Flanagan, in Evans, "*Here I Am*," 112–13, 116.

59. Ford, interview with Paul Newpower, MM, for "*El Mundo de Maryknoll*," Spanish Interview Radio (Program #158), 1978, transcribed by Judith Noone, January 5, 1982, MSA, SFATP: 7-4. Ita's comments were translated by Donna Brett.

60. Mildred Ford, letter to Noone.

61. Gregg and May, audiocassette interview.

62. Ford, "Self-Evaluation," May 1979, in Evans, "*Here I Am*," 134.

63. Meehan, in Noone, *Same Fate*, 79.

64. Penny Lernoux, *Hearts on Fire: The Story of the Maryknoll Sisters*, with Arthur Jones and Robert Ellsberg (Maryknoll, NY: Orbis Books, 1993), 235–36.

65. Noone, *Same Fate*, 82–83.

66. Ibid., 82.

67. Maggiore, *Vessel*, 50.

68. Piette, letter to Betty and Jack Frazier, September 25, 1978, MSA, SFATP: 8-17.

69. Maggiore, *Vessel*, 89–90.

70. Piette, letter to Betty Frazier, February 18, 1979, MSA, SFATP: 8-17.

71. Maggiore, *Vessel*, 93.

72. Ibid., 97–100.

73. Maggiore, *Vessel*, 100–101.

74. Ford, letters to Mildred Ford, January 3 and 11, 1980, MSA, SFATP: 7-7.

75. Pedro Pérez E., OSB, letter to Sister Marlene, September 9, 1996, translation in MSA, Creative Works: 40-3.

76. Piette, letter to Rebecca Quinn, January 22, 1980, MSA, Creative Works: 40-2.

77. Maggiore, *Vessel*, 102.

78. Piette, letter to Quinn, February 24, 1980, MSA, Creative Works: 40-2.

79. Maggiore, *Vessel*, 106.

80. Ford, letter to Mildred Ford, February 10, 1980, MSA, SFATP: 7-7.

81. Ford, letter to Mildred Ford, March 2, 1980, MSA, SFATP: 7-7.

Chapter 11. Maura Clarke: Maryknoll Sister

1. Unless otherwise noted, Maura's early life is compiled from Judith M. Noone, MM, *Same Fate as the Poor* (Maryknoll, NY: 1995); Eileen Markey, *A Radical Faith: The Assassination of Sister Maura* (New York: Nation Books, 2016); and Moises Sandoval, "Four Heroic Lives End in Martyrdom," *National Catholic Reporter* (December 19, 1980): 28.

2. Kay Kelly, MM, letter to Judith Noone, June 25, 1982; a copy of the letter was sent by Kelly to the authors.

3. Sandoval, "Four Heroic Lives," 1.

4. Richard Marie McKinney, MM, recollections on Maura at St. Anthony's, August 2, 1982, Maryknoll Sisters Archives (MSA), Same Fate as the Poor (SFATP): 6-11.

5. [No author], "Bronx Diaries," [n.d.], MSA, SFATP: 6-11.

6. McKinney, recollections.

7. Pat Redmond, MM, recollections on Maura at St. Anthony's, MSA, SFATP: 6-11.

8. McKinney, recollections.

9. Rita Owczarek, MM, recollections on Maura, [n.d.], MSA, SFATP: 6-12.

10. Kay Kelly, MM, letter to the authors, April 21, 1984.

11. Kelly, letter to Noone.

12. Ibid.

13. Ibid. Sister Rita Owczarek, who worked in Siuna, also remembered that Maura was terrified of flying. See Owczarek, recollections.

14. Kelly, letter to Noone.

15. Maura Clarke, letter to parents, December 25, 1963, MSA, SFATP: 8-1.

16. Noone, *Same Fate*, 54.

17. Kelly, letter to Noone.

18. Bea Zaragoza, MM, recollections on Maura, MSA, SFATP: 6-12.

19. Kelly, letter to Noone.

20. Ibid.

21. Ginny Farrell, recollections on Maura, April 6, 1981, MSA, SFATP: 6-11; Sandoval, "Four Heroic Lives," 28; Markey, *Radical Faith*, 86.

22. Laura Glynn, MM, recollections on Maura, MSA, SFATP: 6-12.

23. Zaragoza, recollections.

24. Kelly, letter to the authors.

25. Noone, *Same Fate*, 59–61.

26. Maura Clarke, letter to parents, Palm Sunday 1970, MSA, SFATP: 8-2. The "Family of God" was a new approach to catechizing adults adopted by the Maryknoll sisters worldwide following their 1964 General Chapter. It used the Socratic method to get participants involved in dialogue and sharing ideas. The "Family of God" methodology spread to much of Latin America, where it developed into the Christian base community movement. See Markey, *Radical Faith*, 100–101.

27. Markey, *Radical Faith*, 102–3.

28. Maura Clarke, letter to Bud, Carol, Jimmy, and Johnny Clarke, Palm Sunday 1970, MSA, SFATP: 8-2.

29. Maura Clarke, letter to parents, May 3, 1970, MSA, SFATP: 8-2.

30. Maura Clarke, letter to parents, October 12, 1970, MSA, SFATP: 8-3.

31. Maura Clarke, letter to family, October 15, 1970, MSA, SFATP: 8-3.

32. Maura Clarke, letter to family, October 26, 1970, MSA, SFATP: 8-3.

33. Markey, *Radical Faith*, 135–36.

34. Maura Clarke, letter to family, October 26, 1970, MSA, SFATP: 8-3; Kelly, letter to the authors; Noone, *Same Fate*, 63.

35. Maura Clarke, letter to family, December 25, 1972, MSA, SFATP: 8-3.

36. Kelly, letter to Noone.

37. Noone, *Same Fate*, 65.

38. Maura Clarke, letter to parents, March 15, 1973, MSA, SFATP: 8-5.

39. Maura Clarke, letter to Bud Clarke, March 18, 1973, MSA, SFATP: 8-5.

40. Noone, *Same Fate*, 66.

41. Ibid., 71.

42. Maura Clarke, letter to family, June 9, 1974, MSA, SFATP: 8-6.

43. Maura Clarke, letter to parents, October 16, 1974, MSA, SFATP: 8-7.

44. Maura Clarke, letter to family, July 6, 1973, MSA, SFATP: 8-5.

45. Maura Clarke, letter to family, August 17, 1973, MSA, SFATP: 8-5.

46. Maura Clarke, notes written during an eight-day retreat, quoted in Noone, *Same Fate*, 71.

47. Markey, *Radical Faith*, 188–90.

48. Noone, *Same Fate*, 73.

49. Ibid., 80.

50. Maura Clarke, note to the Nicaraguan sisters, [no date but probably written in late August 1979], MSA, SFATP: 8-10. It is not certain that this note was ever mailed.

51. Maura Clarke, "Christmas letter to family and friends," Christmas 1979, MSA, SFATP: 8-10.

52. Maura Clarke, letter to Jennie Burke, January 15, 1980, MSA, SFATP: 8-10.

53. Ana Carrigan, *Salvador Witness: The Life and Calling of Jean Donovan* (New York: Simon and Shuster, 1984), 201–2.

54. Maura Clarke, letter to family and friends, July 28, 1980, MSA, SFATP: 8-10.

55. Maura Clarke, letter to parents, July 28, 1980, MSA, SFATP: 8-10.

Chapter 12. Carla, Ita, and Maura: Chalatenango

1. Carla Piette, letter to Rebecca Quinn, March 28, 1980, Maryknoll Sisters Archives (MSA), Creative Works: 40-2. The four quotations that follow are all from this letter.

2. Ita Ford, letter to Mildred Ford, April 2, 1980, MSA, Same Fate As the Poor: (SFATP): 7-7.

3. Piette, letter to Quinn, April 12, 1980, MSA, Creative Works: 40-2.

4. Ford, letter to Katherine and Mike Gregg, April 13, 1980, MSA, SFATP: 7-7.

5. Ford, letter to Connie Pospisil, April 14, 1980, MSA, SFATP: 7-7.

6. Ford and Piette, "The One Month Plan and Evaluation," April 15–May 15, 1980, Santa Ana, El Salvador, MSA, SFATP: 5-3.

7. Ford, letter to Mildred Ford, April 28, 1980, MSA, SFATP: 7-7.

8. Piette, letter to Quinn, April 30, 1980, MSA, Creative Works: 40-2.

9. Ford, letter to Regina McEvoy, May 3, 1980, MSA, SFATP: 7-7.

10. Ford and Piette, "The One Month Plan"; Judith M. Noone, *The Same Fate As the Poor* (Maryknoll, NY: Orbis Books, 1995), 100–101.

11. Philip Berryman, *Religious Roots of Rebellion: Christians in Central American Revolutions* (Maryknoll, NY: Orbis Books, 1984), 113.

12. Piette, letters to Quinn, June 2 and 15, 1980, MSA, Creative Works: 40-2; Jacqueline Hansen Maggiore, with Catherine McDermott Vint, *Vessel of Clay: The Inspirational Journey of Sister Carla* (Scranton, PA: University of Scranton Press, 2010), 130.

13. Terry L. Karl, "United States Department of Justice, Executive Office for Immigration Review, Immigration Court, Miami, Florida: In the Matter of Garcia-Merino: José Guillermo: In removal proceedings" (Miami, FL: 2015): 14–15, 69–71.

14. Piette, letter to Cecilia Vandal, May 14, 1980, MSA, SFATP: 8-19.

15. Ford, letter to Rachel Lauze, May 17, 1980, MSA, SFATP: 7-7.

16. Ford, letter to Jessie Poynton and Laura Magallanes, June 1, 1980, MSA, SFATP: 7-8.

17. Ford, letter to Rene Sullivan, May 29, 1980, MSA, SFATP: 7-7.

18. Piette, letter to Marlene, May 16, 1980, MSA, SFATP: 8-19.

19. Piette, letter to Connie [Pospisil], Mini, Jessie, and Carolyn, May 17, 1980, MSA, SFATP: 8-13.

20. Ita Ford, letter to Jessie Poynton and Laura Magallanes, June 1, 1980, in *"Here I Am, Lord": The Letters and Writings of Ita Ford*, ed. Jeanne Evans (Maryknoll, NY: Orbis Books, 2005), 177.

21. Piette, letter to Quinn, June 2, 1980, MSA, Creative Works: 40-2.

22. Piette, letter to Quinn, May 17, 1980, MSA, Creative Works: 40-2.

23. Piette, letter to Mildred Ford, May 12, 1980, MSA, SFATP: 8-19.

24. Cynthia Glavac, OSU, *In the Fullness of Life: A Biography of Dorothy Kazel, O.S.U.* (Denville, NJ: Dimension Books, 1996), 85.

25. Maggiore, *Vessel*, 128; Ford, letter to Poynton and Magallanes.

26. Ford and Piette, letters to Melinda Roper and Annette Mulry, June 11, 1980, MSA, SFATP: 7-8.

27. Ford, "Some reflections—6 weeks after arrival in El Salvador and at the beginning of working on the Emergency Refugee Committee in Chalatenango," June 1, 1980, MSA, SFATP: 7-8.

28. Ford, letter to Mildred Ford, June 7, 1980, MSA, SFATP: 7-8.

29. Piette, letter to Quinn, June 15, 1980, MSA, Creative Works: 40-2.

30. Ibid.

31. Ita Ford and Carla Piette, "Three Months Experience in El Salvador," Report to the PANISA and Chile Regions, July 20, 1980, MSA, SFATP: 5-3.

32. Ford, letter to Roper, June 11, 1980, MSA, SFATP: 7-8.

33. Ford and Piette, "Three Months Experience."

34. Ford, letter to Ana May, July 13, 1980, MSA, SFATP: 7-8.

35. Ford, letter to Jennifer Sullivan, August 16, 1980, MSA, SFATP: 7-8.

36. Ford, letters to Carolyn Lehmann, August 21, 1980, and Connie Pospisil, August 21-22, 1980, MSA, SFATP: 7-8.

37. Piette, letter to Quinn, August 18, 1980, MSA, Creative Works: 40-2.

38. Piette, letter to George Ganss, August 18, 1980, MSA, Creative Works: 40-3.

39. Ford, letter to Mildred Ford, September 7, 1980, MSA, SFATP: 7-8; audiocassette letter to Mildred Ford, September 6, 1980, transcribed by Judith M. Noone, MSA, SFATP: 7-4.

40. Maggiore, *Vessel*, 142.

41. Ford, letter to Chilean friends, September 7, 1980, MSA, SFATP: 7-8; Maggiore, *Vessel*, 121.

42. Betty Campbell and Peter Hinde, *Following the Star: The Liberation Process of the People*, ed. Gary MacEoin (Washington, DC: Religious Task Force on Latin America, n.d.), 11.

43. Ford, audiocassette.

44. Ibid.; Campbell and Hinde, *The Star:* 10–11.

45. Ford, letter to Chilean friends.

46. Ford, audiocassette.

47. Maura Clarke, letter to Mary Manning, August 11, 1980, MSA, SFATP: 8-10.

48. Clarke, letter to Dave, August 21, 1980, MSA, SFATP: 8-11.

49. Clarke, letter to Pat Ganly, August 22, 1980, MSA, SFATP: 8-11.

50. Ford, audiocassette.

51. Ford, "Evaluation of Chalatenango Ministry," probably September 1980, MSA, SFATP: 5-3.

52. Campbell and Hinde, *The Star:* 11.

53. Ibid., 8–9.

54. Ibid., 12; Paul Schindler, telephone interview with the authors, May 2, 1986.

55. Campbell and Hinde, *The Star:* 12–13; Dorothy Kazel, audiocassette letter to Martha Owen, October 1980.

56. Campbell and Hinde, *The Star:* 11.

57. Lawyers Committee for International Human Rights, "Justice in El Salvador: A Case Study. A Report on the Investigation into the Killing of Four U.S. Churchwomen in El Salvador" (New York: February 1, 1983): 22.

58. Ford, letter to Mildred Ford, November 13, 1980, MSA, SFATP: 7-9.

59. Ford, letter to Gertrude Vaccaro, November 13, 1980, MSA, SFATP: 7-9.

60. Ford, letter to Mildred Ford, November 18, 1980, MSA, SFATP: 7-9.

61. Clarke, letter to Kay Kelly, October 21, 1980, MSA, SFATP: 8-12.

62. Clarke, letter to parents, (early) October 1980, MSA, SFATP: 8-12.

63. Report of the Lawyers Committee for International Human Rights, 23.

64. Ford, letter to Jean Reardon Baumann, October 27, 1980, MSA, SFATP: 7-7.

65. Noone, *Same Fate*, 129.

66. Campbell and Hinde, *The Star*: 21.

67. Berryman, *Religious Roots*, 133, 157–58.

68. Noone, *Same Fate*, 132, 134.

69. Clarke, letter to parents, November 17, 1980, MSA, SFATP: 8-12.

70. Noone, *Same Fate*, 136.

71. [No author], *Maryknoll* (December 1983): 1.

72. Noone, *Same Fate*, 134.

73. Oscar Romero, *A Martyr's Message of Hope*, trans. Felipe Ortega et al. (Kansas City, MO: Celebration Books, 1981), 105.

Chapter 13. Execution, Cover-up, and U.S. Complicity

1. Ana Carrigan, *Salvador Witness: The Life and Calling of Jean Donovan* (New York: Simon and Schuster, 1984), 242.

2. Lawyers Committee for International Human Rights, "Justice in El Salvador: A Case Study, A Report on the Investigation into the Killing of Four U.S. Churchwomen in El Salvador" (New York: February 1, 1983), 22–23. Hereafter cited as Lawyers Committee Report; see also Harold R. Tyler, Jr., *The Churchwomen Murders: A Report to the Secretary of State* (New York: December 2, 1983), 55–56. Hereafter cited as Tyler Report.

3. Paul Schindler, interview with the authors, May 2, 1986.

4. Tyler Report, 14–15.

5. John Dinges, "New Evidence on Missioners' Deaths in El Salvador Suggests Official Plot," Pacific News Service, July 1981; Judith Noone, *The Same Fate As the Poor* (Maryknoll, NY: Orbis Books, 1995), 135.

6. Tyler Report, 17–21.

7. Madeline M. Dorsey, MM, "Remembering the Martyrs 30 Years Later," *Maryknoll* (December 2010): 32–35.

8. Raymond Bonner, "The Diplomat and the Killer," *The Atlantic* (February 11, 2016), https://www.theatlantic.com/international/archive/2016/02/el-salvador-churchwomen-murders/460320/.

9. Author interview with Clara Margarita Cortes, April 28, 2008. Her testimony supported that of the clerk who spoke with Ambassador White. The authors

thank Neil and Marge Himber, who took notes during this interview, and Father Bernard Survil, who set it up and participated.

10. "U.S. Resumes Military Aid," *The New York Times* (January 15, 1981): 9; Raymond Bonner, *Weakness and Deceit: U.S. Policy and El Salvador* (New York: Times Books, 1984), 224.

11. John Hall, "Ambassador Kirkpatrick: Reagan-Appointed Democrat Speaks Her Mind on World, Domestic Politics," *Tampa Tribune* (December 25, 1980): A–23.

12. Stephanie Russell, "Nuns Hide Machine Guns?" *National Catholic Reporter* (March 13, 1981): 2.

13. See the 1982 documentary film, "Roses in December," directed by Ana Carrigan and Bernard Stone.

14. Carrigan, *Salvador Witness*, 283–84.

15. Bonner, "Diplomat."

16. "Oral Statement by Ambassador Robert White before the Senate Subcommittee on Western Hemisphere Affairs" (March 20, 1984): 6–8.

17. Bonner, "Diplomat."

18. *New York Times* (January 22, 1981): 14.

19. Lawyers Committee Report, 11.

20. Religious Task Force on Central America, *Chronology of a Martyrdom—November 1980 to May 1984* (Washington, DC: 1984): 2.

21. *New York Times* (February 28, 1981): 1; *New York Times* (March 1, 1981): 1.

22. *New York Times* (March 7, 1981): 1.

23. *New York Times* (March 8, 1981): 20.

24. *New York Times* (March 14, 1981): 8.

25. "Oral Statement by Ambassador Robert White before the Senate Subcommittee on Western Hemisphere Affairs" (March 20, 1984): 8.

26. The above can be verified in *New York Times* articles from March 25 and 27, 1981; April 5, 10, 18, 21, 23, and 30, 1981, and May 2, 3, 10, 12, and 13, 1981; Bonner, *Weakness and Deceit*, 230–31, 241.

27. "Oral Statement by Ambassador Robert White before the Senate Subcommittee on Western Hemisphere Affairs," 9.

28. Lawyers Committee Report, 19.

29. *New York Times* (January 22, 1982): 6; (January 29, 1982): 1; (February 11, 1982): 1.

30. *New York Times* (February 14, 1982): 18.

31. *New York Times* (February 15, 1982): 2.

32. Bonner, *Weakness and Deceit*, 80, 374.

33. *New York Times* (February 14, 1982): 18.

34. *New York Times* (March 21, 1982): 22; (June 30, 1982): 20.

35. *New York Times* (August 29, 1982): 10; (November 10, 1982): 1; (May 28, 1983): 1; (May 30, 1983): 4.

36. *New York Times* (March 19, 1983): 4.

37. *New York Times* (October 7, 1983): 6.

38. Anthony Lewis, "Is There No Decency?," *New York Times* (March 19, 1984), https://www.nytimes.com/1984/03/19/opinion/abroad-at-home-is-there-no-decency.html.

39. Tyler Report, 7, 4.

40. *New York Times* (March 10, 1984): 9; Bonner, *Weakness and Deceit*, xix.

41. Tyler Report, 7–8.

42. Ibid., 10.

43. *Albuquerque Journal* (April 6, 1984): 3.

44. *New York Times* (March 22, 1984): 27.

45. *New York Times* (May 22, 1984): 27.

46. *New York Times* (May 6, 1985): 1.

47. *New York Times* (June 4, 1984): 3.

48. *Albuquerque Journal* (June 20, 1984): D8.

49. *Washington Post* (November 23, 1984), https://www.washingtonpost.com/archive/politics/1984/11/23/salvadoran-cleric-is-killed/aa051a71-eaff-49a5-9f92-3ba709ec1450/?utm_term=.1c612b0264f2.

50. *New York Times* (January 7, 1985), A–1.

Chapter 14. El Salvador after 1982

1. Phillip Berryman, *Stubborn Hope: Religion, Politics, and Revolution in Central America* (Maryknoll, NY: Orbis Books, 1994), 89.

2. *New York Times* (November 1, 1989), https://www.nytimes.com/1989/11/01/world/bombing-at-salvadoran-leftists-office-kills-eight.html. Sources differ on number killed, ranging from eight to ten.

3. Report of the Commission on the Truth for El Salvador, *From Madness to Hope: The 12-year war in El Salvador* (March 29, 1993), 45–51. Hereafter cited as UN Truth Commission.

4. *Boston Globe* (December 20, 1989): 17.

5. John Joseph Moakley et al., *Interim [Congressional] Report of the Speaker's Task Force on El Salvador* (April 30, 1990), 22. Hereafter cited as Moakley Report.

6. Ibid., 23.

7. For a detailed, firsthand account of the Cernas' ordeal see: Lucía Cerna and Mary Jo Ignoffo, *La Verdad: A Witness to the Salvadoran Martyrs* (Maryknoll, NY: Orbis Books, 2014).

8. Moakley Report, 23–24.

9. *New York Times* (December 11, 1989): A10; *Washington Post* (December 11, 1989): A23.

10. Moakley Report, 27–31; UN Truth Commission, 51–52.

11. UN Truth Commission, 46.

12. Americas Watch, "El Salvador and Human Rights: The Challenge of Reform," An Americas Watch Report (New York: March 1991), 81–82.

13. Joe Fish, *El Salvador: Testament of Terror* (London: Zed Books, 1988), 107.

14. UN Truth Commission, 43.

15. Ibid., 43–44.

16. For a detailed study of the legacy of Rivera, see Edward T. Brett, "Archbishop Arturo Rivera Damas and the Struggle for Social Justice in El Salvador," *The Catholic Historical Review* (October 2008): 717–39. Bishops Cabrera, Mojica,

and Alas were all pastorally oriented and held in high regard by their priests and the laity as well. All three wrote letters in 1999 calling on the U.S. Congress to close the School of the Americas, which had trained countless Latin American military personnel, including many from El Salvador, who had later committed human rights violations in their home countries. The authors thank Father Bernard Survil, who provided them with photocopies of some of these letters. They also thank Father Joseph Callahan for his recollections on Bishops Cabrera, Mojica, and Alas.

17. Fred Burton, "Mara Salvatrucha: The New Face of Organized Crime?" *Stratfor/Worldview* (March 30, 2006).

18. James R. Brockman, *Romero: A Life* (Maryknoll, NY: Orbis Books, 1989), 248.

Conclusion

1. Today known as the Western Hemisphere Institute for Security Cooperation.

Index